Praise for
A Question of P

MW00776070

CARL BERNSTEIN
Investigative Reporter, Co-Author, ALL THE PRESIDENT'S MEN
David Tereshchuk is one of the great reporters of our era, covering global conflicts and the leaders who have initiated them, from patriots to despots. Now, using the skills he has honed as an investigative journalist, he may have found his most important subject yet: the real story of what happened in his own young life. Tereshchuk's quest for truth, about both his immediate family and the stories he's covered around the world, resonates through the pages of A Question of Paternity, an exceptional memoir that is at once moving, shocking and undeniably heroic.

NEAL ASCHERSON
Journalist and Author, STONE VOICES: THE SEARCH FOR SCOTLAND;
THE BOOK OF LECH WAŁESA
The compelling, often heart-breaking story of one man's search for the stories behind the world's conflicts and for the dark secret of his own birth. He recalls and reflects on many scenes of horror, but the connecting thread is one of haunting suspense. It's his never-ending effort to find out who made his fifteen-year-old mother pregnant and became his secret father.

CARY BARBOR
Host, National Public Radio Book Club (WGCU Radio)
Tereshchuk's vivid writing lands you smack in the middle of a fascinating and heart-rending quest.

LAWRENCE BLOCK
Crime novelist, MATTHEW SCUDDER *series*
David Tereshchuk spent the past half-century chasing through

every hot spot and hellhole in the world. Now he's written a memoir and it's everything I'd hoped it would be—and here's the surprise: the richest story of many in it is his very own.

RICK MOODY

Novelist, THE ICE STORM

Even-handed and reportorial but also deeply moving, complex and very sad. Tereshchuk is committed to the truth even when the truth is challenging. It's refreshing to read a work so knowing, so honest, so wise.

DAVID W. DUNLAP

Newspaper Historian and Author, FROM ABYSSINIAN TO ZION

A harrowing journey, rich in detail, shaped by transcendent longing. I found myself engrossed by the account of Bloody Sunday.

A Question of Paternity
My Life as an Unaffiliated Reporter

David Tereshchuk

ENVELOPE BOOKS

About the Author

David Tereshchuk (b. 1948) is a journalist working mainly in the broadcast media but also for magazines and newspapers (The Guardian, The New York Times, The New Statesman). He spent two decades with British commercial television, reporting, producing and making documentaries, before moving to the US, where he worked for ABC, CBS, CNN, Discovery, A&E and The History Channel. His earliest work included coverage of violence in Northern Ireland, and then extended into international issues, especially in the Third World. Since 2012 he has been a producer and correspondent for PBS, concentrating on ethical issues. He broadcasts a weekly public-radio dispatch of media criticism, The Media Beat, and writes an online column with the same name, at www.themediabeat.us. A graduate of Oxford University, he has been a US citizen since 2002 and lives in New York City and Ireland. He has been honored by Britain's Royal Television Society with its Social Documentary Award, and by the British Association for the Advancement of Science with its Television Award.

For Schellie
Proof for me that another life is possible.

Published 2024 in Great Britain and the USA by EnvelopeBooks
12 Wellfield Avenue, London N10 2EA
www.envelopebooks.co.uk
A New Premises venture in association with Booklaunch

Cover design by Stephen Games | Booklaunch

A CIP catalogue record for this title is available from the
British Library

Edited and designed by Booklaunch
EnvelopeBooks 18
ISBN 9781915023155

I cannot say what portion is in truth
The naked recollection of that time,
And what may rather have been called to life
By after-meditation.

William Wordsworth
The Prelude (1805 edition)
Book 3, lines 650–653

Author's Note

This book is riddled with inconsistencies in style and I apologise—or apologize. After more than thirty years of life as an American, I still swivel between UK and US spellings and usages. Or is it something else? Maybe my upbringing in what has been called the Debatable Land predisposed me to oscillations and uncertainties. Or perhaps, again, it is simply evidence of a divided mind.

DT
New York, 2023

Chapter I
How I Happened

S he would never talk about it. For decades my mother avoided the matter of how I came into being. She also remained unclear about most everything in our earliest life together. She expressed only the vaguest recollections overall.

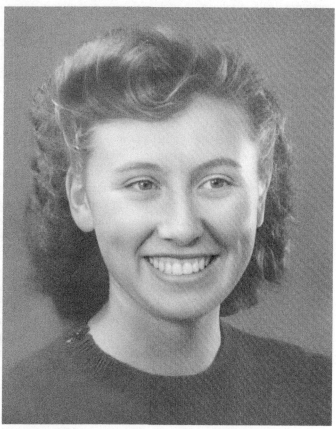

My mother, Hilda Brown, at the age of approximately seventeen.

And I too ended up scarcely able to picture my own growing up, always peering back at it through some sort of hazy scrim.

But a disturbing story—utterly unvoiced at the start, never spoken of when I was a child, and then uttered only a very long time into my adulthood—was that I owed my existence to my mother's being impregnated by a priest who raped her.

In my fifties my mother eventually told me that as a fifteen-year-old high school girl, she accompanied a friend to a Roman Catholic church service. Our family wasn't Catholic. Very few families were, in our large village or small country town in the Scottish Borderland—and there was no Catholic church. We were nominally Anglican, though with only perfunctory observance. Our family might have sometimes attended the parish church, but I have no memory of it if we did. I do have a fuzzy sense of what might have been Sunday School, led a by a sweet young woman; I remember a tall man—of some awe to us kids, but pleasant in manner—once coming in to address the children briefly, wearing a business suit and also what I'd very much later learn to call a clerical collar.

By contrast with us, my mother's school-friend came from an observant Catholic family, Italian immigrants who ran the local ice-cream parlour. It was a place I'd come to love visiting as a child, with its soft, swirly ice cream, round marble-topped tables at chin-height and sugary drinks on tap with tongue-enticing Mediterranean names like Sarsaparilla. Behind the counter were several members of the Italian family, all buoyant and voluble with each other—so utterly different from our generally very quiet home. The Scottish word *dour* comes to mind.

My mother said she'd been curious to discover just how her friend's mysterious faith was celebrated on Sundays. She also found the location the Catholics chose for what they called their 'Mass' to be intriguing. Not an actual church, like our familiar Anglican house of worship, an imposing village landmark on a nearby hill, but instead the obscurity of an ordinary room above the office of a local family doctor, another of the area's few Catholics. A visiting priest would come to conduct the mass, assigned from the sizable city some ten miles away, which had several Catholic parishes.

This particular January Sunday when my mother went along with her friend, the presiding priest, Father Francis (as full a name as she could give me) evidently 'took a liking' to her. I'm not at all sure in what sense she meant that phrase. She said he offered to walk her home after the service, she accepted, and part-way there he raped her.

This account of my conception, learned so late into my life, naturally surprised—no, thoroughly staggered me. I had no reason to doubt her account and I didn't cross-question her about it. Listening quietly and intently, I was anxious not to stop her unaccustomed, vehement flow—and I thought I'd get other chances later to go back over it with her. She was never to give any such chances. And then sixteen years later she died at the age of eighty-five. Since that one day of revelations I've searched in many places for ways to corroborate or check them out. But in essence I continued to have for the story of my conception only my mother's own story to go by.

For the longest time I never told anyone else about my secretive beginnings, nor for that matter did I ever acknowledge to myself what it might have meant to me. The man who 'fathered' me—in one sense only—disappeared around the time of my birth, according to my mother. He was—again, in my mother's account—moved away by his Church superiors to avoid scandal. She said she told no one what had been done to her except for her mother—and that her mother felt it was a shameful event for the family. Silence evidently fell upon us all.

She was sent away to give birth—120 miles to the south, to her elder, married sister's home in England's industrial belt. The shame of her pregnancy had, she told me, brought two strong pressures onto her, which she fully resisted with her fifteen-year-old's determination. One: to have me aborted (a crime at that time, of course, to follow the crime of my creation). Two: to have me adopted as soon as I was born.

But once born, I was allowed into my grandmother's house. Only, though, under terms and conditions. One was that my mother give up her schooling and get a job. She had been on track to go to college and would have been the first in our family to do so. My ever-determined and practical grandmother felt that one more mouth to feed—mine—was too much of a strain on the family budget.

Another condition was the thin veil of a cover-story invented for my sudden appearance. It seems ludicrous looking back, but according to my mother they tried passing me off as just another child in my grandmother's large brood—already nine children, most of whom had grown up and moved away. The ruse took little or no account of the fact that my grandfather had died eight years before, and my grandmother was already entering her fifties.

I saw little of my mother in daylight during my early years. From the age of sixteen, she became our household's only breadwinner. Early each day she left by bus to work as a clerk in one of the city's booksellers. The household was firmly headed by my grandmother, whom along with everyone else in the home I called Mam, the Scottish version of Mom or Mum. I called my mother by her first name, Hilda—and she seemed to be my big sister. There were two uncles there, too, affable boys some years younger than my mother, who were playmates for me—big brothers to all intents and purposes.

As I got older, there must have come a time by when I'd learnt that my mother was indeed my mother—but I can't remember any epiphany. A gradual realisation is much more likely. And I probably deduced it for myself; I don't recall ever being out-loud told anything.

Like many children of unknown parentage, I would fantasise about my origins. Maybe a passing multi-millionaire, or maybe even a royal personage, had tarried long enough in our village to create me, in some fairy-tale relationship with my mother. But I'd always expel such notions abruptly, dismissive of what I saw as childish silliness. 'That's stupid,' I'd say—and, in the phrasing of later generations, I would move on.

Chapter 2
Affliction

For a good slice of my life or, in truth, an undeniably bad slice, I was an active alcoholic. It's a curious phrase, *active alcoholic*, invented by specialists in addiction recovery who want to distinguish between people who have the disease of alcoholism—and drink anyway—and those who manage to stop drinking. The oddity of 'active' as a word, plus some sense of the disaster lying in wait for me if I were ever to drink again, is captured memorably in a trenchant cartoon I keep pinned above my desk, taken from an otherwise rather dry healthcare journal. It shows a woman screaming at her male partner, who is splayed out unconscious on a sofa with empty bottles piled around and on top of him. 'You call this being ACTIVE?' she yells.

I suppose my long active phase began when I was in my early teens, when it might have passed for harmless recreation and rarely involved anything stronger than beer. Actually, that's not true: I was in heaven whenever I managed to score some hard liquor at the age of fourteen. Alcohol use deepened in my college years, dressed with a liberal sprinkling of marijuana as well, and I still regarded it all as utterly innocuous—except, that is, when I crawled back at dawn into my dorm room, after a 'traditional' all-night May Day bout of drinking champagne, whisky and brandy —and helplessly vomited again and again for two hours or more, moaning continually, 'I will never drink again.' This was the first of countless times I would bewail my state with that same forlorn vow.

And did I keep my promise? Never, of course. And just as unstoppably, the cycle of drinking and being violently sick would repeat and repeat.

It's a progressive illness, we are constantly reminded. And in young adulthood I entered a profession, journalism, where I had plenty of cover for it as it progressed. Heavy drinking was some-

5

thing of a rite of passage among colleagues rather than a cause for concern. But the degree to which it was steadily taking me over had to be hidden, and called for determined measures. It's impossible now to say how many mornings, having awakened or come to with a clanging hangover somewhere far from home, I had to sneak in (I hoped unobtrusively) as the day's first customer for the barbershop at Harrods' flagship London store. I'd get a shampoo and a shave, before buying a change of shirt and heading into the TV studios where I worked. Trying to look nonchalant to the front-desk receptionist and security guards, I'd make straight for the dressing room where I kept a change of suit and other clothing. I always bought the extra shirt because I could never remember how many I had left stacked in the dressing-room drawer just for this purpose.

Despite the front I presented as a serious-minded interviewer on camera, there steadily mounted a wretched off-screen toll of bar-room brawls (the pretexts for which I have no memory of), drunk-driving offences (several times making me abjectly beg a favour and, once, hand over a cash bribe to local district reporters not to cover my appearance in court), and car-wrecks that involved massive damage to my own and to others' vehicles. My physical frame was somehow preserved from serious injury but a pallid and eventually florid bloating of both face and body indicated the decay going on inside me. One internist, dramatically if perhaps imprecisely, declared my liver to be 'beyond repair'. So did I stop? I didn't. I couldn't. The disease's grip on me was tenacious and relentless.

My work—always the most important element in my life, I thought—was where the pressure on me to get a grip on myself mounted most persuasively. Brian, one of a few friends I retained from college and who happened to work in the same business, which meant I might listen to him, once spoke a lot more forthrightly to me than I expected or wanted. Sometime in the mid-1980s he and I chanced to meet the day after a TV broadcast I had made—a half-hour report devoted to mental health services, of all things—and he commented: 'Wasn't so bad. You didn't slur your words too much on-air.'

It was one of those excruciating but eventually irrefutable

critiques that my peers came to voice, a lot, about my drinking. It got to the point where the TV company's chief executive had to call me into his office to deliver a damning indictment: 'David, you are paid the highest fees of anyone in this building, second only to me, and we are not getting our money's worth.'

The dull but inescapable fact about an alcoholic's life is that it can be extraordinarily tedious to live and even more tedious, I believe, to narrate to others. Throughout my twenties and thirties I had daily arguments with myself—often more frequent than daily, sometimes minute-by-minute—over whether I could safely pick up a desperately craved glass or bottle, followed by my inevitable defeat and capitulation. And nightly, or ever-earlier in the day, I would end up disappearing into unconsciousness or oblivion. That latter term is a euphemistic misnomer. It suggests I'm forgetting something—but it's never forgotten; the overwhelming compulsion to drink immediately returns, with flatteningly repetitive regularity. There was above all the constant drumbeat of lies to myself that I could still handle the substance that was killing me, despite the growing evidence to the contrary.

It was the blunt professional truths voiced by co-workers that finally got my attention, in a way that all the other serious warning signs never did. I cannot say why. Maybe it was just time. I needed medical help to put the drink down, and extended in-patient treatment. But I still relapsed, many times over. I couldn't stop drinking decisively but it became clear to me that my days of 'activity' were numbered, and mercifully they eventually were. The disease took twenty-seven years to run its course.

Chapter 3
First Home

It was public housing. But because it was in a rural setting, the Scottish Borderland, it didn't earn the label 'housing estate' that is used in England for such developments, often a dominant feature of the country's run-down urban districts. Still less did it resemble the grim 'housing schemes', the term used further north in Scotland's high-density rust belt; these schemes are often likened to what Americans call 'projects'. Our housing tract was by contrast very much smaller, just thirty-four houses. But we fitted the picture. We were poor, the prime qualification for being in such homes. Until my mother started going out to work after I was born, the only income to support all five of us in the house was a widow's pension my grandmother had drawn since her husband, a carpenter, died in 1940. From my earliest days of walking, I would toddle along with her to pick up the pension when it was doled out to her at the village post office on Thursday. I knew it to be an important day for the household. Friday had its significance, too, with the arrival of my mother's paycheck envelope on that day. Small and slim, made of coarse mid-brown paper and containing folded banknotes and a few coins.

The houses were situated around a roughly circular street. The shape was really closer to a squashed oval. But it was called, with inaccuracy that was never questioned, a 'crescent'; and within its curvature was a central 'green' of featureless grass. My grandmother's house was Number 6, and we like every family were attached to our next-door neighbours' house, Number 5. The euphemistic British label is 'semi-detached'. I knew little about those neighbours, but they were often mentioned—usually in terms of 'what would they think ... ?' The concern ranged from what would they think if I went out past their front gate without a coat on a cold day, through to what would they think if my

Grandmother Janet Brown, sixty-three, at Number 6, The Crescent (1958).

'brothers' (actually my uncles, *see page 10*) were noisily boisterous in the evening. The boys were cheery good company to me and I liked being around them, though I didn't really see them much. At twelve and fourteen years older than me, I'd say they had their own world.

What neighbours in general might think—not just those next-door but the whole village, and about many matters, not just the boys' dress or noise-level—seemed an ongoing worry for my grandmother. She was short and a little round—constitutionally fierce, but I sensed perpetual anxiety, too. I cannot remember any events that might have occasioned such anxiety, but I have a strong imprint of her seemingly permanent expression, a knotted

As a baby, with Norrie Brown (left) & Hector Brown (right), whom I grew up thinking of as my brothers when they were in fact my uncles.

brow redolent of puzzlement, and I do recall the alarm in her startled, even scared-looking reaction whenever anyone knocked at our door.

There were three bedrooms upstairs. My mother, for so long appearing to be my big sister, had her own room, my uncle-brothers shared one, and my grandmother had hers overlooking the Green. I remember sleeping in my grandmother's room; but whether that was the regular situation or an effort to offer me extra comfort in one of my periods of illness, I can't be sure. She was a troubled, restless sleeper.

It was she who ran the household—who else could have? Every day seemed filled with her washing and cleaning—and dusting the sparse furniture, especially one dark walnut sideboard with a snowy-white, frequently-laundered, cotton embroidered runner on top. There was floor-scrubbing daily, too, and one day a week a vigorous polishing for the house's outside doorstep, painted red. The wax polish had the brand-name Cardinal, and came in a tin illustrated with a portrait of the appropriate cleric wearing the appropriate bright red cape and hat. She also tended the vegetable garden out back, and she cooked constantly, I thought. Most especially she baked. The smell of warm, slightly crumbly scones would fill the house from the kitchen's small electric oven.

The house's only inbuilt heating source was an open fireplace in the living room where coal and logs burned. In winter we would speedily dash between that warm room and the oven-warmed kitchen, or upstairs to jump into a bed's cold flannel sheets, which were mercifully quick to warm. It took merely our retained body heat, plus aid from a rubber or a stone hot-water bottle wrapped in a worn-out shirt. I learned only later that 'stone' was a misnomer; they were really made of heavy, glazed pottery.

Outside of the house, I had one friend, Edgar—a year or so my junior—who lived on the other side of us at Number 7, with a narrow gap between our houses. One rare but lasting memory is of our fighting, or at least him trying to fight me. I have no idea what might have been the cause at issue, though I do believe he started the fight. My response was not to fight back—instead, to simply restrain him. I pinned his arms to his side in determined, silent containment. Watching from an open window my grandmother called to me, 'What are you doing? Hit him!' 'I can't, Mam,' I answered. 'He's my friend.' I could have made my purpose clearer, I suppose, by yelling an order or just a loud complaint, but I didn't say a thing to him. I could also have taken more aggressive action, but I didn't. As I look back more broadly, my childhood response to anyone or anything troubling me was to clam up; I took little action in response, and said even less.

But I enjoyed a child's quiet delight in the garden, with its peas, potatoes, rhubarb and gooseberry bushes, and a large midden whose compost fed the vegetables and fruit. I enjoyed 'helping' my grandmother, though I doubt I was much use in reality. I probably ate almost as many gooseberries as I picked. And there was at times a particular drawback to being there. The garden backed onto the village's school and its playing fields. In my pre-school years the raucous yells of ebullient schoolkids ricocheted over the high fence and scared me. My uncle-brothers must have gone to that school, too, and they might have been able to reassure me about it. But I didn't register any such reassurance, just the steady build-up of deep apprehension about my future attendance there, which I knew would loom larger once I reached the age of five.

I went to school eventually, of course, full of my long-nurtured fear. And it turned out to be no terrible ordeal. I don't remember any pivotal event happening to dismiss my fear; it must have just melted away. But I didn't exactly develop camaraderie, either. I was quiet and awkward with everyone there, both the kids and the mostly friendly, kindly intentioned adults running the school. I still had my best-friend next door at home, but our age difference reduced our togetherness after I'd become a schoolboy and Edgar still hadn't. I had, at least according to family folklore, the same nominal girlfriend throughout the time I was at the school. She was the butcher's daughter from the village's centre, named Joyce. But I carry no recollection of ever doing anything with her, only of sitting near her in class behind our tiny, heavy oak desks, and the two of us eyeing each other, somewhat expressionless as I recall. I have a fuzzy sense we were not so much bonded by our own wishes but by our teachers' regard as 'the clever pair' of our small class. I can't bring to mind any conversation, no interaction with Joyce, nor with any other children for that matter; no lasting friendships were made.

At home, you might think the absence of a father would at least occasionally have been talked about. I have often thought it strange that we never mentioned it. My uncertainty over whether I even had a father, and if so who he was, never did get voiced in the house. Or I don't think so. My clouded memory is entirely unhelpful here. And elsewhere, whenever anyone in school or at play brought the question up, I would rapidly change the subject.

I kept the curious at bay by sticking to myself a lot, doing my own thing even among group activities. I wasn't one for the informal team games that broke out, like Tag, or Steal the Flag (usually played with a coloured sock for the Flag). I had an intensely private preoccupation to turn to, influenced by my uncle-brothers. They were both eventually to become profess-

Me at about three years old.

ional sailors, one military in the Royal Navy, one civilian in the UK's version of the Merchant Marine. In their teens they each dedicatedly learned knot-tying from complex diagrams in maritime textbooks; I would copy them intently and then carry on practising alone outside the home with my two thin strands of rope.

The scrubby grass in the middle of our Crescent was where we resident children played, along with many other kids from the

Me (left) at four years old with my mother, two of her brothers, and a friend.

village's fringes. Truck drivers made up some of the Crescent's tenant population, so evenings occasionally brought us a very welcome change: a huge alteration to our usual landscape. Enormous eight-wheelers would be parked on the grass's edge during their drivers' occasional overnights at home. They turned the flatness of the Green into an adventure playground, suddenly offering climbing structures, but with few or no hand- or foot-holds. I may have lived in some prevailing low-grade fear, not least an incessantly alert wariness about my more confident or even intimidating playmates, but I felt no fear at all when it came to free-solo bouldering up those lumpy, tarpaulin-shrouded peaks.

I don't imagine for one minute that I was the only fatherless child in that community of a few thousand villagers, but it did seem that every other kid had a dad. A lot were farmers, made clear when the kids spoke with each other knowingly about all the seasonal work they joined in at home, like haymaking, potato-picking, and late autumn ploughing. When I first showed up at school, my name was David Brown—until some years later it changed when my mother married—and the name briefly won me some special cachet among my new peers. It happened to be the same as a sought-after British model of tractor (the UK equivalent, maybe, of a John Deere), but the coincidence's novelty soon wore off among the farmboys and farmgirls. The village was edged immediately by commercial forestry, but was also circled a little further out by low-rolling hills of arable farming, lots of dairy herds—some of whom would be trotted through our streets at milking-times, to Horace the Milkman's dairy—and widely spread flocks of sheep as well. Our classrooms could be heavy some mornings with the imported and sweetish, not at all offensive, smell of the barnyard.

Chapter 4
Debatable Land, Uncertain Waters

In the Debatable Land, so known because neither England nor Scotland had ever decided who owned it, there were virtually no laws—and this made it a stronghold for those who made their living from extortion, kidnapping and rustling. Expert horsemen on the wild and treacherous terrain, the 'Border Reivers' fought each other. Anything that wasn't theirs they stole, anything they couldn't steal they burned, and anyone who tried to stop them they killed. They had names like Geordie... Fingerless Will ... Nebles [meaning 'Nowhere'] Clem ... Buggerback ... and Jock Pott the Bastard.

—*Parish Council Official History*

One benefit of being born to a sixteen-year-old was that I could know my great-grandfather, who was born in 1870. We overlapped in fact by ten years.

My strongest memories of him are from between my fourth and ninth years, and he was in his mid-eighties. Several times through the year, mostly in the summer months and missing out our often frigid winters, my grandmother would take me to his home—seventeen miles westward from our house. He lived in an old fishing village overlooking the Solway Firth, the fjord-like inlet of sea that separates Southwest Scotland from England, and at that point is thirty miles wide. For my grandmother and me, it was a protracted journey each time: packing sandwiches and a Thermos flask of tea for her plus a third-of-a-pint bottle of milk for me, before making the half-mile walk to our village bus-stop —quite an exacting start to an odyssey if even your most determined stride extends only to twenty inches.

Then came an endless, actually forty-five minute, bus ride with countless stops to reach a small county town's busy square, where we waited seemingly forever to catch a squat local bus that

Great-grandfather's home, 'White Row', overlooking Solway Firth, c 1915.

took us the last four miles to the fishing village itself. Or almost. The bus route went past it, not into it; so we disembarked at a wooden bus shelter and then trekked, suddenly with salt wind in our faces, down a much narrower mile-long lane, over a hump-back bridge that spanned a small stream. My grandmother's pace quickened now that our goal of the seafront was in sight, while I had tired and strove hard to keep up.

Inland, our stretch of the country had long ago been given that historians' label, The Debatable Land—somewhat soft phrasing for the violent contestation over territory that the two rival populations engaged in through the centuries. When a formal union was first formed between England and Scotland in 1603, our counties on either side of the previous border were in essence abolished, and the whole region was given the indeterminate name of The Middle Shires. But it didn't stop rival identities being claimed. Was the area really Scottish or English? My grandmother's home-village was sometimes given a tag that's cute but inexact: 'The Olde Border Town'—the border certainly did move around quite a bit over time, but it never ran precisely through the village. At the region's Western end, however, there could be no real argument, since that deep body of Solway water served as an indisputable division between the countries.

On the Scottish side, my great-grandfather's cottage sat on

what was to me a huge clifftop—its actual elevation: twenty-eight feet. It was whitewashed, like the other nine similar houses that made up the short waterfront street. The street's unsurprising name: White Row.

He'd been a fisherman—and his youngest son, my great-uncle Hugh, still fished the Solway in his forties, and lived in the same cottage. It smelled of birch and hazelwood smoke, and grown-up maleness. I knew my logs even at that early age—which tree produced what kind of flame. I felt enveloped in a very different air from what I was used to in my grandmother's home, a bit mysterious and yet somehow comforting. Hugh wasn't around much—at work fishing, no doubt, when I was there. But I relished the stillness of my great-grandfather's presence—a man, anyone could have agreed, of few words. The calm around him gave me the chance, most of all, to study his long ears—astonishingly long, they seemed to me. While I didn't ever find myself really getting to know Great-Uncle Hugh, I felt a distinct closeness to the much older man. I remember myself perking up whenever he entered to take his place as the quiet centre of his low-beamed house.

His occasional visits from a friend, also long-retired, were another a quiet pleasure. They were both called John. They would sit either side of the black iron-grated fireplace where logs first blazed and then glowed orange, and I would sit on the rug between them. The conversation—if that's what it was—consisted of only intermittent phrases.

'Aye, John.' Then a long, long pause.

'Aye, John,' would be the reply.

What felt like another day would stretch out undisturbed.

'Aye well, John,' my great-grandfather might offer.

Then a response, after some considered delay: 'Aye, John.'

And so on for an eternity. I knew what adult conversation normally sounded like—I'd heard customers and counter-staff at the grocer's store sometimes engage in an animated to and fro. But this was of a completely different order. The near-silent ritual would at times be interrupted by my grandmother coming in from the back-kitchen with a vast Brown Betty pot of tea, two big mugs and a small one for me. Other sudden interruptions might occur, but peaceable; one or other of the men might shoot out great gobs of spittle to sizzle loudly on the glowing, red-hot grate. I felt myself glowing, too.

The sea, the Solway, was the biggest determinant of life at my great-grandfather's. I was warned never to venture outward from the waterfront at low-tide. There were salt-marshes and mudflats on which the outgoing tide left beautiful, endless patterns of inch-high furrows that stretched out maybe as far as England. But the incoming tide could take you totally unawares.

As an adult I came across a late-nineteenth-century gazetteer of Scotland with an assessment of the Firth's dangers—and it jolted me into recollecting just how perilous it was.

'The Solway, especially the phenomenon of its tides, differs widely from every other firth in Scotland, or even from every other marine indentation in the world ... All its tides are rapid, and constitute rather a rush, or careering race, than a flow or current of waters ... Even persons best acquainted with the locality are liable to mistake in their calculations of the time when the tide will approach; and, when they are partway across, may suddenly hear the appalling sound of the watery invasion, near and menacing.'

I don't remember exactly how but once, at the age of six or seven, I came to be taking a risky, and forbidden, walk out from the shore. Just as forewarned, I soon found myself trapped on all sides by a fast-returning sea, standing in my Wellington boots on a narrow hummock of slightly higher, hardened sand. A darkening panic overtook me. I couldn't swim. I hadn't learned how.

I'd been kept away from water, as a response to repeated trouble with my ears—eight surgeries in my first six years, as my grandmother recorded the count. My own recall is of repeated visits to ENT specialists. That was the first acronym I ever learned, surprising me but educating me that the ears, the nose and the throat are connected. I may not have been formally taught that fact in biology class until I was in the equivalent of middle-school, but I already knew it through personal experience by the time I was five. I remember deep, almost perpetual pain— wholly agonising if I let water into my ears. And hospitalisations for all those procedures that my grandmother charted, that included two for the exact same operation. I didn't understand how I could have my tonsils taken out twice. It's rare, I was told, but it can happen that they will grow again, if some tonsil tissue gets left behind. And most of all, I recall periods with a terrifying loss of hearing—complete deafness at some times, partial loss but still disorienting and discomfiting at others.

On that slim sandbar it was my sight I seemed to lose. I'm not sure if I physically closed my eyes—but I suddenly saw nothing. I certainly wasn't deaf, though. I could without a doubt hear the rising noise of what must have been fast-moving water, but it sounded to those ears, which I had come to know as unreliable, like something utterly unearthly. I didn't move. Paralysed by fear, I now recognise. And I voiced nothing—no yell for help, no cry of fear.

I've no notion of how long I was there—but the water had topped my wellies and was creeping up well past my knees. Then out of nowhere, it seemed, Great-Uncle Hugh was leaning out of his rowboat to lift me and take me aboard. I was carried back into the cottage safely. And I remember no remonstration, no telling-off. Just an unstated, maybe gruff, sense of relief among the small household.

On every visit there after that, I observed the local community's strictures and kept to dry land. Unless I was in a boat—especially my great-uncle's, of course, forever now a blissful place of safety.

Over the decades since, I've constantly been drawn to the edge of water. The thing about me and water is that I love being by it. I'm awed and calmed by the openness, especially when it's the sea, the infinite possibilities it seems to offer. I'm beguiled by songs of those 'faraway places with strange-sounding names' beyond the horizon I stared at as a child, aware that people did things there I could only imagine ... until one day I would make it to be among them. I just don't want to be in that water.

Chapter 5
Marriage and Move

I n my grandmother's household the ground began to shift.
My fatherless state was going to end, in some sense at least,
with my mother getting married. As an alert seven-year-old I
picked up on a lot of new plans being laid.

How did it begin? Hilda had most likely met him at one of the
weekend dances that were held in the Village Hall. He was a
Ukrainian DP (a 'displaced person') called Mychailo Tereshchuk.
He was working locally and he had reached our homeland after a
remarkable trek. What memories of him I carried from childhood have always been scattered and unformed, perhaps
unsurprisingly given my then-limited grasp of adult matters.
Long after the fact I pieced together his long trans-European
journey with my sister's help, through her connections with his
relatives in Ukraine, and by consulting tomes of sometimes
arcane World War Two history. But his whole story is still far
from clear, as often remains the case with the millions of
families who were uprooted and dislocated by that war.

Mychailo was seventeen years old when the Nazis invaded
Ukraine. Along with many other young men he joined the
Soviets' Red Army in its effort to repulse the Germans. He was
evidently captured by Nazi forces during or shortly after the bitter
fighting of the Lvov–Sandomir Offensive, and held as a prisoner
of war in Southern Germany or Austria. He later somehow—
we're not sure how—fell into the Western Allies' hands as they
made their liberating advance in 1945.

He ended up in a camp in Rimini, Italy, which was maintained by British forces until well after the end of the war. In one of
the earliest conversations I had with Mychailo when I'd turned
eight and we were just getting to know each other, he mentioned
he had also encountered US Army officers in authority at the
Rimini camp, as well as British. I was impressed. As a kid then

devouring cowboy comics whenever I could, as well as the Legend of Davy Crockett, I couldn't help relishing any connection to America, however tenuous. I can't recollect any details he might have described about interactions with those officers—just the ring of that golden word 'American.'

At the war's end the US and Britain had faced a quandary over Eastern European POWs and DPs like Mychailo. Their original home countries now lay behind the line that would become the Iron Curtain, and many among the war's captured and displaced were decidedly reluctant to go home only to live under Communist rule, and very possibly endure harsh persecution. Among the many things I've learned to admire about Eleanor Roosevelt, it was her intervention that helped to change those uprooted people's fate.

Under the infamous Yalta Agreement her husband, by then a terminally ill president, along with Prime Minister Winston Churchill, had yielded to the Soviet leader Joseph Stalin's stipulation that all DPs should be returned to exactly where they had first come from. Newly widowed, in her postwar role of chairing the recently formed United Nations Commission on Human Rights, Eleanor pressed for a much looser application of the Agreement. In a vehement speech she said:

> The sooner those people can be taken where they can become citizens and feel that they are actually building a new life, the better it will be for the whole world.

That was how Mychailo ended up in Britain. At first he was assigned to work on three successive farms in Southern England; he picked up the language as he went. He was then sent further north to be a labourer at a vast arms manufacturing and storage complex, His Majesty's Munitions Depot, that straddled the Scottish–English border. He was housed at a camp where he was united with other Ukrainians—mostly older ones, I imagine—who had served within Nazi forces as part of the SS combat division named 'Galizien' and who like him had been transported from the Rimini camp. In this distinctly militarised stretch of the Borderland he worked his way into a job as an orderly in the British Army Officers' Club at the depot, waiting at table and serving drinks.

It was some seven years into his being stationed in our area, just as he was entering his thirties, that he met Hilda—and ultimately me, her son. I found him fascinatingly exotic. He'd come from an unimaginably far-flung country; through many other different countries on the way, too, compounding in my mind a fantastical odyssey for his life. He was the first non-native English-speaker I'd met; our village was a pretty homogeneous society, after all. The details of his history that he related were few and cryptic, but for me he trailed clouds of dramatic upheaval and mystery. He'd been in battle, seen people killed, I imagined—and many times over he had, to my wonderment, adapted to wholly new surroundings, new worlds.

I remember attempting the impossible. I tried, with very obviously no experience of my own to build on, imagining what it must be like to start life over again completely in a totally strange place, at other people's mercy, far from my family and not even speaking the new place's language. And to do that time and time again. It seemed almost superhuman.

He made an effort to cultivate me a bit. He'd take me for walks occasionally, down by the village's river; I knew no grown man who would have walked with me. I was looking forward to having an adult male around—this intriguing man especially.

I don't recall anyone, least of all him, using the word *father*, still less *stepfather*. I don't remember, either, any talk of a name-change being imminent, any switch from our longstanding family surname, the nondescript 'Brown'. But I was thrilled by all the preparations for the forthcoming wedding ceremony, above all its engrossingly complex protocols and logistics. In my grandmother's front room one afternoon, when the adults were discussing in great detail various practical arrangements, a sudden, long silence fell when I interrupted to ask: 'Which car does the bride's son ride in?' For me it didn't seem at all remarkable, not in any way an out-of-place question.

But there was no word in reply, just the quiet shuffling of paper: guest lists, dress patterns and the Vows pages from an Order of Service.

While I have seen some photos of me at the event in 1956, formally posed in a short-trousered suit with my pocket-square and a boutonnière, I don't recall much if anything of my twenty-four-year-old mother's wedding to Mychailo.

We all called her new husband by the obvious anglicisation, 'Michael'. All of us, that is, except my little sister who arrived within a year of her parents' wedding. As she grew up, Julie called him 'Daddy'. Natural enough and rather sweet, I thought through the years, but it also prompted in me a small, uneasy flinch whenever she said it. Though unintentional, to be sure, it underlined a difference between us as kids.

Another difference was what the two of us called our mother. She said 'Mammy' and I simply continued my ingrained habit of calling her 'Hilda', from the days when she had seemed to be my older sister. No effort, I don't think, was made to change that.

There was much upheaval, though, at least to my mind. With Michael moving in and my sister being born, there was a fresh nuclear unit created within my grandmother's house—two married adults, two sibling children. But pretty swiftly we moved out. When Julie was just a few months old our newly-minted group of four quit the village, leaving my grandmother in the house with only her youngest son, then twenty years old. Our foursome travelled south to England's industrial belt, like many of our region's poor families, Scottish and English, all seeking work. Michael found a manufacturing job and we settled in the then-irredeemably grimy city of Manchester, in a house just off a road with an unpropitious name: Factory Lane. There was indeed a factory at the bottom of the Lane's steep incline, making dyestuffs (chemical colourants for commercial dyes).

The upper reaches of Factory Lane cut through a stretch of decayed slum housing—low Victorian row-houses with no indoor plumbing. The slum-dwellers' outdoor privies were an urban echo of my great-grandfather's home, the fisherman's cottage by the sea—but there the similarities ended. The squalor endured by these city families was more fetid than anything that this country boy could have anticipated. Our life seemed hard; others had it worse.

Ours was a two-storey house, partway down the hill, built of

Me at age twelve with my grandmother, new stepfather and sister (seated).

smoke-stained redbrick, with an indoor toilet, two bedrooms upstairs, plus a small space called a 'box room' where my baby sister would sleep. The house perched unevenly on the hillside, and my upstairs room had an expansive view, at least on breezier days when the smog thinned out, of the dye factory and of other industrial plants and mills that dominated the district.

The abrupt contrast with my earlier rural surroundings couldn't be worse, I felt. What I recall noticing first was Hilda's frustration with hanging laundry outside to dry. It instantly got coated with black soot and grey-green streaks of something else. The dye factory and its neighbours belched out clouds of smoke that I watched taking on varied colours at different hours of the day, marking the addition of extra ingredients in their processing, I guessed. I was most alarmed by one occasional variant, an especially bilious shade of greenish yellow that was rippled with angry purple wheals.

I had previously of course lived only in the Scottish Borders, and I missed their gentle hills achingly. I'd seen little if anything of the more dramatic beauty of Scotland's lochs and Highlands further north, but I'd heard and read about them extensively. And from within the murk of Manchester it was for those romanticised uplands, as well as my familiar, real home region, that I worked up a deep sentimental longing—deep for a boy on the point of entering his teens. My longing soon came to embrace just about anything that carried the label 'Scottish'. BBC radio at the time would often broadcast the traditional Scots song 'The Banks of Loch Lomond', historically a lament after the 1745 Jacobite rebellion's defeat by English troops. And whenever I heard it I was embarrassed to find myself in teary snuffles, especially at the lines:

> Oh, ye'll tak' the high road,
> And I'll tak' the low road
> And I'll be in Scotland afore ye.

There were new Manchester schools to attend. First a 'primary' (or elementary) school, which was a hulking and blackened building on a small lot. Then within two years I was in a vastly more extensive 'grammar' school, the equivalent of an American middle- and high-school combined. At both transitions, I remember that my perpetual, generalised trepidation, a deep-seated anxious apartness, came to be sharply intensified.

As testimony to superior educational standards in my home village—at least in my biased mind—I was bumped up a grade after my arrival in the city. In consequence, although I wasn't short for my age I repeatedly became the smallest boy in whatever class I joined, simply by being the youngest. I got physically bullied a lot until I learned after many humiliations to fight back. One of the insults that accompanied my beatings was a Northern English dialect word entirely new to me: *mardy*, meaning 'soft' or 'spoiled'. By the time I got to the grammar school, hostilities became subterranean, in a battleground of basement cloakrooms; in addition to our bare fists they now involved 'flick-knives' ('switchblades' to Americans) and what we called 'knuckledusters' in our softening British euphemism. They were made of hard metal, of course—brass or steel. It was all much scarier than anything I'd known in lower school, rural or urban.

But my fear would vanish in the fury and tumult of a gang-fight. I soon understood there can be no room for fear when knives are slicing the air and bigger people than you are gut-punching and kicking you. The priority is to punch and kick your own way out.

I embarked on a silent programme of self-training over I don't know what length of time—some weeks, maybe months. Early on, when taking a beating, I would in my mind step outside myself and imagine that the pain of each blow was less with each one, until I actually believed it and the punches really did feel bearable. More than that, the overcoming of my own hurt seemed to give me the capacity to lash out and hurt others.

Bigger boys picked on me for other reasons besides my size. They cited as just cause for a beating my Scottish Borders accent. It was, they said, 'really weird' among the prevailing flattened vowels of Manchester-speak. Also classed in the really weird category, and deserving a dose of corporal punishment, was my new Eastern European last name. I'd gained it 'for convenience', my mother had said vaguely. The change also served, I'm aware, to provide another even more desirable commodity: respec-tability. In place of bearing my mother's maiden name, that simple, earth-toned 'Brown' as I had for nine years, I was now made to adopt my stepfather's multisyllabic patronym. This despite the fact that, as I learned only many years later, he did not legally adopt me.

Tereshchuk was admittedly more interesting a name than plain old Brown, but I found its extra syllables cumbersome. And besides, Brown was mine, and I liked it; it was straightforward and it suited me. I began to think, though, that the very strange-ness of Tereshchuk could be used to offset my misgiving about it; it could possibly work to render me more interesting to others. I decided to trade on its relative exoticness even while inwardly resenting it. I would methodically explain the cluster of conson-ants in the middle of Tereshchuk: 'S-H-C-H, and yes there are two Hs.' Although now Anglicised as four letters, I pointed out earnestly, these represented simply one single if complex letter: Щ in the original Cyrillic alphabet as used by Ukrainians. And for its pronunciation, it should sound exactly the same as—and I would demonstrate vocally—the cluster formed in phrases like 'EngliSH CHurch' or 'freSH CHeese.' But my determined treatise won little traction among Manchester's teenagers. Few if any were motivated to get the name right.

So I moved on and constructed a wisecrack that could perhaps edge out, or at least cover up my resentment. I would say, 'If I just had a penny for every time I have to spell out my name, I'd be very rich.' It somehow made me feel better as a kid, whether or not it amused anybody else. And though I may, in my seventies, now be finally over my childhood discomfort, I still find myself slipping back into it. If I'm on the phone dictating my name and address to someone about to mail me something, there's a reflex to make the same old, tired attempt at a joke. How many pennies could I have piled up by now?

Chapter 6
City Teen

NOVEMBER, 2018

An evening flight to Los Angeles. Next morning I awake slowly from a gauzy dream of my rural childhood. I'm walking with my grandmother to the village post office where she picks up her weekly widow's pension, and then tut-tuts her way along the sidewalk to Horace the Milkman, worrying under her breath if she has enough to pay his delivery bill. Drawn from history as lived, my dream even includes a small herd of cows strolling alongside us, till they make with ingrained habit a right turn into Horace's milking shed.

Once fully awake and caffeinated by pre-ordered room service, I'm of course in a Beverly Hills hotel. I unthinkingly call for my car to be readied by the valet, and then drive it to the high-security parking garage of California's State Courts. A private elevator with a white-gloved attendant takes me up to the Appeal Court Justice's chambers, and I sit to talk with the Justice about his life and career. I'm on assignment for national television to profile America's highest-ranking judge professing the faith of Islam—and to ask the inevitable question: 'What's it like to be a Muslim judge in the age of Trump?' We also discuss other, broader matters of jurisprudence and governance. One of his staff brings in Lapsang tea for us.

An occasionally familiar reflection surfaces for me: What's a bastard boy from the rural borderlands and city slum districts doing here? How strange it is to have passed between such divergent worlds.

My morning's task completed, I drive out of the Hall of Justice and turn onto Santa Monica Boulevard. The car radio plays—with perfect timing and banality—the local Angelino band Weezer. They're singing one of their Nineties hits, 'Beverly Hills', a song I loosely recognise from my early days after arriving in America and tuning to Q104.3—Classic Rock:

Where I come from ain't all that great.
I didn't go to boarding schools.
Got nothing in my pocket.
The truth is I don't stand a chance.
It's something that you're born into.
And I just don't belong.
Beverly Hills, Beverly Hills—that's where I wanna be.

My teen years in Manchester, England during the 1960s were an oscillating mix of deep uncertainty and the beginnings of self-confidence. With puberty, I fast came to want a way to get along with my fellows. At my new, urban high school for boys I turned determinedly to sports. I was athletically built and felt sure that the previously unfamiliar sport of rugby, with all its associations of hearty camaraderie, would provide my entrée into convivial male society.

Home life still lacked any great comfort for me. My sister was growing up and now also attending school, an elementary school in her case. This enabled our mother to go out to work, as a clerical assistant. We all still lived in the same modest house, not actually in the city slums, but close enough to them to be affordable. My sister and I had a fond if slightly distant relationship; I enjoyed reading stories to her, notably *Winnie the Pooh* and later *The Chronicles of Narnia*. But with eight years between us we were not close companions. My peers at my high-school had become my priority.

I came to be pretty good at school rugby. I provided strong pushing power at the back of the scrum and some fair speed running with the ball. I enjoyed feeling the strength in my shoulders, and the ability to help in a combined effort—in winning a point or two, or even better a whole game. Truth be told, though, no great sense of fellowship developed with my teammates. For all my desire to be in this in-crowd, I could never summon the easy-going openness that it seemed to require of me, and which others so clearly possessed. Despite my strong ambition to be likeable, I seemed stuck with a reserved nature.

And the sport that I turned out to be best at was solo cross-country running. 'Cross-country' was an ambitious misnomer. The races were actually held through a Manchester park with the gloomy-sounding name of Boggart Hole Clough, *clough* being an old Northern-English word (pronounced cluff) which meant a steep-sided gully, and *boggart* reputedly being a malicious kind of local goblin. The parkland was thick with rhododendron bushes, but they had a darker colour than rural naturalists would recognise, their leaves covered in the city's filmy soot.

I got a rush from the running itself, and from my sense of personal, unaided achievement in staying the arduous course, even sometimes finishing first. But I had to admit it did nothing at all to help my clubbability. It just served to further underline my aloneness. I wanted to stop feeling alone, and I believed I had some real potential for changing into a social being. It appeared I was a good-looking boy. It was reassuring to be told so, especially when it came from a girl—a pretty girl. I was by this stage fairly tall and, although slim, I carried myself in what I heard described as a 'strapping' fashion. I made an effort with my grooming. Popular older boys were the natural model to copy in their styles of dress and hair. I sensed them to be richer, too, even though our school uniforms were intended to level out differences between the prosperous and the poor.

Cultivating a good look was a tricky path to tread. Those few of us who looked sharp, even incorporating a dash of trendiness into our uniforms, could end up standing out too distinctly, and we'd be decried as fops or 'nancy-boys', whatever that may have meant to us at our sexually under-informed age. It was clearly at the least a label to be avoided, even if we were hazy on what specifics might be involved.

There were among us a lot of slum kids who were scornful of appearances that might come off as slick; they maintained a slovenliness and an unwashed look, almost like a badge of honour or maybe some form of protest—it was hard to tell which.

For myself, as part of my drive to be well-presented I was an eager tub-user, bathing daily if I could get away with it in my economy-conscious family. Our water was heated by natural gas,

31

and that was costly. I really appreciated that tub; and if I'd known then about showers in the home, I would have wanted one.

Appearance was one thing. Conversation was quite another. Keeping up with the banter and chatter of my fellow mid-teenagers presented difficulties. Unsurprisingly for the time, talk at school was peppered with references to TV shows. Imported American series like *Bonanza*, *Seahunt*, *Gunsmoke* and anglicised versions of US game-shows like *Beat The Clock*—these were the titles I would hear about all the time. However, my family's budget didn't extend to a TV set, and I lived in ignorance of all the shows' content.

The local public library came to my rescue. One upside—maybe the only upside I'd yet discovered—to life in the city that I still hated for its grim edifices, its filth and acrid smells, was the presence of this astonishing repository of knowledge. And it was accessible—amazingly enough—in a grand public building open to all. I'd come to regularly sink myself among its treasures for many hours after school. But specifically to deal with my telly-illiteracy, I would get up extra early in the morning and make a quick but essential library stop on the way to school, speed-reading the daily papers, in particular their reviews of broadcasts from the previous night. I could usually glean enough highlights about the programmes to pass muster with my peers, as long as our chats didn't get too detailed. If the twists of a particular plot-line came up—'*Wasn't it fab how Little Joe dealt with that snobby new girl from the other ranch?*'—I had nothing to contribute, and I'd have to change the subject rapidly.

Dating called for similar subterfuge. My eagerness to fit in with others was mounting to a kind of desperation, constantly feeling held back by my family circumstances. I came to resent bitterly the absence from our house of another mass-market product: the telephone—one more humiliation that I felt was unmentionable and had to be hidden. A desirable girl may have given me her phone number, and I may have saved up my newspaper-delivery wages for a movie or a fairground visit. But in order to call the girl and propose a date, I had to use one of the few public pay-phones in our neighbourhood. At that time, those phones would emit tell-tale beeps that required the caller to drop in coins to pay for the connection. Agonisingly for me these beeps could also be heard at the other end of the line. So I figured out a way to conceal or bypass this all-too-audible giveaway. I'm not sure where I learned it, but it involved a fast tapping-out of a complex numeric code on the receiver-rest just as the connection was meant to go through.

It was just a few years into the 60s and Britain's revolution in rock music was well under way, home-grown but heavily influenced by Chicago's Maxwell Street Blues. I've never been totally sure just how that transatlantic linkage began. I know we as teenagers conducted a fervent trade among ourselves, borrowing back-and-forth some rare imported records by Muddy Waters and his ilk. God help you if you scratched anyone else's precious vinyl.

I gained a notion of how America's Great Migration had carried the laments and protests of Southern rural blues into a resonant fusion with the more urgent rhythms of city life, and how the form developed most resonantly among the busking musicians of Chicago's vast open-air street-market. We were a ready audience for this powerful new mix. We too knew something about migration: our urban region was a magnet for the poor and unemployed who flowed in from Ireland, from the farther Northern parts of England and of course from Scotland.

Manchester is only forty miles or so from Liverpool and each rival city had its febrile undergrowth of aspiring rock stars. And eventually there were some very successful emerging stars—The Beatles in 'The Pool', and The Hollies among us in Manchester. The world now knows the ultimate victors in that intercity competition.

For the young in both urban centres there was a mush-rooming of what Americans might have called garage bands. Except that we practised in tolerant parents' back rooms, or in empty church halls. Few of my peers' parents had garages; street parking was more the norm as car-ownership grew, if slowly, in our neighbourhood—almost always second-hand models, and as often sitting on bricks as on wheels. My own family didn't acquire a car until I was seventeen and leaving the home. The absence of a car was something else I'd never mention among my fellows. If I agreed to join a schoolboys' outing to a movie, I'd run the risk that my journey there by bus, involving some uncertain connections, would make me late for the show. One time I arrived a good fifty minutes into the screening, walked around the theatre's block several times over, worsening my lateness, incapable of facing my friends with the reason for my delay. I bailed on the whole thing, walking all the way back home again. From then on I worked hard at fully mastering Manchester's complex bus timetable and would carve out an extra hour or more for making any cross-town trip.

Car or no car, the compelling draw of the music scene was irresistible. Like innumerable other city youngsters, mostly at that time just the boys, I bought a guitar with money saved from my part-time jobs—a small but steady bedrock of newspaper delivery earnings plus occasional add-ons from a bit of yardwork. I consulted the requisite 'Learn Three Chords In A Day' booklets and I joined up promiscuously with any band that would have me. I didn't seem able to remain faithful to a particular set of musicians for very long. But Manchester's fledgling rocker world boasted a fluid and extensive personnel pool, so I kept moving and I'd soon find my place in the line-up of a new group, trio, quartet, or even one of the combos that we were sometimes quaintly called. The name for one four-person band that I stuck with a bit longer than most was chosen with some stunning creativity: we became The Four. Our graphic logo, boldly printed in the circle of our big bass-drum, spelled it out in Roman numerals, IV. This was an effort at some edgy punning on 'intravenous', even though our acquaintance with drug-use was pretty limited in our midteens.

Pubs and basement nightclubs were the semi-professional setting for our gigs. I don't know about the others but, for me, the two intoxicants of alcohol and marijuana unquestionably helped to boost the greater social ease I was beginning to experience. While much of that teenage period is now a blur, I remember with complete clarity what drink I drank. I'm strongly imprinted with the brand of beer that predominated in almost every pub and all the city's liquor stores. It was Worthington's Pale Ale, brewed not far away in Burton-on-Trent, a town proud

34

to be known as The Capital of British Beer. My very first taste was of the bottled variety (it was of course widely available on tap as well) and it came in a wooden crate of maybe twelve bottles. The crate had been carried in by one of my bandmates to a practice session in a youth-club's rec room. I recall the club as unsupervised, or perhaps it was just liberally or laxly supervised. No great fuss was made about the drink. I didn't register any thunderclap

Me performing in 'The IV' rock band at the the age of fifteen, approximately.

on swallowing it or even just a jolt. But clearly the beer was desirable, because our consumption continued and mounted. I believe every band-practice from then on was accompanied by Worthington's.

It was also our regular companion whenever we were paid cash (a little) to perform in the music-room of a pub, or in the downscale clubs where we occasionally got gigs. Free booze was also a currency of payment for us, topping up the meagre sums of money involved.

I remember being greatly stirred by a girl a couple of years older than me; she was maybe seventeen and named—I think— Caroline. With the help of shared bottles and maybe the seductive power of our band's music (though that's a stretch of a claim to make) I succeeded in 'pulling' her, in the ugly phrasing of my adolescent cohort, meaning of course bedding her.

'Caroline', if that's correct, became a kind-of regular girl- friend for a while. Though she was an attractive and sexy-enough young woman in her own right, my real excitement about her surged when I learned early on that her surname was the highly- resonant Worthington. I actually thought I might be stepping into a family of valuable connections. It turned out, though, not to be the right branch of Worthingtons. Her father, a good- natured man who seemed to like me a lot, was a dustman—a sanitation worker.

My disappointment wasn't too great. There were consola- tions. Caroline's father was no ordinary garbage collector. As well as emptying the district's dustbins (trashcans) daily, he also held the keys to the sanitation trucks' depot, and with his job as superintendent came a house, which faced onto some of Man- chester's worst slum housing. I soon learned to ignore the pervasive slummy smell, plus the even more pungent stink of garbage, as Caroline and I got completely distracted in our hot- and-heavy trysts in the depot's hidden corners and crannies. She had access to her father's keys, so we could slink easily from her family home into the empty depot.

But about that drink itself. The other band members and I were relaxing with the ever-available beer after playing a set when I was overtaken and puzzled by a previously unknown sensation.

It came to me not in a lightning-bolt of perception, but a gradual dawning—a growing appreciation that I did not feel alien, did not feel out-of-place, did not feel at odds with my surroundings, did not feel in some undefined danger, did not feel inadequate, not sidelined, not judged and found wanting. It was so unfamiliar—and wonderful—that I tried to hold on to the feeling, but it dissipated as dawn approached and I had to get home. I dived into a deep but narrow cleft of sleep before waking again soon to the plateau of another school-day.

The sheer abandon of playing in the band was a simple all-encompassing joy, a losing of myself in the pounding rhythm and defiant noise. And I could hardly fail to feel flattered by the crowds of young girls below, craning upward, wildly tossing their heads and screaming.

But subterfuge was still a necessary part of my repertoire. My vocal skills were even more rudimentary than my guitar-playing —indeed they were well-nigh non-existent. I was occasionally required to join our bass-player and the lead vocalist in 'harmonizing'—except that, to conceal my inability to hit any note accurately, I had to resort to surreptitious lip-syncing.

Things didn't go so well at home. While my stepfather had once made efforts to engage with me in a friendly manner, he changed once he had successfully wooed and married my mother, fathered a child of his own and moved his new family to the big city. Michael's relations with me cooled fast, and in the ten years or so that he and I lived together, my attitude towards him in return became in succession resentful, distant and rebellious.

On his side, he was dead-set upon self-improvement, and he attended night-school diligently. He'd got a job as laboratory assistant in the chemical factory near our house—a menial position that he was anxious to advance out of. His evening studies, several nights a week, were to increase his skills in translation, especially for scientific articles. His wish for upward mobility was resolutely expressed, and repeatedly: 'Next year I'll make a thousand pounds,' he'd say. (This was 1964; the equivalent in today's money would be roughly US $25,000.) It was a serious amount of cash for our family, sounding to my ears way too high to be reached. Michael's ringing aspirational vow would have meant a doubling of his income inside a year—and we lived among factory workers, labourers, bus- and truck-drivers, plus some warehouse hands and retail staff. I never saw any evidence of hard work and dedication resulting in great economic self-improvement.

Silence predominated in the house, much heavier to me than the quiet I'd known in my grandmother's home. Michael seemed to have lost any interest in me except when he felt the need to reprimand me, and I had no desire to communicate with him. My mother had come to maintain an impotently anxious middle position between us, saying little.

From his secure base and determined self-application, Michael couldn't understand or tolerate my unreliability; my staying out late, my sleeping off the late nights on weekend mornings. I managed to hide from him actual drunkenness or being high. I felt sure he would take an even darker view of all that; I rarely saw him touch alcohol. On the other hand, I for my part threw myself determinedly into drinking, on performance nights, in the many practice sessions and in the secretive parties we'd move on to with their booze, drugs and fervent sexual exploration.

I was sixteen. There was an argument—in all likelihood about my arriving home at an unacceptable time, maybe the next morning or another day entirely: I don't remember. It escalated. Verbal jousting was frustrating for Michael since English was the least fluent of his several proficient languages. For myself, I was by then revelling in my expanding vocabulary; I'd come to delight in achieving sharp verbal felicities, especially the sly extra impact of unexpectedly mixing in Latinate words with blunt Anglo-Saxon terms. I'd also found a new willingness to use my broadening language skills in a downright, forthright fashion—something that would have been unthinkable for me in my younger, shy, more withdrawn days. While unable now to quote any exact phrasing, I still acutely recall the heady, powerful feeling of pressing a spoken onslaught against Michael with confidence. Often in those days, scorn and ridicule would surge in me whenever he struggled to assert something like, 'I am head of family. Your job is do what I say.' In this day's encounter I was once again throwing his lack of fluency and his clumsy efforts to express authority back at him—verbally hard and unremitting.

At one moment in our dispute, probably provoked beyond what he could bear in dialogue, he turned to action and advanced with his open right hand in a swing at me. I sidestepped and swiveled to take on his exposed left-side with my fists raised and clenched, ready—my blood racing—to pummel him.

Hilda, whose presence I'd blanked out, now rushed between us—and Michael and I both stepped back, but with fixed stares of fury. I don't know what if any words were voiced at that point. But I still carry with me the frozen tableau and the image of his dark and tightened face, a trembling jaw especially, that read to me not just as anger but as sheer outrage that I had evaded his blow and was even daring to fight back.

For the next year we scarcely spoke a word to each other. Eventually, the chance of a breakaway from this simmering state of perpetual stand-off appeared when I turned seventeen. A sardonic phrase would often run around my head at the time. A *Manchester Guardian* writer named William Bolitho, who was friends with both Nöel Coward and Walter Lippman, had targeted that hated hometown of my teens with a well-turned quip. Being the dedicated drinker that I already was, I heartily resonated to his words: 'The shortest way out of Manchester,' Bolitho wrote, 'is notoriously a bottle of Gordon's Gin.' In the event, though, my escape route was to be a little different. I won a scholarship to Oxford University.

Chapter 7
Chasm

On reaching Oxford at the age of seventeen I thought, perhaps unsurprisingly given my new surroundings, that I
had alighted in a kind of heaven. The oft-cited 'dreaming
spires' of the university meant just that for me: a dreamland. My
admission into a college and the scholarship award that made it
financially feasible owed a lot to the instruction and encouragement that my high school had provided—especially its dedicated
English, Latin and French masters whose classes I was lucky
enough to have taken. The school was not all social deprivation
and gang fights, after all; academics were taken seriously.

I was very open to the university working its reputed magic on
me, with both faculty members and fellow students helping to
bolster my intellectual arrogance. That had started to develop, I
suspect, back when I first arrived in Manchester from the Border
countryside. The city school system administered aptitude tests
and I was judged to be a grade ahead of my age. I certainly felt
myself to be brighter than anyone around me.

Oxford had an entrenched tradition of inspiring in students a
reliance on their own mental self-sufficiency, and I felt encouraged to maintain a headstrong confidence in my innate abilities.
'Innate' was just how this institution considered our intellects to
be. I don't recall anyone suggesting the need to exert effort or
apply industry in our studies. We should just be naturally
brilliant, we supposed. Brilliance seemed to comprise simply
spotting allusions, recognising sources, connecting references,
and presenting them all of a piece as evidence of coherent
comprehension. Our tutorials, accompanied sometimes with a
glass of sherry, had the feeling of a gentlemanly exchange of
ideas about the texts under review, be they Shakespeare, Dryden,
or Wordsworth, and there was little sense of any mental training
being imparted.

'Don't work too hard,' a tutor would say on ending a session with us, as he issued our essay assignments for the following week. Such warnings were delivered with an arched eyebrow, serious but not serious. In keeping with the university's broadly generous student-teacher ratio, our tutorial groups were always small, usually two, rarely more than four undergrads—and we would repeat to each other as a farewell until next time that same injunction against hard work.

If I only could, I'd like to be original in describing the wonder of Oxford and its unworldliness but it's hard. Autobiographies by Oxford graduates rarely fail to devote thousands of words to their alma mater's elegant grandeur and to the air of languid superiority that she could instill in her denizens. Try as they might to be innovative, they often end up little more than variations on Oscar Wilde's late-nineteenth-century reminiscences ('the most flower-like period of one's life') or the aesthetic idealism of wealth and privilege in Evelyn Waugh's *Brideshead Revisited*. Wilde the undergraduate, still talked about fondly in my day, had cultivated a decidedly flippant persona for himself. While he was perhaps unexpectedly an earnest boxer at college (his bouts likely to have been in the light-heavyweight class) he also lovingly adorned his rooms with peacock feathers, lilies and delicate porcelain. With the truly false modesty of an Oxford man he claimed: 'I find it harder and harder every day to live up to my blue china.' And as for Waugh, sixty years after Wilde, he accomplished even less academic work than was loosely required and behaved in a manner that he himself later described as 'fatuously haughty'.

I too was besotted by the place. It brought me, after all, three long, luxuriant years of developing and fully indulging a taste for knowledge, beauty, social conviviality and sexual adventure. And without yet knowing then about the precedent set by Wilde the decorator, I even pasted and hung my own hessian-tawny wallpaper on the slightly crumbling walls of my seventeenth-century rooms.

I remember strolling along Queen's Lane one Spring day with an oddly-combined sensation of sheer bliss about my good fortune in being there, along with a premonition that I would never again in my life feel so good. The lane was hardly one of

Oxford's majestic sights, at less than thirteen-feet wide. Hemmed in by high limestone walls, it permitted no entry to vehicles except bicycles. It started out from the front gate of my own college, St Edmund Hall, and wound its way past the backsides, as it were, of neighbouring seats of learning: Queen's College, which dated back to the 1340s, New College ('new' only in relative terms, since it was founded in 1379), Hertford and Wadham colleges, and eventually to our highest temple of knowledge, the imposing Bodleian Library that served the entire university.

It was a commonplace route for me to take, but on this day's walk I made time to commune with the faces of gargoyles high up on the college buildings. Although practically speaking they were only drainage-spouts, many had an encouraging carved smile just for me or even an outright cheering laugh. Others, though, wore grimaces of obscure pain or a contemplative gaze up into the clouds that prompted me too to stare heavenward. Over the walls from New College's garden wafted the always-soothing scent of lilac.

At ground level, a discreet door to the carefully symmetrical lodgings where the provost (president) of Queen's had his private residence was painted a rich cobalt blue and topped with a classically Georgian transom that bore the three eagles of the college's coat-of-arms. Pretty damn elegant for just a back-entrance, I thought. I passed under the arch of our Bridge of Sighs, England's answer to the one in Venice and, atypically amid Oxford's general devotion to full-blown antiquity, relatively juvenile, some 300 years younger than the Italian original. It connects two separate quadrangles of Hertford College on either side of the lane and I recall my heart trilling to the buoyant sound of undergraduates chattering their way across it. I could even make out, I told myself, the swishing of their black academic gowns, always worn *de rigueur* when we attended lectures or class. At moments like these, I would feel fully at home.

Over time I mastered a passable imitation of the nonchalance that Oxford seemed to require about life in its enchanted universe. I eased my voice into a lazy drawl and a careless, undemonstrative shrug of the shoulders was my only response whenever anything resembling praise came my way for an essay, an interpretive idea or a suggestion for new lines of scholastic inquiry. The same studied casualness appeared to be mandatory among all my peers.

I developed a capacity for dismissing my poverty and father-lessness from my mind. In my determined settling-in to Oxford's rarified and smug air, both of those troubling conditions were successfully—I believed—waved away as quite irrelevant to my current life, and even more so to my expanding future.

But in the here-and-now among my fellow undergraduates I would often get overcome with anger at myself for a lingering insecurity in my make-up. I'd thought I'd beaten down my chronic introversion during my late high-school years, only to find it surging again now when surrounded by so many others apparently more accomplished than I was, and certainly wealth-ier, exuding much greater ease in their lives. I came across a group of four or five freshmen chatting around our college's stone fountain at the centre of the main quadrangle. From a slight distance I heard a reference to some proceedings at an athenaeum. I came a little closer, thinking that if I hovered a while I might be able to step into what could be a discussion of Emperor Hadrian's arts-and-sciences school in ancient Rome. But it became clear it was all just banter about how many of them had fathers who were members of the Athenaeum, at that time London's most respected gentlemen's club in Pall Mall. I veered away fast, as if I had simply been aiming for the dining hall.

In that same first term (semester), an entirely undramatic but illuminating encounter made a sharp impression on me. Another student—to my mind the infuriatingly confident product of an expensive boarding school—joined me to shave at an adjoining sink in our communal bathroom. My answers to his evidently genuine curiosity about me were far from forthcoming; they were flat and curt. I simply wasn't much used to people talking to me in a way that seemed affable, kind and relaxed.

'Who are your people, then?' was one question I found hard to take in, let alone answer. After a pause, I volunteered, 'They're from Scotland,' though I knew it wouldn't have been geography that he meant. 'But I've ... moved around a bit.'

To his credit he didn't seem put off by my gruffness and we parted agreeing to have a pint later that day in the buttery. That quaint college term was our somewhat risible historical euphemism for the undergraduates' bar; once upon a time its half-cellar space would have housed barrels of butter as well as beer, cider and mead. I felt a little looser as the pair of us downed our beers together, just two among a crowd of smokers and drinkers—a gaggle of 1960s male youth flicking their cigarette butts now and again out of the medieval mullioned windows. But for days afterwards I was tortured with self-criticism about the whole episode: Why couldn't I have been the one to begin that bathroom-sink conversation? Why couldn't I have been more easy-going once it had started?

The new cure I prescribed for myself was to go into journalism—becoming a reporter on the student newspaper. This way, I figured, I would have to talk to people, no matter how intimidating I found them, otherwise I wouldn't get the interviews and the quotes I needed as a wannabe-professional.

It turned out to be a good career move for the future. I spent some time pounding the pavement as a newshound, one of several on the undergraduate team. Promotion came rather easily, working my way up through the small newsroom to become first the news editor, and then finally taking the lead position as the paper's overall editor. One well-known function our publication fulfilled was to serve as a kind of feeder-farm for the country's national newspapers in Fleet Street. That wasn't where I was going to end up, though. I had decided—ahead of the truth and for the wrong reason—that newspapers were a dying species. I was sure that television would do the killing-off, with of course no notion at the time that the real killer, the internet, lay farther ahead in the future.

I tried a taste of television work when I was still an undergraduate. During one long summer vacation I got an internship at a local commercial station that served, of all places, my original home territory of the Borders. I told no one at the company that I once came from that same area: Oxford schooling seemed to outweigh the need for any local knowledge. In my job interview, the station's head of news asked me, if only as a late afterthought, what I might know about their broadcast footprint and joked back, 'I've heard that you have more sheep than human viewers.' He took it well, laughing and saying he often said the same at cocktail parties. I was hired, as a news-desk lackey. The job title on my payslip: 'copy-boy'.

A couple of weeks later, out of the blue, one of the senior news anchors was poached by the rival BBC and I suddenly found myself taking his place on-screen for the nightly broadcasts. This happened, astonishingly for me and many others watching my efforts, when I was still nineteen.

Other fortuitous bonuses came along as well, including one that catapulted me onto the national network with a regionally-angled story. More than that, it unexpectedly sidelighted a major international event, the Soviet invasion of Czechoslovakia. Our surprising local angle was that the teenage daughter of a Czech Communist Party leader happened just then, a politically very inconvenient time, to be doing volunteer work in the West, digging ditches at an international work-camp in our area, which I filmed. The camp was newsworthy in our terms: a team of well-meaning foreigners sent to our region by a charitable aid agency to upgrade some of our more benighted living conditions. But a dramatic new development occurred after I had filmed the ditch-digging and interviewed the girl along with other volunteers. It was an extra twist that thrilled me as an eager journalist.

On the very eve of Russian tanks rolling into Prague, a pair of KGB agents arrived in our Borderland and kidnapped the official's daughter, bundling her eventually onto a flight to Moscow. I hurriedly interviewed all the local people who'd been eye witnesses to the kidnapping, and I traced the agents' journey, taking the girl, evidently dazed and probably drugged, to London airport and aboard an Aeroflot plane. I documented the whole cloak-and-dagger story in my report for the country-wide prime-time broadcast. My joy was complete; I got to sign off, saying, 'From the Border region, this is David Tereshchuk for News at Ten.' There could be no crown more glorious for a young reporter.

I became an ever-more-motivated TV journalist after I finally left Oxford and entered the real world as a full-time professional, first covering metropolitan news in London, then the national news, and eventually international issues.

At college I had opened as broad and as deep a chasm between me and my origins as I could, and I now put an even greater distance between myself and my mother. It was physically sizeable since a three-hour car ride separated London from her home near Manchester. We were separate in other ways, too. I would phone her only very rarely. The cost in those days of any call beyond the merely local was a strong disincentive to phoning, and an easy excuse for not calling. Outwardly I justified our separation as an inevitable result of my hectic, constantly travelling work-life, while inwardly I quite simply didn't want to be associated with Hilda.

The distancing had begun gradually back in my teens. Ever since she had gone out to work again when my sister had reached school age, her clerking jobs grew in importance through a succession of workplaces, beginning with a junior position in a hospital and eventually reaching a job with fuller responsibilities on a university campus. Her focus shifted perceptibly from home to profession. Meanwhile my hostility to my stepfather and my growing teenage unruliness—the late nights, the disappearances —provoked in her a frustration about me that took the form of tight-lipped coldness and an untargetted, angry stare.

I admired her aspiration to improve her life (all our lives really, while I still lived in the family) but it was outweighed by my disgruntlement with her for not taking my side in my private warfare against Michael. She and I ended up being little more than cordial and proper with each other.

It now appears to me a very bleak family landscape. She was discontent, that much seemed clear, but about what I couldn't fully be sure. Michael, meanwhile, concentrated on his own aspirations, pursuing certificates and diplomas. I just wanted escape, of almost any kind. Were we all so preoccupied in our different ways with getting out of where we were that simple human tenderness between us just got pushed out of the picture?

Hilda's professional progress achieved its intended aim, a boost to the family income, and my stepfather's earnings climbed too, until the couple eventually bought a new house far from the slums and the factories. It was in a clean, lower-middle class, well-lawned suburb of cookie-cutter houses, which I judged whenever I might show up—as the superior Oxford snob I'd by then become—to be as repellent as I'd found our previous smog-shrouded home.

My twenties and thirties were dedicated wholeheartedly to gaining national prominence in my industry, and Hilda and I ended up communicating with little more than Christmas and birthday cards, and not always prompt ones on my part. I was in commercial TV, so I wasn't working for the BBC, but it was that grand public institution which came to play a role in preserving our slender mother-and-son connection. In whatever country I might have gone to on assignment, the 'Beeb' would jolt me into a guilty realisation that I had once again missed my mother's birthday. Its World Service broadcasts always patriotically marked the British queen's birthday, which happened to fall on the day after Hilda's. Cursorily apologetic greetings would then arrive one day late at her house from Uganda, Bangladesh, Lebanon, Sri Lanka or wherever—by whichever close-to-instantaneous medium I could lay my hands on locally. I'd send international telegrams at the outset of my travelling days, later

At Thames Television in 1974, flanked on both sides by fellow on-screen hosts: cool John Stapleton, left, and the affable Bill Grundy, right.

turning to faxes after Hilda had taken to those machines (rather early on, in a sign of her business efficiency), and eventually on to emails once she acquired an iPad and an internet account.

The path of her life only tangentially touched mine. She divorced my stepfather—I guess I should retrospectively call him my first stepfather. That happened when my younger sister and I had both left the family home. From my out-of-range standpoint I could claim no knowledge, still less any understanding, of what marital tensions may have been building up. Hilda soon got married again, to a Scot named Norman, and she continued building her career, by now running the administration side of a business school where he (my second stepfather) worked as a teacher. His specialty was the engineering business.

As years and then decades passed I grew less constant in my avoidance of her, or them. I would even make occasional trips to their home, though regarding the visits as dutiful more than affectionate. With Norman a constant presence, I found it hard to have one-on-one conversations with my mother, and I noticed in her a need to have him always close by, serving—it appeared— as a kind of buffer. Our exchanges whether in person, or written, or in the occasional phone call, all seemed stilted affairs. The few times when she and I were alone together she would never refer to our early days—and for my part I rarely brought them up, either. I see now that I was maintaining my long-ingrained habit of avoiding the topic, the always unclear topic of how I came to be her son in the first place.

Then something changed—or rather two things, maybe three. First, I stopped drinking alcohol. My abuse of it and other addictive drugs had come—in the classic phrase of clinical specialists—'to seriously affect my life'. My own way of summar-ising it was that I crashed and burned. In my new-found and liberating sobriety, I also got married and moved to New York, the hometown of my new wife Melissa.

The new willingness that can come with recovery from addic-tion to look square-on at life, instead of avoiding its challenges, prompted in me a totally fresh hunger for knowledge about my father. I abandoned the ostensible lack of curiosity I'd professed for so long. I now viewed my well-cultivated indifference to the matter as a fake, a creation of my early conditioning, and indeed a toxic fake that had no place in the healthy life I was now trying to live.

Melissa supported me eagerly in my new spirit of inquiry. And then a surprise pregnancy early on in our marriage made us both even more eager, as now parents-to-be, for as much information as we could get about my genetic history, not least for reasons of pediatric healthcare in the future.

So I resolved to just briskly 'get to the bottom' of the mystery. I could have no idea then that the process of prising open my mother's secrecy would become so lengthy, spanning yet more decades—or so tortuous in its zigzags.

Chapter 8
Glimmers

SEPTEMBER, 1997

Hilda and I sit down at a sidewalk café just off Broadway. We've been to see Christopher Plummer at the Music Box Theater, his masterful and ultimately Tony-winning portrayal of the classical actor and legendary drunk of the 1930s, John Barrymore. Not long before his death, Barrymore tries to recreate a triumph from more than twenty years earlier in his career—a once widely-praised Richard III—even though he's now suffering from late-stage cirrhosis of the liver, and his brain is too fried to remember his lines.

It's two years, probably more, since I last saw my mother. She is visiting me from England for the first time since I came to live in the US. I'd remembered she enjoys the stage, so I'm pleased to have seen her watching Plummer intently, her eyes agleam with fascination. Now in her sixties, she is putting on some weight, but has dressed for the theatre and at five-foot-nine, neat in her businesswoman's suit, is a striking, rather handsome woman, recalling the pretty girlish woman she was when I was boy.

As we take our sidewalk seats Hilda voices something rare, a question about my feelings. In a tone I hear as deliberate motherliness, she wonders if I am 'bothered' by having seen in the play such a true-to-life account of alcohol's effects on one of its slaves. Barrymore was undoubtedly a helpless slave to booze, as I too once became and as Hilda eventually came to know.

'Were you upset,' she asks, 'to be reminded of what you used to be like yourself?'

I say, 'No, I wasn't, not unbearably.' I tell her what I often remind myself: 'It's good for me to face up to the truth of my drinking history honestly—a vital part of my staying away from alcohol, a day at a time.' And I add, with what I aim to be some lightness, that this approach has been working well for me. 'For nearly six-and-a-half years now, in fact.'

It seems a long time since her arrival at the addiction rehabilitation centre tucked away in Southwest England where I was first treated for alcoholism. It was called Barleywood, carrying an ironic but surely unintended echo of the extra-strong concoction, barleywine. She'd been invited to attend a 'family weekend' that was facilitated by counselors, and she was stunned to discover what my life in London, two hundred miles away from her, had become. Her successful son was in fact a shambling drunk, often to be found passed out in derelict buildings and on park benches. I remember her weeping, asking me and the counselors if it was somehow her fault that I'd become an alcoholic; and when reassured that it wasn't, sighing and saying she was glad I was 'getting help' for my problem.

She recalled, in her contribution to the therapeutic session, that her father had been a 'pretty hopeless' drunk, leading her mother to impose virtually complete teetotalism in the household after he died, and that one of her younger brothers had become a self-admitted alcoholic, something I hadn't known till then. My slowly detoxing brain still didn't function too clearly, but I had some notion that outside of her time seeing me she also joined other patients' family members attending lectures about alcoholism and had discussions with the staff in my absence about my prospects for recovery.

Her perplexity at Barleywood comes back to me as we order our Broadway drinks: mine a coffee, hers an iced tea. I remember how she reacted during the therapeutic session not just with shock—a pained look of distaste creasing her face as if at a sudden bad smell—but also with incomprehension on learning that I had come to behave, in part at least, like a homeless street-person.

She was puzzled why I hadn't gone home at nights, since I wasn't technically homeless. I still had one of my homes left, after all, even as my life and finances plummeted. I had become an acquisitive young man and had greedily bought up several properties in a gawky display of my prosperity, only to speedily lose most of it. My vagrant ways after dark were hard to explain. Alongside her on a counselor's sofa I tried to convey the absurd inanity of what had passed for my mental processes: the blurry indecision about what to do next when cash had all been spent at the bar, or everywhere was closing. Hailing a cab to go home seemed an impossible task; getting a train ticket at a kiosk even more so; and a bench in one of the many little parks that dot London's inner areas seemed so much easier. Or, if it was raining, a better option could be a still-roofed section in one of the decaying empty buildings I knew around the broken-down neighbourhoods where I mainly drank by that stage. It was a huge relief to take off my shoes and put them under my head as a pillow.

My mother grew more horrified as I began relating specifics. She lowered her gaze and raised her hand to silence me as I wandered into unwelcome detail about my toilet arrangements while out on the street. I remember little else about her during that rehab visit, except that on leaving she promised that she and her (second) husband would look after my cottage, eighty miles to the north, while I completed a stay that ended up lasting another three months of in-patient treatment.

Talking now on West Forty-Sixth Street I reprise our Barleywood meeting a little, as I remind her how tenuous a grip any drunk, including me, can keep on the reality of his surroundings. 'I was like Barrymore,' I say, 'when he recited those obscene verses, totally out-of-place and inappropriate. He had no idea where he was in reality.' I'm referring—imprecisely and not verbatim because I know how much she dislikes vulgarity—to a limerick composed by Barrymore about a girl visiting a zoo. He said she was:

> Seized by the nape,
> And humped by an ape,
> As she sighed: 'What a heavenly screw!'

Barrymore blurted out this extraneous material while supposedly doing serious prep-work on his Shakespearean dialogue. 'I was as bad,' I say, 'maybe not versifying out-loud like him, but every bit as divorced in my mind from what was going on around me in the actual world.'

I suddenly see an opportunity. The unaccustomed candor and

the air of empathy in our Barrymore-centred chat encourages me to broach the topic that I never have with her.

Not ever broached in person at least. I have tried it once, and quite recently, but at a distance. A few months ago, I very tentatively posed the long-unanswered question of my origins in an airmail letter to Hilda, since it somehow seemed easier to do it on paper. I had written: 'In my current, sober life many things are coming into new focus. My mental confusion as an alcoholic blinded me to the importance of some matters, and I simply avoided them. Now I just can't avoid them. One important matter is: who was my father? That's something I know we have never talked about, but it could now be the time to do so. For my part I dearly want to have that discussion. Can we please talk about it?'

By return mail came an angry refusal. She blamed my wife: 'You were never interested in all this until you met Melissa. She said her 'nerves' were badly affected by my letter, and 'I never want to hear about it again.'

I wrote nothing in reply. And my only spoken words of reaction, voiced only to Melissa as we both sat reading Hilda's note, came out as merely: 'Well that's it, I guess.' I was disappointed and hurt, more than I wanted to immediately admit, but not really surprised. Melissa said, 'It's time to leave it alone,' and I agreed.

Now, though, twelve weeks later, one-on-one with Hilda under the curiously warm neon lights of the theatre district, and after our talk together about unreality versus reality, it seems to me possible, just possible, that I can try raising the subject afresh.

'It's like a dark cloud making things difficult between you and me,' is how I begin, 'my not knowing who my father was.'

'Oh, David,' she answers. 'It's very hard.' And she says she's sorry for being so angry at the letter I wrote her. 'But it's very upsetting for me.'

That ostensibly mild word, 'upsetting'. It's been so familiar from our exchanges throughout the years, and it's highly charged. She never uses it with any specificity, indicating for instance the particular cause of any upset or what kind of upset might be the result; instead, I've come to recognise that it serves a generic, blanketing function. It will cover any subject with a label signifying the unapproachable, the not-to-be-talked-about.

But I press my inquiry, albeit gently. At least I'm intending to be gentle. I can see, though, that even the softest of questioning is distressing her. Her hands and her upper lip are quivering, something I don't think I've ever seen. I lay out in as careful a manner as I can my sense that the continuing ignorance I've been kept in, stretching now over five decades, has blocked us from having what could be a real mother-and-son relationship. I don't try to describe what such a relationship might exactly consist of —that would be beyond me.

I'm at pains to avoid phrases like 'I deserve to know,' or that begin, 'You ought to ... .' 'I just want us,' I say, 'to have an open and free way of talking to each other, which this unending secret seems to prevent us from having.'

There's tactical thinking in my approach, of course—and I'm deliberately drawing on journalistic practice: the wiles by which I can sometimes get a reluctant interviewee to talk. But arcing fiercely behind my calm stratagem, is one silent howl of protest after another: 'It's outrageous, keeping this secret from me!' and 'What right do you have you to protect yourself like this, if protection is what it is?' and 'You're utterly selfish' and 'What about me?'

However angry I feel at heart, my reasoning has consciously undergone some changes in recent times. I've passed through differing stages since I first came round in my earliest sobriety (that's how it felt: 'coming round' from being in many ways unconscious) to addressing what was previously never addressed. Early on I had feverishly permutated a multitude of possibilities about my paternity—often fantastical ones. Maybe my father was a passing GI. I knew that more than two million US troops passed through the UK during and after the War, though to be realistic there were no American bases set up anywhere in our own region. But having 'a Yank' as my father could maybe explain my fascination with US culture (as if just about every other British boy of my generation wasn't also immersed in superhero comic books and Hollywood Westerns). Alternatively, in a flashback to some childhood reveries, I imagined that he could have been an aristocrat. But by what kind of happenstance this duke or earl could possibly have met my mother exceeded my adult powers of imagination. A horde of potential kinds of father, ultimately and theoretically infinite in range, ended up just bewildering me, and I had to firmly chase out of my mind all the scurrying speculations.

Taking a different tack now, six years later, I've graduated to believing I'm unconcerned about the particulars of his identity. To my thinking at this stage, it's the sheer existence and maintenance of the secret that is troubling me, not the specific detail that has been hidden, name, age, profession and suchlike. My father could be anybody, I am now convinced; it's unimportant exactly who.

But none of this do I voice to Hilda as we talk, and instead I just emphasise—steadily but not contentiously, I hope—the unhappy murkiness that I keep attributing to our dark secret being still locked in place, a murkiness that (as I can't help repeating) keeps us separate from each other.

'I see that,' she eventually says, slightly shifting the glass in front of her. 'I will tell you.'

She pauses with a quick breath, not quite a sigh. 'But not here; not now. I need to be back in my own home, surrounded by my own things where I feel comfortable.'

I'm astonished. Inwardly excited and elated. But I don't show it. I'm anxious to signal that her new willingness, after all this time, is just perfectly normal. I reach to take her hand on the table between us. I stand and hug her shoulders to my waist as she remains sitting, a little stiffly. We hail a cab to take her to her midtown hotel, and me to my West Side apartment.

Chapter 9

Motherhood and Childhood

Trying to find who might have been my father inevitably meant learning more about my mother's life story. It's of course hard for me to picture what she was like before I made my appearance. But I feel sure that one passage in her younger years must have been especially important, even though she herself didn't dwell on it much. Perhaps tellingly, for my part too, I never asked her about it for many years. Describing it as an 'important' passage is a distinct understatement. It was the time she was sent away as a foster child.

In her adult life, during our everyday family conversations, she would only ever obliquely refer to that period of separation. She would occasionally mention 'when I was living away,' but only to signal a particular point in chronology, not to open up any account of the experience itself.

The background. I was not the first child that my hard-pressed grandmother regarded as a drain on her meagre family resources. My unexpected arrival, making her send my mother out to work at age sixteen to pay for the extra mouth to feed, may well have counted as a serious family emergency. But there had been an earlier, perhaps even bigger emergency. Eight years previously, shortly after the Second World War broke out, my grandfather had died—of alcohol-exacerbated illnesses, I was to learn much later.

His death left Mam looking after three children under nine, and without her husband's income as a carpenter, haphazard though it had been. She'd previously raised six children, one of them dying in childhood, one soon to die in the war at the age of twenty-six. The youngest ones still living at home were the two small boys aged six and four—my future uncles—and the eight-year-old daughter who would become my mother.

Financially strapped and in all likelihood quite exhausted, she decided—untypically, from what I came to know of her gritty self-sufficiency—to accept help in raising the girl child. Mam was much more accustomed to boys; among her older brood only one, her third, had been a girl: my mother's big sister by eleven years, my Aunt Doris.

Later it was to my aunt's house, a hundred miles away in England, that my mother would be sent, in some secrecy, to spend her pregnancy, almost as soon as it was discovered and before it began to show. I thus came to be born in Aunt Doris's home. Aunt Doris developed quite an attachment to me (perhaps helped by my happening to arrive on her birthday) and I evidently fell for her too. When learning to talk I called her by a toddler's stuttering effort at Doris, 'Dodo', which was to become her informal moniker across the whole family. By contrast, the best I could do with Hilda's name was something like 'Ninga', which never stuck. Dodo had married an English machinist in the textile industry, whose skills would in the 1950s take their family (including two boy-cousins of mine) to the British colony of Southern Rhodesia, nowadays Zimbabwe. Their emigration was typical of our family's diaspora across different English-speaking parts of the globe. My uncle Wilfred, for example, an older brother among the siblings, became a copper-miner in neigh-bouring Northern Rhodesia, now Zambia. Some thirty years later, as it happened, both of those African countries would become stamping grounds for my own form of adventurism, my reporting and filmmaking on the regions' liberation wars. Back as that toddler in my grandmother's home I thrilled to the periodic arrival of blue airmail letters from the relatives in Africa, most especially their gloriously coloured pictorial postage stamps showing zebras, antelopes and elephants.

Mam's fostering of my mother sent her to the home of three charitable, middle-aged sisters named Blackburn, 'spinsters' in that period's vernacular, who lived together in the nearby city, the county seat that lay ten miles to the south, an hour's bus-ride on the English side of the border. 'The Blackburns', always referred to as that, were prominent among local Methodists, known for their piety, their connections at a high level in the national Methodist Church, and for their good works in our region. They inculcated in Hilda a degree of prim properness—a subject of sniggery jokes from her younger brothers, as I observed later on in a not-quite-understanding fashion, when I was growing up amid all three of them. She would sometimes try, vainly, to get the boys to straighten their backs whenever they slouched during meals—something that only happened when Mam left the room to get something from the kitchen. They'd deliver a sing-song gibe at Hilda, 'Bossy Little Miss B!' which I came to recognise as a taunt that she'd turned into a miniature copy of the older Blackburns.

Who knows how such a connection had ever been made between our two households, us and the Blackburns? It's lost in the mists of family history. I'm aware, though, that the tie was genuine and loving, and for all the spinsters' great emphasis on propriety, the connection survived the upheaval and scandal of my out-of-wedlock birth to their former young ward. I remember Hilda sometimes taking me, in the early 1950s when I was six or seven years' old, to tea at the sisters' home, and being fussed over by the religious trio.

At one teatime there was an honoured guest whom the sisters fawned upon even more than me. It was the preacher Reverend Donald Soper, sometimes referred to in those days as 'Britain's Billy Graham'. He enthralled me as he told us about how he practised his preaching arts, in between major evangelical tours. He would go to London's famous Speakers' Corner in Hyde Park and step onto a literal soapbox to expound spontaneously on the gospel. He wanted, he said, to hone his skills at dealing with hecklers, which Speakers' Corner could be counted on to supply. 'One young fellow thought he'd got me,' Soper told us. 'He yelled, "If you know so much, what shape is the soul?" I paused —but only for a second—and shouted back, "Oval!" That shut him up and I just carried on regardless.' I can still feel the simple joy of laughing with the adults in their amusement at a witticism I thought I got.

While I'm pretty sure that Hilda was treated with care and affection while among the sisters, it pains me now to think of her being taken from her family home for what became a total of five years out of her childhood. That separation was leavened a bit by infrequent trips back to Mam's house. She would then briefly see Mam and her little brothers and, more importantly for her, she would sometimes even get to be with her eldest and absolute favourite brother, Tom. Talking to me in her seventies, she recalled him as a great strapping fellow, a hero-figure at thirteen years older than her who'd enlisted in the Army, looking 'so handsome in his uniform', she said. Whenever he had home-leave, and she was able to travel back from the Blackburns, he favoured her with small gifts and much loving, big-brother attention—until he was killed in 1945.

It happened when his Short Stirling troop-transporter plane crashed behind German lines in Norway. I remember Mam often saying that she blamed personally and would never forgive the prime minister, Winston Churchill, for insisting that Tom's unit, the Border Regiment, First Airborne Battalion, should carry out the mission. Perhaps ominously codenamed Operation Doomsday, it was part of the Allies' liberation of Nazi-occupied Norway during the very last throes of the war. Churchill reportedly enforced his will in defiance of warnings from his military staff that severe weather was making the venture far too dangerous. Tom's plane was one of fifteen that took off from Eastern England bound for an airfield near Oslo. It was one of two that crashed in the dense fog that quickly enveloped them. The crash killed Tom, nineteen of his contingent, and 24 soldiers in the other plane. All the remaining aircraft turned back home, totally thwarted by the fog. They were to complete the mission some days later, safely after the bad weather finally cleared.

Norwegian Resistance members and civilians buried the British dead at the crash-site, and later they were exhumed and re-interred in the Commonwealth War Graves section of Oslo's Vestre Cemetery. Mam's bitterness was compounded with some cruel irony; by the time Tom was killed, the German officers at High Command level had already formally surrendered. 'A needless death,' Mam would say, with a tsk of her tongue and an abrupt shake of her head.

The death of the grown-up brother on whom Hilda had doted couldn't fail to exact an emotional toll. She expressed mixed feelings on one rare occasion when we did talk about her time with The Blackburns. She recalled her shock and lonely grief over losing Tom, endured away from the home where her mother and her youngest brothers were all grieving together. 'I felt I was all on my own,' she said. 'The Blackburns were kind, but they didn't really understand.' She also laughed, though, and moved on to make light of the entire fostering period.

She contrived to sound merely amused about her strict regimen of chores for the sisters: 'Everything had to be done at a specific time of day,' she said, her tone finding fun in the memory, 'and in exactly the right order. Sweeping before the dusting—never, ever, the other way round, of course'. She had to join in much religious observance, too, that included daily Bible-readings under the women's tutelage, something that was far from a feature of life in our family's house. Another of the chores she recalled was to set the table before bedtime for the household's breakfast next day. It was a habit that she took up again in her own later years with her second husband; I confess I found it, as an occasional visiting guest, more than a shade finicky. Perhaps it's just me, but I'd never seen such overnight pre-arranging conducted in anyone's home that I'd been in, and it reminded me of a hotel's dining-room procedures, not simple domestic living.

Another time she told me—almost in passing, even a bit absent-mindedly—that the experience of living away from home at that young age had taught her independence. She went on to link that notion with the way she raised me and my sister: 'Because of that I always tried to bring up you two to stand on your own two feet.'

From my viewpoint of today, I see aspects of her make-up that might have had their origins in that separation from her family and in an emotional rigidity that rightly or wrongly I attribute to The Blackburns. To cite a possibly minor matter, my mother was never a hugger. And probably unsurprisingly neither was I. Until, that is, I stopped drinking. I was joining a new circle of sober people, and I noted a little quizzically that they tended to hug each other on meeting and on parting, and sometimes in between. It struck me as a bit strange, but it was unquestionably a currency of exchange among these folks, and so I joined in.

Someone I didn't even know would hug me, just being friendly, and I found it okay. More than okay; it was positively heartening in some unaccustomed fashion. Oh, and I was getting American-ised into the bargain, too. To someone from Britain, whose social customs could be said to lead the world in stiff-upper-lippery, a demonstratively hugging American can be rather alarming, but in my circumstances and in this new circle, I soon settled fully into the genial habit.

A short while after my own initiation, I introduced Hilda to hugging, when I was in my forties and she turning sixty. She greeted it gingerly at first, smiling with awkward embarrassment and eventually getting accustomed to it as a regular meeting ritual, though never lingering in the hug. I reflect a little ruefully, for both my mother and myself, on the long hug-less expanse of my upbringing and through many of my adult years.

I wonder, too, about my mother's return to the family at the age of thirteen. By then Mam evidently felt able to take her back. Maybe the young boys had become less demanding at eleven and ten. And maybe, though I have only conjecture for this, The Blackburns were leery about keeping Hilda with them any further into her teen years.

She trailed a wake behind her of loss and loneliness just as she faced whatever adolescent changes were beginning. And I don't doubt she could have been distinctly vulnerable to the attentions of an older male who might take an interest in her. I obviously cannot say with any certainty, but perhaps it was in such a state of susceptibility that at fifteen she encountered the man who would, at least in one sense, 'father' me.

Chapter 10
Raising Me

The landscape of my young memories appears crowded, though lacking in sharp focus. You might think one's mother should stand out strongly from the formless crowd; it doesn't seem to. My brain furrows to recall any more than just a few scenes out of Hilda's time with me as an infant, a toddler, an eight-year-old adventurer on a bike, a pre-teen, a teenager. Despite every effort, little emerges to represent her.

There are some repeated rituals that do stand out. She washed her hair on Friday nights. Memory is helped here by an auditory imprint: our family—not normally musical at all—made a repeating refrain out of a popular radio tune. Even though our broadcasting choices were constrained in 1950s Britain, we were nevertheless able, when weather conditions didn't garble the signal, to hear an alternative to the publicly funded and then rather dull BBC. We would tune to a pop music station of debatable legality that transmitted all the way from Europe's Grand Duchy of Luxembourg, a jurisdiction that was so free enterprise-friendly that it allowed brazen, almost piratical use of its wavelengths, reaching across many national borders with impunity. Amazingly to our ears, and utterly unlike the BBC, it even carried commercials. 'Friday night is Amami night,' Hilda would say, quoting lyrics from an ad for her favoured brand of shampoo that played on Radio Luxembourg. Definitely a non-singer, she prosaically just spoke the words, but her young brothers would take them as a cue to part-sing, part-yell the whole jingle over and over again. It was all in a spirit of light mockery at the very predictable routine maintained by their sister, that singular creature in the house: a teenage girl with all the special requirements such a creature would need. For all of us, it also marked emphatically and rather joyfully the end of the work and school week.

From the period, I think, when I was still unsure that Hilda was my mother and maybe was my sister, another ritual has stayed with me. On workdays at 7:15 am, she'd always seem in a hurry to catch the bus to her job in the city. But even so she would take time to sit alongside me, and from her own breakfast plate divide off some of her scrambled eggs on toast for me—carefully cut into little square sections, each one a toddler's mouthful. And after she'd seen me take a few and chew each one fully, she would dash away.

When a bit older I would sometimes accompany Hilda to the city, but not to her work. These trips were among my frequent visits to doctors' offices to have examinations or treatment for my troublesome ears. Mostly I was taken by my grandmother, but occasionally (and I imagine these were times specially allowed by Hilda's employers) it could be a mother-and-son journey on the bus. From the city bus terminal, the last leg was an awe-inspiring zigzag of a walk. We'd make our usually hurried way through certain half-deserted, grand, late-Georgian streets where lawyers, accountants and doctors all displayed their well-polished brass nameplates. No spoken exchanges between us have survived in my head, just the rare and reassuring hold of her hand on mine.

I remember far fewer occasions of being with my mother after we swapped our rural and small-city surroundings for the industrialised big city. We now lived as what I felt to be an isolated household; just the four of us, mother, son, stepfather, and little sister, that to me contrasted greatly with my memory of an extended family spread out across our home village. Even in the new, tighter-knit setting I recollect being away from Hilda much more strongly than being with her—and many a time, indeed, actively hiding from her, not to escape exactly, but to avoid troubling her. My loneliness and homesickness for the Scottish Border country would sometimes make sudden, helpless tears spurt from me. But I didn't want to 'upset' my mother. This was my earliest conscious understanding of the term that came to be such a resonant word of warning in our home.

So I'd shield my tears from her—or her from them—by making hurriedly upstairs for the bathroom, the only lockable room in the house, private, and mine to myself for a while. Thus barricaded in solitary, I would shake my head into some dry-eyed calm, and then hum Scottish folksongs under my breath until I felt able to face the rest of the household again.

When older—about eleven, I think—I joined the swelling ranks of British youngsters who passionately followed the exploits of American comic-book superheroes, except that I made a deliberate choice for my special hero. It was Batman—because he was not superhuman. Just a regular human, though endowed with a vast range of amazingly effective, near-magical gadgets and machines (the Batmobile, the Batarang, Bat-Skates, BatCopter and the like) all of which helped to provide the impact of superpowers. It meant a lot to me, too, that his alternate, regular persona, the suave Bruce Wayne, was a millionaire (I guess these days he'd have to be a billionaire). That struck me as a highly desirable superpower in itself.

Naturally enough my deeply serious child's play involved faithfully emulating Batman, running around the house and our steeply sloped Manchester backyard in pursuit of imaginary villains cast in the mould of Batman's nemeses: the Joker, the Penguin, the Riddler. But there were limits to my imitation. I dressed appropriately enough, I thought, in a tightly belted sweater and shorts but as a caped crusader I was completely and all-too-obviously in want of a cape. And here my mother came to my rescue. A worn-out bedsheet, once it had exhausted her stitched repairs to the many rips it had suffered over time, was pressed into new service. She scissored it into a shape that billowed convincingly behind me and fixed it around my neck with ribbon-like extensions, fastened by tiny, round metal poppers that would secure it over my shoulders.

Her cape-making sits firmly in my memory, her feet working the treadle, her shoulders hunched as she squinted over the Singer sewing machine on which she always made clothing for my sister and me—her summer sundresses, my short-sleeved shirts. For this job as precisely as for any other, her fingers guided the fabric past a clattering, jumping needle, to ensure such a strong, un-fraying double hem to the cape that it could endure the stresses I'd put it through in my strenuous crime-fighting. My hero's original in the comics was bat-black, of course; my homage of a facsimile was white or, by that stage of the bedsheet's life, an off-white grey. But with my imagination filling in the darker colour, that cape did the job just fine. And oh, was I grateful! A mother's love could not have run more deeply.

Chapter 11
Overseas—Poland

I had reached my nation's capital but I was working in purely metropolitan television; no one from my family in the regions farther north would ever see my work. There was a brash and rather mean-spirited observation, as I reflect on it, that I employed when joking with my new colleagues, most of whom were Londoners. I'd point out that as far as my mother was concerned, I could be earning my living in a brothel. She would certainly never see any evidence that I was engaged in a respectable enterprise, if that's what TV journalism counted as.

In the job I won some bright spurs pretty quickly, getting noticed especially for my reports on homelessness in London (a problem that never seemed to move out of crisis mode) and I was soon rewarded with a promotion to cover broader, countrywide issues. Since our network transmitted these reports nationally, my family would now have the chance to see how I spent my working hours.

One of those national reports was about what became known as 'The Rolls-Royce Crash'. Not an expensive car-wreck, but the dramatic collapse of the totemic British engineering company. The crash didn't affect the firm's more famous, luxury car-making business, but it did fatally threaten its important, if more humdrum jet-engine manufacturing plant, which was then failing disastrously to compete globally with the likes of America's Boeing Company.

The looming closure of Rolls-Royce's massive factory in the town of Derby endangered the economy of England's entire North Midlands region; my job was to find and film workers' families and small supply-line engineering firms to illustrate how all these many livelihoods now suddenly stood at risk. In the end, after our report was shown, the government nationalised the company, thus rescuing something like 80,000 local jobs. My mother did see this broadcast, although I didn't know it at the time. Nearly fifty years later, after she died, I found among her things a postcard that she'd addressed to me in London, but hadn't mailed, and yet a little oddly had still kept. She wrote that my report was 'very interesting' and that she was sorry I had not visited her during my filming. Derby, after all, was a mere fifty miles' drive from her house.

I had decided to repress what I regarded as a childish need to call home and alert my mother whenever my output might be appearing on her living room TV set; I trusted to chance that she might just happen to catch the broadcasts. I told myself I didn't greatly care if she saw them or didn't.

At another point in that same period, I covered a neo-Nazis' march through the dead centre of Manchester, just seven miles from her, and didn't visit her then, either. Just too busy.

Such national coverage impressed my bosses enough to make them unexpectedly decide to send me on an international story, even though I was the youngest and still least-experienced guy on the staff. This first foreign assignment was naturally very welcome but it created an awkward problem for me, prompted by, of all irritating things, my murky family background.

My mission would be to cover an outbreak of violent unrest in Communist Poland—a shipyard workers' uprising that pre-figured, though we couldn't know this at the time, Lech Wałęsa's Solidarność movement that developed over a decade later and helped to finally topple Communism. The strike and protests whose significance we wanted to investigate had been crushed in a murderous hail of police machine-gun fire. Nearly fifty strikers were killed. I was awed and a little scared by the seriousness and importance of my imminent reporting responsibilities but mostly I was just plain excited. However, in order to travel to the shipyard city of Gdansk as assigned and report on the killings' aftermath, I naturally enough needed a passport. I kicked myself for lack of foresight in not already possessing one.

Thoroughly flustered, I remonstrated inwardly that any self-respecting globetrotting reporter should always be on standby and always fully equipped with the documentation needed for a sudden departure overseas. Instead, here I was, belatedly submitting a first-time passport application. What would normally be a routine official transaction turned out in my case to be more complicated than I could have realised.

I'd spent all my high-school years bearing my Ukrainian step-father's name. It was also under that name that I was admitted to college, gained my degree, applied for and found work in television, authored articles published in national newspapers and magazines, signed the lease on my new flat—and so much more in terms of my everyday life. I had no idea, until I was trying to obtain the passport, that the name I used was not my legal name.

To my self-sufficient 22-year-old's annoyance, I now needed my mother's help. She moved with alacrity, though, and signed an affidavit declaring that she and her husband had taken (through 'custom and practice', in lawyers' parlance) to calling me by her husband's last name, even though he had not legally adopted me. Ever since their marriage I had always believed Michael to be my adoptive father, so it was a surprise that he turned out not to be, but I didn't delve with my mother into why things had gone that way. I was simply in a hurry to get my grown-up journalist's travel papers in order.

Along with my mother's affidavit, my lawyer prepared what in Britain is called a 'deed poll', a well-nigh inexplicable term from the Middle Ages; this arcane instrument enabled me now to legally use the Ukrainian name I'd already been using de facto for about twelve years. In the light of my surprise discovery, I briefly considered reverting to my original, simple, monosyllabic name of Brown. I had for sure never liked the cumbersome Slavic one very much but I had put a lot of effort into mastering its spelling and pronunciation and getting other people to master it too, so I decided to stick with the longer option. I also thought—and I smile to recall this—that I'd be messing with my national and international career if I set about changing names at this point; that career was then all of two years old and I can't now imagine that any damage would really have been all that serious. I simply wanted in my youthful ambition to get on briskly with my first-ever foreign trip, and just regularising the status quo of being called Tereshchuk appeared to be the speedier solution.

So, brandishing my shiny, stiff passport emblazoned with the words 'Her Britannic Majesty', I flew to Poland and faced the novel task of trying to practise journalism under a dictatorship. My team and I inevitably had minders appointed to watch over us; assembling the elements of our story on film entailed a fair amount of evading our official supervision.

I was helped by a lucky chance. A college contemporary of mine, a promising English composer, was now doing his post-graduate studies in the Polish capital at the renowned Warsaw Conservatory of Music (its most illustrious alumnus: the francophile Frédéric Chopin). My friend's study mates, perhaps unsurprisingly for a community of musicians, included some distinctly rebellious twenty-somethings. They were strong-minded and brave dissidents, so I quickly got plugged into their underground network, or small circle, of anti-regime activists, all of about my age. Introductions and meetings were arranged covertly and we even managed to conduct a few filmed interviews (though anonymous, perforce, and conducted with shadowy lighting) in my room on the fifth floor of the Hotel Bristol, once majestic but now decidedly drab in an all-pervasive People's Republic kind of way. Our helpers included a recording engineer from the conservatory, who was also a piccolo player and led a rising folk-rock band. He scanned for listening devices in all our team's rooms and found that mine was unaccountably the only one not being bugged. I felt a little insulted—or at least under-valued by the state security service. Was it, I wondered, because I was clearly the juvenile in the visiting team and therefore of little significance?

After almost three weeks of filming our crew returned to the UK with as much material as we were ever likely to get, and I was left behind to follow a 'hot tip' I'd received. From one of my young dissident sources I'd learned that there existed some state television footage (never publicly shown, predictably enough) of the striking workers being massacred in Gdansk. And I went earnestly on the hunt for it.

It was a doomed effort, even though I got close, I believe. I managed to slip past a lazy-looking minder who was yawning and nodding near the hotel's main door, took a taxi and then caught a train to the far south of the country. I was in pursuit of a highly placed official in the monolithic broadcasting authority's TV division. When I had tried to meet him at his office, I was told he'd gone to his ski chalet retreat near the winter resort of Zakopane.

In addition to my formal inquiries lodged with the monolith, I had been widening my unofficial, underground sources. One contact had led to another, in the way they always do, resulting in some new dissident connections, now among workers in the country's film and TV industries; it was through them that I had learned that this particular broadcasting apparatchik had been put in personal charge of the massacre footage (hence my eagerness to meet him) and that the film was stashed in his office safe. I was also assured that it would have gone with him wherever he went, even on a short vacation.

When I arrived at the resort I asked around for his whereabouts—he was a noted and regular visitor in each skiing season, it seemed—and I was directed to his chalet. His doorbell rang out with a curiously suburban ding-dong chime and one of his security detail opened the door left-handedly, his right hand hovering over a sidearm at his belt. Unlike the guard, the official himself fully understood my English when he quickly joined us, but loudly denied the existence of the sensitive film I was seeking and the doorman plus a second guard who then appeared very decisively gave me the bum's rush and shooed me off the property. They unholstered their weapons and waved them at me as part of the eviction procedure.

On my return to the capital, I was arrested for exceeding the limits of my permitted travel. It wasn't the first time I'd been arrested for doing my job. That had been in the sedate English county of Kent, while trying to get a good viewpoint from which my crew could film a nuclear power plant on the coast. In a development that government nuclear experts had scandalously not foreseen, the plant had come to be threatened by rising sea levels (as early as the 1970s), and we needed to show the dangerous erosion process at work. Who knew—I didn't—that approaching so close to a crucial public facility like this constituted 'trespassing on Crown Property'? The only consequence for me, though, was spending a few hours as a guest of the (really quite friendly) Kent Constabulary. My Warsaw arrest would be very different, I realised. And indeed it did prove to be an unpleasant introduction to authoritarian enforcers putting the frighteners on me. It was the first in a range of similar experiences in various oppressive countries, but here in this Polish initiation it was complicated by that familiar, vexed question of my identity, and my vexing name in particular.

Probably only opportunistically and almost certainly amping it up a lot, my captors made a big thing of the name on my passport. In my drafty cell (a single, unshaded lightbulb dangling overhead, in total caricature of every film or TV interrogation scene I'd ever watched) they warned me that because of my name I would not be receiving any consular services from Her Britannic Majesty's embassy. I was completely on my own. The offspring of Ukrainian parents in 'your father's generation', as they put it, were considered Polish citizens when on Polish soil, and I could even be compulsorily drafted into the People's Army of Poland. The thinnest of justifications from history lay behind this threat; part of Ukraine, indeed the very region where my stepfather's patronym was common, had come under Polish rule during an earlier part of the twentieth century. A little disconcertingly I had already come across many examples of my name when I was looking through the national phone directory, appearing in a Polish version of its spelling, with Zs instead of the Hs.

The interrogators' intention was clearly to alarm me. And it worked. I spent a day and a night in my cell with a mounting cold fear that was hard to dismiss, no matter how fanciful their threats might appear when I thought about them rationally. It's a recurring anxiety for any travelling journalist who might find themself at the mercy of an oppressive regime: that their home country's diplomats may not be able to rescue them from trouble. And now my current circumstances seemed to be turning that nightmare into reality. My cell conditions were of a predictable kind—the temperature barely above zero and no blanket, one small bowl for food, not warmed, containing something watery and of a pale mauve colour (possibly a meatless borscht)—all of which combined to reinforce the scenario of me as a hapless Pole under Poland's harsh authority.

After nightfall I was even picturing, a tad hysterically, a Slavic sergeant-major screaming unintelligibly at me in my grey-green camo fatigues as I paced out endless marching drills for him. The scene got elaborated into maybe a half-dozing dream, or else some overactive wide-awake imaginings: I now saw myself squelching in leaky combat boots through a boggy Silesian forest, laden with a sixty-pound backpack.

Thankfully, with daylight, an entirely different character entered the scene. He was a well-dressed party official, in contrast to the shabby-looking thugs my case had merited the previous day. He gave his name as Konrad Kozlowski from the party's Committee for Control of Radio and Television. The name sounded suspiciously stereotypical (maybe a Polish equivalent of, say, 'Joe Johnson') but when I much later checked with a CIA contact it turned out that a man of that name had indeed been one of the committee's five vice-chairmen. Konrad, if that's who he genuinely was, gave me back my seized passport and went on to bring up—in the tones of a reasonable man—the delicate matter of my search for the all-revealing news film.

He acknowledged, somewhat tenderly and with a sad look of sympathy, that the footage did indeed exist. But there was no way in God's good heaven that I or anyone else in the world was ever going to see it, and there was a Polish Airlines flight leaving for London in three hours: here was a ticket for it and outside was a Party car to take you gladly to your hotel for your luggage and on to the airport.

Chapter 12
Overseas again—Bangladesh

I felt penned-in, because I was—along with twenty or so other more experienced and more blasé journalists.

I was scared, though for public consumption I was merely restless and frustrated. Scared I'd taken on much more than I'd bargained for or knew how to handle. At the back of it all, scared I might be shot dead or killed some other way, since I had chosen to work in my first foreign warzone. We were all restricted by military command to the grounds of our hotel, the Intercontinental, in the Bengali city of Dhaka, while beyond the perimeter, out in the countryside, we had reason to believe unspeakable mayhem was being inflicted on a helpless population.

I was proud, enthralled that my TV bosses had given me this assignment late in London's long, cold spring of 1971. Still aged just twenty-two, I'd recently demonstrated some journalistic tenacity in an even chillier Poland and was not so much resting as cruising on my new laurels. And suddenly I was being shipped out to an adventure in the steamy tropics of East Bengal. It felt exhilarating, though I knew it would be no jaunt. I was to document that territory's violent transition into the new-born and blood-drenched nation of Bangladesh.

The Bengalis' leader, Sheikh Mujibur Rahman, had proclaimed their separatist independence from Pakistan, and immediately the ruling Pakistani military junta launched its scorched-earth Operation Searchlight to put down the rebellion. I flew in via Pakistan's administrative centre, Karachi in the west of the country, where I was given press accreditation by the military and when I finally reached Dhaka (the capital of what was still officially known as the East Pakistan region) it was firmly under the command of Pakistani generals. For a start, journalists were 'cantoned' within the Intercontinental Hotel—an intriguing piece of soldierly jargon, redolent of England's

Royal Military College, Sandhurst, where many senior officers from both Pakistan and India had trained. I was to be there for a little more than four weeks, the other journalists much longer. It was the furthest east in the world I'd ever gone, yet I was disappointed I hadn't penetrated further. My real ambition was to be reporting on the globally attention-getting Vietnam War. I had an inevitable youthful desire to get myself into the middle of the most important action, and—I hoped—the most dramatic. I didn't consciously want to put my life in danger, and though I'd often heard the label 'thrill-seeker' being applied to members of my profession, I wouldn't have said I was ever that reckless. But I did consider a rush of excitement to be one of the just rewards of my job. It seemed perfectly natural to me and not up for question. I was keen, well-nigh desperate to witness at first hand and up close exactly what soldiers were doing in the conflict I'd been sent to cover. It was my duty on behalf of the audience at home, for whom I considered myself to be working.

For the moment, however, the 'action' of war was distinctly absent. Our military hosts kept insisting on what they called the 'regularity' of the situation, even though it was clear that the city was on a war footing. Most readily obvious was the disruption in food supplies; for us that meant a drastically curtailed bill of fare in the Intercon's restaurant. We journalists as well as the senior army men who shared hotel quarters with us survived on an almost unrelieved diet comprising a new dish to me: curry omelets. Every mealtime, a waiter would present the tall, ornate menu to each of us.

'Could I have the sirloin, please?'
'I'm sorry, Sir. The sirloin is unavailable today.'
'Hmm, okay. How about the chicken? It says chicken fricassée here.'
'Yes, Sir. But unfortunately the chicken fricassée is unavailable.
     Sorry.'
'Any other kind of chicken?'
'No, Sir. I am afraid not.'
'Well, what is available?'
'We have omelet, Sir. Curry omelet.'
'Just like last time?'

'Yes, Sir.'

'Ah well. Okay then. Please ask the chef to go easy on the curry.'

At the hotel's entrances and exits, sepoys (the 'grunt' rank in Pakistani forces) stood on guard with their antique-looking but in fact new and locally manufactured Lee-Enfield rifles. Armoured cars mounted with machine guns patrolled the streets outside. Inside, a phony normality was maintained. A stiff-backed pianist with a bristly moustache serenaded us; we suspected a military background, given his refusal to slouch even while his hands were lazily stroking the keys for one familiar standard after another, all getting rendered almost characterless. Among them was 'The Shadow of Your Smile', which came round so often it got to haunt me. It was rather weirdly to keep on repeating in my future, too, whether from a lone pianist once again, or from a jazz trio or just as piped Muzak in far too many fly-blown taprooms, seamy nightspots or so-called cocktail bars that all came to form a backdrop to my overseas field work.

Given our circumstances in Dhaka, conducting basic journalism was challenging at best. Visits were allowed outside the hotel to approved sites only, with accompanying army officers who called these supervised forays 'tours.' They included meetings solely with pro-Pakistan lackeys, like the civil servants in the regional Ministry for Transportation who professed absolutely no knowledge of any upsurge in separatism among the Bengali population—the very reason of course for the Army's massive presence there.

But individual Bengalis would sometimes slip into the hotel at great risk to themselves, and give us some sense of what might really be going on. I was the first reporter to be greeted, in whispers, by the campaigning secessionist Ajit Choudhury. He smuggled in a few copies of his pro-independence newspaper with *Joi Bangla* ('Victory to Bengal') emblazoned in capital letters on every page. I think I was merely the first foreigner he saw, and he rightly assumed I was a journalist. I got a hurried briefing from him as we retreated to the relative obscurity of a service corridor, where he gave me names and locations of villages where he said the army had carried out massacres.

The strained atmosphere in the hotel turned more uncomfortable and ominous after the country was hit by one of its all-too-frequent and massive floods, the result of a battering cyclone, and a rampant epidemic of cholera also broke out. A reporter expert in the region's commerce (from The Economist?, the Far Eastern Economic Review?—maybe the Financial Times?) took on an assignment from the rest of us to check out the supply-chain reliability of all the bottled water that Intercon staff now started issuing to us. I've no idea how he made his checks, but we trusted him, and none of us to my knowledge fell ill.

Amid the general unease and discomfort, I got a pleasurable kick out of the distinguished stature of my journalistic company. My companions were mostly war-weary old-timers from Vietnam transferred temporarily out of Saigon. I was acutely conscious of my youth and inexperience compared with them. But all the same, I had made it out from London under my own insistent steam to this new far-flung theatre of war; in the office I'd stepped up as the sole volunteer for this task from among the junior research staff and had figured out my own flight-plan since many airlines had started to avoid the region. Since my arrival I'd been working hard to fit in, cockily injecting into my manner as much worldly-wise confidence as I could. While the action I was impatient for still eluded me, just being among these weathered old pros persuaded me I was taking part in a big story. As a group they emanated an easy, fraternal conviviality, and I was surprised and flattered by their egalitarian manner, their lack, as far as I could tell, of any condescension towards me as the newbie. For my part I managed, or so I thought at the time, to prevent my sense of awe from becoming too evident.

But I was inescapably agog at the presence of one reporter in particular: Clare Hollingworth. She was the London Telegraph's legendary war correspondent and before Vietnam she had covered the Algerian liberation war and the Arab-Israeli conflict, and had even been credited—way, way back—as the first journalist to report the outbreak of World War Two. Her 'scoop of the century', as everyone called it, came when she'd been travelling along Poland's border with Germany in 1939 and had seen, thanks to some freak winds dislodging their camouflage, massed ranks of Nazi tanks preparing to roll across the frontier that night.

By the time I was working alongside Clare she was sixty years old, which to my mind was unimaginably elderly for a reporter. Though I would have liked to spend some one-on-one time chatting with her, it wasn't possible; Clare was all business. But I did get to walk with her; and then my callow thoughts about her ageing got firmly quashed. I found myself struggling hard to keep up with her in the 98-degree heat and 70-per-cent humidity as she made long, determined strides through one of the cholera-ridden refugee camps around Dhaka which—under guard, as ever—we were permitted to visit. Clare was clearly built of hardier stuff than I, and to my utter lack of surprise she went on to live, as a fixture in Hong Kong's Foreign Correspondents' Club, until she was 105.

The Saigon-habituated reporters like Clare, among them her fellow-Brit Dick West, the Australian Murray Sayle, and the American Sydney Schanberg, all well-known names to me before I met them, contrived to be both angered and jaded by the Vietnam echoes they found in Dhaka. These came in the form of preposterous press conferences held almost daily by Pakistani officers. I sat next to Murray in my first such conference and learned that in his Strine dialect we were being submitted to *drongoes* and *flamin' galahs* giving us *furphies*—idiots and clowns feeding us bullshit, of course. Just like the circuses I'd read about being mounted daily by US commanders in Saigon, which Murray recalled to me as 'the five-o'clock follies', our Pakistani grandees regaled us with summaries of their 'encounters with the enemy'. They meant the Mukti Bahini, the few-in-number, scattered and poorly armed force of Bengali liberation fighters. After these purported battles, the major-generals or occasional lieutenant-generals would always announce that they'd scored complete victories. No casualties were ever suffered by the Pakistani side, and an entire wipe-out of rebel groups was always claimed.

A lack of Pakistani casualties was possibly credible to us, but nothing else was. We were hearing, from a wide variety of Bengali sources, not about military engagements, but more and more reports of the wholesale destruction of villages, and the rape and killing of civilians. I felt impelled to attempt some truth-testing of my own, and that inevitably meant escaping the cantonment that the military maintained upon us.

I looked for support. While in Dhaka I made what became a lifelong friendship with Colin Smith from London's The Observer, older than me but closer to my age than the surrounding titans of our trade. I'd met him earlier while covering the violence in Belfast. We found there that we shared a mainly sophomoric strain of humour. On hearing a report in the journalists' bar that a soldier had been shot in the Ardoyne (one of the city's hardline Irish Republican districts), we each simultaneously reacted with the same heartless, smart-ass crack: 'That sounds painful!' We would meet again many times over in places like Beirut, Gaza, Jerusalem, Harare, Pretoria and more. Colin's impish wisecracks always resonated with me—fittingly or not.

Colin had a nickname among colleagues generally—'The Boy Soldier'—for he had enlisted at sixteen as a cadet in the British Army, but came to cherish writing more than 'square-bashing', the ritual formation marches that typified basic training in the UK. He was valued by his editors as an enthusiastic and always accurately detailed reporter of battles. I had other Observer friends besides him and they had their own in-house moniker for him: 'The Bang-Bang Boy'. It was both patronising and born of some envy; they knew that no one else on the paper could ever match Colin's adventurous derring-do. If anything, their jealousy was heightened by having to acknowledge his other considerable talent: turning in cogent, well-reasoned 'think-pieces', our term for the analytical situation reports and overviews that a weekly newspaper (and indeed my weekly TV programme) would often require.

So it was to Colin, the bang-bang boy-soldier, that I turned with my notion of splitting off from our press corps and venturing into the countryside to witness and verify the Pakistani Army's real actions. To my surprise and disappointment, he said flatly: 'You must be crazy.' I'd been hoping for an endorsement, and frankly for some company. But I didn't go on to argue with him or try to press my case any further. Colin was the least risk-averse individual I had ever known and yet here he was, tight-lipped and dismissive, refusing point-blank to entertain my eager plan. Frowning and tight-lipped myself, I conceded inwardly that he was probably right. But undeterred, I nevertheless decided to set out alone.

I was impelled by the hungry journalistic need for original material. The desire common to many a reporter, of course, to scoop others. And in my case, still pretty raw and unseasoned as I was, the chance to get one over on my elders felt especially appealing. Those other, more senior correspondents were, I realised, not being fearful or timid in their reluctance to escape our confines; rather, they were pinned on the horns of a common professional dilemma. They needed to keep in close touch with official news sources (even the generals' ridiculous battle bulletins), however enticed they might be by the scent of powerful, unofficial news elsewhere. I respected their concentrated intensity, not least for its being combined with a judiciousness that was well beyond my young reach.

My new forty-five-year-old friend, Murray from Sydney, was an amiable, shambolic-looking character, tall and dramatically beak-nosed, who defied the unspoken rule—one that anybody would think obvious and necessary—to travel light in a warzone. He cut a very different figure, for instance, from the safari-suited Martin Woollacott of the *Guardian*, a physically trim specialist in Far East conflicts who looked sleekly prepared for anything. Murray had brought an extensive and heavy library with him. When the army had gained more confident control over the sprawling city and was allowing us to go a little greater distance on our 'tours', Murray would lumber along with a book-bag slung across his shoulders filled with thick volumes like *The Great Game*, about six hundred pages long, on Victorian Britain's and Czarist Russia's long contest for control of Afghanistan and India; or something bulky on South Asia's Wars, 1839–1880. While it may have been ostentatious and it did look a tad ridiculous, I still marvelled at Murray's studious effort to ground himself in deep historical background, no matter how immediate the conflict was that he had to cover right now. Seeing such high-minded and broad-ranging professionalism simply reinforced my own far more elementary urge to score a straightforward, baseline news exclusive, out in what we all knew to be the killing fields.

I left the group just as another unsurprising mealtime was getting under way, slipping out of the hotel at one of its back exits. I succeeded in passing the checkpoints unchecked. It was oddly easy; maybe it was every rank of soldier's mealtime. I found a car and driver to take me out towards the area of the army's advance. That, too, turned out to be easy. All that was necessary was simply to be the inescapably conspicuous figure that I was and would be again and again in many countries of the developing world: a white man in need of something, and in possession of US dollars in cash. I didn't have to hunt. Eager helpers came to me. I chose from among the small crowd of potential drivers the one who seemed to speak English somewhat better than the rest.

Well away from the city where roads had become impassable in the wake of flooding, I then 'found' a boatman whom I came to know as Hamid, though he must have had a fuller real name. In his large dinghy (originally a Bengali word, I learned) or small sampan—he used both terms for his flat-bottomed craft—we searched for indications of the Pakistani soldiers' onslaught. That wasn't hard, either. Every village had a story; account after account of vicious, seemingly mindless, mass cruelty was relayed to us from along the network of waterways. After three days and nights we found ourselves getting close behind the army as it moved north and east, roughly towards the town of Narsingdi. Everything I encountered in this somber landscape was new for me, and most overpowering of all was quite simply a smell. It nearly obliterated all my mental efforts at processing the information we gathered, and the growing corroboration of the massacres we heard about. The stench combined the pungent tang of overripe, often putrid vegetation with that of human and animal diarrhea. Until I became sort of used to it, I found note-taking and even thinking almost impossible.

Two nights in succession we slept on a riverbank, and then once in the boat instead of onshore, for reasons which Hamid couldn't explain to me in his sign-language and limited English, and which I didn't feel I should question. He was short, strong and very dark, an intense, marron-like colour common to many Bengalis, deepened in those living and working mainly outdoors. In river stretches too shallow or reed-entangled for his low-powered outboard motor, he propelled and steered us with a hefty pole, and his huge exertions raised his muscles and tendons into peaked ridges along his upper back, his shoulders and arms. During our stopovers, though, he expended little energy, moving economically, minimally. He warmed dahl for us both on a Primus stove, and offered me a small tarp as we prepared to sleep. I had brought no kit of any kind with me, staying true to the 'travelling light' principle that I had thought appropriate. And of course I'd been trying when I left the hotel to look as if I wasn't going anywhere far. I gave him back his tarp; it made me even sweatier than I already was, more than I'd ever been in my life. Something else without parallel for this new-comer to the subcontinent was the totally blanketing soundscape around us, the never-ending, raucous calls of gibbons, tree frogs, fish eagles, mynas and more, every creature in a contending chorus. It's a wonder that I slept at all, but I did.

In our daytime progress, villages were now no longer sources for information; they'd been destroyed. It was rare we found anyone alive to tell us anything. When we occasionally did, we heard not hearsay testimony, but now vivid and direct eye-witness accounts. An aged survivor in his eighties described his daughter and two grand-daughters being dragged out of their house and gang-raped, then sliced apart with rifle bayonets. A middle-aged man in furious grief gestured horrifically with stabs of a stick to show how his wife had been bayonetted to death; he had watched helplessly, hidden in the bush and terrified for his own life. Hamid and I had our own direct encounters now, not with soldiers but certainly with their handiwork: countless dead bodies, male and female of all ages. Many were badly charred; their homes had been razed to the ground.

We came across one house that was only partly burned but collapsed, its palm-leaf thatched roof lying flattened, and I saw a pair of man's legs sticking out from under the thatch. With Hamid's help I lifted the stiff bamboo pole that formed the roof's edge, propping the whole thing up with first my knee and then my shoulder, and I tried to pull the body free. The legs came away in my hands, separating, it seemed, at mid-thigh. This has become a looped image in my consciousness, repeating itself nowadays in my thankfully rare nightmares; it's become a predictable accompaniment to my occasional periods of heightened stress.

Other kinds of sensory flashback have accompanied me, too. With some incongruousness born of my inexperience, I guess, the odour of charred bodies initially reminded me of my girlfriends' hair-curling wands or heated rollers whenever they had cranked them up too high. Now decades later, it happens in reverse; the slightest whiff of some accidental singeing—like a cigarette-lighter catching a wisp of a woman's bangs, or the burnt hairs on my forearm over a stove's gas flame—will rocket my nerves back to the scorched Bengal countryside.

When I returned to Dhaka after my week of logging the aftermath of atrocities, my film crew of three had arrived from London. (That's how my network did things in those days, rather than hiring locally; and the crew had travelled first-class, thanks to our union contracts.) I now had a well-plotted, image-filled itinerary for them to follow. With Hamid working full-tilt again at gathering village witnesses, along with some local people who had a smattering of interpreting skills, we had no shortage of compelling spoken narrative to accompany the ghastly visual evidence we were gathering. All five of us were retracing together the grim territory that Hamid and I had scouted, but now we were filming, filming incessantly, it felt.

Getting the filmed material back to London was a tense exercise. When the army censors demanded to examine it, I gave them a set of cans containing still-unused film, telling them with studied nonchalance that they would have to process it themselves, but I would be happy for them to send it on to me in London after they had viewed it. Meanwhile our real footage was concealed under a false bottom in my carry-on bag. The modified bag was frequent issue for any of our assignments that might involve subterfuge.

Full-scale international war between Pakistan and India was about to break out, which would eventually result in Pakistan's defeat and the creation of the independent country of Bangla-desh. Just as we were beginning our return home, the looming cross-border conflict radically altered our journey's course. Indian airspace was suddenly a no-fly zone for PIA, the Pakistan airline we were to use, and indeed the only company that by then would fly in or out of Dhaka.

The circuitous route now imposed on our flight, travelling all the way around India, took us an anxious fourteen hours. Then came a six-hour lay-over, still on Pakistani soil at Karachi Airport, before changing onto British Airways heading for Heathrow. Throughout that total of twenty hours, each one of which I counted off fretfully, I became increasingly convinced the censors would have developed the blank film and discovered my ruse. The riflemen who glowered at us in Karachi Airport looked especially menacing to me. Nevertheless, they let us through unchallenged. Dealing with our film cans had not been a matter of military urgency back in Dhaka.

Once finally in London, I was more than relieved; utterly exultant in fact. But not for long. It turned out when our film was developed that our cameraman had been suffering—inexplicably and without ever telling me or other colleagues—from a serious eye-infection. Everything imaginable that could be wrong with our images was wrong. Out of focus, shaky to the point of rendering the scene unreadable, badly over-exposed, vastly under-exposed. Altogether the footage was useless; it couldn't be broadcast.

I didn't know what to do except kick furniture, and even in my stunned state I knew that that was pretty pointless. Then I remembered that I had another commitment, and still in a daze of rage I left my network's offices to carry it out.

In some ways, journalistically speaking, all was not lost. Beneath that same false bottom in my bag I'd also carried still pictures from the ravaged villages taken by other photographers. As a piece of collegiality that I learned we can sometimes practise, especially in wartime, I had promised to deliver these photos to the London *Sunday Times*.

In the paper's hallowed newsroom (hallowed to me, at least) I handed the film to the magisterial figure of the foreign editor,

Godfrey Hodgson; he was gravely smoking a pipe as he thanked me for the delivery. My senses were swirling in confusion. I'd certainly been bloodied by my grim tropical fieldwork and was now feeling horribly crushed by one of journalism's cruel realities—you can lose a story more easily than getting one—but I found myself one more time stirred by the superior coolness of my elders and professional betters, especially here in one of the engine-rooms of their craft. Hodgson calmly evaluated the horrific images I'd brought and went on to employ them as a graphically potent framework for the written exposé that was filed by his correspondent, Anthony Mascarenhas. It was a world-exclusive which authoritatively documented the Bengal massacres in full. The paper famously gave the story a huge and stark headline—'GENOCIDE'—and it came to be known in newspaper circles as 'the story that changed history'.

I knew I'd played a small, purely logistical role in bringing to the world the major revelation that rolled off the Sunday Times presses. It was consoling to some extent but it was to be a long time before I found myself able to let go—to a degree, at least—of my fury at our own team's failure.

Back at the TV company, appalled incredulity at what had happened spread fast. My boss, the weekly show's executive producer, raised holy hell with the company's camera department but couldn't get to the cameraman himself. He'd been admitted to the hospital. I paused only a little to consider the cameraman's position. The guy had been ill, and who knows what had been going on in his sick, maybe delirious mind? But the shithead had just single-handedly destroyed my first-ever foreign war coverage: dramatic headlining stuff, all of it—coulda-been award-winning. He ended up getting fired. I ended up getting drunk.

Chapter 13
Bloody Sunday

No one expected there to be shooting, let alone killings. One recollection is fixed in my mind sharper than any other: a soldier in a red beret, down on one knee, leveling his SLR in my direction and firing. I was in Derry, the Northern Irish town I felt I understood best, but I was mystified by how this could be happening.

It was very early 1972 and I had been assigned by my TV network to keep a general, watchful eye on Northern Ireland developments. Ours was a weekly current events broadcast. Indeed, its name was simply *This Week*, and grabbing 'hard news' for each day was not our job; instead, we were meant to provide viewers with explanatory analysis on a wider canvas. I was conducting my watchful mission alone, by now a familiar enough role for me, and I was pleased to be so trusted by my bosses.

For the last weekend of January, I knew there was to be a big civil-rights protest march through Derry. At most, I figured there would be the customary low-level standoff between protesters and British soldiers, the kind of skirmish we had all grown familiar with: some stone-throwing from one side, maybe some tear-gas from the other. We were now a couple of years into what the Irish with typical wryness were already calling 'The Troubles'. Every afternoon when school was let out some of Derry's Catholic teenagers would gather at an intersection where William Street met Rossville Street and then lob bricks and stones at the soldiers, who would respond—if the mini-bombardment grew troublesome enough—with tear gas and sometimes water cannon. Local people had unofficially renamed the spot 'Aggro Corner', in the way that civil unrest and turmoil will often breed nicknames.

'Aggro' was for aggression, or perhaps aggravation; either one would be a good fit. Nicknaming being infectious, some of

Frame from my documentary for CBS on Derry's embattled history (1998).

us reporters had taken to calling these predictable and relatively harmless encounters the 'Four O'Clock Jam Sessions', possibly riffing on the idea of both afternoon tea and hard percussive music. During the days preceding the march, my Catholic, nationalist contacts and some police sources were all forecasting no serious trouble, only the probability of that same weekday ritual occurring again, albeit this time over a weekend. And so I reported to my bosses that I would not be needing a film crew. 'Uneventful,' I predicted. 'Good for coverage on the nightly news, but nothing for us.'

And indeed, on the day itself the march began innocuously enough. Very cheerfully, in fact, even though it had a serious political purpose: to protest against the authorities' recent imposition of imprisonment without trial in the province. Reading back now over contemporary news coverage, I'm struck by the number of English reporters who chose the phrase 'carnival atmosphere' to describe the marchers' bright mood; it evidently reminded them of a summer fair bringing good humour to a country town back home. But as the march reached Aggro Corner the customary skirmishes did break out, young tearaways doing their usual thing and getting chastised for doing it by the main body of marchers and the stewards in charge of marshalling the crowd. The march as a whole took a rightward turn, in an orderly move towards what was known as Free Derry Corner, the area's traditional spot for speechmaking. Speeches had been planned as the final element in the two-hour-long demonstration.

Suddenly firearms came into play. And from then on, this day —30 January 1972—was destined to be known as 'Bloody Sunday'. Like every other observer and marcher, I was taken completely by surprise when British paratroopers burst through barriers lining the route, ran towards the crowd and almost instantly began firing. This is the last fucking straw! I thought, as I crushed my nose into the roadway's asphalt, with high-velocity bullets cracking and whining over me. I was twenty-three and scared witless but my thoughts came fast and embroidered with bravado. I had by then covered enough of The Troubles to have been variously threatened at gunpoint by Protestant para-militaries and forced to run from Irish Republican Army sniper fire. Now, I blustered to myself in outrage, it's my own national army that's firing at me.

I ran and dived for cover, tearing my jeans and cutting my knee, and I huddled behind a rubble barricade feeling as foolish and professionally humiliated as I felt frightened. My job, after all, was to make television, and all I had was a notepad. Wanting to do something of use, I scribbled notes: the time according to my cracked watch-face (4:16 pm), the fractured sobbing of a woman nearby, the number of shots that I was trying to count— an impossible task since they overlapped so much. It was during that notetaking that my eyes locked on the one soldier I remember so well, levelling his rifle at my group of cowering youngsters and pulling the trigger. Like anybody would, I imagine, I dropped my gaze and flattened myself to the ground again.

When a break in the firing came, I ran from the danger area. Around me others lay still; whether they were hit or just being cautious I couldn't tell. Thirteen men, all Catholic residents of Derry, were shot dead that cold January day, six of them under the age of twenty-one on my side of the rubble barricade. A fourteenth would die of his wounds some weeks later.

Though I wasn't at first even conscious of choosing a direction, the dash I made for safety somehow led me to the home of John Hume, leader of Derry's 'constitutional' Irish nationalists (as opposed to the IRA, who represented the 'armed struggle' brand of nationalism). The door was open, and John's wife, Pat, took me into their kitchen to bathe and dress my absurdly small injury, while the house filled with all kinds and ages of Derry men and women, many trembling in shock and fury. I heard John roaring on the phone—something this peaceable community organiser hadn't previously seemed capable of —as he castigated the prime minister's chief adviser in 10 Downing Street. I heard him repeat the word 'massacre' many times, sometimes more fully as 'unprovoked massacre.'

I went back to work on the streets, hoping to make sense of what had just happened, and I met some colleagues and friends on the way, all trying to do the same. We almost immediately encountered the military's lie-making machinery start to rev up. At an impromptu roadside press conference, a British officer gave us the first official account of what he called 'the incident'. Just a few of the reporters, including myself, had been on the crowd's side of the barriers; most had been with the Army and police on their side. But wherever we had been, none of us had seen or heard anyone use a weapon apart from the paratroopers.

'We came under fire from seven snipers,' said the officer.

'Of whom we killed thirteen,' muttered a *Guardian* reporter, a friend who would be celebrated in later years for his biting sketches of proceedings in Parliament.

Later in the day BBC News filmed an interview with the paratroopers' most senior officer on-site, Lieutenant-Colonel Derek Wilford. The no-nonsense interviewer emphasised to the colonel that there was no evidence of any armed attack from the crowd's side. Wilford contradicted him, embellishing the official lie further. 'There was a Thompson sub-machine gun fired, between fifteen and twenty rounds, I would say—and an M1 carbine was fired at me as I traversed across the open ground.'

Though I can often be guilty of some abstruse verbosity, I've

With Nobel Peace Laureate John Hume, Derry, 1997.

remained puzzled through the years by the colonel's odd usage, 'traversed'—not 'ran' or anything simpler. Was it the outcome of some previous brainstorming in the officers' mess, or maybe a coaching session? Did Wilford always talk that way? Or did he summon up the word specially, in the hope of sounding more formal and official, more authoritative, more credible?

The killings quickly became a cause for global protest. Britain was condemned in many quarters. At the UN there were demands that an international peacekeeping force be sent to pacify the province. In Dublin the British Embassy was burned down by angry demonstrators.

Amid the heightened tension, I was busy covering the aftermath on Derry's streets. Perhaps to compensate for having had no film crew present during the actual killings, my TV show now sent me two crews from London. When I finally got a call through to our office, even though the whole of Derry's meagre telephone exchange seemed to be ringing off the hook, my first words to the executive producer, John Edwards, were close to a sob: 'I'm sorry, John. I got it wrong. Telling you there'd be nothing big.' His response was as brusque as I'd always known him to be: 'Who gives a fuck now? Here's what we're gonna do ... .' I now had to scamper fast, along with more reporting staff who were rushing over to help: I was to prepare fresh material for filming by both incoming crews. I also had some moonlighting to do. The national weekly magazine, the *New Statesman*, for whom I'd become a contributor, wanted an immediate eyewitness article from me, including some assessment of the massacre's impact on the overall Northern Irish situation. The work in every direction was intense.

Somehow or other a dogged member of our team managed to get a call through to the Parachute Regiment's HQ, talked his way into the barracks with one of our crews and filmed interviews in the sergeants' mess with some of the shooters themselves. My task, meanwhile, was to film civilian eyewitnesses giving their accounts of the shootings. I shipped out to London one day's worth of such material, and the next evening—somewhat miraculously, given the ever-increasing overload on phone lines—a call reached me from the office about the film's arrival. It wasn't good news: sound tapes were missing for some of the rolls of film. The practice in those days (when location material was still shot on film, not videotape) was to capture sound and vision separately and sync them together back at base. Filmed interviews with no sound were of course useless to our editors— a calamity. I really thought my work was being cursed with technical problems; it was still only months since the footage disaster of my Bangladesh coverage. With more experience, I'd come to see my industry as rife with such crises. TV technology, whatever the period and whatever advances it may have brought, has often been a blight as well as an indispensable tool. But whatever may have happened with our Derry sound tapes, I was now charged with locating the backups that our bosses hoped we had made. I felt quite sure our reliable recordist would, as a matter of course, have created a safety copy for all our interviews. Pretty sure, at least.

Heavy rain, blowing in cold from the Atlantic, was falling on a darkened city in military lockdown. Searchlights panned back and forth across the glistening Victorian buildings. My home-base, the venerable City Hotel (which was to be destroyed in a bombing two years later) had filled up with journalists arriving from many countries so our crew members had been billeted out in one of Derry's B&B guest houses, the sound recordist among them. I strode round, since my phone calls hadn't been picked up. Perhaps unsurprisingly, given the curfew conditions, no one opened the front door, no matter how hard I banged on it. It was 1:30 am. I went to the rear of the guest house and began to climb a slippery drainpipe towards the window of what I believed was the soundman's room, on the top floor of the four-storey building. I tried to anticipate the swings of the army searchlight that crisscrossed our section of town and I climbed only when I felt I wouldn't get picked out by it. A few days before in broad daylight, I'd miraculously survived this army's gunfire; I had no wish now to die at their hands in the dark up a drainpipe. As I was just making it past the third floor, the light beam suddenly switched its pattern and swung back on itself, taking me by such surprise that I lost my footing and slithered back downward about ten feet, scraping flesh off the base of my thumb.

I came to a stop at a joint in the pipe at second-floor level. Four feet or so to my left was a smallish, frosted window, presumably to a bathroom, which had been dark when I passed it going upward, but now was lighted. I stretched to lean over and rap on it, hanging on agonisingly with my bloodied right hand. A middle-aged woman, looking terrified but self-possessed enough to open the window—something I'm not sure I would have done in the same circumstances—listened to my unlikely account of what I was doing there and hauled me, scrambling, inside.

Upstairs, Brian, the burly, red-bearded soundman, was astonished to hear and then see me at his door. He was mortified to learn of the missing tapes. But their loss may well not have been his fault and anyway it was no time for fault-finding. Together on the floor of his room we sorted through his many reels of tape. Sure enough, he had followed protocol to a tee and made a safety copy of every interview, labeling each one in full detail. We found the safeties we needed and made a new copy of them all—a lengthy job that would nowadays seem hopelessly archaic, hooking up Brian's two Uher tape machines, one playing out each interview's audio, the other recording it afresh. I ran with our package of new tapes to the home of a local cabbie we'd hired as our location driver for the whole assignment, woke him, and had him rush the vital material to Belfast Airport sixty miles away, just in time for the first London flight of the day.

I t took just one more day for all of our filmed material, both civilian and military interviews, to arrive in London and move upward in our company's chain of command, well beyond my pay grade and into the realm of politics and the law. The government's response to the domestic and worldwide uproar over Bloody Sunday was to set up a public inquiry, which had in many ways the legal authority of a High Court trial. Senior justice officials then tried to enforce a gag-rule on our company broadcasting anything about Bloody Sunday, arguing that it would be a crime for us to broadcast any statements about the killings, on the grounds that we'd be committing contempt of court, by prejudging the Inquiry's outcome.

Our bosses urgently sought their company lawyers' advice. At first, I feared they would cave under the government's pressure. In my still limited experience of national journalism, I'd been disheartened at times to see attorneys for newspapers and broadcast networks acting over-cautiously, chickening out of worthy fights; too often they'd simply urge their clients to avoid taking serious risks. But our legal eagles turned out to be made of sterner stuff, and with surprising speed, in little more than a day and a half, they came up with some smart legal arguments to use in the service of bold journalism.

They analysed years of contempt-of-court statutes and case-law precedents, looking to isolate exactly what element of media coverage resulted in prejudice to a court's proceedings. They concluded that it was specifically the selection of evidence—editing material in a particular way—that 'settled law' had found to lie at the heart of influencing people's thinking in a courtroom. In essence, it was the process of selection that threatened to sway the decisions of jurors, or (as in our present case) the findings of a presiding judge. The very act of selecting was what produced contempt of court. Armed now with this fresh legal assessment, our team leader, the brash John Edwards, decided to transmit our material over the air in a novel and striking fashion. He broadcast

Continued on Page Two

the footage simply in the form of uncut 'rushes', without any editing at all. He even retained all the film clapperboards, sound-checks being called out, errors, retakes, camera reframing, everything that would normally get left onto the cutting-room floor. 'No editing means no selection of the evidence,' he said, 'and no selection of evidence means no prejudice, no contempt of court.' The gambit worked. The government withdrew its threat to ban our broadcast ahead of time or to prosecute us after it aired.

Public reaction was its usual mix. The kind of viewers who phone a network company immediately after a broadcast (or even during it—and believe me, they do, or certainly used to) are mostly disposed to just complain; our company switchboard's log of incoming calls for that evening recorded many people asking 'What is this mess?' and 'What's gone wrong?' and 'Why are we seeing all these mistakes?' As for viewer approval, this was long before the days of the Nielsen Ratings that track viewers' so-called 'engagement' by the quarter-hour, but we did hear anecdotally that many in the estimated audience of 18 million— exactly how many we couldn't know—were moved by being shown direct and raw eyewitness accounts. TV critics in the press remarked that the presentation had originality and an unexpected forcefulness.

Within a few weeks I was testifying at the public inquiry, giving my first account in an official setting of what I'd seen on Bloody Sunday. I was nervous, self-conscious about my youth among the suave lawyers of national repute and all the military brass. But I was firmly assured of my own recollections and I apparently held up creditably, according to court reporters and observing lawyers, against some vigorous, hostile cross-examination by the military's chief counsel.

At one point during my testimony, I said I had looked up at the high-rise apartment building behind me, the Rossville Flats. The attorney pounced on this as an opportunity to suggest there had been IRA snipers up there and that the soldiers were justifiably returning terrorists' fire. My scanning upward, the attorney claimed, contradicted my earlier description of the soldier I'd been focused on, and other soldiers, too, who held their rifles horizontal, aimed towards the crowd in the street.

Counsel: Did you look up there to see where firing had come from?

Tereshchuk: No. I did not hear any sound from up there.

Counsel: How high did you look up?

Tereshchuk: Up to the top.

Counsel: Why did you look up to that level when you told us that at all times the [soldiers'] rifles were held parallel to the ground and were not facing upwards at all?

Tereshchuk: I was there for some time. I was looking around me in all directions.

I'd evidently turned quite sarcastic. For his part, the lawyer moved on to a well-worn tactic among prosecutors, warning me in severe, admonishing tones against committing perjury, a jailable offence in this quasi-judicial setting.

> Counsel: You must be very careful about the answers you give, because you told [the Inquiry] that at all times the rifles were aimed horizontally to the ground and not pointed upwards. Would it be right to say that, at times, they were apparently firing up into the higher reaches of the block of flats?
>
> Tereshchuk: I cannot say that I saw them fire their rifles at any angle other than the horizontal.

Reading this decades-old transcript, I'm struck not just by my testiness but even more by my twenty-three-year-old's mimicking of the formal sentence structure so characteristic of British courtroom exchanges, even down to dicing with double-negatives.

Many other eyewitnesses gave testimony that affirmed, like mine, that the crowd had done nothing to warrant the army shooting at them. Regardless of this, the Inquiry ended just two months later—appallingly in our view—with the soldiers being absolved of any wrongdoing. The strongest criticism from the chairman was an almost offhand acknowledgement that some soldiers' shooting had 'bordered on the reckless'.

We need not have been surprised. In establishing his inquiry Prime Minister Edward Heath had chosen as its chairman the most senior judge in the land, Lord Chief Justice John Widgery, who just happened to be a retired army brigadier. Furthermore, as we were only to learn thirty years later, after the public release of secret Downing Street records for 1972, the PM had given the Chief Justice a one-to-one warning: 'It has to be remembered,' he said, 'that we are in Northern Ireland fighting not only a military war but a propaganda war.'

When these previously hidden details of history finally emerged, they came as further infuriating confirmation that Widgery's inquiry, so swift to convene and swift to report, had been a cynical fix. For propaganda reasons more than any other, just as the prime minster clearly intended, the army had to be exonerated. But of course—and this was outrageous for me and countless others—there was no exoneration for the fourteen dead of Bloody Sunday. In essence, the opposite applied. They remained besmirched with the suspicion that they had somehow brought about their own deaths. By what actions? Firing a gun? Throwing a bomb? Nobody would or could officially say.

This unacceptable murkiness lingered over the dead citizens of Derry as years passed. But eventually after a quarter-century, another prime minister, by this time Tony Blair, responded to the Catholic community's deep-rooted sense of injustice. Soon after he took office in 1997, he set up a whole new inquiry. He had been powerfully influenced by the work of a man who at the age of fifteen had been huddled near me behind the same barricade. I met Don Mullan only after he had grown up to become a crusading journalist; he had amassed hundreds of contemporaneously recorded eyewitness accounts of Bloody Sunday that had been 'overlooked' by the Widgery Inquiry, or the Widgery Whitewash, as it became known. Don and I both gave evidence to Blair's new inquiry, and together we participated in a documentary film about the fateful day and its subsequent history.

In the years that followed, I had done more Northern Irish reporting but went on to pound a broader international beat, most often in Africa. Whenever I did get back to Ireland, something—and during those years I couldn't have said what—had kept me away from that particular grim stretch of Derry's Bogside district where the killings had happened.

Now, with my testimony being required once more, I was suddenly in Derry again and this time among many others who'd also been there on the day. With Don Mullan and with the others, whom I was meeting for the first time, I repeatedly found a very unexpected bond. At least unexpected for me; Don said he wasn't surprised.

Sudden kinship would develop with each encounter. Exchanges like 'Where were you?' bounced between us. 'Sure, you must have been just twenty yards from me!' And we often turned out to share an onerous sense of having unaccountably escaped—even somehow unjustifiably—while others had died. 'Survivor guilt', though, was a phrase that hadn't even occurred to me until it was plain-spokenly voiced by Don, who we figured out together had been about seventy feet from me when the shooting started. Another fellow-witness, Terence McClements, who had been seventeen at the time, said: 'My instinct for self-preservation took over and I ran. I've felt guilty that a fella I knew, two feet from my shoulder, was shot and why was I not shot?' I was realising now just how strong and simple a fellow-feeling I shared with these men. How come I lived to tell the tale? How did I deserve such astonishing good luck?

This wasn't the only surprise I had about my own mind's workings. In preparation for the public hearing, a team of investigators recruited by the new presiding judge, Lord Justice Saville, travelled to my New York home and took a deposition from me in great detail. They asked me one apparently simple question that I had never been asked before, about my most vivid single memory, the soldier firing towards me. 'What was on his head?' Without a moment's pause I recalled: a red beret. It might have seemed an odd, out-of-left-field question. Even perhaps a trick question of some kind. But through the long hours I spent with these patient questioners, I grew assured that they were simply trying to build up as full a picture of the event from my point of view as they could, putting each visual element in place bit by bit. Unexpectedly, though, the matter of the soldier's headgear became a tripping point for me. The deposition team gathered all available photographs capturing the particular quadrant of paratroopers that advanced towards the barricade where I had crouched and the pictures plainly showed that the soldier in question was wearing not a beret but a helmet. However certain my memory had been, it seemed clear that I was just wrong.

My conviction that I carried a crystal-clear memory of the Bloody Sunday massacre was severely shaken. In my predictable fashion, I turned to the tools of my trade to find some answer to my perplexity, and carried out my own picture research. I dug out more visual material in American media archives and in Irish and other European sources, as well as in the very full British ones. Photojournalists from much of the outside world had been drawn to the Irish Troubles, including a surprising number of French cameramen. Gilles Peress, for instance, from the Magnum Agency in Paris, took a painstakingly full array of Bloody Sunday pictures. As I reviewed images from every kind of source, they confirmed what the Inquiry team had noted; the soldier firing in my direction was indeed wearing a helmet, not the beret I recalled. How could I be remembering it so inaccurately?

I was puzzled and confused. I contacted a range of experts on memory and eyewitness evidence. Unconnected with Northern Ireland, the 1990s had seen a mushrooming of psychological and neurological research into the malleability of people's memory. Many American criminal cases had rested on the accused being identified by eyewitnesses, sometimes wholly mistakenly, and questionable convictions had resulted; much of this new research had been provoked by these unsound verdicts. Whenever a published study about the deceptiveness of memory struck me as especially illuminating I would email or phone the researchers who'd conducted it. My mission felt peculiar. I wasn't chasing the details of a story in my usual professional way; instead I was on a search to understand my own brain's functioning. As I introduced myself to each scientist and explained my troubled recollecting of Bloody Sunday, it felt at the least awkward, maybe even humiliating for me as a pro. Was I not confessing to a shameful error, a weakness or at least some incompetence? Of course no scientist I reached gave the slightest hint they judged me for making a mistake, but the possibility that they might stayed top-of-mind for me with every fresh call I made.

Not all the specialists remained worth pursuing. Some appeared more concerned with what people forget than what they remember. Happy to be whittling down my checklist of interviewees, I put aside the 'experts in forgetting', as I had classified them. The experts I maintained contact with, and called repeatedly with follow-up questions, eventually began to shrink in number as well.

I suspect I came over as something of a caricature, the over-persistent reporter. I would vary my phrasing in hope of gaining further clarity, but in essence I kept posing the same question. 'If photographs and video all recorded the soldier one way, how come I saw him, or at least remember seeing him, quite differently?' A half-dozen interviewees, possibly tiring of my insistence and repetitiveness, excused themselves from the ongoing conversation; one Ohio-based academic, very prominent in his field, just abruptly stopped answering my emails and voicemails.

Professor Elizabeth Loftus, on the other hand, in Washington State and later in California's university system, stayed with me. And I found her explanations persuasive. She was the psychologist whose work seemed most directly relevant to my concerns and she was decidedly the most helpful. Widely known as a pioneering doyenne of human memory research, she had a welcome directness to her, and even gave a blunt name to what had become her main specialty: 'false memories'. She made herself fully available to my layperson's inquiries, however crude or simplistic they might have seemed. When I recounted my Bloody Sunday experience down the phoneline, the questions she asked were often repeats from my interview by the Inquiry lawyers, though she had some state-of-mind queries of her own to add. 'What could you hear when you were looking at the soldier?', 'Do you remember holding your gaze on him, or did you ever look away?', and 'Could something have taken your attention off him, if only for a moment?'

As we talked on the phone, long gaps would occur. I imagined her eyebrows rising as she took these pauses for thought, arching even above the frames of her sizeable glasses. I felt I knew that occasional mannerism. These were pre-YouTube days, before it became everybody's indispensable research tool, but in preparation for any important interview by phone I would habitually try to 'get a visual' of my target. I found many photographs of Loftus, and located some videotape of her in lectures and a panel discussion. I reckoned that her frequent reflective lulls, plus her loose, reddish-blonde hair and perpetual half-smile all served to soften the severity that her darts of incisiveness could at times carry.

She broadened my understanding of the mental processes by which memories are captured, especially under stress or during trauma. If I'd ever previously considered how my own brain worked, I had somewhat unthinkingly applied a label suggested by a 1950s movie-title that sounded apt to me: *I Am A Camera*.

Long before the musical *Cabaret* appeared, this British film told, without any songs, the now-familiar Christopher Isherwood and Sally Bowles story from Weimar-era Berlin. I guess that, like Isherwood, I saw myself as purely a passive recipient of experiences and events; it keyed in with my self-image then as one of life's continual observers. In utter contrast, Loftus pointed out to me how very actively—not passively at all—our brain is always working in assembling its memories. It will often, she said, take elements from disparate sources and merge them together, and it's often the merged version that we mostly rely upon later.

For my confusing beret memory, she had a working hypothesis. She suggested that my mind could have 'superimposed' one snapshot recollection on top of another during the tumult of gunfire. Among all of us in the blindsided, panicked crowd, it came as an abrupt and extra-frightening realisation that it was now Paratroopers who had arrived. They were the Paras, a regiment that carried an especially fearsome reputation. I heard several voices yelling 'It's the Paras!' as we all ran. A distinguishing feature of the Parachute Regiment's uniform is the regulation red beret. When going into action, their officers wore those identifying berets even while the so-called 'other ranks' in the front line might switch to riot headgear or even combat helmets. I had evidently transferred that newly significant, highly resonant detail—the bright red beret, one I'd probably seen on an officer's head—onto the helmeted man firing towards me. Or at least that's what the professor said, and I came, if a bit uneasily, to accept her theory. I certainly did now acknowledge that I was not just a camera.

For the Inquiry in its broad, painstaking work, my evident loss of precision about a visual detail, while troubling for me individually, did not of course have any great significance. The headgear of one soldier as imprinted on my mind's eye did not detract from the more important overall thrust of my testimony. And that testimony was also echoed by many other witnesses' recollections, often more forceful than mine. They all coalesced to present the same irrefutable message: that the Army's shooting at people in the crowd had been unprovoked. But my brain, even while it was ready in logic to put aside its confusion over a detail as unimportant in the grand scheme of things, would just not let go of its troubling conundrum. To this day, whenever I think of Bloody Sunday and I close my eyes, I indelibly still see that red beret, which I really could not have seen in the way I remember it.

I felt a broader uneasiness growing about that troublesome brain of mine. The distressing fallibility of my memory, as I saw it, made me unsure about the way I'd viewed the world in general throughout my adult life. I'd been a reporter at this point for over thirty years and had always insisted that facts are facts and supposition is something else. My mind's involuntary fudging of what I had believed to be an utterly unambiguous recollection was now cruelly mocking my ingrained attachment to certainty. Since I'd just entered my fifties, it's possible that age played a role in this, too; maybe some kind of mid-life crisis of confidence was overdue anyway. My consternation started to feel almost existential. 'Am I who I think I am?' I found myself wondering before I fell asleep. 'Am I as reliable an individual, as trustworthy, as I believe?' On awakening, this unaccustomed, unwelcome challenge to my self-assurance would haunt my days.

I winced during the Inquiry's public hearings to hear the chairman singling out my and other journalists' usefulness because we were professional and practised observers. 'Reporters often make excellent witnesses,' was the Lord Justice's assessment. I certainly didn't feel excellent.

During this phase of the Inquiry, The New York Times commissioned me to write a personal reflection on my problems of recall. To my own surprise, though not to my friends', it turned to be one of my most difficult pieces of journalism to write. I may have felt I'd confidently reported on just about everything from a local parish sewing circle to international conference tables, but at that point I was dismayingly unused to writing about myself.

When the piece was published, Times editors gave it a strong but unwelcome headline. 'An Unreliable Witness' was emblazoned in bold type just above my name. That, I thought with some bruised annoyance, was putting it a bit strong. But I had to recognise it was literally, strictly speaking, true.

The Saville Inquiry continued for an extraordinary total of twelve years. It must rank as one of the most thorough-going official efforts to re-examine any episode of a nation's history. Eventually Lord Justice Saville formally concluded in 2010 that the fourteen dead of Bloody Sunday were indeed blameless, and that responsibility for the killings fell solely upon the British soldiers. It fell to yet another prime minister by this stage, David Cameron, to deliver an unprecedented apology in Parliament:

> There is no doubt. There is nothing equivocal, there are no ambiguities. What happened on Bloody Sunday was both unjustified and unjustifiable. It was wrong. ... On behalf of our country, I am deeply sorry.

For the bereaved families of Derry this was of course welcome news—in part. They are not all of the same mind, but many family members have consistently demanded criminal account-ability for their loved ones' deaths. Only now, another thirteen years (at the time of writing) after Saville's decisive conclusion, has one single British soldier—one lone Paratroop lance-corporal—been charged with murder. In public he has been known only as 'Soldier F'. All the paratroopers involved in the shootings were granted anonymity for the investigations, though the cloak of secrecy got torn a little at times; some crowd-members said they heard one of his fellow-paratroopers call him 'Dave'.

Getting charges pressed against any of the shooters proved to be an agonising legal roller coaster. Seventeen Paras came under suspicion as the individual culprits, but the building of cases against them was a patchy, complicated process. After Saville reported, the Prosecution Service said it would need four years to prepare charges, but the effort stretched out very much longer. In the case of Soldier F, forensic ballistics succeeded in matching his rifle to a bullet found in the body of one victim, a seventeen-year-old who had been about thirty feet from me behind the rubble barricade. In all, Soldier F loosed off thirteen shots out of the 108 that the Paras fired in total. Ultimately, though, prosecutors were able to charge him with murdering just two men in their twenties, both shot in the back around eighty feet from the barricade. They also charged him with wounding (in actual legal terms, committing attempted murder) a further five others. During the investigation a surprise witness, a lieutenant from a different regiment who had been at an observation post above the action, emerged as willing to give evidence against Soldier F—but then the prospective witness died, evidently of natural causes.

Developments elsewhere in Northern Ireland also affected the Soldier F prosecution. Another case entirely—a killing that took place in Belfast, quite separate from Bloody Sunday—had led to murder charges against two soldiers but those charges unexpectedly had to be dropped. The legal reasoning was complicated, but (if I can cite a very rough American analogy) it approximated to the accused men not being read their Miranda Rights. Civilian law-enforcement officers in the UK call it 'reciting the Police Caution' to an arrested person. The precedent set by that failed Belfast prosecution led the Bloody Sunday prosecutors to suddenly abandon their charges against Soldier F.

Lawyers for the families tried, and are still trying (again, as I write now) to get a judicial review of the prosecutors' decision, in hope it will be reversed and the case against F reinstated.

Meanwhile, lawyers have also pursued judicial review for cases involving other paratroopers, who unlike F were never indicted in the first place because prosecutors feared the evidence wasn't strong enough to secure a conviction. The dead in these cases were three seventeen-year-olds, a twenty-year-old and a twenty-six-year-old who had variously been behind the barricade, or at the base of the Rossville Flats or nearby, beside some low-rise buildings.

Time will tell if the British justice system can ever provide a satisfactory reckoning for Bloody Sunday's families. In the words of a formulaic phrase that UK reporters conventionally use about court proceedings, 'the case continues'. Even if, as in these killings, more than half a century has elapsed.

As for me, deep in my own personal denial for the longest time, I didn't think that Bloody Sunday affected me to any deep or substantial extent mentally—apart, of course, from my utter disgust at the long injustice. I first dealt with that disgust by compartmentalising it professionally in the public realm of sharp but not screeching news commentary. Back when the original 'Widgery Whitewash' finding was announced, I wrote for a London periodical that, given what I and others had seen at first hand of the soldiers' unwarranted actions and the lack of any evidence against the civilians who were killed, it was indisputable that the soldiers had committed crimes. Later, I presented the same unreserved conclusion, buttressed with careful reasoning, I hope, when I treated Bloody Sunday as distant history, in archive-based documentaries and some occasional magazine articles.

If I looked inward, which I did very rarely through those years, I could readily acknowledge that back in 1972 my youthful self had already been badly rattled by the atrocities of the Bangladesh war. I'd also been imprisoned, briefly but scarily, by some roughneck bruisers of Poland's authoritarian regime. And during my first year in Northern Ireland, before Bloody Sunday, I had lived through dangerous firefights and been menaced by masked gunmen. But I believed and went on believing that the Derry massacre amounted to simply one more frightening event to slot into my growing ledger of alarming happenings. Just part of the unavoidably hectic fabric of a journalist's life.

In Chicago sometime during the early 2000s, someone tossed a question at me that I wasn't prepared for. I was taking part in a panel discussion on Northern Ireland issues when the query was voiced: 'What effect did Bloody Sunday have on your reporting work?' I didn't really have an answer. I fell back, as I often can, on a flip kind of truism, something like: 'Well, it certainly was a shock to my system. And since then I always pay very close attention whenever I come into contact with armed soldiers.' In truth, I do reflexively find myself uneasy among uniforms and loaded weaponry, no matter how innocuous the setting might seem; even mere military parades can get me a bit edgy.

As I reflected alone after the discussion was over, an unacknowledged truth tumbled out. I am by no means a specialist in the coverage of mass murders—God forbid—but the record looked telling, once I stepped back to consider it. While my TV and print journalism has inevitably ranged widely in topics covered, that evening I realised there is one undeniable thread weaving its way through it all.

Here I am in 1974 in the pages of the *Times* of London, embroiled in controversy over Portuguese colonial soldiers mowing down nearly four hundred residents of a Mozambican village, a massacre that American commentators compared to the Vietnam War barbarity of My Lai.

And in 1976 here I am on British television pointing out frame after condemnatory frame of footage that has captured South African policemen firing at schoolchildren during the Soweto uprising. Later, for a 1980s TV history of South Africa's long battle against racist rule, I'm reconstructing the terrible details of the Sharpeville massacre in 1960, when sixty-nine unarmed protestors were gunned down by police.

In the 1990s here is my first television documentary for an American network, the result of my visiting Florida and hearing about an under-reported but horrifying historical subject. Insistently and successfully, I pitch the story to the network, and end up producing a film that depicts a 1923 lynch-mob rampage wiping out the African-American community of Rosewood, a rare pocket of black prosperity near the Gulf Coast. In Rosewood's case it took seventy years for the victims' descendants to receive any legal redress.

Like it or not, aware of it or not, I have clearly been drawn back again and again to the peculiarly compulsive narrative of a powerful, armed group of men ruthlessly destroying the lives of ordinary people, initially with complete impunity. And there follows, as it must, the never easy, and sometimes hopelessly protracted, search for justice. It offends me; and I guess, for reasons that undoubtedly go way, way back, I have been taking it personally.

During one of my first visits to white-ruled South Africa, when I was just beginning thirty years of reporting the country's turbulent struggle, I travelled several hours east of Johannesburg to a small Afrikaaner town. I was jolted to see a bulky white farmer coming out of the local post office, only to knock to the ground and start kicking a slightly-built black man who had simply been unlucky enough to be walking on the same pavement.

My gorge rose just as it had in high school when I was the target of bullies until I learned to fight back. Up to that point I had been regular prey for a squad of thugs drawn from my class and from older classes too. Six or seven of them would lie in wait to ambush me at a scrubby piece of landfill on my way home. To foil them I varied my route and my timing, but they'd often catch me all the same. Outweighed and overpowered, I had to submit limply to punches and kicks. I was in a helpless frenzy of anger; I just couldn't get out of their grip or escape their blows. These came mostly to my belly, sometimes to the back of my head. In the end, after I did acquire the ability to retaliate, it was amplified powerfully by my volcanic outrage and fury. I perfected my own home-grown form of a roundhouse kick, swiveling on one foot and slamming the other very effectively into my tormentors' kidneys. Eventually they left me alone as too much trouble.

On that Transvaal pavement, I felt as powerless as when the teenaged bullies first menaced me. I watched the farmer's assault, my body rigid while my brain frantically tried to figure out what I could possibly do. I was a twenty-four-year-old incomer to this hardline apartheid heartland; if I intervened, what would happen? I had some experience of reacting impetuously when my dander was up over something I found outrageous; it would sometimes detonate into a riot of punched-out teeth and broken bones, or at least fingers. Alcohol usually figured in those eruptions. But this was different. I was stone-cold sober in the sharp, subtropical morning light. Calculations had to be made. Two-hundred-and-thirty pounds of Boer farmer would likely floor my much leaner frame. Other sturdy specimens of white manhood were standing close by, looking ready to join in, and it wouldn't be on my side, or still less on the black man's. I stayed rooted to the spot, guilt coursing through me at my inaction, until the farmer delivered one last kick of his steel-capped boot to the victim's ribcage and strode on to his truck parked nearby.

Five or six black men and women who had also been watching, at first immobile and outwardly impassive, now rushed forward to help the beaten man. They half-walked, half-carried him to the shaded bench of a bus-stop, clearly intending to take him somewhere safe and get treatment. He looked to be in caring hands. I saw him appear to pass out, but I wished all the same to somehow connect with him. There had been nothing I could do and now there was nothing I could say; but I impossibly wanted him to know that I was a sympathiser, however much or little that might mean.

I turned away, now palpably shaking with shock and guilt, along with the onset of sheer relief at the violence ending. I remembered I had been on my way to an official appointment. Disquietingly, it was at the police station, a matter of formally registering my presence in town. Once there, I knew that it would serve no purpose to report the attack I'd just witnessed.

Men with power overwhelming, even killing others who are powerless. Yes, I've reported on massacres, as the record shows. And I've covered oppressive totalitarian regimes. In my simplistic, perhaps even trite way, I have mentally categorised both—murdering a group of people, menacing an entire population—as simply organised, institutional bullying. It's common enough among all decent human beings, and I'll willingly include many reporters in that designation, to be thoroughly outraged by bullies. My own fixation with them is hardly distinctive. But something else about bullying—a completely off-the-wall, even melodramatic, idea—has tugged at me insistently. It would take hold during those moments over the years when I wondered, without ever getting an answer, just what kind of man had first caused me to grow in my fifteen-year-old mother's womb. My work experience was teaching me very clearly what kind of men will stoke in me the fires of disgust. I would find myself angrily asking: 'That man, whoever he is who "fathered" me: was he a bully?'

Chapter 14
Dictator

While still a young man but already well-travelled, Winston Churchill labeled Uganda 'the pearl of Africa' and 'a fairy tale'. On this, my first visit to any African nation, the very beginning of my career-long familiarity with the continent, I too was entranced by the place. There's a deep aromatic richness to Uganda's densely forested hills, and its lush, dark-green vistas are dotted with stunning waterfalls and crystalline streams. As a son of the Scottish Borders, I had come to regard every trip to a hot country as overdue recompense for growing up cold and damp, and I found this East African country's climate deliciously cosseting. It sits on the equator but at a 4,000-foot elevation, so the nearly 100-degree Fahrenheit temperatures that greeted me at Entebbe Airport brought a strangely fresher tropical sensation than I'd known so far—certainly a world away from swampy Bengal. Uganda was warm, intensely hot at times, but never sticky or saturating.

The thirty-mile highway into the capital city, Kampala, was garlanded with huge WELCOME! signs spelled out in colourful flowers, along with Ugandan national flags on every light pole, entwined with another flag I didn't recognise. My taxi-driver, always the journalist's first source, told me the festive arrangements were temporary and intended for an imminent state visit by a neighbouring country's president. I regarded them all the same as a personal message, or at the least an encouraging omen for my own stay.

Forty-eight hours later, the forthcoming state occasion offered me my first sighting of the man in charge: the bulky, six-foot-six-inches-tall leader who had designed his own title:

His Excellency President for Life, Field Marshal Al-Haji Doctor
Idi Amin Dada, VC, DSO, MC, Lord of all the Beasts of the Earth

and Fishes of the Sea and Conqueror of the British Empire in
Africa in General and Uganda in Particular.

For what it's worth, the abbreviations that might have suggested
the Victoria Cross, Distinguished Service Order and Military
Cross were all counterfeits of genuine British honours, which Idi
Amin conferred upon himself. From about thirty feet away what
struck me apart from his sheer mass was his rock-rigid stance, as
a bead of sweat trickled slowly down his rounded left cheek. His
brows furrowed in static concentration but his eyes darted
almost jerkily from side to side. He seemed a disconcerting
mixture: simultaneously tenacious and mercurial.

A brass band cracked out of tune occasionally while a march-
past of troops saluted him as he stood at attention alongside his
guest, President Jean-Bedel Bokassa of the Central African
Republic. Both men had taken power in military coups and today
in downtown Kampala they both wore elaborate dress uniforms
encrusted with rows of extravagant medals on each man's chest,
in what looked like competitive mockery of each other. A much
shorter man than his host, Bokassa added to his height by
wearing an odd high-rise version of a general's peaked cap. The
whole ceremony looked and sounded ridiculous, but it bore an
inescapable air of menace.

Bokassa had also recently declared himself President for Life
and as well as the broad repression of his entire population, he
was already notorious for a habit of razor-slashing any
subordinate who angered him. For his part, Amin was still in the
process of becoming the bloodthirsty tyrant the world now
remembers, responsible in the end for the deaths of 300,000 of
his fellow citizens. But back in mid-1972, the Ugandan president
could still appear as merely the hearty buffoon that many people,
especially overseas, took him for.

One intriguing, somewhat creepy element to their pompous
celebrations was Amin's renaming of a major street in honour of
his fellow dictator. The new 'Bokassa Street' had previously been
Alidina Visram Street, commemorating an influential nineteenth-
century trader who, like many East African businesspeople, was
born in India.

I was instantly seized with the idea that this particular businessman, or at any rate his modern-day descendants, might well form the human heart of the story I was there to cover. And indeed, the Visram family was not hard to find. They were one of Uganda's more prominent Asian dynasties and their phone number was easily discovered in Kampala's slim directory. When I called, saying how my interest had been piqued by seeing their forefather's name ignominiously erased in the business district, they immediately invited me to dinner at their rambling villa on the city's outskirts.

An elaborately laid-out, long oval mahogany table was awaiting us. I was the only guest and was surrounded by a score or more of Visrams spanning three generations. A fourth generation, several children aged between, I'd say, four and eleven were on their way to bed as I arrived around 7 pm. Upon gentle instruction they all said a polite goodnight to me. We adults— and I sensed I was the youngest adult in the room—then sat down to eat. I was glad that I had thought to dress quite formally. In London I had packed one lightweight tropical suit in a pale cream colour with peaked, double-breasted lapels. It had been mocked as over-fancy by my more casual fellow-reporters in their dun-coloured safari-jackets (four practical patch-pockets on the front and who knows how many pockets inside) but my dress-sense now felt wholly vindicated. A bonus, in fact; I'd intended the suit for meetings with government officials and now it did double-duty at a family event that turned out to be more formal and elevated than I could have anticipated.

I was no stranger to South Asian food after my time in Bengal and Karachi, and long before that I had frequented Oxford's and Manchester's so-called curry-houses, which in the 1960s were among the earliest in Britain's growing influx of Indian restaurants. But in Kampala I encountered novelty in the sweet-salty dishes of India's Gujarat region. There was a superior delicacy to them, small as they were but astonishingly numerous; they just kept on appearing one after another as the evening went on, each one tickling the palate with subtly different flavors. The stand-out dish, one I'd never come across until that night, was bhugo: minced game bird that had been baked twice with spices. In

India it would probably have been partridge but here in Uganda the local sandgrouse was used. It was decidedly hot, in the spicy sense, and very dry, but came complemented with some *khadi*, a thin ginger-and-chili flavoured gravy or soup with yogurt added in.

I was seated just where I was supposed to be, on the right hand of my host's wife, and opposite the host himself, the current head of both the family and the business, Heiderali Visram. Like several of his male relatives he wore an *achkan* buttoning high at the neck, though some younger ones sported Western-style business suits, all much darker than my pastel affair. The women, perhaps seven or so, were all in boldly coloured *sarees*, several with tiny, stitched-in *sheesha* mirrors that caught and multiplied the flickers from three candelabras on the table. The most resplendent *saree*, in a bright magenta, was worn by Heiderali's wife, Sugra, who mentioned to me early on that she had been a member of Uganda's parliament, and had started the nation's still-new family-planning programme.

I settled in comfortably and listened to the tale of the family's history, with Heiderali doing most of the telling. A trim man in his fifties with shiny boot-black hair greying at his temples and behind his ears, he spoke quietly, sounding very accustomed to having people listen. 'Nearly a century ago now ... ,' he started; his discursive style was conspicuous. 'My grandfather, Alidina Visram, walked inland for eleven hundred miles from Dar-es-Salaam on the coast to make his way here, setting up trading posts all along the way.' I sensed he was reciting a well-rehearsed chronicle. 'Here in the interior, Kampala and Entebbe became the essential kernel for his business, and eventually we embraced all of East Africa.'

It was certainly a striking origin story. Alidina Visram had left India as a penniless twelve-year-old boarding a cargo ship to the East African island of Zanzibar. He was clearly a hard-driven youngster, finding work in the caravan trade and moving up fast from his porter and messenger roles to managerial positions. He soon branched out, parlaying his own earnings plus loans he convinced established traders to advance him, and founded his own entrepreneurial caravan business. The growing ivory trade offered him his big commercial break, when he had the idea of selling packaged food to big-game hunters. I was learning all this some time before I'd develop my own fascination with elephants—living ones, that is—and at the time I passed no moral judgement on this questionable source of Visram wealth. I was merely, and somewhat innocently, agog at the founder's business acumen, not least when I heard how he cannily anticipated the growth of East African Railways across the entire region.

Along the new routes inland he began opening general stores called *dukas*, selling food and essentials to construction workers laying the tracks. He steadily kept one rail-stop ahead of the railroad builders. Alidina Visram & Company then had more than one-hundred-and-seventy branches. He expanded into the trucking business and then into processing agricultural commodities. He built, for instance, Uganda's first cotton gin and exported its products around the world.

I noticed the honoured forefather's name was always invoked in full as Alidina Visram; he was never called by merely his fore-name, Alidina, even though every person in the room was also a Visram, except for me of course. Some of the historical details came from brothers and cousins around the table, who judged with careful courtesy when an appropriate pause might come in Heiderali's flow.

Sugra commanded her own respectful silences, just as when her husband had spoken, and she was greeted with much affirmative murmuring after she said: 'Alidina Visram established his first Kampala *duka* even before the British colonialists arrived here.' She also pointed out that, while the great man had belonged to the Ismaili sect of Islam, he employed thousands of Indian immigrants who were Hindus as well as his fellow Muslims, and provided jobs for many more native Africans into the bargain.

This was all excellent material, I thought—perfectly matching the very reason I had come to Uganda in the first place. My bosses had urgently deployed me there because Idi Amin had provoked a sudden international crisis. He had announced he would banish all Ugandan Asians from the country within ninety days, seizing their assets in the process. He shocked foreign ambassadors with some ugly, undiplomatic language, spitting out the word 'parasites' to label the entire Asian business sector. Amin's brand of populism was leading him to stir up resentment among his impoverished African followers against the smaller and (often, though not always) much richer Asian population. He clearly intended to ride the wave of racial and class envy, with the Asians as scapegoats, to secure his position politically among the country's black majority.

The wider world was aghast at Amin's plans, not least Britain as Uganda's former colonial rulers. Hectic measures were sought to provide safe harbour for the expelled families, many of whom held British passports as a hangover from colonial times. Many, however, did not have the right to enter the UK and they consequently looked like becoming stateless refugees. India, Pakistan, Canada and other East African nations, plus some European countries, would soon step up to offer refuge. The US would eventually play a part, too, accepting about 9,000 for resettlement.

(Not everyone was resettled, though. The following winter I traced hundreds, mostly men separated from their families, who had ended up shivering in the snow-covered refugee camp of Traiskirchen in Austria, many of them wearing layer upon layer of their equatorial clothing.)

Such international scattering of the Asians was still in the future as we sat together at dinner; the impact of Amin's expulsion announcement was just starting to register. With each fresh dish, and each new snippet from their family history, my enthusiasm to feature them in my report was mounting. I grew convinced that the Visrams were the perfect case-history. I was a novice tele-journalist of just three years standing, but I'd fast come to value the storytelling device of focusing tightly on individuals to illustrate a more widely applicable truth. Understanding the plight of 80,000 threatened human beings would be easier if the viewer could see exactly how a single family was dealing, or having trouble dealing, with the threat that loomed over their entire community.

Our evening stretched out longer, three hours, then four, without any sign of ending yet; dinner plates were discreetly removed and replaced with *jagghery*-sweetened desserts. African staff did the serving and clearing, I noted. Some family members, the younger men in particular, became increasingly animated about the injustice of what faced them. Their language loosened up; no actual curses escaped their lips though I made a mental note that their exclamations were at times 'a close-run thing', each one a victory of politeness over profanity, but only by a very narrow squeak. Like my own phrasing, perhaps, their English was decidedly colonial, an affect of formality for them, I thought; it barely masked their fury. One vocal thirtysomething got to mid-sentence before having to correct himself. 'And this is what we get, after we've built up their economy, provided so many jobs for the b—, the Africans ... this is what we get.' It was the only time that the obvious racial element in the nation's tensions came near to surfacing openly. After a moment the anger in the air dissipated, and the overall mood subsided into a kind of forlorn dismay, resignation even, though undertowed with deep apprehension about the future.

I asked a direct question at one point, trying not to sound crude in the elegant room's restrained ambience: 'Where will you go?'

Sugra replied softly, 'We have absolutely no idea where in the world we can relocate.'

The poignancy of their fate moved me, as well as quickening my filmmaker's hopes. I could vividly picture them being shoved up a gangway onto a steamer in the sweltering port of Mombasa, classic refugee figures carrying just one suitcase each—a compelling contrast with this handsome, comfortable home. Occasionally through the evening I mentioned under a cloak of some casualness that I had to start shooting a film very soon; now with greater specificity I asked a couple of times if I could interview family members on camera. My request was politely evaded, with yet more family background information being quickly laid out, or the virtues of another fine dish explained to me. I began to get anxious that the deepening need I felt for their participation in my film was going to be disappointed.

Around midnight, with the arrival of Uganda's native robusta coffee and digestif drinks, everyone suddenly got very firm with me. They had no desire whatever to appear on international television to illustrate their and all the other Asians' predicament. They were unpersuadable. 'It's simply too risky,' Heiderali said flatly. I didn't give up. I broached the idea again even more earnestly, though in truth I was offering them little beyond the reporter's cliché of 'an opportunity to tell the world your story'. I even attempted the dubious claim that publicising their case globally could possibly make powerful nations pressurise Amin into changing his mind; this too fell unconvincingly on all ears. For the entire table, and Heiderali took the lead decisively here, fear of what vicious punishment Amin could exact upon any one of their many extended family members and associates was simply too great. I felt admiration for Heiderali's firm control of the situation, his fatherly protectiveness over his whole clan, and I couldn't blame any of them for their reluctance to help me. In my four short days in the country, I had already heard sporadic reports of Asian homes being invaded by Amin's thugs, husbands beaten, wives and daughters raped, possessions and money taken.

Eventually when all was said and done, the Visrams and I began to rise from the table and I took my leave amid friendly but subdued farewells.

Thwarted in my plans, I returned to the International Hotel and my new temporary 'gang'—the group of correspondents with whom once again I would form an alliance, partly of convenience, partly of friendship, forged in challenging circumstances. The task at hand was difficult for us all; reporting on a dictatorship always is.

After a few days my film crew arrived from London, and we shot an interview with Makerere University's Professor Ali Mazrui. He was later to become a giant among Africa's forthright public intellectuals, but at that time with us he was a modest academic, sounding just cautiously critical of Amin for stirring up black resentment of the richer Asians. For secrecy and safety's sake we chose to talk with him on a sailboat, far out on Lake Victoria. We set sail from a jetty outside the city, picking up

Mazrui at a prearranged point a couple of miles along the shoreline. I'm surprised now at our thinking we could get away with this ploy, since we'd already often heard versions of that phrase so common in Big Man autocracies: 'He has eyes and ears everywhere.' (And Mazrui's anxiety about being seen with us was entirely justified by subsequent events—a month afterward, his university's vice-chancellor was 'disappeared' and then killed, the result of incurring Amin's wrath.) The professor picked his words carefully in our nautical setting, but between the lines he bravely made it clear he felt Amin was endangering the economy by expelling the valuable business community.

'It's inevitable,' he said, 'that there should be black-versus-brown prejudices in Uganda. But to cut out our country's economic heart in service of those prejudices is a highly risky course to take.' Without saying it outright, he was assisting us in painting a picture of Amin as a racist, crazy and destructively divisive of his own country.

I had my own, private anxieties on the boat. At twenty-three, I still hadn't learned to swim—something my pride couldn't let me tell my crew. Every sharp squall brought on by the tropical lake's erratic winds threw me into a panic. I was glad, though, that we now had in the can at least one authoritative piece of well-informed commentary to include in our expulsion story.

We did the rest of our reporting, mercifully for me, on dry land. But perforce, it was limited. We were reduced to filming quickly snatched interviews around the capital, talking with not especially prominent Africans and Asians. Nobody prominent would talk to us on the record besides Mazrui. With the ordinary people we filmed on the street it was rare for any to give us their names. I was learning the journalistic art of making the best out of whatever could be found.

I was grateful for advice from one particular senior reporter among the gang at the International: David Holden, who was chief foreign correspondent for London's *Sunday Times*. To me David seemed very senior, in that he was all of forty-eight years old, more than twice my age, as I ruefully calculate from my current septuagenarian standpoint. Our talks became more frequent after my team had gone back to London and was preparing to broadcast our material across the UK and the other territories where we syndicated our show. My task was to remain on the ground to simply keep, as often, a watchful eye on developments.

David and I, albeit in our respectively different media and with widely opposite degrees of experience, were both 'weekly men', relieved of any pressure to report-in daily with immediate, hard news, so it was quite easy for us to find time for leisurely meals together. On 14 September, the night when my team's report would be airing in London, we went for a late dinner in an Italian restaurant on one of the seven hills that surround Kampala—like Rome, as Ugandans often say. Africa on this night was far outdoing Southern Europe; a tropical storm was raging, a spectacular light show with streaked lightning crackling over the hills, attacking each one of the seven in turn, it seemed. The waiters, evidently trained by a Neapolitan boss who'd been a settler in Ethiopia before moving south to Uganda's much lusher climes, sang extravagant operatic arias as they delivered dishes. They were surprisingly good, the tenors rather more than the baritones, and all were certainly having fun even as they worked attentively.

My mood matched the unsettled weather more than the merriment immediately around us. I confessed to David I was jittery about my show's broadcast. Amin's embassy staff in London, I thought, could well take offence. I imagined them seizing on our portrait of Amin as capricious and maybe mentally unbalanced. I could see them sending their negative report back to an outraged Amin ... and his order going out that I should be made to pay for the insulting broadcast. But David was at pains to reassure me.

He had a languid manner, all of a piece with his reputation among us for possibly being a gentleman-spy. Britain's MI6 had a habit of employing such types, working undercover as journalists. The infamously defecting Soviet double-agent Kim Philby, for instance, was employed by both MI6 and The Observer newspaper. I'd seen David give a graciously resigned smile and change the subject whenever anyone had the bad manners to suggest his frequently impressive insider scoops owed anything to an intelligence agency. Over our meal my anxiety about the risk of Amin exacting revenge on me made David push aside his glass of waragi, Uganda's banana-based answer to gin. Not for the first time with me, he imparted an avuncular concern for my worries. He leaned forward on one elbow, closing our heads together as he spoke in soothing tones: 'A bad reaction in London is quite possible of course, but it's not that likely. Amin's diplomats abroad are under pressure, and they wouldn't want to attract his attention especially. They'd fear him blaming them for the broadcast themselves. And besides, if anything were to happen, it would be a while before it took effect back here, even longer to centre on you. You'd have time.' (This was of course well before today's globally shared, instantaneously accessed news-cycles.)

I might have broken into a relieved smile, except that his voice then took on a fresh tinge of seriousness. 'But all the same,' he said, 'for other reasons entirely you might consider this. Tomorrow I'm catching the dawn flight to Nairobi. I strongly advise you be on that flight with me.'

'What do you know?' I rather stupidly asked. I realised I shouldn't expect an answer.

'Just feeling cautious,' he said. I questioned no further and agreed to go with him.

We returned to the International and to bed for a very few hours. By 6:00 am we were lifting off from Entebbe to meet the sun rising over the Indian Ocean. Less than two hours later we were in a different country, Kenya. As I took a taxi headed for Nairobi's Stanley Hotel, David waved me off airily, saying he was going to meet 'some planter friends' from Happy Valley, well north of the city.

Meanwhile back in Kampala, armed men from Amin's retinue charged into the International looking for journalists. They dragged off nineteen of my colleagues to the Makindye Military Prison on the edge of the city.

Amin was reacting, flailing his violence in different directions, to an unexpected insurgency. Ugandan exiles in Tanzania who opposed his regime had launched an invasion from the south. Amin ordered a phalanx of MIG jet fighters to strike at them from the air. In his capital it was a simple reflex for him to grab, and lock away, well out of contact, all the foreign reporters who'd come to his country.

For four days, until international diplomatic pressure managed to free them, my colleagues suffered vicious beatings in what had come to be called 'Amin's Dungeon'. They also witnessed other prisoners, all Africans, being killed—especially gruesomely, by having their skulls crushed. John Fairhall, a long-time Africa hand with the *Guardian*, another somewhat older man to my mind at all of forty-four, was utterly changed by the experience. He would give up on foreign reporting completely and become his newspaper's home-based education specialist. In his hallmark, dispassionate style John later wrote that Makindye was 'the prison with the highest mortality rate in Amin's Uganda. Of about twenty-five men in my cell, fifteen were taken out over the four days and killed, usually with sledgehammers.'

For my part, safe next door in Kenya, I felt much inevitable relief. My London bosses, saying it was partly to reward me for good shoe-leather research, and partly to celebrate my narrow escape, gave me a month off, or even more if I wanted it. Our network company's CEO even sent me what we called a 'hero-gram', a label born of the ironic false modesty required of us on-the-ground guys:

> CONGRATS GETTING GREAT STORY OUT
> [STOP] AND SELF TOO [STOP]

I asked a girlfriend in England to fly out soon and join me and, in the meantime, I set off on an extended safari into the bush, aiming to meet her later on the coast for a beach vacation. I seemed to feel no guilt about having run away while others ended up being traumatised. But I did ask myself why I hadn't woken any of the gang early that morning before the flight to tell them we were leaving. My rationale was that whatever knowledge lay behind David's decision to depart, it was his own secret to share. And he had shared it, or at least pointedly hinted at it, solely with me—for whatever reasons.

Later, back in London, I saw David again only rarely, and only at cocktail parties, and never alone. On one occasion, I rather tipsily introduced him to my companion for the evening as 'the man who saved me from Idi Amin'. He laughed it off good-naturedly and sidled his way past us.

Five years after our Kampala episode David was dead. Not long before hearing news of his death I read a reflection he'd written about the occasional dangers involved in newsgathering: 'I have felt the boots going in and I have heard the prison door close behind me; and I know how sickening the fear of such moments can be.' He also wrote, 'Thank God, I have never suffered either bullets or the steel tearing into my flesh.'

David's body was found with a 9mm bullet through his heart; he was lying on the ground alongside a construction site in Cairo. At first he couldn't be identified; his wallet and passport were missing, and even labels on his clothing had been cut out. Eventually three stolen cars, all small Fiats abandoned in different locations, were found to be connected with his death. He'd been shot in one of the cars, from behind at close range— so close, in fact, that his jacket was scorched below his left shoulder. His briefcase, identification documents and luggage were all found in the second car and some of his work-papers in the third. A somewhat sophisticated abduction operation had evidently been conducted.

There has been speculation that maybe Israel's Mossad agency, or possibly the CIA, were involved. A sinister discovery was made elsewhere; ahead of the killing, telexes had been stolen from the Sunday Times offices in London that detailed its chief correspondent's Middle East travel itinerary, and this would certainly suggest the work of an organisation with international reach. But to this day no one has been charged with David's murder and no reason ever established for his death.

Chapter 15
Cottage—A Rural Interlude

I first saw the cottage in the winter of 1990 and it was enchanting.' she recalled. 'But I spent our whole week there totally huddled by the fireplace.' She was from California, and in cold weather she said she needed central heating. It was undeniably 'authentic', she would agree, but a cottage in the hills without central heating? That had to change.

My still-new wife, Melissa, had perhaps unsurprisingly been captivated by the stone house that I'd owned for the previous fifteen years. It was built in the mid-eighteenth century and was tucked away in the delightful landscape of England's Cotswold Hills. And I was glad she was going to make changes. The cottage had played a chequered role in my life, dating back to a different time and a different relationship.

My girlfriend in the late 1970s, Jane, was helping me take an unaccustomed step into a business enterprise. Like me, she worked in television but at a different national network company, and not as a journalist but as a programme organiser. She was a slender brunette with a pretty, heart-tugging smile that could flash out suddenly from her mostly quiet demeanour. She would appear reserved, perhaps even that passé description, 'demure', but as soon as we were alone she could turn on an exciting sexy foxiness that I found irresistible—plus an unquenchable sense of fun, about sex or anything else. She wasn't ever the foremost humorist in any group, but I enjoyed the ease with which she could join in the flow of social banter. She was much more of a natural at it than I was. And although by my mid-to-late twenties I'd become pretty well Anglicised, I was a little in awe of what I considered her quintessential Englishness. A certain type of Englishness, for sure; she'd been a contemporary at the same girls' boarding school as Margaret Thatcher's daughter. I don't know if that schooling was responsible, but she also had a practical kind of briskness to her. In the words of one of her colleagues, Jane was 'a great fixer, a just-get-things-done kind of girl'. She became my main source of encouragement when I joined with my diverse bunch of friends and some previous co-workers to make our bold leap into the relatively unknown.

The idea was for us to create an independent production house, initially making documentaries, but then (if all went well commercially) we would branch into feature-movies, network drama series ... and who knew what other entertainment industry heights we might conquer. The immediate target of docu-mentaries felt very reachable given our combined experience, but when it came to theatrical films and other fiction-based output we didn't have any concrete ideas or, as I recall, any actual screenplays. Nor had we acquired any literary properties ripe for turning into screenplays or treatments.

We were sure, though, that we had all the necessary skills, well-proven across a range of different, but complementary areas. One of us was an ace cinematographer, greatly valued in both TV and film. Another was a production manager well-versed in the ways of both British television and Hollywood. We had a highly versatile film and video editor who'd brought fluidity to many powerful factual series, period dramas and even some zany comedy shows. The creative team was rounded out by an audio dubbing-mixer who was acclaimed in the business for his precise, bat-like hearing and a fastidious talent for matching music evocatively with visuals.

The finance side of our planned operation comprised two deep-pocketed City investors ('The City' being the square-mile of east-central London that forms the capital's business district, our equivalent to Wall Street). The slickers, as the rest of us called them, sensed great monetary potential in our creativity. I'd first met one of them by chance in the infamous wine bar, El Vino's, a watering hole for both journalists and City types; he'd recognised me from my TV reports and introduced himself. He said he liked how I'd been dissecting one of London's property-development scandals of the period. We fell to discussing our respective trades over a bottle or two, and I'm almost certain it was he who suggested we might collaborate. Within a week or so he brought along a former colleague who had already amassed some solid show-business connections; this was during another heady El Vino's session. The two were quick to present to our whole group a business plan, one that envisioned a considerable 'value-added' operation; the so-called added value would come from their successful marketing of our creative output. They wouldn't be the first city slickers to think they'd make fortunes out of film and TV production. And it wouldn't be the first such plan to be hatched over too much Alsatian hock and Scotch whisky.

The venture's attraction for me was double-headed. I hankered after being my own boss. I was inescapably titillated, too, by the simpler notion of making a lot of money. As the rather absurdly well-paid young man I'd become, I had fast developed a taste for conspicuous consumption. Reacting no doubt to what I saw as a youth spent in deprivation, my acquis-itiveness was a signal of my complete and successful escape into prosperity. But I could always use yet more moolah.

The plan needed 'plant', in the slickers' lingo, but plant without heavy overheads. We would put together our own dedic-ated media-centre, comprising studios, high-end editing and post-production facilities which we'd of course use ourselves; but we'd also rent them out to other creative teams to keep the place humming and make it pay for itself even when we were not producing our own output there. To avoid London's exorbitant real-estate costs we'd locate the business out of town—far enough away to be affordable, but close enough to limit trans-portation costs and allow our renters to still feel reasonably close to the centre of things. The geography sparked another induce-ment for me, the undoubted delight of gaining a foothold for myself in the countryside, in the kind of rural setting I hadn't known since my early childhood.

So Jane and I were deputed to find a site; it was one of those down-to-earth things she was good at. We diligently began crisscrossing the Cotswolds, only ninety minutes northwest of London, in search of just the right property. The recruiting of investors and some repeated re-honing of our business plan to meet changing market conditions (which called for more meetings in City wine bars), plus our intense location-scouting, all preoccupied us for about a year and a half. It was beautiful, rolling countryside through which Jane and I travelled and where we spent many weekends in guesthouses and hotels, some amusingly basic, some outright opulent. The landscape's allure was an important consideration, and in retrospect I realise that to some degree it echoed my old Scottish Borderlands, which is something I didn't consciously observe at the time.

I also discovered some helpful local information while reporting on matters religious and ethical, which was my main job in those days. Here was religion intervening in my life in an unexpected way; a recurring phenomenon that I still find strange. In later times I would reflect on the oddity that other people's faith became so central to my life, or certainly to my work-life, even though I had no faith of my own. But at this point all that mattered was a secular, economic truth I learned about the English Methodist Church, as founded by Charles Wesley back in the eighteenth century. The Church was now falling into serious decline. This was most notable in the Cotswolds, where its growing congregations had once spawned a great deal of church-building, but the flock was now dwindling fast, in some places even dying out completely. The real-estate consequence of this demographic shrinkage was a wave of unused churches being deconsecrated and sold off at something close to fire-sale prices, along with unwanted ministers' residences. We could as a business quite easily buy such a church and convert the main building into a studio and associated workspaces. And as a couple we had the fancy notion of reserving any possible side-chapel, or—more likely—manse (the one-time clergyman's home), for our own personal use, remodelling it as a country residence, a retreat from our London home.

But the whole enterprise soon collapsed. It turned out our partnership was divided within itself on how to actually run a business. I was outnumbered by colleagues who in financial questions were considerably more cautious than I—and perhaps wiser—and consequently we parted company. It's probably fair to say that I was usually the one pushing to take on bigger gambles, more expensive ones at that, and I'd often get blocked by risk-averse opposition from the others. My disappointment over the split wasn't great. I was discovering I didn't have a great liking for business anyway, and I was content enough to resume paying full-time attention to my broadcasting job at the network.

All the same, during our search Jane and I had made contact with a whole slew of Cotswold realtors, and one of them drew our attention to an exquisite, three-storey, honey-coloured stone cottage, originally a farmworker's home, with walls that were two feet thick. It was part of a tiny unspoiled village just a half-hour beyond Oxford, and so still within easy reach of London. It had picturesque appeal, being flanked on one side by fruit trees that gave it the ridiculously quaint name of Plum Cottage. It also had its own pear and apple orchard out back, and was surrounded by fields of grazing sheep, cows and horses. Irresistible. We bought it instantly, and we modernised it substantially if not luxuriously, preserving its unvarnished rustic quality.

It was a sweet dream. Jane was able to enjoy the cottage for another three years. Almost from the outset of my knowing her a decade previously, she'd been diagnosed with a degenerative disease, NF, or in full, Neurofibromatosis. The diagnosis came three years after her mother had died of multiple sclerosis, which might be genetically related to NF (the science is inconclusive on this). Originally on meeting her, I had been touched to learn about her losing her mother. I was both intrigued and attracted to her by her sadness, or perhaps more by the way that she valiantly masked the sadness with her reserved demeanour. When later she was abruptly told that she now had to live with a chronic illness just as her mother had, she resolutely minimised it. At first it hardly affected our life together at all; she was determined that it shouldn't.

NF can result in a baffling array of symptoms, ranging from small café-au-lait coloured patches on the skin to sometimes massive deformities. For quite some time, through four or even five years, her symptoms were minor, but we shuddered when we saw David Lynch's movie, The Elephant Man. Some medical historians believe that Joseph Merrick, the film's Victorian character with a hugely swollen head, was the victim of an extreme case of NF.

In Jane's case, the minor symptoms slowly but progressively got worse, and were much more than skin-deep. They required a series of internal surgeries, ever more serious over a period of twelve years. Small tumours, and later bigger ones, would grow in different parts of her body, including her neck, her left leg, her abdomen—each in turn needing to be swiftly excised. She reacted to the successive crises in a phlegmatic and stoic way and after each surgery was freshly determined to get on with life as normal, while I tried simply not to think about it. A walking stick entered the picture, then crutches, then a wheelchair.

I confess, now, to being sorely tempted to leave her as her condition grew worse. That's a terrible thing to admit and one that challenges any assumption—especially her assumption—that I loved her. I certainly loved her when she was healthy; when she wasn't, and needed me to be supportive and caring, my love wasn't quite so reliable. I did stay with her, in the sense that I didn't actually walk out and leave, but I escaped from her plight in a way she could not, by resorting to drink and the company of others.

Even when I told myself I was rising to the challenge, I was cheating. I would busily visit European and American research laboratories in a fervid search for a miracle cure without acknowledging to myself that my travelling was in fact a form of escape disguised as devotion. Jane could have come with me more than once; in fact, she joined me on only one journey, to a drug firm's sanatorium in Switzerland; otherwise I would travel alone, and inevitably return with no good news. At home, what I offered gave her little in the way of either comfort or company. I got drunk much of the time, missed accompanying her to medical appointments and dallied with other women when she was hospitalised. I was drunk in bed with somebody else when the 2:30 am phone call came telling me that Jane was dead.

Almost a decade later, life had mercifully become very different. I had become sober—and married. A short while into our marriage, what had now become our cottage was having the central heating installed that Melissa declared to be so essential. Other changes were taking place, too, as she turned the house into a home of far greater comfort and stylish beauty.

Melissa unquestionably had an eye, as they say. She had made her career in the art world, first with the New York branch of Christie's auction house and later running private Upper East Side art galleries. All her remodelling and redecorating decisions for the cottage were made in New York but were carried out in a lengthy and remarkable long-distance exercise. Our main home was her existing Manhattan apartment, and we were able to make only rare visits to Britain. But we had a project manager on site, a Cotswold master of construction we knew only as Mr Crump. We never learned any forename. Via endless phone calls and faxes back and forth with him and with bathroom suppliers, furniture warehouses, appliance-makers, carpet-sellers and other ancillary sources, Melissa tirelessly brought about a complete overhaul of the house.

She was a devotee of England's so-called Bloomsbury Group of the early twentieth century, the artists and writers who included Virginia Woolf and E.M. Forster. Indeed, her interest in them was how we originally came together. We had both gone to a gathering in London where the hosts were people we each had as friends without either of us knowing it. When the friends introduced us and we talked, it emerged that she'd crossed the Atlantic to attend a summer school dedicated to the Bloomsburys being held at an Oxford college. I told her frankly that I hadn't myself taken much interest in the group as a whole, though I admired Forster's novels for their power in exploring human connections across barriers of race and class. I said I did know something about Oxford and that when travelling between London and my cottage I frequently broke my journey in that city of dreaming spires, sometimes for coffee or lunch. I suggested a date, for after one of her classes; we could go boating on Oxford's almost unbearably pretty River Cherwell. I reckoned this graceful and evidently aesthetically minded American would enjoy the picture-perfect sight: the ancient university's idiosyncratic flat-bottomed punts each gliding languorously, propelled with a pole, past riverbanks overhung with cascading willow trees. It seemed to have the desired effect, maybe even more than I'd bargained for. Our afternoon boat trip was to take us in a direction I was very happy with. In less than a year we were married.

Some of Melissa's choices for the cottage were influenced by her many trips, occasionally with me, more often alone, to the Bloomsbury Group's country retreat, the well-maintained, historic Charleston Farmhouse in Sussex. Evidence abounded there of work by the group's visual artists, the painters and craftspeople who formed a sub-set of their own, the creative collective called the Omega Workshops. Like many a mid-twentieth-century young woman, Melissa had been excited to discover the freshly assertive 1920s feminism of Woolf's book, A Room of One's Own, but she seemed to me a lot more interested in the visual world created by the Bloomsburys than in their written output. There was also something we turned out to share, a liking for salacious gossip, and we both took delight in the group's reputation for louche behaviour and sexual liaisons at Charleston that seemed dizzyingly multi-directional. We could quote to each other one critic's assessment that the group members were much more interested in themselves than in anything else. According to the critic, their preoccupations amounted to: what Virginia had to say about Lytton, or whether Duncan was sleeping with Vanessa or with Maynard, and whether Roger and Clive actually knew it was going on anyway. He of course meant in turn: Woolf, the novelist; Strachey, the biographer; Grant, the painter and designer; Bell, the other painter; Keynes, the economist; Fry, the designer; and finally Clive Bell, the art critic and husband to the painter, Vanessa (who was also Virginia's sister).

But tittle-tattle aside, aesthetics was the main matter for Melissa and I was somewhat handicapped in comparison by being colour-blind, and thus couldn't ever be a hundred-per-cent definitive in my visual judgements. All the same, I did have a strong sense that the interiors and furnishings at Charleston were an uneasy melding of homespun Arts-and-Crafts design along with some exuberant use—'overuse', I'd say—of unexpectedly strident colours. Our banter as a couple included a running joke: that my red-green optical deficiency meant I couldn't possibly know what I was talking about whenever we discussed decorating. But all the same it never stopped Melissa from seeking my views on a colour-scheme she might want to employ.

While she started out from a more enthusiastic standpoint than mine about Charleston's rooms, she didn't merely want to copy them. Much more interestingly and creatively, she translated the group's sometimes clumsy extravagance into an elegant and soothing overall balance, as she artfully combined the eye-catching with the comfortable.

Perhaps she was reserving her innate audaciousness, sometimes even outright flamboyance and zaniness, for her own appearance rather than rooms or hallways. That first date on Oxford's river had begun with my eyes popping; as I steadied my punt she stepped into it wearing black suede shoes with flat heels and pointed toes that curled upward, in what I took to be a parody of those worn by Renaissance court jesters. There was also a matching straw hat adorned with a huge silk bow. I had never gone out with anyone so strikingly dressed. But I tried to be cool and, avoiding any specifics, I just said, 'You look great.'

Melissa's fondness for the Bloomsbury aesthetic was to create at least one troubling episode for Mr Crump. He phoned us one day in distress. 'There's been a big mistake,' he said. A delivery of paint had come for some of our interior walls and it was black. The cans' contents were a bespoke product from Farrow & Ball. The company headed Melissa's list—a short list, naturally—of traditional English paint-makers of whom she approved, and they had developed a particular colour under the name 'Off-Black'. It was inspired by eighteenth-century estates whose smoking rooms could use some camouflage for their coats of tobacco staining. The Bloomsburys had dramatically hand-stencilled Charleston's dining-room walls in black, and this boldness had inspired Melissa to have Mr Crump use black for the walls in one of our remodelled bedrooms. It took her some earnest coaxing to get him to apply it, but in time he did, if still a tad reluctantly.

Mr Crump's qualms vanished completely in the end, but only after neighbours began dropping in for a peek, since news of the decorating oddity had spread through the village. He admitted to us that all the visitors had approved, once they saw how well the black walls went with the printed-chintz curtains Melissa had also decreed: a deep pink-on-black fabric by the nonconformist designer, Rose Cumming. Sometime later, Melissa wrote a design-journalism essay about the whole operation (she'd by then left the art world and joined The New York Times) and the paper headlined it, 'When Love of a House Is Long-Distance'.

She summed up the black bedroom's final success in a way that could be read as a small tribute to my aesthetic taste, of all things: 'The one person who had harboured no doubts about it, my husband, never slept better than in that room.' Harboured no doubts? Really? The truth was of course that I couldn't be at all sure about what was being planned but I completely trusted her anyway, always, no matter how oddball her choices might seem.

There were absolutely no doubts, for real his time, about the joy that the finished cottage gave us. For her, it was a proud creative achievement and some fulfilment of a Californian Anglophile's dream: an aged stone arcadia amid England's greenery. And for me? Maybe a sweeping aside of unwelcome memories from a few years before. Maybe also a more distant reminder—and along with it an elaborate, deeply satisfying, almost magical transfiguration—of my childhood in rural, low-income housing.

Over the next few years we visited and stayed in the cottage frequently, and always for as long as we possibly could, enjoying pretty well every minute. We spent the turn of the millennium there—memorably on the last night of 1999, watching huge bonfires burning as beacons on every hilltop of the Cotswolds in a chain that stretched hundreds of miles, with the wood-smoked air suggestive of continuity—of Shakespeare's time or Chaucer's.

But our life became steadily more and more New York-centred, and with many mixed feelings we ended up selling our English home. We bought in its place a late-nineteenth century, grey, cedar-shingled saltbox on the Southern shore of Long Island. As Melissa wrote in another, later article about that new home, 'If we were going to have a country house, it really ought to be in the country where we lived.'

Her deft knack for décor did not desert her. All the English furniture from the cottage—even including what she wrote of as 'my husband's Regency chest-of-drawers' and for that matter our early-nineteenth-century, Gloucestershire cherrywood dresser—were settled snugly into their American surroundings. And many of the English wall-colours, though not our bedroom's infamous off-black, were repeated exactly. Our Atlantic seaboard home, while new to us, looked and felt reassuringly familiar.

Chapter 16
Life-Changing

So it had been a *girl* who had brought me to New York. To be accurate rather than casually disrespectful, or for that matter politically or culturally incorrect, Melissa was a woman and well into her thirties: a beautiful, kind and insightful woman. At the time we fell in love and married, when I was forty-two, it was almost a toss of a coin that decided where we should live together.

It was definitely a fifty-fifty matter. Our two professional lives had hitherto been spent in big-city settings that to each of us seemed pretty equivalent as a place to settle. Her fine-art career for twelve years in New York led shortly after our wedding to an art-dealers' firm hiring her to manage galleries it owned in both New York and London. My career in broadcasting had been based for twenty years in London and that same trade's American capital—some would say its world capital—is of course New York. It boasted media companies aplenty, big and small, all needing expert professionals. At this point my work in the UK had become entirely freelance in nature: no exclusive single contract any more with a broadcast network, just plugging away at getting occasional gigs in all three mass-media outlets of the time: print, radio and TV. There was no sign yet of the internet and the social-media network.

I feel I won the notional coin-toss, in that I was the one who relocated. I moved into Melissa's existing Manhattan home, a tiny one-bedroom Upper West Side apartment (but with both an outdoor terrace and a working fireplace indoors, she was at pains to emphasise to me). Emigrating to the US was one of the best decisions I ever made in my life; that, and marrying her at all. We often reflected in subsequent years that for all the tough life-passages that came along, we ended up with a far happier life overall than if we'd made our home in the UK. Like many a transplanted Brit, I felt liberated from England's still-stifling class system. And Melissa, though always an adaptive soul, was too much of a free spirit to have been comfortable long-term in an England that she saw as charming but also fusty and often blithely unaware of its own rigidities.

My transition, however, was not at all easy in one area that mattered to me a lot, my professional life. I wasn't, clearly, making a career move; it was absolutely a move for love. I had no new job lined up. For quite a while I struggled hard to find any TV work, having at some points to take fairly unexpected, non-television jobs, like being a filing clerk in the New York Public Library. Some well-meaning connections got me that gig; it wasn't an enactment of my teenage passion for libraries, though it's a nice coincidence that I should be hired as an adult by a towering example of the same public service I'd learned to value so much as a boy. I have never been surrounded by so much Carrara marble as when I worked in New York Public Library's Beaux Arts temple on Fifth Avenue, but the work itself was probably the most numbingly tedious that I have ever experienced. I had little to do with the books. Most of the time I was repetitively transferring information from index cards into a newly-digitised cataloguing system.

I very nearly got a job as an overnight building guard, until the watch-keeping company (it had the valiant name of Epic Security) discovered I didn't have a New York State gun licence. Perhaps one measure of my desperation to find work was how disappointed I felt to get turned down by United Parcel Service (UPS) as a driver's helper. I was trying for pretty well any kind of job, as long as it would give me a pay cheque. One job I did get— one thankfully more related to my experience and offering the beginnings of a foothold in the American media world—was to teach broadcast news and documentary-making at Columbia University's Graduate School of Journalism.

Finally after almost two years—not an eternity, but too long for someone of my impatience—I slipped into actually making TV documentaries again, for the news division of one of the major commercial networks. I had been trying to pitch the long-hidden story of Rosewood, the prosperous African-American community in Florida that was wiped out in a lynch-mob rampage in 1923. I'd sent lots of ideas to many different TV companies. Executives at that one network liked this one idea, and I was hired. But once I was working on the project, specifically once I'd shot my material in Florida and then had to edit and write the finished film at the network's New York HQ, I did not find the acclimation smooth.

I fear I harboured an all-too-British sense of superiority, smugly certain that our form of broadcasting, from both the venerable BBC and its rival commercial networks where I had mostly worked, was universally and unquestioningly admired. I was distressed to find my scripts repeatedly thrown back at me by my new bosses and a do-over demanded. I couldn't figure out what was wrong with my efforts and no one could quite explain it, either. Then a kindly and witty senior producer took me aside and said, 'It's probably just British-American miscommunication, maybe even simple mishearing. You might have heard them say they wanted *class* from you; they really want *crass*.'

I found the quip funny enough to give me pause, and it lightened my growing anxiety about not succeeding at something I was convinced I knew how to do. I became more willing to chameleon my way into greater Americanisation, deliberately pouring many more US-oriented references into my scripts, along with a snappier vocabulary and delivery. Early on I had labelled the contemporary background to Rosewood's massacre as simply 'post-World War One', using some generalising shorthand out of my European history studies. But in my conscious adoption of deliberate Americanisms, my writing conveyed instead something of the early 1920s, a time of over-excited Wall Street traders, flappers dancing the Charleston and biplanes doing stunning aerobatics, while my voice-over narration spoke of an exuberant country electing 'a series of strongly pro-business presidents'.

The film was rated a success and my career started to build again. I got to make many more documentaries, a lot of them historical, some of them on contemporary subjects, and I now moved pretty confidently between different networks as an independent contractor.

My marrying, my switching of countries and my total overhaul of how I worked could all be said to be part of a pretty massive midlife readjustment. One big readjustment, though, was still to come. In New York I embarked determinedly on a broad mission to quite simply banish secrecy from my life. I'd become sickened by the lies and evasions that were so characteristic of how I'd lived up to that point.

Though only 300 square feet, my new home nonetheless boasted two windows, and through either one of them I could stare at the tops of our neighbours' bamboo plants and feel sick. Almost literally so. We were four storeys up from where the invasive species had taken root and then grown, as bamboo always does, fast and high. In the micro-climate of our building's courtyard, the tiniest change in the wind made the tallest leaf-clusters sway vertiginously off to the right or to the left, swing close towards me or far away, and then back again in an instant. Rarely could they ever stay true and straight upright. 'Sick of it all,' was my repeated, self-involved thought. I could have likened myself to the bamboo in a positive way, seeing us both as ambitious, eager for growth and flexible—but I didn't. Instead what I saw nauseated me with my own history of weaving and dodging, dodging and weaving.

As a child getting riled by the question, 'Watchyer dad do? Is he a farmer?' I had hidden my anger and feinted with a counter-suggestion that we play marbles instead. As a college student I had darted into diversionary stories to evade someone's speculation: 'Your last name sounds Eastern European—is that where you're from?' I concocted a range of stories around my Ukrainian stepfather's marriage to my mother, some that included the invented death of my 'real' father, or my mother's equally fictional divorce from that nebulous figure. In my story-weaving I had to avoid the matter of my biological father, whoever he was, and I couldn't bring myself to say that I was Michael's offspring, even though I had the convenient (but unwelcome) cover of bearing his name.

In my adult life working on TV, when newspapers prepared articles profiling me as a minor celebrity, I connived to twist the interviews they conducted with me away from probes into my personal background. I was doggedly certain that my appearing every night on a screen in people's family rooms should not entitle them to learn about my family. All this unceasingly evasive struggle had been tiring as well as sickening. I was sick and tired.

I had hidden and lied about a lot of things: sexual infidelity of course; my lack of real, relevant experience early on whenever I applied for a job; the closeness I'd claim to top politicians or captains of industry so I'd be the one to get assigned to interview them; and most of all, of course, the laborious efforts to conceal my drinking. All until I reached the point where I just didn't want to lie anymore.

But among all my secrets and evasions, it was my family secret that turned out to be the most daunting for me to tackle. It took six years—with a lot of help from Melissa, from friends, and from two successive, both very shrewd psychotherapists—to sort out my uncertain feelings towards my mother and gather up the courage to raise with her the question of who had fathered me. What was it, through those years, that held me back from fully getting to grips with what I called 'the paternity issue'? That's how I filed the matter, still holding it at arm's length with my quasi-clinical phrasing. The answer, I suspect, lay in another question, a fundamental self-analysing question that's familiar to many: who genuinely wishes to be rigorously honest and open? Certainly not I, the evidence suggested.

No matter how much I told myself I should embrace this honesty business, and do so unconditionally, I retained an edgy resistance to it—downright fear, more like. Certainly that was true when it came to my mother. Trying to approach her with assertive openness seemed doomed to failure. When I made my first attempt, using transatlantic airmail to pose what I hoped were my simple queries, Who was my father? and Can we please talk about it? it prompted Hilda to retort with an angry rebuff, written with such insistent pen-pushing that it nearly tore through the flimsy blue paper. And I'll admit that part of me was actually relieved.

My fear that I would get nowhere with her had proved self-fulfilling. Thank God I can now gracefully retreat, I sighed to myself: I don't have to press my case any longer. I didn't know exactly what I dreaded she might do if I did press on. Cut me off without a penny? That's a comical notion. Raise her voice at me from across the Atlantic? Refuse to speak to me ever again?

Or was something else restraining me? Did I want to avoid being punishing towards her? Would I be inflicting undeserved pain by making her confront the truth, whatever it actually was, hold it up to the light and deliver it to me?

I didn't want to hurt her, and I didn't want a fight with her. But it all came down, once again, to the essential underlying mystery that demanded an answer. Just what was this hidden truth anyway—how could it be so horrible, godammit, that it made both of us unwilling to address it?

So a state of hiatus ensued, maybe a stalemate. But my retreat from the quest didn't last too long. Within little more than three months, my drive to get at the truth had reasserted itself, and I was making another, somewhat more successful attempt—what Melissa and I came to label 'The Broadway Café Talk'. That conversation with Hilda gave me a new, pleasing warmth of anticipation, since I believed a true and full account was now within sight. She did, after all, say across the café table that she would tell me the truth when she was back in her own British home, surrounded by the things that made her feel comfortable. I imagined that would mean her sitting in her favourite armchair facing me, with her cherished teapot and cups on hand, and what we'd call with a smile her collection of 'geejaws', some of them small ebony carvings I'd brought her from African trips, all doing homely decorative duty on the shelves behind her.

But very soon after she returned to that home from her New York visit, she and her husband, Norman, sold their house. It was a lengthy process, and so was what followed: the finding of a new home, closing on it, and moving to it, a distance of about 120 miles to the north.

It was a retirement move, back to the small city that lay close to our original home village. It was, in my strongest memory of it, where I had been treated for my painful ears as a child. And perhaps touchingly for her, it was where she and Norman (unknown to each other at the time, they told me) had each attended their respective girls' and boys' high schools. Melissa and I speculated that Hilda was trying to maximise the comfort she'd take from her surroundings: maybe she wanted a return to where she had known a simple schoolgirl's life, before her biggest upheavals began—with her conceiving me, of course. Perhaps that same modest and far from hectic city would now be a place of rest, her safe haven where I would finally learn about my father from a mother enjoying some new-found tranquility.

But the invitations to visit her that I tried to wangle (subtly, I hoped) simply did not come. Perhaps I wasn't all that subtle. My work on occasion required flying to the UK, usually to videotape stories in London, and I'd point out in a phone call ahead of time that I could easily extend my journey and make an extra trip north to her new home. 'I have the time,' I'd say when she worried I'd be abandoning my work to travel in her direction. I'd reassure her it wasn't a problem. 'I can certainly make the time—if it's to see you,' I'd insist. It repeatedly turned out, though, that my assignment coincided inconveniently with a trip she herself was to make with her husband; usually to further north in Scotland. I was patient, never expressing anything but disappointment solely at having to miss her. I would never suggest I had any other aim than simply for us to be together. I voiced no hint of my nursing an agenda, though of course I did have one; it was based on her own earlier willingness to reveal my paternity sometime when she was comfortable.

Meanwhile, there was a break in the strongest link Melissa and I still had with the UK: our house there. While we had happily held on to the cottage for some time after Melissa renovated it, we were finding it less easy to get away from New York to enjoy it, and by the time 2001 arrived we had made our decision to sell. A somewhat hurried completion meant we had to empty the house on a deadline. Its last role in our lives was to be featured in the 'House and Home' section of *The New York Times*—and a photographer from the newspaper's London bureau was sent to cover it. We lit a log fire in the grate to cast a warm light on the eighteenth-century beams and we 'dressed the set' with some of the more photogenic of our antiques. Only then, after pictures were taken, could we set about dividing up the entire contents, some for sale, some to gift to British friends, and some for shipping over to our new American house. The international movers would arrive within a few hours.

We had a simple plan. Once the house was emptied Melissa would go to stay in a London hotel, I would drive north to see my mother and after that border country trip, I would reunite with Melissa at Heathrow to fly home to New York. But suddenly, early in the morning before the photographer and then the movers were due, my mother told me on the phone that she now could not see me. Some new and unspecific things to do, and people to see were preventing her.

I didn't have time to develop resentment, though I rolled my eyes a little at what I saw as yet one more bit of avoidance. I got focused along with Melissa on the house-primping, the photography and then the clearing-out.

In the quiet that fell after the movers' truck groaned heavily along our drive and away, we stood in our empty rooms. Empty except for one ungainly item on the floor—a fax machine of UK-only voltage, which we would not be transporting but hadn't yet thought to unplug. It suddenly whirred into action.

It stuttered out a single handwritten page from my mother:

Dear David,

I know you just want a name. So here it is. He was called Father Francis.

That is all I know.

He was a Roman Catholic priest and he raped me when I was an innocent schoolgirl.

He was sent away. I have no idea where.

—Hilda

Chapter 17
Phoning

We read my mother's fax in silence. Then a further silence. Melissa spoke first. She seemed struck by the medium as much as the message: 'She sends you a fax?' I was somehow less surprised: 'Umm ... yes. She sends a fax.'

'You have to call her,' said Melissa. 'Jesus! Poor Hilda!— That's what happened?'

I didn't rush to the phone, didn't prevaricate either. I had no definite purpose in mind. As I was dialing, a weird, maybe numb emptiness seemed to overtake me.

'Thanks for the fax, Hilda,' I said. It seemed the only way to start. The emptiness ballooned and hung in the air. I was operating on automatic, still with no specific or lucid intent, though I did feel even in my overall fogginess a need to come up with a fresh approach of some kind, something new. For chrissakes, I thought, let me say something different from what I have been saying—endlessly, it seems. Here and now, from Hilda, had arrived something that was utterly new, something terrible. Let me try to be up to it.

I think or hope, but can't be wholly certain, that I said, 'I'm so sorry that you had to suffer what happened to you.' Whatever clumsy words of sympathy I may have attempted, they were greeted by silence at her end. It deepened the emptiness hanging between us. In an effort to steady myself, I fixed on her actual words on the slightly waxy paper in my hand. She had, after all, despite half a century of avoiding the entire subject, just sent me a message. This was progress.

I wasn't making a conscious calculation, but I had a feeling the fax could mean she was ready to talk with me, despite her clear suggestion of finality, 'That is all I know.'

My voice formed a slow sentence: 'You wrote in the fax: I

know you just want a name.' A name from her was undeniably something definite for me, certainly better than the long, immutable nothing of before. And along with the name had come horrific drama: a priest and a rape. This all needed—maybe she herself needed—something fuller than just a few brief sentences.

'I am very grateful, yes, for the information,' I said, still picking my words awkwardly. 'And I really have to thank you for it. But I promise you, besides me wanting straightforward facts, there's more, much more.' I realised I was slipping back towards a refrain I'd been voicing, delicately or pushily, for years.

'Overall, I have wanted,' I couldn't help adding, 'simply to find a way we can talk with each other without that secret always blocking us.' Rightly or not, I felt her message to be achingly incomplete; there must be more to say, for her and for me.

My mind darted about for another tack to take while she stayed silent. And then, as the emptiness billowed about form-lessly, a habit from my work-life asserted itself, a very basic piece of long-honed journalistic craft. Sometimes the job can be really simple.

I said: 'Could you just tell me ... what was it like for you?' It was one of those interviewer's vacuous little prompts, deliber-ately disingenuous but sometimes surprisingly useful. The 'it' being asked about can be as specific as the interviewee wants to take it or as all-encompassing. Being raped one Sunday morning in early 1948 ... or living that entire inscrutable life of yours.

A key seemed to turn. What followed was possibly the longest conversation I had ever had with my mother—without any doubt the longest phone call. One hour and forty-eight minutes, according to my cellphone's global roaming charges. Once it got going it went rapidly—and it was almost entirely her.

'My best friend in high-school was Alba—you know, from the Asti family at the Italian ice-cream parlour. They were Catholics, of course, and they would have these Sunday morning masses in a room above the doctor's surgery.'

I had to translate, silently, since my own vocabulary had by those days become fully Americanised. She meant the mass was held above the office where our village's general practitioner examined his patients; he wasn't a surgeon wielding a scalpel in the downstairs room. The doctor happened to be a Catholic, and he made his building's upper floor available to his relatively few co-religionists in the area for their weekly worship. Hilda said that a roster of priests, one per week—usually 'a young junior priest'—was sent to conduct the service from the nearby city where there were several Catholic parishes.

'I was just fascinated to know what went on. I didn't know anything about it. We weren't taught anything regarding Catholicism in school. But Alba said it was a nice occasion, with families all going together, and lovely rituals and hymns, so I really wanted to see what happened. That's why I went with her.'

I absorbed this beginning of her story on an upstairs floor of the cottage. I'd gone up—in the absence of any furniture—to lean on a deep bedroom windowsill, with one elbow supporting the phone to my ear, the other hand scribbling on my pocket notepad.

I noted Hilda saying she found herself fully engrossed in the mass, just as she'd hoped—though she didn't describe any particulars. She was introduced to the priest as 'Father Francis' after the service. She remembered that he looked young ('not an old priest'), was Scottish—by which I assumed she meant his accent—and that 'he took a liking to me'. The phrase leaped up to lodge in my mind. Here as at many points during this story unfolding down the phoneline I wanted to interject, to ask in this instance just what those words meant. Was this a clearly sexual liking, I wondered? Hilda's tone sounded so indeterminate. Was there possibly something complicit in the fifteen-year old girl? I couldn't tell if the liking had become evident instantly. My conjectures grew broader, though I had no basis for them, and I wondered if this liking applied to more than this one occasion. Who knows, I thought a little wildly, maybe they met at other times, too? As I re-read her fax's bald words—'he raped me when I was an innocent schoolgirl'—I couldn't help speculate that there could be more to it than that. But the picture she drew of this one winter morning was so immediate and vehement that I let such queries lie unspoken, and the urgings of my reporter's trained scepticism went unanswered.

She said the Father 'offered me a walk home'. And that he 'was so nice and friendly that I just went with him'. But the walk didn't lead home. 'He drew me into a garden—one of those big gardens up the Moor Road. He pushed me to the ground and raped me.' I remembered that row of houses and their spacious rear gardens; I felt sick.

She understandably described no details here and I didn't press her. Inwardly I nonetheless queried: was there a lengthy subterfuge, any softness of approach at all, any attempt at a willing seduction? Just how did initial friendliness turn into a predatory attack?

She also said nothing about how he left her. From here on, she spoke purely of fear, a deep, all-embracing fear. 'I was just terrified to tell Mam what had happened.'

She became even more frightened a couple of months later when she found she was pregnant. 'You'll remember Mam as a sweet old granny—but I was very scared of her. She could be really fierce,' she said.

Once she did summon her courage and told her mother, and once Mam did indeed react furiously, according to Hilda, a plan was hurriedly hatched to dispatch my mother to my aunt's house for me to be born. I learned, somewhat in passing as Hilda pressed on, now straining to catch her breath at times, how they at least briefly considered aborting me. 'But we didn't know how to find anyone to do it,' she said. Abortion would remain a crime in Britain until another twenty years had passed.

A different plan had also come up for a short while. 'Mam told me we should have you adopted as soon as you were born. But I wouldn't put up with that. I really wanted to have you—and I have never regretted it for one minute.'

I started to voice a thank-you for her not giving me up, but she almost hushed me to get on with the story: 'Oh yes, I really wanted you—and I took the train to Dodo's house to have you in secret.' Her sister's, my aunt's home was in Northern England's textile-making region. 'Dodo was just lovely. Very businesslike, but just lovely. She took such good care of me—and of you when you came. You probably never knew this but that's why I gave you her married name as that middle name of yours.' Stansfield: a name that she knew I liked, though she may not have known my reasons. It was rural-sounding, and certainly home-grown (not cumbersome and Slavonic, like the surname I'd eventually have to live with) and it carried a connotation of standing sturdily.

She described something I felt I was hearing for the first time, though I can't be totally sure: that I had been a remarkably quiet child, even from my very first appearance. 'You hardly cried at all, ever. Dodo was amazed at how you simply never made a fuss, even when she said you must have been hungry. I didn't know what to expect, but you just seemed so very still and peaceable to me.'

We—my mother and the brand-new me—travelled back north to our home village after a few weeks. 'Mam allowed us back into the house but only on condition that I went out to work and earned your keep. So I found that clerking job in Thurnhams the booksellers.' The store formed a well-known landmark in our nearby city's commercial and cultural life.

I asked if she wasn't disappointed to have to give up her schooling; I'd always thought she'd must have been a good student. 'Yes, I was upset a bit. Our teachers said I had a very good chance of going on to college. Amazing, since none of us had ever gone. But Mam was adamant, and I couldn't argue against her, so I went along with it. And I came to like the job in the end, though I missed being with you in the daytime.'

And how was it for her being such a young—and unmarried —mother in the village? 'In those days, everybody looked down on you having a child out of wedlock. Mam had said from the beginning that we had to tell everyone she was your mother, not me. It seems silly now, but that's what we did.'

I agreed it sounded unlikely, and asked a little incredulously, 'Did you really think it could be a convincing story?'

'I was fifteen—what did I know about things? Mam said it would work. I don't remember how old you were when we decided the story wasn't working—or even if it was ever a decision that we took. Maybe the truth was so obvious all along, and maybe everybody knew, so we just dropped the whole notion. And anyway, I soon found I wanted people to know you were mine; I couldn't keep up the pretence.'

My rapid notes were sketchy as I made them, and I filled them out from still-sharp memory over the next day or so. Alongside the verbatim quotes, I wrote and then circled in a margin the single word, 'Fast' to highlight her very untypical, hurtling pace.

I know full well that the notes are incomplete. As interviews go, and have gone in my working life, this would not count as one of my most incisive. I was hardly at the top of my game in that emptied, echoing room, listening to my mother and trying to direct and yet not direct the flow of her memories. Over the years since that conversation, I've worked to pursue further the information my notes recorded, using my full kit of tools for journalistic and historical research. But the notes remain the sole —and frankly uncorroborated—core for this origin story of mine.

As the afternoon light began to fade, Hilda eventually ran out of steam. I said I should travel up to her house and be with her. It would have been only a four-hour drive along England's northwest motorways. But she demurred. 'No. I think I just want to sit back and think awhile.' After a moment she added: 'And besides, Norman will be home soon—and it would all be too much with the both of you.'

I didn't try to elicit anything more from her. I'm not sure what further specifics I could have hoped for. It seemed right to stop. The two of us in each of our limited ways had made an effort to connect, undoubtedly a deeper effort than any we'd ever seemed capable of before.

I told her again how grateful I was for her breaking the silence and hoped she would take good care of herself that evening and onward. I think I even recommended hot chocolate —my repertoire of self-care measures felt somewhat enfeebled at this point. I was pretty exhausted myself.

Melissa and I made ready for our drive to the London hotel and our flight the next day to New York. We were both stilled, a bit stunned perhaps by the heightened emotions of the day. As we set off, I braked slowly at the driveway's end to bid a final farewell to our English country haven, a cherished source of rest and restoration through all the eleven years we'd known each other.

In the car and later in our hotel room, I relayed to Melissa all of Hilda's story. We recognised there were still many blanks to be filled in, with time perhaps. But in that one intense afternoon the dam had decisively burst, we felt.

Chapter 18
Priests

I'm not conscious of having undergone any sort of spiritual evolution, if that's even the right term to use. Just hearing those four short syllables—*spiritual*—can make me wince, a token of my ingrained discomfort. I know I'm not a hardcore atheist, although that is certainly how I saw myself in my student days and well into adulthood. The time and professional effort I spent covering religion from my thirties onward may have softened my atheism a bit.

Hindsight suggests that, over time, a kind of vaulting arch was being built, one that would connect my later years back to my childhood, while in between, at ground level, my young man's insistent rational materialism went on operating stubbornly. In that ground-level material life, all the same, I found some ethical sensitivities that would get activated in an intriguing, possibly significant way. There were hard-to-deny echoes of my upbringing: whenever I did something I knew to be wrong, I found myself churned by a vague but strong sense that I was somehow offending against the whole world, against all human life as it should be lived, against even (in my wilder, more expansive bouts of guilt) the entire universe. It owed something, I feel sure, to the way I had been so greatly affected, indeed truly frightened, when as a young teenager I had read William Wordsworth's famous account of feeling somehow admonished as a boy by an ominously overhanging, craggy mountain soon after he had committed 'an act of stealth'—stealing someone else's boat.

Wordsworth also poured into my consciousness an appreciation, again vague and yet portentous, of grandeur and power in the natural world that was beyond me, but that nevertheless could act upon me:

> ... a sense sublime
> Of something far more deeply interfused,
> Whose dwelling is the light of setting suns
> And the round ocean and the living air,
> And the blue sky, and in the mind of man:
> A motion and a spirit that impels
> All thinking things, all objects of all thought,
> And rolls through all things.

Here's what I find so unshakably memorable about those lines, which now carry even greater force than when I first learned them at age fourteen. W. Wordsworth used a vast and multi-sourced vocabulary; it comes a very close second to W. Shakespeare's world-beating stockpile of nearly 900,000 words: that's according to the number-crunchers who compile writers' so-called 'concordances'. But out of all the options he had available to him, the later William deliberately chose—as a label for his great rolling power, entity or whatever it might have been—a perfectly wonderfully plain and simultaneously imprecise word: *something*.

The full and clear effect of 'something' is that I simply don't know what it is; if I knew, I'd be using another, more specific word. It lays out for me a great unknown, maybe a great unknowable. I cannot chart the course of my development with particular incidents or specific epiphanies, but I am broadly aware that I have today arrived, somehow or other, at being remarkably comfortable with not knowing things. That's maybe an odd notion for a journalist to express—and perhaps especially for this one. When younger I harboured an edgy need, often an unstoppable compulsion, to know everything I could possibly learn, to arm myself and be prepared for absolutely anything that might happen, with some protective foreknowledge tucked safely into my knapsack for self-defence.

Nowadays I am more open to the possibility of surprise, to what I don't know and couldn't have predicted. The unexpected dawning of an emotional truth. The recognition, for instance, that here in my present-day life I'm wholly at ease when I find myself still talking confidingly with my wife, Melissa, seven years after her death. And, in virtually the same moment, I'm wholly at ease with remembering, and sadly accepting, just how perturbed I was in my befuddled form of bereavement forty years previously, when my girlfriend, Jane, kept coming into my guilt-laden thoughts after she died—so perturbed, indeed, that I tried to shoo her away.

Living with, being at one with reality. With the present, including all its uncertainties. Less troubled by the past and unthreatened by the future. I believe that's the extent of my faith. I feel well-attuned to Flannery O'Connor's words written a hundred and fifty years after Wordsworth's educative encounter with his mountain: 'Faith is what someone knows to be true, whether they believe it or not.'

I spent years in some bemusement that, even though I never intended it, I became thoroughly entangled in religion. At least, my work-life got entangled with it. It started back in the early 1980s, when I unexpectedly took the lead in a new form of broadcasting developed by the British TV company where I worked. My mandate was to cover religious faith and associated matters like ethical questions by adopting a novel, determinedly journalistic approach.

It was a big change from previous practice. British radio and television's long-established custom had been to treat the realm of faith as (almost literally) sacrosanct. Religion occupied a special, protected place—meaning in practical terms that our broadcast schedules even had a slice of time explicitly carved out for it. It was called, in our office slang, 'The God Slot'. The contents of the slot, generally the holy hour from 6 pm on a Sunday, were most obviously exemplified by one long-running BBC programme, *Songs of Praise*, which was just that—a half-hour of lustily-sung hymns emanating each week from a usually very beautiful church somewhere in the British Isles. The lucky house of worship would be descended upon with great fanfare by a multi-camera live-coverage unit, a rare privilege for which local parishes would fiercely compete.

It seemed especially radical for me to be chosen to run our new and very different religion programmes, since I had no religious background at all. During my childhood the Church—in our village's case an Anglican parish church—was for my family purely the site of perfunctory Sunday gatherings that were more social than devotional. I do remember the well-spoken and kindly vicar, but mainly because I had such trouble saying his name. For years I couldn't pronounce Reverend Frith's tricky end-consonant, 'th', reducing it to the comical-sounding Friff that became a lasting embarrassment to me.

As I grew up I gained no education in theology or related disciplines, and frankly no great interest in them. At the age of thirty-two, when I was given my surprise professional assignment, a London girlfriend threw me a party, renting as her venue the revolving restaurant atop the city's Telecommunications Tower. She said: 'It's the nearest you'll ever get to God, David.'

My well-known distance from religion was part of the point, my bosses told me. I and the team I was to lead were charged with always taking, on behalf of a general, secular audience, an objectively questioning viewpoint. I had my doubts about this mission, born mainly of lack of acquaintance with the subject-matter, but it turned out to be a successful experiment for the TV company and for me.

The tenor of the times certainly helped. Our first really big, dramatic story came when a would-be assassin attacked the new and charismatic Polish Pope, John Paul II. As he entered a crowded St Peter's Square standing and waving in his open Popemobile, he was hit by four shots from a Browning Hi-Power 9mm handgun. His attacker was a member of a Turkish right-wing terrorist group, the Grey Wolves, who'd been hired by the Bulgarian Communists' secret service on the apparent orders of the Soviet KGB. A news-junkie's wet-dream, you might say—and we did, among ourselves. My team earned kudos for the coverage, and our sturdy kind of reporting continued with many other major stories of the period. The new revolutionary leader in Iran, Ayatollah Ruhollah Khomeini, was building a theocratic state after overthrowing the Shah's secular regime. He made a particular enemy of the United States, condemning it to Iranians and all his followers elsewhere as 'The Great Satan.' Christian Churches of various stripes, and across much of the globe, were being forced to respond to women's pressure to play a greater role in their organisations. Northern Ireland's violence—already a familiar subject for me—was boiling fiercely, and it called for discerning reportage that accurately explained the role of religious sectarianism in the island's divisions.

In a word, it was invigorating journalism. I perhaps shouldn't have been surprised, but I was quite taken aback by the mounting piles of job applications on my desk from young reporters, all eager to work in this once rather derided 'special interest' area. We were demonstrating to both the viewing public and our fellow professionals that the field of religion and ethics will constantly offer up issues and stories of striking impact, well deserving of sharp journalistic inquiry.

The flagship in our output was a regular weekly show called *Credo*, devoted to topical matters, and once it had made its mark, we soon began producing a flotilla of spin-off 'specials' with varied themes. Under a series subtitle, *Behind the Veil*, one of those limited-run series examined the challenging impact of women on traditionally patriarchal faiths. I could scarcely believe my editorial luck when, for an early episode, one of our teams brought back footage from the US featuring an unconventional community of nuns—definitely not cloistered—who roared around northern New England doing their pastoral work on Harley-Davidson bikes. 'Whose Angels were they?' we had to wonder.

For me individually, a significant shift came in 1982, one that I wouldn't, and probably couldn't, have articulated at the time. Looking back, I see it as the beginnings of a move away from my viewing the world in purely material terms, towards recognising that there are indeed other, perhaps broader dimensions to human existence—something that the people I reported on clearly already deeply believed, in all their own disparate ways.

I embarked on what turned out to be an intense piece of television, a six-part documentary series called *Facing Death*, which candidly portrayed several terminal cancer patients in their journeys towards the end of their lives. It gained for its time an unprecedented audience response to our on-screen 1-800 phone number (this was of course long before the immediate interactivity of social media and the internet in general). Thousands of viewers phoned to request copies of the booklet of practical guidance we published to accompany the documentaries, written by expert thanatologists, grief counselors and other end-of-life professionals.

Taking on this difficult and sensitive topic was, I now reflect, the first time I became interested in what I would then tentatively label the non-material aspects of life—and death, unavoidably. In deciding to make the series I'd become newly fascinated by what thought processes and reactions people might go through when they knew they were dying. I also wanted to explore the experiences, while death was looming, of those immediately close to the dying, their family members and friends—and then see how life went for the bereaved afterward, as they dealt with the loss of their loved one. At the time, there was in both Europe and America a rising zeitgeist that formed the background to my project. Under the influence of a compassionate and determined campaigner, the terminal-care physician and researcher Cecily Saunders, the hospice movement was just getting established in England, and the study of end-of-life issues was gaining wider appreciation through the work of the Swiss-American psychiatrist Elisabeth Kübler-Ross (she of the now-well-known 'five stages of grief').

My interior motives for venturing into the field of human mortality were not clear to me at the time. My embedded habit was to firmly compartmentalise my private life away from the world of my work. I really did not make any connection—though it looks balefully obvious to me now—between my new interest in death and dying, for a TV project, and what was happening in my own home. My live-in girlfriend, Jane, who'd been with me for about a decade, was becoming increasingly debilitated by her incurable disease, neurofibromatosis. Without appreciating then quite how fully, I was hungry for knowledge about what to expect, for both of us, as the illness brought her death ever closer. I think I wanted a template for how to handle what I foresaw as a challenge that would be frighteningly beyond my capabilities.

When Jane eventually died two years after I completed work on the *Facing Death* programmes, I was to some extent prepared for the loss, or as prepared as I could be, mentally, at least. My heavy drinking, seriously ratcheting up at this point, took care of the emotional side, or so I believed. It was a fast-acting way to blank out unwelcome feelings, and so was my work. Alongside the booze, I relied a lot on the diversionary stimulation of exciting journalism.

Through the 1980s, religion and associated topics continued to exert their hold on me, a strong hold but still purely professional, never personal. That crowd-pulling pontiff, John Paul II, decided to make a historically unprecedented papal visit to Britain. In the midst of our nation's then serious-looking economic troubles, one newspaper carried a cartoon of the pope with the cynical questioning caption: 'Can he give the last rites to an entire country?' Our more earnest response at the TV network was to produce a pair of one-hour specials devoted to the state of the Catholic Church world-wide. In the two hours respectively, our team explored first the global and then solely the British dimensions of the overarching subject. I have to confess that my most lasting memory of the whole exercise is simply my most personal, and (I will admit) most gleeful moment.

Like generations of British schoolkids, I'd been taught about our country's historic, and fractured, relations with the pope in Rome—a story dominated, at least in the telling we received, by the compelling and egotistical figure of King Henry VIII. He swaggered through the first fifty years of the sixteenth century, famously marrying six wives. My high-school history teacher, a hard-charging educator aptly named Mr Ram, aimed to open up our vocabulary as well as our historical awareness, and he grandly proclaimed to us that King Henry was 'a man of great appetites, for sex and other forms of carnality, including gourmandizing; he burgeoned to a weight of four hundred pounds.' To be fair, Henry had been tall, trim and handsome in his younger days but a lingering leg injury, incurred while he was jousting, turned him into a sedentary older man unable to exercise the way he once had. And regarding sex, again to be fair, there was more than just appetite involved. Henry felt a desperate need, in tune with the patriarchal times, for a male heir, and his first wife, Catherine of Aragon, could not provide him with one, despite her six pregnancies: three miscarriages, two boys who died in early infancy and one surviving girl.

Henry wanted the then pope, Clement VII of Italy's power-broking Medici family, to dissolve his marriage to Catherine so he could marry his mistress, whom he expected to give him his much-needed son. When the Pope refused, Henry simply created his own Church authority. He took advantage of Europe's then-swelling theological turbulence, the surging tide of Protestant separatism, and brought into being a completely independent Church of England, one we now know worldwide as the Anglican Church. And to quote again from Mr Ram's bombastic lessons: 'Henry then appointed as head of the new Church of England … guess whom? Henry himself, of course.' Once he'd grabbed power over all Church matters, Henry officially permitted his own marriage annulment. Quite a slam dunk, we schoolboys thought.

Another outcome was that succeeding English monarchs, down to Charles III today, have carried the title Supreme Governor of the Church of England. But with a greater sense of decorum maybe setting in, and maybe a wish for a less triumphalist monarchy, day-to-day, administrative Church leadership came to be placed in the hands of not the king but England's leading clergyman, the Archbishop of Canterbury. Down through the centuries there has been a lingering unease in Christian circles about this massive splitting-off of Anglicanism from Roman Catholicism.

The unease came to be expressed in the twentieth century as 'Ecumenism,' a movement that has embodied everything from a simple desire for closer cooperation across the divide all the way to idealistic hopes for complete Church unity again, a belief that the long separation could be finally erased. All this made me very eager to interview the Englishman who had only quite recently, in 1980, been appointed Canterbury's archbishop, the Most Reverend and Right Honorable Robert Runcie. He was said to favour Church reunification, though with great caution, not ostentatiously; a common assumption was that he saw it as only a very long-term prospect.

My moment of glee came when the two of us talked on camera, and I got from Runcie a startled silence for a sharp breath or two, with his eyes suddenly widened. This was in response to a question I'd honed with some care: 'When the Pope kisses the ground at Gatwick Airport, will you be in any sense the branch-manager finally welcoming a visit from the boss at headquarters?' I wish I could now find archive video of this exchange, but as I recall it Runcie's answer—after his prolonged stare—began with, 'Well, I wouldn't quite use that phrasing, exactly ... .' The interview's style and tone typified what we liked to think was our direct and brisk, sometimes peppy approach to matters that had too often been clouded, among broadcasters at least, with excessive reverence.

We offered British viewers journalism that they evidently found engaging. One example was a documentary we made on the Mormons, a faith that struck many as intriguing and exotic. The Church of Latter-Day Saints was known mainly in the UK for its tidily-dressed American missionaries, polite young men who regarded the old country as a land ripe for conversion. When aired, Nielsen ratings and other indicators showed there was a favourable reaction among viewers but our programme deeply offended the Church elders, even though (or perhaps because)— it had relied heavily on their own public educational videos, including 'dramatic reconstructions' that showed newly-deceased Mormons joyfully meeting—in very literal, photo-realistic scenes—their long-dead ancestors in the celestial kingdom, all decked out in flowing white robes. We endeavoured to be objectively cool while providing context for these images, but it was hard to maintain a totally serious tone.

I suspect we compounded our offence to the Church hier-archy by bracketing our portrait of Mormonism within a whole season of programmes devoted to out-of-the-ordinary beliefs. The season bore a probably over-simplistic umbrella title: Cults. The Mormons took their place in our catalogue along with Scientology, Transcendental Meditation (TM) and the Bhagwan

Shree Rajneesh Movement. A senior Mormon based in Britain—a bishop as I recall him—wrote to me personally to announce that I was 'condemned to everlasting perdition' for ridiculing their faith. I had the letter framed and hung in a bathroom at home, pointing it out to visitors as my Perdition Certificate. It's a lasting regret of mine that the redolent keepsake got lost in one of my later house moves.

Our probing of Transcendental Meditation was different. The purely meditative element of TM's practices has evidently brought great benefits, notably a welcome peace of mind, to many people I've known over the years, mostly in the US. But I have to report that my team's 1981 investigation into the movement—my first-ever encounter with it—had me scratching my head.

Its foundational beliefs, at least in the way their ideas were promoted at their British HQ, seemed to us fanciful at the least. The imposing and richly fitted-out mansion in Southern England's countryside was staffed by earnest young people, the senior ones all male and predominantly American. They were called ministers; I'm pretty sure the one nominated for us to interview was named Bruce something, but his official title was definitely Minister for All Possibilities. He was part of TM's World Government for the Age of Enlightenment. This we duly accepted and described him as such on air.

(There was also a Minister for Prosperity and Progress, and a Minister for Cultural Integrity, Invincibility and World Harmony, but my disappointed team didn't get to meet either of them in person.)

As reporters we felt we had to draw the line of credulity at the point where the leaders made striking claims for one element in what they called 'advanced' TM. This involved the Sidhi—allegedly special powers that derived from the Sutras, the aphorisms of the ancient Indian sage, Patanjali, and from the Rigveda sacred texts originally written in Sanskrit. If fully internalised, the leaders asserted, TM's Sidhi would enable their followers to fly. When we filmed the training process it looked, unimpressively, a lot more like jumping.

To this day, to friends who extol the virtues of TM as an aid to relaxation, I nod in acknowledgment but remain uneasy about what farther reaches of absurdity the beliefs behind their meditation practice might have taken them.

All in all, I covered a great many adherents of varying faiths and persuasions, and I kept having to acknowledge one simple truth. The best of them did a lot of good in the world—often with heavy odds stacked against them. In this at least, there was some resonance with my own growing interests and concerns. While reporting on ethics and belief, I also found myself doing more and more broadcasting and magazine-writing about Africa, coming to concentrate on Southern Africa's struggles against racist white regimes. The racists had desperately, often viciously, clung to power in South Africa, Zimbabwe and the Portuguese colonies of Mozambique and Angola. That coverage led me on to a wider, more global view—highlighting the world's widespread inequities and unfairness. I would frequently present extensive examinations of the deep overall divide between the so-called developed world and developing countries. In blunter language, rich versus poor.

This sharpening focus led me to leave the ranks of Britain's commercial TV companies. I was headhunted to run a new non-profit alliance of overseas aid organisations called the International Broadcasting Trust (IBT). Its membership brought together Oxfam, Save the Children, War on Want and other such charities. Our purpose was to use television for educating rich-world audiences about the realities of life in the poor world—and about how the unequal relationship between those two worlds worked out in day-to-day terms. I was now finally freed from the constant connection to religion.

Or so I thought. For a while I felt unfettered but a dozen years later, religion, spiritual practices and ethical quandaries of belief all contrived to ambush me again, after I had moved to the US. I became a correspondent for the Public Broadcasting Service's weekly programme specially devoted to that same old subject realm. Again, it wasn't a deliberate choice on my part. I was introduced at a cocktail party to the programme's executive producer, who knew of my British work, and he invited me to start making videoed contributions, solely on the basis of that previous track record.

The PBS show's name contrasted intriguingly with my previous flagship output, *Credo*, a title I had considered pretty snappy. The American programme sat solemnly in the *TV Guide* schedules under the banner *Religion and Ethics NewsWeekly*. It must count as one of the most boring TV titles ever but it had the virtue of presenting in three nouns (or was it four?) a completely, even laboriously accurate label. In time I moved on to a less specifically targeted programme elsewhere in PBS, the wholly mainstream PBS *NewsHour*. There, newly-minted as a so-called special correspondent, I was meant to maintain my religion and ethics concentration among all the general-interest coverage that the *NewsHour* offered.

In my New York career perhaps the oddest development came when I was hired by, of all things, a Catholic religious order. In its formal function as the American Catholic Church's overseas-

At London's Regent's Park Mosque, reporting for PBS on UK government measures against violent extremism.

7/7 Memorial
Hyde Park, London

RELIGION
& ETHICS
NEWSWEEKLY

DAVID TERESHCHUK
Contributing Correspondent

TOP: *A still from a PBS report from London's memorial for the bombing victims of 7 July 2005. Fifty-two pillars were put up to represent fifty-two people killed.* ABOVE: *Conducting interviews, Louisiana, 2014.*

aid division, the order carried out educational, health-related, and anti-poverty work in Asia, Africa and Latin America—the same geographic and socio-economic fields in which I'd operated when running IBT from London. While providing the priests with my media-related services I had no real interest in the worshipful dimension of their lives. I was just glad for the chance to be constantly addressing international issues; in one memorable instance I travelled to Namibia to report on the astonishingly effective reversal of that country's once rampant HIV/AIDS epidemic. It was a success achieved with the considerable help, gratefully acknowledged by the Namibian health authorities, of dedicated Catholic priests and nuns, both local and from overseas. It was inevitably a decidedly pragmatic effort, oblivious to their religion's doctrine; I found it privately satisfying to see hundreds of men and women in clerical garb handing out millions of life-saving condoms, in total disregard of the Vatican's unyielding and unrealistic prohibition.

Fundamentally, I simply could not get comfortable with religion. Its supernatural dimension, the much-vaunted impenetrable mystery of it all, offended the well-trained and hardheaded intellect I believed I possessed. The piety of religion's many believers struck me more like pomposity and my egalitarian instincts disdained the unquestioned authority so often enjoyed by religious leaders. I was to continue in the self-appointed role of uninvolved outsider, even as religion kept being woven into my avowedly irreligious life as the years went by. And then unexpectedly I was fifty-two years old and my mother was telling me my father had been a priest.

Chapter 19
Search

I returned to our New York home still jarred by the news I had received in the UK. Four years had passed since my mother first promised she would tell me the truth about my origins. As I now absorbed what she finally had told me, I realised with some surprise that my ingrained habits were not kicking in—those of my profession, that is. It seemed odd, but I didn't take any investigative-journalist action, like for instance diving immediately into 1940s Catholic church records to find traces of my alleged rapist-priest-father. Instead, I simply phoned my sister at her home in Texas.

'There's something you need to know,' I began. Julie was aware I'd been in England, and would have talked with Hilda. I passed on just what our mother had told me. She listened; no interjections of wonder or surprise, no questions either. I heard the concentration behind her silence, as carefully registered as the story I was laying out.

'Essentially,' I summarised, 'Hilda said a priest raped her and that was how I was conceived.'

Julie's response was calm and calming: 'So that's what it is, David.' I could feel her folding our family's fifty years of secrecy into her innocuous phrase.

'Uh-huh ... that's evidently what it is,' I said.

Julie and I had much in common, though in some ways we were quite different. No surprise in that, perhaps, since we shared a mother but not a father. She moved to America before I did, quite separately. And while she became a pretty dedicated world-traveller along with her husband, their home-base in the Lone Star state remained for a long time a simple tract house in a suburban subdivision. Overall, Julie's demeanour was modest, her manners were quiet and her approach to life was undramatic. The only time I've seen her in any extreme of emotion—and even then it was more bafflement than voluble distress—came when she learned with horror what depths I'd sunk to in my alcohol addiction. In my later sober life I grew increasingly happy that she and I became close friends as adults, fully making up for the distance between us as children eight years apart.

'You know,' said Julie, 'I'm listening to you in my kitchen, looking out over the canyon. And there's no crashing of thunder, no flashes of lightning.' I knew what she meant. My news was not world-shattering; life was obviously going on as always, whatever I might have just learned about my beginnings. She wasn't minimising my unexpected news, just applying a measured assessment with some sisterly warmth.

We slipped into pensive reflections. Almost as one, we spoke the words 'poor Hilda' about our mother clinging onto the mystery for so long. Julie couldn't help faulting Hilda for using a fax to convey her weighty announcement. I said I felt the terseness of her message had been allayed by the long phone conversation that followed it—unprecedentedly long, astonishingly full. When I relayed Hilda's description of our grandmother's angry reaction to the pregnancy, Julie and I naturally couldn't decide whether that fury might have included outrage at a churchman assaulting her daughter. But in Hilda's own telling, as I recalled it, Mam's anger was expressed solely against herself for getting pregnant. I went on to relate how they hatched the plot to pass me off as my mother's youngest baby brother, and then how she was sent out to work at sixteen to pay for my keep —everything, in sum, that I could recite of Hilda's account. 'What a life she's had,' Julie remarked, and I was gently nudged towards a little empathy, among my erratic mix of other feelings.

In the initial wake of Hilda's revelations I had experienced a rush of heady excitement, even some giddy elation at finally hearing a secret given up. But along with that came renewed anger that I'd been kept in the dark as a child and throughout my life until now. I was also assailed by vying emotions about the man whose son I apparently was: revulsion at this evident criminal and at the same time a strange but undoubted pleasure in at last having a father I could maybe name. Whatever confused thoughts careened through my brain, they were infused with dark fury at the man for raping my mother. It didn't quench my anger to acknowledge, as I had to, the seemingly glaring, indisputable fact: without that rape I just wouldn't exist; there would be no me. It was weird, overwhelming, confounding.

So our siblings' matter-of-fact conversation, coming three days later, acted as a welcome salve to my inner turbulence. Though Julie wouldn't necessarily have known it, she was reaffirming in me the strength of a resonant maxim that I already valued and now found more apt than ever. I had heard it from both an esteemed news editor whom I once worked for, and an alcoholism specialist who'd counseled me for a while. From their differing standpoints, they had each said that any new information we ever get is initially merely that. 'It's just information.'

I sensed an intimation of some resolution to our long-lasting family secret. A secret that I regarded, with maybe a child-like sense of ownership, as my secret. It had now been definitively opened up, and in a gratifying way: directly to me myself, and by the very person who'd been keeping it from me. But along with being self-centredly gratified by a victory of some kind, quite another response began to surge that extended beyond simply myself. I'd been informed that an unconscionable crime had been committed against my mother, and by a man, this Father Francis, who had gotten away with it.

The Catholic Church across many countries was then reeling from exposés of priests sexually abusing minors, both boys and girls. Here was yet one more individual case that had evidently stayed long concealed by the clerical authorities. My journalist's spirit now couldn't fail to be stirred. By rights it was a case that must be fully, comprehensively excavated.

In taking this broader view I strove to put aside my personal involvement, but it couldn't be forgotten. I kept devising impetuous fantasies of confronting the perpetrator myself, though my imaginings didn't extend to precisely what I might ever say to him. All of this assumed he was still alive; signs were that he'd be at least in his eighties at this point, if he had survived. A fellow journalist I talked with who also specialised in religion, and who was not normally the most cynical in outlook, said: 'He's probably a cardinal by now.'

Other colleagues who worked the 'abuse beat' (the issue had even become a sub-specialty in religion coverage) emphasised the difficulties facing me. A prohibitively long time had elapsed. The reporters' experience of how efficiently the Church often scrubbed its historical records about sexual offenders made them say I'd be wasting my time if I started to make 'front-door', official inquiries of the Church about my particular story. It would be a mistake, they said, to directly approach the diocese where my alleged father could have worked.

There were other, less direct ways that might be more effective. My own years of reporting on religion had provided me with some contacts, even a few friends among the clergy. They could perhaps offer me just what I knew I needed: 'insider' operating skills, and in some cases private access to official and confidential archives.

Almost immediately, there was Father Jack. I met him when out of curiosity I attended a weekend retreat for ex-drunks like myself, held in New Jersey. He was another ex-drunk and was performing the visiting role that Catholics call Retreat Master. Here was perhaps another instance of religion's unplanned hold on me; it was purely my interest in a strengthened recovery from alcoholism that nudged me into this proximity with the Christian faith once again—mere proximity, I'd stress, not intimacy, and just for three days: hardly a full embrace.

The gathering was in a Benedictine retreat house and involved around eighty one-time problem drinkers, all male. Father Jack guided us through long days of reflection that included informal seminars that he conducted about living a sober life. These were interspersed with quiet time for contemplation, communal meals and walks alone or in fraternal company around the house's restful, rustic grounds. Jack's heartening personality made the proceedings even more informal; he was blessed with a sharp kind of humour that I warmed to: ironical but rarely sarcastic. He would sometimes address us as 'My dear reprobates ... .' He'd then pause before adding: 'And I speak as a reprobate myself.'

In a custom evidently expected of retreat masters, Jack made himself available for private twenty-minute sessions with individual attendees. In his droll phrasing, 'You could have something to get off your chests, or any other part of your anatomy in which it might currently reside.' My scepticism told me these one-on-one talks would likely take the unwelcome form of a Catholic confessional. On the other hand our crowd included only a few Catholics and far more representatives of other faiths. One of them, a friend of mine who'd flown from Singapore for the event, was a Buddhist. Several of us, myself included of course, were men of no formal faith at all. Putting my uncertainty to one side, I decided to book a session with Father Jack. It was now only weeks since I'd heard my mother's account of being attacked by a priest, and here was a chance to talk directly with an example—in this case an approachable, even likable example—of that same profession.

The small, monastic guest-room Jack was sleeping in doubled as a temporary office. As he welcomed me inside I imagined it as less of a confessional and more of a consulting room—the consulting room, indeed, of a somewhat elvish therapist: so he seemed now, this short, rather portly man who snapped off his clerical collar and tossed it onto his desk as he settled onto a ladderback chair. He spoke in that angular accent of Southern New Jersey, its edges softened with echoes of his Irish origins.

'How's it going?' he asked.

I made an abrupt start: 'I've been told I'm the son of a priest who raped my mother when she was fifteen.'

I expected some surprise, even some shock. But no; it was just all in a weekend's work for Jack. He merely inquired, 'When was this?' and 'How did it happen?' He also wanted to know where it had taken place.

Factual details duly taken in, he moved on quickly, saying, 'How have you felt about all this?' I now don't recall the actual words I used but I expect I dwelled on my lifelong puzzlement and my anger at having been kept in the dark.

He surprised me with a sudden, 'Have you forgiven your mother?' Though unexpected, it was an obvious question as I thought about it. And in the instant my answer came surprisingly clear and wholehearted: 'For keeping the truth from me? Yes. Yes, I have.'

He paused to register this—for both of us to register it, I'd say. I think I understood even at this early point that forgiveness is a process, not a momentary event, but I certainly felt in that moment that I was making a commitment.

Jack's pause wasn't long. 'And do you want to find out more about him?' was his next brisk query.

'Well, I'm in two minds. Several minds, really. I think he should be exposed and the authorities who concealed what he did should be exposed. Maybe they moved him to somewhere that meant he could do it again. That too should be exposed.'

Jack broke in almost impatiently: 'As a matter of policy and of sheer justice, that's exactly right: I would agree.' He was eager to move on. 'But what about your other mind or minds. As a son, say.'

'I just don't know. I'm furious at him for raping Hilda.' Unthinkingly, I'd found myself using her name, no longer 'my mother'. I tried hesitantly to clarify my feelings: 'I don't know if I want to have anything to do with him. But then I think I do want to. I could maybe tell him to his face what I think of him. If he's still around to hear it.'

'I'm not sure you know what you think of him,' Jack mused. 'Yet.'

I felt I had to consider this notion, and I told him that I would. Then came the weekend's most unforeseen words. 'I could find out more, if you'd like,' he said.

He really could, it seemed. Jack turned out to have responsibility, in his own home diocese, for what he described—loosely, at least to me—as 'erring priests'. He was an official of many parts. Part frontline investigator of allegations, part assessor of evidence and liaison officer with police and other secular agencies like prosecutors' offices, part advisor to bishops in charge ... and part counselor to the guilty men, as long as they were, as he put it, 'truly repentant'. He was involved in the occasional process of sending offenders for treatment, if it seemed likely that it might reform their future conduct. But he admitted: 'Frankly, it rarely makes any difference. Sex abusers can build up a skilful wall of denial for themselves. And they often put on a convincing show of compliance with their treatment. But generally, in my experience ... if someone rapes once they're highly likely to rape again, if allowed the opportunity.'

About starting a search for Father Francis, Jack felt confident that, diocese to diocese, he could prise details out of the English church authorities, even after five decades. 'I know which vaults they hide the bodies in, as it were,' he said, in a way that might have included a wink, if he had been a winking man.

I placed my confidence in his confidence. And awaited a new chapter of revelations, so to speak.

Chapter 20
Mother in the Dark

My mother often fades from the scene while I'm recalling our history on the page. It's hard to deny she forms an important part of my life, and this was inescapably true throughout my childhood years. By my late teens, though, I'd say she was still significant but with a twist: she became conspicuous by her absence.

In earlier pages I've reconstructed my memories of living with her, however few and sketchy they might be; I've also gone back much earlier, trying to picture her own disrupted younger life in the years before my clearly scandalous conception. But in my twenties, a period when I know other people often experience a life still shared between parent and grown offspring, my mother was simply no part of the picture. I made sure of that while I forged my determinedly self-reliant way in the world.

There were points in time when we might have reconnected more closely; Bloody Sunday, when I was twenty-three, could have been one of them. After news broke of the massacre in Derry, Hilda apparently threw herself into a flurry of efforts to locate me. She must have had a deep maternal terror that I was in danger. She would have learned through seeing my previous broadcasts that I was specialising more and more in the Irish 'Troubles', so she had good reason to believe I would have been in Derry on that terrible day.

I learned later that she had contacted my office and some of my friends and neighbours. I have no idea how she could have got hold of their phone numbers. She also reached a couple of ex-girlfriends; again, it was amazing to me that she found them. I had no comprehension then of the extremes to which a mother can go when her child is in any way imperilled. I wouldn't normally compare Hilda to a wild animal, but a year or so later I did think of her urgent reactions to Bloody Sunday when I was in

East Africa, watching completely awestruck as a mother leopard dived hell-bent into deep savannah thickets and pulled to safety an injured cub who'd come under fire from a pair of angry brushtail porcupines.

Back on Derry's streets in 1972, working in high-intensity mode to gather footage—and possibly still in shock—I gave no heed at all to Hilda. I did notice that some of my colleagues, even action-hardened veterans, were getting in touch with their families to give assurances they were safe. I shrugged off their example as somehow not applicable to me.

After my long night spent rescuing our interview tapes that had gone missing, when I returned to the City Hotel the reception clerk handed me a note from the pigeon-holes behind him. He said my mother had finally got through to the hotel switchboard after two days of calling and getting only a busy signal. The note, from the board operator, said she'd told her I was okay, and was out working—which may or may not have reassured her at 4:30 am. I felt not the slightest need to call her back.

A few days later, I think when our team and myself were all back in the London office, I did have a phone conversation with her, recounting very vaguely what had happened to me, minimising any risks the events might have included. 'But you could at least have told me where you were,' she said inevitably, 'and that you were all right.' I acknowledged, if a bit unwillingly, that she had a point. But I didn't want to engage with her concern. I was badly shaken, as I was starting to admit to myself, if only begrudgingly. But I didn't want anyone else to know how shaken I was, certainly not my mother.

My prevailing habit, once I'd started travelling for my work, was that I simply never told Hilda where I was going. Sometime late into an overseas assignment I might send a picture postcard, with the location looking bland and untroubled. But since it was usually outbursts of trouble that had provoked my reporting trip in the first place, the cards could seem disingenuous, so I abandoned the practice. I wouldn't have said at the time that I hated her or even disliked her. At some level I knew I was angry with her, though I never formulated exactly why. To all intents and purposes I was merely dismissing her from my busy life. I wanted her kept in the dark and insofar as I thought about her at all, I would tell myself I didn't want her 'upset'—that freighted word again in our family—or to be worrying about what might happen to me. It never occurred to me that knowing nothing whatever about my movements might in itself worry or upset her.

Entirely unspoken then was my desire, quite plain as I look back, to minimise all connections with her that I could in my London-based and international life. I had an inexpressible embarrassment about her, about my family in general. There was that old, seemingly irradicable shame about our background in poverty and yet a fascination with poor communities, locally and globally, in my journalism.

It seems inconsistent and contradictory to me now, but back in my twenties I would spend much of my reporting work amid poverty, and yet never identify myself as coming from poor beginnings myself. I was now pulling in an income much greater than all my recently graduated peers and—in a cliché favoured by those same contemporaries, dating back to Samuel Johnson in the eighteenth century—had become 'rich beyond the dreams of avarice' compared with my own family. I felt entirely disconnected from my financial history.

Putting that history to one side, I frequently dipped deep into the lives of other people caught in a cycle of poverty, like homeless families on the streets of inner-city London boroughs like Camden and Hackney. I spent a little over a year (for a TV documentary I recall, just one of several such projects) charting the course of children's lives that social-services agencies were monitoring because their parents' poverty, among other factors, put them 'at risk', to use the specialists' jargon. I was affronted by the degrading conditions of their life, and powerfully energised as a reporter by the sheer unfairness of it all. I was surprised to hear that my senior colleagues were impressed by my interview questions, calling them not just detailed but 'insightful' and even 'penetrating'. They seemed merely simple and basic to me, like my wanting to know how often a family of four was able to buy a loaf of bread at one shilling and nine pence, when the father's daily labouring wage was scarcely more than four pounds a day. (The equivalents in today's money would be $2.50 for bread and a daily wage of about $35.00.)

Overseas and on a broader canvas I would portray the often institutional, systemic nature of poverty. Like the economic cramping of a developing country's population as it relies upon trade in basic commodities. An African country like Burundi, for instance, could be utterly dependent on a single commodity, in its case coffee, for well over ninety per cent of its national income. This obviously made the country intolerably vulnerable to the vagaries of the international coffee prices. The individual small farmer, and her husband, were grotesquely at the mercy of multinational companies and their manoeuvres in the global market. For their part the mega-corporations rarely struggled to factor any notion of fairness into the prices they 'offered' to those farming families. I would report on this phenomenon in different countries with different commodities, but the process was infuriatingly similar everywhere. As the opening to one such report I made for TV, I used jagged, bold lettering across the screen: 'The Staying Poor Machine'. Over-simplistic perhaps, but it summed up my reaction to the never-changing inequity.

I found it inconceivable to let my colleagues know, or my

With UK prime minister Tony Blair, right, and Harold Evans, centre, the then publishing head of Random House Books, 1998.

subjects with whom I sat in lengthy explorations of their daily condition, or still less my watching audiences, anything at all about my own experience of growing up poor. I sidelined my own beginnings as irrelevant. Of course I knew the truism that all poverty is relative, and while I sat with the severely disadvantaged subjects of my reporting I could mentally swerve into the evasive comparison, 'I didn't have it as bad as they do.' Fluttering over all of this was the banner of my vaunted journalist's objectivity. Sympathy for the poor was okay, within limits. But personal identification with them was not. It would compromise the impartial authority of my reporting.

Other considerations were more influential. Foremost among them was an infatuation, combined tellingly with fear, about my professional cohort, not least when I began socialising with its members. Thankfully, things have at long last changed, but in those past decades British broadcasting was largely run by a class of individuals whom I could only regard as 'posh' ... and I devoutly wished to merge seamlessly into that class. I was scared of being found out, of being exposed as an upstart outsider. As if anybody would really have cared in the end.

I would self-servingly quote to myself an ironic pun: 'to the manor born'. It was a common enough piece of wordplay based on a phrase from Hamlet, in which the prince says that he is 'to the manner born', meaning simply that he's accustomed from birth to certain local habits. Our modern-day pun, manor for manner, altered the meaning into a suggestion that someone has claims to upper-class origins. (Funnily enough, at least to me as a former heavy drinker, the actual 'manner' or habit that Hamlet singled out was riotous consumption of alcohol in his native Denmark.) With its -or spelling, the phrase later became the title of a popular BBC sitcom that laid a laugh-track over dialogue crackling with jokes about class differences.

For me the words served as a kind of mental spur to my upward social mobility; I thought myself clever in the way I could get by socially, even though I could be haunted by the sense that I was a phony. At two different points in that early phase of my life —when acting like a chameleon in new surroundings came naturally, and when I still possessed a now-lost gift for vocal mimicry—I switched my accent from the previous, dead give-away dialects that bedevilled me. My twenty-something's taste in expensive clothing helped a bit as well; I ordered my suits from Savile Row tailors, very traditional but with an edgy cut, albeit limited to the lapels and pocket-flaps. But my conscious adoption of a superior demeanour counted for more than anything I would wear. My Oxford days had taught me to play-act a complacent air of ease when among those I regarded as my 'betters'—even among those accustomed to employing servants, it would seem.

I recall how the tectonic plates first moved when I was seventeen, almost immediately after I was installed in my mediaeval college rooms. A modest knock at the door announced the arrival of a seemingly much older man—probably in his fifties, I now recognise—wearing a short white jacket. 'I am Bill, Sir, and I am to be your Scout' (Oxford-speak for 'manservant', to serve the 'young gentleman' that I had suddenly become). My first reaction was a mix of shock and horror. My second—and it wasn't long in coming—was to take to this new relationship as a duck to water. In fact, I now see this early acclimatisation to a master-servant arrangement as contributing greatly to the sense

In the historic Eastern State Penitentiary in Philadelphia, reporting on the US's continuing use of solitary confinement. ESP closed in 1971.

of entitlement that became an unattractive part of my make-up in early adulthood, and maybe for quite a bit longer. My high-handedness, though, was always accompanied by the nagging whisper that I really was a fake, a whisper that I'd counter by straining harder to talk loudly and confidently.

Behind it all there was my continuing shame about being illegitimate. I didn't seem able to shake it. It made no logical sense. I had nothing, after all, to be ashamed of. It was hardly my fault. I had no responsibility for being 'a bastard', 'misbegotten', 'born out of wedlock' or any of the other pejoratives that remained in common use throughout the early years of my life. I once had to suppress a shudder in a London gentlemen's club, when a member of our young drinkers' group referred to a relative as 'base-born, from the wrong side of the bedsheet'. The speaker's own perfectly validated pedigree, as the thirteenth marquess of his line, made me cringe even more at his archaisms —everyday parlance in his family, from the sound of it. I knew full well that shame doesn't work in any logical fashion, so logic provided me with no real defence. My approach simply remained that of determinedly keeping my family background a complete secret. I had to avoid the subject absolutely, even within the confines of my own mind.

With the passage of time, I am glad to say that attitudes have shifted. Being born illegitimate doesn't carry a stigma any more because marriage is no longer venerated as it once was. My attitudes have shifted too, and in recent years I have had opportunities, and taken them, to walk in that once-taboo territory quite comfortably and openly.

Here's one example. For one of my fairly frequent TV reports on America's epidemic of mass incarceration, I wanted in 2019 to focus on one under-reported aspect: a significant growth in the proportion of women in the country's prison system. As my team and I conducted our research, a noted Los Angeles campaigner for criminal-law reform, Susan Burton, emerged as an ideal person to include among our interviewees. She had once lived a self-confessedly miserable life on the streets of South Central, with an addiction to drugs that led to arrests and incarceration. The pattern of separations from her daughter resulted in a complete estrangement between the two of them. Along with my professional assessment that she'd be a relevant and strong presence in our report, I felt an undertow of personal connection to some of her life-story.

Unlike her, I was never incarcerated, other than a few scattered overnights in jail cells, but I had a rap sheet of sorts. I'd been known, when without a car for whatever reason, to 'borrow' neighbours' vehicles so I could drive, drunk of course, to a liquor store after my home supply had run out. Once, predictably enough, I crashed, totalling the borrowed car, and inevitably I was arrested. I pilfered cash from others—like girlfriends too careless with their purses—to buy booze when my own funds

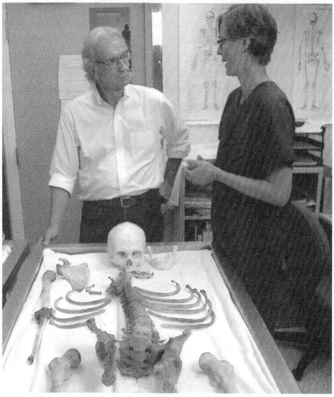

In an Arizona medical examiner's laboratory discussing the remains of an unidentified migrant who died in the Sonoran Desert after crossing the border.

were depleted. I amassed quite a sizeable criminal record, based on my drunk-driving offences alone, and these grew more serious with each arrest. I eventually faced a prison sentence of six months to a year, but at the last minute, thanks to an agile, persuasive defence attorney, the sentence was mercifully reduced to two years' probation.

On site in Watts with Ms Burton, as everyone called her, we videoed a sit-down interview for about thirty minutes. She presented her compelling argument that the right place for women when they got arrested, especially if they were addicts, was not jail but a supportive home base, well settled in a community. She ran a small network of sheltering group-homes for such women, plus professional support for addiction recovery whenever it was needed. My crew then went off to capture the additional 'visuals' offered by those group-homes, leaving the two of us to talk over mugs of coffee in her office.

'I went badly off the rails,' Susan told me. 'Bringing up Toni was hard.' Toni was the daughter she had given birth to after she was raped in her early teens. 'Later I had a little boy too, K.K.— but he was killed in a car accident when he was five.' Her son had run without warning onto a crosswalk and a minivan had run him down.

She said her daughter had lost a brother and then, in a way, lost her mother as well. Susan fell into depression and worsening drug-use after the young boy died. 'I couldn't sleep. I'd see his face at night, hear him calling to me. I tried everything I could to alleviate my pain. It was the early 1980s, beginning of the crack epidemic, and here on the streets there was a lot that someone like me could get her hands on.'

For once, my usual professional reserve and distance dissolved; my feeling of connection with her spilled into a simple openness that reflected hers. 'Yes, I can imagine,' I said. 'I got addicted to alcohol and drugs, too. Drank my way out of what was once a useful career.'

Her eyebrows rose just a little, she made a slow nod of recognition ... and we soon found ourselves swapping early life details.

She told me that when she was a girl, her housing complex in

East L.A. was called Aliso Village. The rustic name sounded to me, as a one-time country boy, like a bit of a stretch; absurd for a city neighbourhood. 'I grew up in a village, too,' I said, 'but a real village, in the countryside—a sleepy little town, really.'

Aliso was never quite like genuine countryside, Susan said, but it had originally been a settled neighbourhood for working families. It soon changed, though, into what she called 'a territory for black and Mexican gangs, and knife-fights in daylight'. She said the gang-members 'fought around the clothes-lines where all our families hung our laundry'.

I told her my family home was also in a public housing project, though rural and without any knife-fights that I could remember. But my grandmother had warned me against mixing with some bigger kids who had violent reputations. 'Actual knifings came later,' I said. 'After we moved to the big city, I ended up in a huge new high school and I was terrified by the fights that went on—mostly in our underground cloakrooms.'

There was greater physical danger for Susan. She described the Christmas Eve of her fifteenth year when she was ambushed by a group of six or seven bigger boys. 'I was with my friend, Cupcake. I was wearing my Christmas outfit, purple pants.' The boys pushed the two girls into a basement and raped them both.

'I went home, took off my Christmas clothes and buried them in the trash.' Her face took on a distant gaze, but she spoke emphatically. 'And then I buried myself, too. I stepped out of my body and went to another place. I never spoke of that night, and no one around me noticed a thing.'

Some weeks later a schoolteacher realised that Susan was pregnant. Her mother's reaction as she outlined it to me sounded familiar. 'Having had six children,' Susan said, 'Mama certainly knew how to care for a pregnant daughter. But it wasn't about care; it was about shame ... and then her shame became mine.'

There was a short silence and I said flatly, 'My mother told me she had been raped at fifteen years old.'

Susan said nothing for a moment, glanced up, held her stare at the ceiling, and then down again. 'That's bad,' she said. She asked, 'Was it one of the neighbourhood boys?'

'No,' I said. 'My mother said it was a priest.'

'Oh my,' she replied. 'That's worse. Or maybe not.'

'Yes, maybe—I don't know,' I said, feeling foolish. 'But then, how could I?'

We both laughed, uncomfortably—and then more fully, at ourselves, in the manner of isn't-it-crazy-to-be-laughing-at-all?

Her smile dropped. 'And you're the child of that rape,' she said.

It wasn't a question. And I wondered for a moment at her assumption. I took a slow gulp of coffee and then told her, 'My grandmother took it as a mark of great shame, like you said your mother did. She tried at first to pass me off as her own child.'

'Yes,' Susan said, 'that's very common in families, or it used to be. And yeah, we can get so completely conditioned to feel shame. We'll believe we're a bad person who doesn't deserve a better life.'

The professional purpose for our being together then intervened. She remembered she had promised me some case-histories for the young women in her group-homes, those at least who agreed to be featured. She wanted to find the information in time for my crew's return from filming the homes, so our private chat became a little hurried, tossing a few short bulletins back and forth between us.

She grinned: 'So you're not drinking now, right?'

'Right,' I said, 'not for twenty-eight years.' She reached out her hand, clasping mine in congratulation, saying, 'And it's twenty-five years for me. Aren't we lucky?'

'Totally agree about our luck,' I said.

Sizing each other up and down, as if now we were just meeting for the first time, we joshed each other about our completely contrasting looks, for all the commonalities that we'd been discovering. Me, a seventy-year-old white male in my customary uniform, an old-school TV correspondent's dark suit with a navy-and-burgundy necktie; she, a late-fifties African-American woman in large, owlish glasses, dreads halfway down her bright scarlet overblouse, plus black tights and box-fresh white sneakers to complete her street-hip look.

'Get a load of us,' she said. 'Kinda Laurel and Hardy!'

'You're too cool to be Hardy,' I said. 'Though I do fit as Laurel, the British half of the pair.' She looked puzzled, then laughed to hear that the thinner of the two comics was born in the same county where I grew up. Then as my crew came back into the room, we wrapped up all the journalistic business we had to complete.

Later that afternoon I was driving the twenty miles to a restaurant on Santa Monica's shoreline for an indulgent meal with my team—the kind of reward I give myself and colleagues while on location—and I felt a surge of regret about just one thing in our South Central conversation. I wished I'd told Susan what kind of relationship my mother and her 'child of rape', if that's what I was, had experienced over the years; how long I had pursued my efforts to get that relationship onto a good footing, like the one Susan had regained with her child. 'I'm so glad for you two,' I had said, about the warm and ever-deepening mother-daughter reconciliation that she'd described to me.

I would have told her that while relations between my mother and me had unquestionably been distant and strained when I was a young man, I had tried hard—once I found a better life as a sober middle-aged man—to then re-establish those relations on better terms. They improved, I would have said, but they didn't really become what I could honestly call a strong connection.

Chapter 21
Tenterhooks

I couldn't rest content with Father Jack's plan to investigate, probing within the Church's institutions on my behalf. My inner reporter kept urging me to dig further. So I reached out, in other, different directions, with what my trade calls 'feelers'—though the word is cringe-making here in the context of sexual predation. Jack had promised to proceed with great care as he searched for the priest who had allegedly fathered me by raping an underage girl.

I had reason to feel such caution was essential. The English Church authorities, once alerted to such a search going on, could easily cover up any still-traceable tracks; it was just such adept cover-ups that had foiled other journalistic and judicial investigators who pursued cases of clerical abuse. An Irish reporter and, separately, an English one, plus a frustrated American prosecutor had told me of instances of relevant church records mysteriously going missing and some other archives being suspiciously but not provably altered. It seemed wise that my new avenues for research should be just as discreet as Jack's.

My line of work had given me a contacts-book well stocked with religious people in general, and these included a British priest whom I'd befriended early on. He'd since moved up to a pretty elevated position in the Catholic hierarchy. He was well acquainted with the corridors of power in Westminster, the major diocese presided over by the Cardinal Archbishop leading all of England's Catholics. Like my existing American ally, Father Jack, my English clerical friend also promised to use his discretion and to go as unnoticed as he could while probing the mystery of 'Father Francis'.

I also turned to a reliable contact in British law-enforcement. I understood that no crime would have been reported to secular authorities back in the year of my conception. But since then, as my contact emphasised to me, Britain's police forces, courts of law and successive ad-hoc government commissions of inquiry had all established a new body of knowledge about sexual abusers in the Church, both present-day and historical. Some of these probes had successfully cut through Church efforts at concealment and had even in some cases ended up delivering a measure of justice to the victims. My contact's area of responsibility conveniently covered much of the north of England, extending right up to the Scottish border. Such a highly placed officer had as good a chance as any investigator, perhaps more than most, of uncovering the truth.

Since both these new lines of inquiry continued without my direct personal involvement, I was in a constant state of frustration, even while I could see that my expert friends would almost certainly make a better job of it than I would. On my own I could all too easily become the stock figure that I abhor, a clumsy journalist committing missteps because he lacks an expert's familiarity with an arcane territory and its nuances. Unable to steer the search in detail, I lived on tenterhooks—feeling, quite palpably, as if I was being stretched out on a frame, made tense and attenuated like a tightening fabric.

Father Jack reported back first, after six months of searching, to tell me there was no discernible record of any Father Francis. 'Not as far as I can find,' he was at pains to stress. 'That doesn't mean that he didn't exist. Just that I couldn't find him.'

I slumped into disappointment. My eager hopes seemed thoroughly dashed. Perhaps disproportionately so, I realised; if this had been one of my journalistic pursuits, I doubt I would ever have become as deflated as I was by Jack's findings, which he himself had stressed were not absolute, not entirely conclusive. And hope still resided in the two other investigators who continued working on the case in their separate ways. My state of suspense over just how these newer probes by the English churchman and by the law officer might be proceeding became ever more taut.

Another whole year was to elapse before first one, and then soon afterwards the other, contacted me with their conclusions. Their work, as well as Jack's, had come to nothing; they each told me with regret that they had hit a dead end. They too had found no evidence of a Father Francis.

Melissa Bellinelli Tereshchuk and me, both holding umbrellas.

I was felled by disappointment once more, but then I shifted into a kind of wearied resignation. What did I really expect? I thought. The odds, I must have realised, were stacked against any successful result, in view of the sheer expanse of history being dragnetted. Nearly three years had passed since my mother told me of her alleged rape, and my desire for further deep inquiry now felt robbed of its urgency. I didn't make a deliberate choice to abandon the chase; it felt more like involuntary slippage back to the time before my hopes had first been raised, back to the avoidance behaviour I'd allowed myself to practise for forty years, utterly sidelining 'the paternity issue'. And I certainly did have other mainstream matters to fully occupy my attention: an increasingly busy work-life, plus a marriage which was now blooming into its twelfth year and becoming wonderfully all-encompassing.

After another four years I became aware that a new player had entered the ecclesiastical scene, suddenly changing the landscape for me and even rekindling some hope. I learned that a self-help network had sprung into being, representing a population which was not widely acknowledged to even exist: the children of Catholic priests.

It had begun in Ireland—another country rife with sexual misconduct by priests, of course—and it used as its name a title based on the initial letters of the very phrase itself, direct and shocking as it would be to strict Catholics: 'Children of Priests'. The group called itself 'COPing'.

'We want people to know we do cope with the shame, the secrets and mysteries, and all the confused feelings that will accompany our situation,' the organisation's founder, Vincent Doyle told me. He was a psychotherapist, and the son of a priest himself. In the early 1980s, an Irish member of the international Spiritans order, or Holy Ghost Fathers, had an affair in his forties with Vincent's mother, who was married and already had three children. Thus Vincent was born. The priest became the boy's godfather and they knew each other purely on those terms until the priest died when Vincent was twelve. It wasn't until he was twenty-eight that his mother admitted that his real father had been not her husband, but the priest-godfather. His disgust at the long-maintained secrecy was a compelling drive behind his creation of Coping. He and I seemed to have much in common.

By the time I came across him, Vincent's group had become Coping International, extending over many countries where more and more such children were emerging into public view. I felt boosted by the somewhat comforting message that if I was a priest's son, then I'd obviously be far from alone—indeed I could be one of about 50,000, so far as Coping had yet tallied. This sizable problem, or issue, or whatever it ought to be called, was starting to get a thorough airing across much of the world, in large part thanks to Coping. As I looked at it from a Church out-sider's standpoint, all these awkward new arrivals in the world (like me?) seemed simply the inevitable consequence—given how human biology works—of any organisation blind enough to apply as a condition of employment the requirement that staff must abstain from sex. There were bound to be employees who broke the rule, and any sensible employer should, you'd think, make allowance for that happening—especially when a whole new human life was created by the rule-breaking.

In his role as Coping's leader, Vincent chose the more neutral term 'phenomenon' to label these thousands of priests' children, and he faulted the Catholic celibacy vow as much as I did, but publicly he put greater priority on getting the Church to change its attitude towards the innocent children involved—and indeed towards their mothers. For him, the stigma was the phenomenon's most unacceptable feature.

For me the sheer uncovering of hidden truths was the most appealing part of Coping's purpose. I was thrilled, and not merely as a reporter who loves a good story, to learn how Coping helped bring into the open so many individual cases of hidden priestly paternity. I found them refreshing in their demonstrating that even the heaviest cloak of concealment could sometimes—maybe including the cover-up in my own story—be conclusively ripped away.

One especially startling, extended crusade against such secrecy grabbed my attention. It was the odyssey pursued by Jim Graham, a near-contemporary of mine. Jim was conceived and born in 1945, in Buffalo, New York and had been an airline pilot before becoming a businessman. Despite an elaborate blurring of his origins, he gathered some clues about the identity of the man who might have fathered him, a parish priest. He pursued those tips tenaciously, to the point of forcing the Church, through legal action, to exhume the body of the man his search had pinpointed, a certain Father Thomas Sullivan. A DNA comparison then finally established that Jim had been right: Fr Sullivan was his father. A lifetime of lies was finally replaced by truth.

I was moved and inspired by Jim's story. But in my case I still had, even after getting expert help from others, only the merest smatterings—fewer than Jim had to work with—that might hint at my alleged father's identity. Although it was now close on ten years since I was first told about 'Father Francis,' there remained little more than that single, incomplete and tantalising name.

With my past still looking as unclear as ever, more pressing matters started to preoccupy my present. Just as we were marking eighteen years of marriage, Melissa unexpectedly fell ill, and was diagnosed with late-stage ovarian cancer. Our lives now became very eventful as the inevitable personal drama of cancer's progression took us over, but intensive treatments held the disease at bay and kept her alive for the next seven years.

We would say to each other, as well as to friends whenever they asked, that of course the cancer's grim presence dominated our existence, but perhaps surprisingly not a hundred per cent. We still lived our lives. We held a party to celebrate our twentieth wedding anniversary at which we renewed our vows. Melissa wore her own offbeat variant of a silk turban, a natty response to chemotherapy's unheeding theft of her rich, golden mane.

In her stronger moments at least, she would check on my progress with various projects, including my paternity search. While it wasn't top-of-mind for me, I did check in periodically with Coping International, as they maintained an alert lookout for any signs of the priest who might have fathered me. Melissa always wanted to know the news, even though it continued to be no news. She once also caught me extricating myself from an opportunity I'd been offered to produce a public television profile of Sadiq Khan, the promising new mayor of London, the first-ever Muslim to preside over that capital city. I felt I should cancel my assignment because Melissa's next bout of treatment was imminent and I needed to be by her side. 'No, you have to go to London,' she chided me, 'Americans have got to learn about that guy.' She was just as firm that I should continue paying attention to our Father Francis mystery.

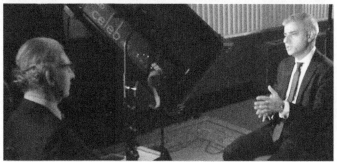

Interviewing the new mayor of London, Sadiq Khan, 2016.

But inescapably Melissa died. And then during my dazed, near-catatonic state of bereavement, Hilda also died. In a miasma of mixed feelings, my sister and I returned briefly to the UK and buried our mother. Back in New York, as I set about adjusting far from easily to a whole new life alone, I gave little or no priority to the still-unanswered questions about my beginnings.

Suddenly, though, Coping came up with a possible new answer. Vincent Doyle called to tell me that some informal sources had discovered a possible match for Father Francis. His presence had been perhaps cunningly obscured in the archives under an altered identity. It was possible, this new evidence suggested, that he was in fact a priest who had moved away, about two months after I was born, from a parish in the city near my home village. And a year or so later he seemed to reappear in the records but using a variant of his name and working for another parish in a more distant part of the diocese.

I was excited—and at the same time I got angry at my earlier helpers on both sides of the Atlantic. I rushed to judge them as too easily fobbed off by Church sources, for not having pursued their searches assiduously enough. But the enticing new possibility that the truth might finally be at hand pushed my recriminations aside. Another event diverted my anger, too: the saddening death of my expert in 'erring priests', Father Jack, an abrupt and sudden death after a short illness.

In the meantime as well, I was learning in my professional capacity about institutional changes inside the Catholic Church. The repeating sexual scandals in many countries had led the Vatican to set up new procedures that were called, in the British Church at least, 'safeguarding'—meaning measures to protect children and vulnerable adults who might be at risk from an abusive priest. Every diocese in Britain was now under orders to create a Safeguarding team that could investigate suspicions of abuse that arose. Such investigations could also be triggered by retrospective, historic allegations, without any time-limit or statute of limitations.

Another development arose, too, surprising many analysts of

Church affairs. Under Pope Francis, the Vatican devised some new though secret guidelines for errant clergy themselves. Priests who violated their celibacy vow were now being ordered to take some responsibility for any resulting children—and for the mothers, too. According to attentive Church observers, this unprecedented change in policy could be largely attributed to the agitation and pressure created by Coping. Vincent Doyle himself told me he was one of the few outsiders granted sight of the new guidelines in written form, while he was on a visit to Rome. The Church came eventually to admit publicly that the document existed, but would still not reveal its detailed contents. According to the Vatican spokesman, it was 'for internal use ... and is not intended for publication'.

In the matter of my own case, Vincent and his Coping team now felt they could take some action with the only circumstantial but in their view reliable evidence they'd uncovered about my likely father. They had established a working relationship in both the UK and Ireland with the Church's safeguarding apparatus and were thus ready to present to the particular diocese in question the claim that my mother had been raped by one of its priests. 'All we need, said Vincent, 'is your consent for us to contact the diocese.'

'Go right ahead,' I said. So Coping lodged an official complaint with the diocesan Safeguarding Officer. The officer was a social worker by previous profession, and had as her first name Jane. Somehow that very ordinariness and familiarity reassured me. She contacted me directly some days later. She asked if I would confirm my consent for the inquiries to be opened, and then promised us (Coping and myself, that is) that we could 'soon', she said, count on a full report regarding the Church's own discoveries, whatever they might turn out to be. I was once again on tenterhooks.

Chapter 22
Zimbabweans

It wasn't really my thing but an insistent group of friends suggested a week's hike in the Rockies. 'Come join us,' said one. 'We'll be eight guys doing trails around Maroon Peak, above Aspen. Some of them challenging, others fairly easy— some just a walk-in-the-park.' The group had made an annual tradition of hiking trips, and habitually invited me along. But since their destination had previously always been Switzerland, I regularly declined; it struck me as an ocean too far and, worse, some forbiddingly serious terrain. Their unaccustomed switch this particular year to a mountain range in our own continent helped somewhat in persuading me to go along with them.

But what really swayed me was something else entirely— more to do with my head than my feet. A couple of the guys said kindly that the hike would take my mind off the impatient wait I was undergoing, my wait for an answer from the British Catholic diocese that might bring fresh information about my father.

Their ploy worked; I got nicely distracted from my impatience. Of course I opted much of the time for those easier trails on offer; I am, after all, the kind of outdoorsman who just once took a bicycling vacation in France, but only after I learned that the tour company was called 'Cycling for Softies'. Colorado's majestic landscape won me over completely. Almost anywhere I reached along the Continental Divide between eight and ten thousand feet up, I was repeatedly staggered by jaw-dropping vistas and ever-changing cloud formations, themselves mountainous in their grandeur. The company was diverting, too. There were dinners each night at our risibly nicknamed 'base-camp', in fact the very comfortable mountainside ranch-house owned by one of our members. The meals were often an affable riot of mere badinage, but occasionally there were heartfelt reflections on our own companionship and the perceived (possibly self-satisfied?) rewards of having made it to all of our advanced ages.

We were a mixed bunch, a small cross-section of the men friends in my life after living in the US for nearly thirty years. I took note, though, that there was one element of incompleteness. We were all white. I also felt a rising of my habitual uncertainty—all too common when I'm in a group of any sort, even people I know quite well—about whether I truly belonged. But the simple warmth of all these men's camaraderie kept those feelings largely at bay.

There was Bob, extra-tall and gangly, conversationally hesitant but sternly passionate in his environmentalist views. He had been a hard-headed stock-market trader but was now retired and active as a board member for non-profits with an emphatic tilt towards saving the planet. And there was Rob, the son of a Lutheran pastor who had bucked the family trend and, unlike his brother who also became a pastor, had instead made a career in accountancy. But he'd led a life of headstrong exploits of an unruly kind, cutting sharply against his profession's reputed dullness. There'd been a few run-ins with the law. Not financial malpractice (he was squeaky clean in that department), more a matter of what he nonchalantly described as his youthful exuberance. That's despite at least one case of disorderly conduct occurring, I understood, in his fifties. Overseeing all our proceedings was Walter, the host at our ultra-easeful basecamp. He was a Southern lawyer still greatly in demand despite being another of the group who'd supposedly retired. His mainly corporate clients valued his meticulously prepared and elegantly argued feats of advocacy at trial. Walter was, I'd have to say, my closest friend out of the bunch. There were other lawyers too, and other financial wizards, all with their individual quirks and eccentricities. I was the only journalist among them.

One morning early on I was caught unawares by some news, but not from the Catholic diocese as I expected. This was public news, information on a very different plane. For all its relative isolation, our basecamp had good broadband connectivity. Going online just before dawn, I heard the BBC's World Service announcing that Robert Mugabe had died, after nearly four decades of rule and misrule in Zimbabwe. I went downstairs and fixed myself a light breakfast, joining two other early risers. They were Bob, the retired financier, and Mark, another money-man but younger and still working the property mortgage markets. Both knew of my long involvement with Africa, and I knew of their shared taste for keeping up with the news, domestic and foreign.

'You see Mugabe's dead?' was the first remark, from Bob.

'Yes. Can't say I'm heart-broken,' I answered, in tune with the inevitable recitation I'd just heard the BBC provide of Mugabe's tyrannical history. I wasn't really awake enough to fully acknowledge my own truth, that I harboured in reality a mass of mixed feelings about the dead dictator.

'Did you know him?' asked Mark.

'A bit. From a long time ago. Hard man to know. And I saw less and less of him as he got entrenched as the boss man.'

It came to me that I'd first ever registered the name of Mugabe almost fifty years previously, as a fighter against white supremacist rule who'd been thrown in prison. That was more than a decade before he rose to power. As I mused now on the BBC's unremitting indictment of his despotism, I acknowledged to myself that I had once admired him. I was impressed by his self-propelled rise from rural poverty in the country's South, his sharp intellect and his political skills in confronting racist domination.

The kitchen filled with the bustle of others much less concerned with international news. The group's plan was to go out for a hearty American diner breakfast in the nearby town, and then head off on a trail that presented a bigger challenge than the day before. I wasn't as enthusiastic as the cognoscenti among us to hear that this excursion offered substantial 'elevation-gain'. Such hikers' jargon meant to me simply that we'd be walking, or clambering, uphill most of the way. I opted to stay at basecamp. Good spiritedly they all took their leave for the breakfast and the hike, and I was left with my thoughts of Southern Africa.

Across our host's back deck I could make out Sopris Mountain a tad indistinctly through the rising morning mist. If only because of my introspective mood, it seemed to mimic the tropical heat-haze that once shimmered my view of Zimbabwe's dark Vumba and Nyanga mountains. Those two ranges had formed a lowering backdrop to the long guerrilla war of liberation that I reported on.

I remembered Peter Niesewand, who had been my first guide in that reporting. He was only four years older than me but seemed a towering journalistic powerhouse. Rangy and agile, with wayward fair hair and a ready, winning smile, his easy-going appearance belied a determination and industriousness that I found daunting. I met him in 1972 on my first assignment to white minority-ruled Rhodesia (as it still was) and we began a friendship that ended up being all too short. It started over drinks in the Quill Club, a journalists' hang-out tucked away within the Ambassador Hotel in Salisbury, the capital city. The first person Peter introduced me to was one of the country's very few black lawyers, Edison Sithole. When I arrived at the club they were laughing together, wryly and maybe a little forcedly, about both of them being clumsily surveilled by the regime's security police. I never met Sithole again. Not long after this he disappeared, his car abandoned in an area of military operations. He was rumoured to have been abducted by agents of the regime, but the truth has never been established.

Like most white Rhodesian males, Peter had been conscripted into military service when eighteen years old, and he'd maintained many of his contacts within the army's ranks. This gave him a seemingly endless fund of insider information about the guerrilla war being waged against that army. He was unflinching and thorough as he gathered and stored his barroom overhearings and casual confidences. These he would process into carefully double-checked, compellingly told stories that he'd dispatch to his many global media clients. That intentness in feeding off his sources went along with an unbending absolutism about never revealing who the sources were.

For all his sociability he seemed to me a solitary figure; in his world of white privilege, he stood out as the only reporter who could to any degree unnerve its arrogant rulers. The local press corps generally seemed cowed by the government, but Peter just kept on asking awkward questions. These ranged from inquiries about secret army operations to one pointed occasion during a live TV panel-interview when he insistently questioned the regime's prime minister about whether some expensive remodelling of bedrooms at the PM's official residence was really justified on grounds of national security, as the leader had tried to claim. Peter later told me, with a disingenuousness I found hard to believe: 'I was surprised to learn the prime minister actually disliked me intensely.'

A visiting correspondent from *Time* magazine described Peter as 'a protean freelancer'. He ran his own one-person bureau that served the BBC, Reuters, the *Guardian* newspaper, United Press International, Agence France Press and Australia's ABC network. His small, untidy office overflowed with expanding concertina-folders, mountains of newspapers and unsteady wooden file-cabinets. I learned from him how to operate his vintage but reliable Teletype machines for sending dispatches, with yard upon yard of hole-punched paper tape spurting from each machine in narrow ribbons. On mastering the keyboard I helped him one night, feeling great collaborative glee in the game, to double or even triple his output as we delivered a running scoop almost simultaneously to both London and Paris, plus an extra version of the same story to Sydney.

Unlike some resident journalists in the world's hotspots, Peter was generous in giving aid to incoming reporters like me, who were often lightly slandered as 'parachutists'. The term was expressive of the resentment we could often provoke among the local press gang. This was understandable, given our sometimes blithe ignorance of the terrain into which we dropped. Part of our job description was of course to be a quick study. I had arrived from working on a story about neighbouring Mozambique's racial repression, under the Portuguese colonists who were still in power, and I was eager to find evidence of cross-border military collusion with the Rhodesians. Peter had of course already been digging into those transnational connections, and the two of us worked together productively for a couple of weeks. It was a cheerful give-and-take process, made exciting by the knowledge we were dealing in material that the authorities absolutely did not want us to have. He passed on to me his latest gleanings about new army manoeuvres getting closer to, and possibly deep into Mozambique. I in turn told him about the Portuguese defences I'd seen put in place (with South African assistance, I could report) around a massive development project which was then being built on the Mozambican side of the border. The project was intended, in part, to provide hydro-electricity to Rhodesia, via a high-voltage power-line that would be 150 miles long; a tempting target for two countries' insurgent liberation armies.

Together one afternoon we drank some locally distilled mockery of Scotch whisky with a middle-ranking white army officer. The obnoxious but powerful homemade product was a response to Rhodesia being economically isolated, struggling under severe international sanctions. Peter knew the officer well and they had agreed he'd wear civvies for his meeting with us. We had some cover for the clandestine conversation, as the out-of-the-way bar steadily filled with boisterous tobacco-farmers newly in town for an auction, and we pumped our informant for details of upcoming troop movements in the border country.

So it was eventually with a well-researched story about triangular white racist collaboration, implicating South Africa as well as Rhodesia and Portugal, that I finally flew home to London and told it all on television. And meanwhile, on-site, Peter continued to chronicle determinedly the racists' obstinate entrenchment against the surging forces of change and freedom.

I was happy about my Zimbabwean collaboration with Peter, and along with it the beginnings of our friendship. But it was to be my last African assignment for a while. Early the following year, 1973, soon after I'd turned twenty-four, I was taken off the road by my TV bosses. They had what they regarded as a promotion for me.

I had to quit international coverage, and instead take up the post of a metropolitan London and national correspondent. This brought a whole new dimension to my work, in that I was now to be regularly on camera in the nation's capital. During my few years of global journalism, I had functioned as what American networks call an 'associate producer' and I found it hard making the transition from always being behind the camera. I was disdainful of, maybe scared of, and certainly deeply resistant to, acquiring the performance skills required in my new on-screen role. But with constantly repeated practice, since I was on a daily evening broadcast, I got better at it, and eventually became reasonably competent, though with an undercurrent of nervous hesitancy that has never totally left me.

Meanwhile in Rhodesia, Peter's self-assured work was now getting him into real trouble. State authorities arrested and imprisoned him for breaking their so-called Official Secrets Act, causing damage to their efforts at defeating the country's black liberation movement. He was sentenced to two years' hard labour for 'the communication of information likely to be of value to an enemy'. At the heart of the case against him, heard in a secret trial, was his sweeping exposure of how Rhodesian troops were operating in Mozambique in collaboration with the Portuguese war-effort. Peter had greatly expanded the storyline that he and I worked on together the previous year.

I had met Peter's wife, Nonie, only briefly while I was in Salisbury. I would now get to know her more fully, at first purely by transcontinental phone. With Peter's imprisonment she leaped into vigorous action. She had at home their son, Oliver, who was under a year old, and she was now heavily pregnant with their second child, but all the same she repeatedly drove 350 miles to see Peter. He was being held in solitary confinement, and she was permitted only a one-hour visitation. She would then connect with journalists throughout the world in a determined mission to maintain global attention on her husband's plight. One of the journalists she contacted, naturally enough, was me; I would televise our phone conversations along with pictures of Peter. This was my small but very willing contribution to a global 'Free Peter Niesewand!' campaign.

As weeks went on, though, I came to be troubled by the single-minded focus of the campaign. I didn't want to be disloyal to Peter, but my earlier work on the ground made me all too aware that the white regime had also imprisoned thousands of black activists. They were being kept, often for years, in conditions worse than Peter's confinement, many in cells with tin roofs located out in the scorching savannah, and almost never receiving family visits. Among the captives was Robert Mugabe, then a political organiser hardly known at all internationally. I was aware of him, but at that point we had not met; he'd been beyond all contact since his arrest in 1964, eight years before my first arrival in-country.

In London I'd met and befriended Mugabe's wife, Sally Hayfron Mugabe. She was living in necessary exile following his arrest. She was originally from Ghana and had married Robert in 1961. They'd met as fellow college teachers in her home country, which was already independent from British colonial control. She told me Robert had been impressed by the self-confidence of Ghanaian citizens like her, after just a few years of self-rule. I'd come across Sally almost by accident because, although a high-credentialed teacher in Ghana's education system, she was having to earn her living in London by working as a secretary—at the Africa Centre, in the capital's Covent Garden district. Set up as a cultural institution, it served as a meeting place for politically active pan-African exiles. It also possessed an excellent library where I'd go to maintain my familiarity with the continent, sorely missing my once-frequent trips there.

Sally was a very subdued presence in the Center. Our mutual friends, both Zimbabwean and Ghanaian, told me she was vivacious by nature but had become deeply depressed. The Mugabes' only child, a son called Nhamodzenyika, had died of malaria at three years old, and the Rhodesian regime refused to allow Robert out of prison to attend his burial. Sally found herself, the friends said, desperately lonely in London. She also felt harassed by British authorities. They threatened to deport her because of some visa irregularities. This provoked Robert to write from his prison cell some angry but incisively phrased letters appealing to the British prime minister on her behalf. Robert's efforts, along with British supporters' help, eventually won the argument and she got to stay; but his bitterness against Britain never faded, and her depression was never entirely abated while living there. As she and I talked in her Covent Garden office, I told her I was eager to amass information about her husband and his fellow-inmates; she brightened a little and grew resolved to help me. I wanted to highlight the imprisoned liberation fighters in one of my broadcasts.

As I worked on the idea, it was a delicate phone call that I had to make to Nonie, asking if she'd agree to broadening the story to raise awareness of all the black prisoners. Peter's release understandably remained Nonie's prime and foremost objective, but she agreed to go along with my plan, especially once she knew I'd by then put together a list of several hundred other prisoners; not an exhaustive accounting, we both recognised, but sizable. And when we came to record our interview for broadcast, she was bold and outspoken about how fully she recognised that the other, black, prisoners' conditions far exceeded her husband's in authoritarian brutality.

With Sally's help I pulled together some pictures as well as more biographical details for the men being held. Images were findable for only a handful, but these few did include Mugabe; Sally lent me their wedding photos. I earnestly wanted her to do an interview with me. I envisioned for my broadcast a journalistically neat balance: two prisoners' wives appealing for their husbands' freedom, one white, one black. But it proved impossible. Sally worked hard to provide me with all the information she could uncover, but she resolutely refused, even shuddering in distress while we talked about it, to speak on the record herself. She couldn't bring herself to talk about her husband and her life without him. 'I just cannot,' she said. 'It is too much.'

In the end we compiled a broadcast which firmly underlined the Niesewand case once more, but moved on to intertwine it with the previously untold story (at least in Britain) of the countless others with black skins. And here the televisual talents of my colleagues came through to help me. In place of my plan for a personalising, individual and emotional balance—one husbandless wife matched by another—our sharp programme-director suggested we simply make a storytelling virtue of the inherent imbalance. 'Let's just emphasise,' said the director, 'the sheer contrast in numbers: one white man, countless black men.'

There then followed the laborious, painstaking process that was necessary in those pre-digital days. Our graphic artists imprinted my list of all the names we'd been able to identify onto an extraordinarily long roll of jet-black 100-pound cardstock paper, I'd say about thirty-five-feet long. In the end there were 544 names, each in stark white-on-black capital lettering, plus a one-sentence description of each man. The whole list was unrolled on camera as the final shot of our broadcast, without any narration or music or sound-effects, all the names moving upward over the TV screen at a slow reader's pace. It lasted a full three-and-a-half minutes, an unheard-of expanse of dead silence to appear on commercial television, with only unrelieved monochrome wording to look at.

It had its impact. Newspapers reported on the unaccustomed and soundless sight that had appeared on viewers' screens. They reported, too, the many puzzled phone calls to our broadcast centre complaining about a serious technical problem, the sudden, inexplicable audio dropout. And within a week, fuller stories began appearing in British papers and magazines devoting attention to the many black Zimbabwean prisoners being held in addition to Peter.

Diplomatic pressure built up globally, not least from the Nixon Administration in Washington, a tad surprisingly but certainly welcome. The pressure was brought to bear upon the white-minority governments of South Africa and colonial Portugal, who in turn leaned on the Rhodesian leadership, a small clique that was always dependent on support from those bigger racist regimes. After seventy-three days in solitary confinement, Peter was released. But—and I needn't have been surprised, though I naïvely felt angry and disappointed—the fate of not a single one of the black prisoners, including Robert Mugabe, was in any way altered.

Pandemonium broke out in London about Peter, especially among the tabloid press. And amid happy tears of relief, Nonie had told me that he was being shipped out of Rhodesia via one of the few airlines (because of international sanctions) that still operated at Salisbury airport. This was Portugal's national line, TAP. The plan was for him to switch planes at Portugal's capital, Lisbon, and then go on to London. Nonie would follow separately along with Oliver, in the hope they could set up a whole new British home for the three of them, plus the imminently arriving baby.

I thoughtlessly assumed I was the only one to know about Peter's itinerary, and I hurriedly booked a flight to Lisbon with a film crew and producer to catch him there. I'd be first, way ahead of my professional competitors, I imagined. But inevitably we turned out to be among a horde of over forty London-based 'hacks' who flew to Lisbon, all similarly intent on being first.

Into the Lisbon terminal walked Peter, with a burly attendant on each side of him; I was told later they were British agents who came aboard at a West African stopover. He looked drained, sallow and decidedly bemused by the welcome, or assault, that greeted him as he blinked in the crews' lights. He gazed vaguely around him and strained to hear what was being yelled in his direction by contending, overlapping questioners.

My producer, a relentless colleague named Lyn Gambles, could see I was intimidated by my fiercer rivals. Two sharp elbows are needed to be an effective onscreen presence, especially amid the competition of a press conference, if that's what this was. But my arms seemed paralysed by the clamorous uproar. 'Get out front,' Lyn hissed into my ear. 'We'll keep rolling film and cover you—just get forward. Peter knows you, for God's sake!'

I'm not sure that I forced myself through. It felt more like Lyn was shoving me all the way to the front. When I called out 'Peter!' it seemed like he couldn't quite hear me. He was scanning uncertainly from side to side. But when his face did meet mine, those blinking eyes abruptly widened. I couldn't form a question. It was far from a yell and yet I somehow made myself heard with just a simple declaration: 'Nonie says she'll be joining you soon.' The blinking went faster and there was a sudden moistness to his eyes; then a smile lightly twitching his mouth. A strange silence settled briefly on the jam-packed transit lounge. In that quiet gap before the tumult of voices surged again, I lamely asked, 'How are you, Peter?'

'Mmm ... I'm okay,' he said. 'I think.' Another pause. 'It's good to see you.'

The Niesewands settled in a London neighbourhood not far from mine, and for a few years we would get together quite often. Peter rapidly found his professional feet in the UK and by the mid-1970s was a globe-trotting correspondent for the *Guardian* newspaper. He had also developed a new talent for writing mystery and espionage novels. Once during the unusually hot British summer of 1976 (a rare case of country-wide drought) he had to miss coming to Sunday lunch at my house because he had once again been sent overseas at short notice. I heard a scuffling noise at my front door, then a couple of thuds either side of a strangely abrupt and short ring of the doorbell. On opening up I found Oliver, now four years old and barely over three feet tall, jumping to stab at my bell-button. He pointed down the street with one hand, wiped a trickle of sweat from his reddened cheek with the other and gasped: 'The car is boiling!'

Nonie had been driving him and his three-year-old brother, James, the few miles from their home but she'd jarred to a sudden halt about 800 feet short of my house. Her radiator had overheated and the engine completely seized. Oliver had leaped out and run to my door for help. His succinct message galvanised me. I filled a garden watering can and carried it along the street, with Oliver stomping alongside in a supervisory fashion, to where Nonie had opened the hood. Together the two grown-ups, neither of us adept mechanics, were at least able to top up the radiator. Leaving the vehicle to cool down, we all went inside and ate lunch, mainly a salad I'd thrown together. I was catering alone in the absence of my girlfriend, Jane. She was in the hospital for one of her more minor surgeries, which would later get more serious.

Oliver's resourceful initiative had impressed me and I was touched by his purposeful action. A fellow feeling rose in me; for a young boy without a father (though in his case just temporarily, but repeatedly) who jumped into responsibility when his mother needed him. At lunch and as we talked through the long, warm afternoon, he was quiet and reserved, quite different from his noisy arrival; he observed but did not engage. It seemed like he'd been impelled to be outgoing only by the sudden family emergency. At twenty-eight, I still had the clumsiness of a childless adult male unused to chatting with preschoolers, and I made the mistake of trying to draw him out a little. I asked, 'Are you missing your Dad?' He didn't answer; just looked down and withdrew into deeper silence.

Peter was distinguishing himself in his global coverage. It included post-revolutionary Portugal, Lebanon's civil war and the Soviet invasion of Afghanistan. He was twice named the UK's International Journalist of the Year, the awards coming three years apart. Nonie, too, entered British journalism, focusing her writing on architecture and design, both great passions of hers. Like many busy Londoners, we all, the adults at least, would constantly say we never saw enough of each other. The four Niesewands eventually moved to India when Peter was appointed the Guardian's Asia correspondent. And then, in one of those blows that seemed to us in our thirties to be savagely incomprehensible, Peter suddenly died of a heart attack, two years short of turning forty. A poleaxed Nonie emerged gradually from bereavement to create a solo life for herself, finding what solace she could in her writing. Oliver and James, by then in their mid-teens, were jolted into premature adulthood, becoming independent and assertive young men after being permanently robbed of their father. To my great regret, I saw less and less of all three of them.

Now and then, though, I saw that other Zimbabwean friend in London, Sally Mugabe. That is, until she left Britain and went home when her husband's sentence eventually ended after ten years' imprisonment. Later, when I resumed making visits to Zimbabwe, she was always a must-see, and also a friendly and willing conduit towards her increasingly powerful husband. She was cheerful once more, more cheerful than I'd ever seen her, and already becoming well-known and popular in her own right. She would eventually be called Amai, the much-loved Mother of the Nation. When we met it was mostly for tea in the afternoon, warm and reflective times.

Robert was meanwhile advancing skilfully to the fore of the liberation movement, ascending indeed towards the topmost leadership in ZANU, the Zimbabwe African National Union. I observed him mostly from afar, only occasionally gaining somewhat closer access, and then purely thanks to his wife. These had to be, at his insistence, absolutely off-the-record meetings. His temperament seemed intense, as much as his size was compact, just five-feet-seven-inches tall, with a proportionate, lean physique. He displayed a lawyerly mind; two of the four college degrees he achieved in prison via correspondence courses were in law. To his background of a Jesuit mission education, he had added some self-taught grounding in Marxist theory. It was impressive to see him sometimes at work with colleagues, patiently taking in the views of activists and advisers, synthesizing them seamlessly and voicing them back to the team in a way that seemed to satisfy everyone about having been heard. Occasionally he would firmly quash sharp disagreements among them, using reason not just authority.

He did not remain that agreeable. I saw him again back in London for the 1980 Lancaster House Conference which negotiated an end to his and his allies' liberation war. The negotiations finally settled on full legal independence for a Zimbabwe in which he would become prime minister, and eventually president almost for life. During the conference he threw a furious fit, angrier than suited a realistically minded politician, I thought, and maybe cranked up for theatrical effect. He had discovered that the British intelligence service was bugging his and other Africans' hotel rooms to learn details of their bargaining positions and strategies.

A couple of years after he became prime minister, by which time I was running my TV network's coverage of religion, I produced and broadcast a documentary about him. It examined the arguably paradoxical make-up of his politics: his combining of Catholic education and beliefs along with an avowed and deepening commitment to Marxism. He gave us a cursory and barely engaged interview. In fact my professional cool got severely rattled as he dismissively stonewalled us, flatly denying there could be any tension between those two very different world-views. It was left to others I interviewed, including Catholic teachers from his old school, to point out contradictions in his mindset.

He went on to tilt more and more towards the communists' 'dictatorship of the proletariat' concept, with his emphasis settling more firmly on the 'dictator' part. He certainly had no real wish to place the people in charge of anything—that was his role. He had a particular fondness for North Korea and its then leader, Kim Il-Sung. He commissioned North Korean architects to design what he named Heroes' Acre, a grandiose monument and burial area to commemorate fighters from the liberation war. He increasingly claimed sole leadership in that wartime effort, retrospectively and insupportably. He created a new brigade of the Zimbabwean Army, specially trained by the North Korean military, and then employed them to carry out a series of vicious massacres. These formed part of his bloodily successful effort to stamp out political rivals, in effect eliminating regional and ethnic opposition in the country's Western provinces.

The last time I saw Sally was at the Presidential Residence. She had become a modest and gracious occupant of the edifice to which Robert gave the name, 'The Blue Roof', his parody in colour, I figured, of America's White House, with his building bring roofed in blue Chinese tiling. Her welcoming demeanour contrasted sharply with her husband, who was becoming ever more high-handed, irascible and petulant. As I entered their lavish stateroom, he brushed past me in leaving. He grudgingly stopped and turned to me only when his wife reminded him who I was. His one word 'Hello' was all the welcome I got.

An aproned maid brought in a tray, and I was surprised when she poured the tea. Normally Sally would do that herself. She told me she'd been diagnosed with degenerative kidney disease. As we sat together her voice gradually weakened and we talked only in gentle banalities. It was a frail hand that I finally took to say farewell, and I left through their tall front gates in a state of misty sorrow.

Sally's health continued to worsen, and Robert fathered two children with his secretary, Grace Ntombizodwa. Grace became known, in whispers at least, as 'disGrace' and she went on to distinguish herself with some phenomenally expensive shopaholism in foreign capitals, plus a surprising handiness with her fists against underlings. This reached the point that a

Blue Roof domestic worker had to file charges against Grace for smashing her in the face with a shoe, giving her a bloodied, broken nose. All this behaviour developed once Robert had married Grace, after Sally finally died and was buried in Heroes' Acre.

Robert's excesses only increased with time, as he practised stupefying mismanagement of the country's economy, brutally suppressed all dissidents and surrounded himself with sycophants, allowing corruption and incompetence to run riot. His paranoid autocracy only ended when he was finally deposed by army officers and some of his own top cabinet members, after thirty long years in office. He then died two years later ... and I heard the news in the Colorado Rockies. I ended up feeling a grim awe at the making of this ninety-five year-old monster, so utterly changed from the adroit campaigner I had known, though never very well, in his forties.

Chapter 23
Diocese

The letter came emblazoned with an imposing coat-of-arms, redolent of authority stretching back centuries. The graphic, though in a modern, streamlined style, drew heavily on medieval roots: visual devices suggestive of a cross and of a bishop's crook to evoke shepherding a flock. The inter-twined emblems were set on a background of papal yellow-gold conveying the broad supremacy of Rome.

In contrast, the bold typed letterhead seemed purely secular: SAFEGUARDING COMMISSION. This was twenty-first century vocabulary of the type used in the social-work and law-enforcement fields. A careful scan of some fine print in the front page's footer was needed to confirm that it originated from an ecclesiastical entity: a Roman Catholic diocese.

On my behalf the global support organisation Coping International (Children of Priests) had officially referred to the diocese in my mother's story and formally asked for the man who may have been my father to be identified. Coping's referral or complaint had been signed by Vincent Doyle both as director of the referring institution (Coping itself) and as a practising psychotherapist who had the legal duty in both Britain and Ireland's jurisdictions to report any possible child abuse he became aware of, even if it had occurred long ago.

One Sunday in January, 1948, Hilda Brown (then aged fifteen) accompanied a high-school friend to observe a Catholic mass conducted on the premises of the local GP doctor, who was Catholic. There was no Catholic parish church in her village. There she met the priest conducting the mass, whom she sensed to be 'a young priest, not old'. After the service he offered to walk her home and in a neighbour's garden allegedly raped her. She knew his name as only 'Father Francis,' perceived him to be Scottish, and learned that he came from a city parish, one of several priests assigned in turn to conduct the village mass.

The complaint followed Coping's usual format in picking out the most salient pieces of information that 'may help identify this priest'. They were numbered:

1. Priest's name: 'Father Francis'.
2. Hilda perceived him to be Scottish.
3. Hilda perceived him to be 'a young priest'.
4. Hilda believed 'Father Francis' came from a nearby city parish.
5. It is believed by the family that the priest was 'sent away' following the birth of Hilda's child.
6. Hilda gave birth to David in October, 1948.

Vincent ended with a demand which, as Coping's leader, he was all too accustomed to addressing to dioceses:

> I am asking you to examine the diocesan archives to seek out a priest who possibly matches this priest as described above. Following this, we can discuss examining DNA matches via a genealogist.

Now the diocese's official answer had come. It was sent formally to Coping, but of course the group immediately forwarded it to me, initially by email, with a hard copy following soon after.

In one detail at least, the answer was unexpectedly forthcoming, and the detail was compelling. The diocese covers a thousand square miles of England, with its northern limit touching the Scottish border, and I'd already discovered that at the time of my conception it had employed nearly 250 priests. In response to my mother's recollection of the priest's name being 'Father Francis', the diocese gave this specific piece of information:

> Father Francis Leo Caron was a priest during the 1940s. His date of birth is recorded as 23 August, 1917. He died on 26 January, 1995.

(For anonymity's sake, I am using a somewhat altered version of his surname, which the diocese gave exactly. My reasons for the anonymising will become clear.)

When I first glimpsed the name, my sudden reaction sounded like a young boy long stifled and denied the truth. I spluttered, 'Gotcha!' The name's three parts almost glowed on the page, and detonated in me a blast of feverish speculation. The last name suggested a French origin, which gave me pause in light of my mother's recollection that the man had been Scottish. My thoughts ran in wayward directions. I tried picturing what Gallic facial features he might have had and I wondered about my own. Do I look at all French? I don't think so.

Rushing to mind came everything I'd learned about the overlaps, historical, cultural and linguistic, that connect the Gallic French and the Gaelic Scots. Every Scottish schoolkid was taught, like me, that The Auld Alliance between our two countries dates all the way back to the thirteenth century. It cemented a common cause to oppose the English. Our tragic heroine, Mary Queen of Scots, grew up in France and married the French king's young son. In the fifteenth century, Scottish and French people had the right (highly unusual in mediaeval Europe) to be regarded as citizens of either country. Our long cultural exchange left many traces in our everyday vocabulary. The Scottish word 'scullery', for a kind of side-kitchen, comes from the Old French escueillier. The ubiquitous Scots name, Jock, echoes the French Jacques. Our generic term for something attractive or nice, 'bonnie', is clearly connected to the French bon or bonne. And in even my grandmother's repeated order to us as children, 'dinna fash yer'sel' ('don't get yourself worked up') we can hear the French word fâché, meaning angered.

We the Scots—I can get quite carried away in my Gaelicness —developed a distinctive legal system, quite separate from the English, with many similarities to the French still evident today. The Scottish version of a district attorney is called a Procurator, in adaptation of the French term Procureur. Courtroom lawyers in general are called advocates, like the French avocat. And, perhaps very relevantly to my own ongoing investigation, Scottish criminal law possesses a feature that's unique. When a case comes to trial in Scotland, an accused person who is not convicted will still face, unlike in other jurisdictions, one of two alternative verdicts. The accused might be found straight-forwardly 'Not Guilty', as elsewhere, or they might be given a special Scottish verdict: 'Not Proven'. It's an interesting subtlety; it perhaps reflects more fully the complex realities of human affairs than does the purely binary choice, just guilty or innocent, that prevails in other countries.

My mental scurrying did not diminish the blunt shock effect of seeing the priest's name on paper. Whatever national antecedents he may have had, Scottish, French, or even English or something else entirely, I felt a wince or a jolt every time I re-read those words: *Father Francis Leo Caron*. I was perturbed that while earlier investigations on my behalf a decade previously, by the American Father Jack and my British clerical and legal contacts, had never discovered this man, his name was now being readily handed over by the authorities, and with such evident ease. The letter also noted that whatever his full name may actually have been, it was officially the case that he was 'known as Father Leo'. His middle name had been given promin-ence over his first name, Francis, which had of course been our starting point for the inquiry. They were offering us a reason why searching for 'Francis' would not have found him. Leo may have been a cover, however thin, to obscure his identity deliberately as a Francis. The Francis, I couldn't help but think. So here, almost certainly, was finally the man we were looking for.

Then came some separate evidence to support the idea of him as the culpable individual. Working independently, Coping's team of researchers quickly identified the specific parish this 'Father Leo' had worked in. They also discovered that he had left that parish, which was in the city close to my home village, very soon after the time of my birth. It was not immediately clear to which other position, or in what new parish he might have been moved, but the timing strongly suggested to me and to the Coping team that he knew about my mother's pregnancy and my birth, and that his superiors did too. It wasn't definite proof, of course, and it was all purely circumstantial but I found it highly suggestive.

My ingrained journalistic caution began to assert itself. The letter did refer a little vaguely to 'other priests' who could also have been visiting my home village at the time, but it seemed to me striking that the diocese itself had clearly—and in an openly transmitted document—decided to single out this one specific individual. As I thought about it more, it had the feel of an almost casual offering of information.

What if it wasn't him? demanded my inner fact-checker. Wasn't it irresponsible, to put it mildly, of the diocese to be naming him? What about his own family—his officially acknowledged family, that is, who might still bear the same last name? How would they like his identity being bandied about as an accused rapist? I felt uneasy about hounding a dead man who still wasn't totally, incontrovertibly confirmed as my father, and still might not be.

As a step towards more conclusive confirmation, Coping also asked the Diocese for help in searching for what genetic connections might exist between Francis Leo and myself, if any. It was at this point that the diocese stopped being helpful.

In previous investigations on behalf of possible priests' offspring, Coping had successfully gained the cooperation of dioceses in the UK and overseas. Those dioceses had helpfully identified living relatives of likely priests so that DNA comparisons could be made with the supposed offspring. No such help was forthcoming from this diocese. Its wording struck me as curt. 'The Diocese is not prepared to consider providing assistance,' it said.

Vincent told me he found this attitude 'weird'. I was a lot less temperate: bordering on furious, more like it. I told Vincent I wanted to demand the details of Father Francis Leo's family, so I could commission my own DNA comparison tests. I'd been amassing a broad sense of how DNA-based genealogical networks function, the likes of Ancestry.com, MyHeritage.com and others, the way they take and analyse DNA samples from their enrolled members, adding them to databases that were already made up of tens of millions of individuals. The extraordinary volume of such DNA resources had proved useful to many people seeking knowledge of their parents. They included of course some of the many priests' children that Coping had acted for. Quite separately, facing different issues, adopted children in search of their biological parents would also turn, often successfully, to these online networks.

I could recall some startling instances where those same databases had helped in criminal investigations as well. There was the dramatic cold case in which Oregon police had finally identified a serial killer with the help of the cross-referencing online service named GEDmatch.com. The crimes dated back forty years, but they were nonetheless solved because relatives of the killer had recently, in all innocence, uploaded their DNA details in search of their ancestry. All the police had to do was pay the Gedmatch membership fee and upload the DNA sample they were hoping to match, which had come from traces of the attacker that were left behind on his victim's bodies. The detectives were then able to find a match with the family's DNA, and consequently trace the killer himself. It was grim stuff but it gave me an encouraging vision of how I might be able to check if my DNA matched any that had been uploaded by relatives of my possible father. The easiest thing would be for the diocese to reveal any relatives they knew about, and I could then ask to make a direct comparison of my DNA with theirs.

The Church authority's resistance to cooperating with us stirred in me some lust for combat. Or, at the least, a strong desire for hostile cross-examination. In my mind's interrogation-room, I was looming over the cowering cleric in charge, his Lordship the Most Reverend Bishop, giving full vent to my anger:

> What's so different about you? Other dioceses have provided the names. You've given up the priest's name. Why don't you just identify his family as well? What is it you have against me?

I was really taking it personally that I couldn't get what other dioceses had offered Coping.

The angry fantasy faded and then, thinking more strategically, I looked for a feasible way to shift the diocese's resistance. How could I build up pressure and induce them to name the priest's relatives? My ideas ran—as I expect they would for many a journalist—to immediately phoning the regional newspaper that served the diocese's area. I could spin a story to the newsdesk about the search for my origins and complain about the Church authorities being 'not prepared to consider' helping me. I could cite the buzzwords of our trade—cover-up, obstruction, smokescreen and the like. The local reporters, once primed, would easily come up with more scandal-raising phrases of their own to make strong headlines. A prominent splash of the story could cause quite a stir in the region, embarrass the diocese and thus bring about an official change of heart—or so I thought.

At Coping, Vincent counselled me otherwise. 'They're being tactical,' he said, 'and it's not surprising that since they know they're supposed to be transparent these days, they're giving some info, withholding other facts and generally obfuscating as much as they can.' He suggested an alternative approach. 'You know, it's amazing how much genealogical information there is out there nowadays in the public domain. We don't necessarily need the diocese to help with the family connections.'

He advised that I simply trust Coping's own researchers to work on my case further, seeking out possible relatives for Father Francis Leo. 'It's better to gather more intel ourselves, before engaging in battle. And then we may not even have to fight with them at all, given what we learn ourselves.' This gathering of 'intel', Vincent assured me, wouldn't take that long.

So I agreed that we'd courteously thank the diocese for their information so far, express regret that they wouldn't help us further, but say we'd now pursue our own inquiries and maybe talk with them again at some future point. This became our new strategy. Perhaps I was reaching for a bland and clichéd thought to calm me down but I did remind myself that I had lived a good many decades knowing absolutely nothing about my father. I could probably wait a little longer for the last few details—if that's what they were—to be filled in.

It felt good, relaxingly so in fact, to be doing 'nothing hasty, nothing combative', as Vincent described it, in the calm voice of a campaigning veteran with experience of getting the Church to change its ways.

I didn't completely relax. I hitched my reporting skills to the genealogical expertise assembled by Coping. Chief among the experts was Linda Lawless, a professional genealogist in South Australia who herself had learned, though only after her mother had died, that her father had been a priest. To neither's surprise, we readily formed a bond, though there was some difference in our ostensibly similar experiences. She had been born the outcome of an apparently loving relationship, though short. And unlike me, she'd enjoyed good relations with her stepfather, who moved into a parenting role when she was too young to remember her previous upbringing.

With Linda as the prime mover, and myself the willing observer-learner, we began building a profile of Father Francis Leo. Scrutinising whatever family trees were available online, as well as official public records, we were able to begin at the end, so to speak. Thanks to a published death notice, we identified where Father Francis Leo had died in 1995. It turned out to be Blackpool, Lancashire, a famously downscale resort-town on England's northwest coast: rather a boisterous, even raucous place for a clergyman to retire, I thought. It also lay within that same diocese that Francis Leo belonged to back in 1948. Once he had left my home area those few months after I was born, it seemed that he hadn't travelled very far.

We launched a search for his priest's 'Memorandum'—the clerical equivalent of a résumé or C.V.—which could be found via other Church sources besides the uncooperative diocese and which would show just where else he had held positions. If he was indeed a child-rapist, all available evidence about sexual abuse told us that he probably didn't abuse merely once. Other parishes may have become fresh fields of opportunity for him, in a pattern that is known all too well by investigators. If (again if) he was my father, I might have half-siblings dotted across the ecclesiastical map—the result of other possibly underage girls falling victim to him.

I gave a sample of my DNA to Ancestry.com. I had long ago (just out of what seemed like idle interest at the time) given a sample to the smaller genealogical network, MyHeritage.com. I think someone had given me membership of the network as a birthday present. I now went on to send my spittle in a vial to still more and more sites until the combination of all the networks meant my genes could eventually be compared with an inordinate 60 million individuals worldwide. And at this point I needed to relax again.

I had to sit back patiently and wait for my DNA to be analysed, which could be several weeks or perhaps months. Only then could matches possibly start to emerge. It was a matter of watching out for people in the networks whose DNA had 'high scores' in matching mine. In technical terms, they have to would score well up the scale in centiMorgans, the unit of calibration for genetic linkage that was named after the early-twentieth-century geneticist, Thomas Hunt Morgan.

Though I may have sat back, my mind still couldn't take it easy. Independently of my giving samples to the database networks, Linda was busily plotting all of Father Francis Leo's findable family connections, her work being conducted within the private confines of a confidential website guarded by pass-word-only access. It was disquieting to see these specifics of his life being shown in clear graphic form and naming his forbears and his siblings. A sister and two brothers, evidently.

These details soon had me picturing a little family group for him, back in 1920s Northern England. That was where birth-certificate records had placed his origins—once again something at odds with my mother remembering him as a Scot, at least by his accent. This was a possible anomaly that should perhaps have raised our caution-level as researchers. But then, in the Debatable Land of the border-country where Francis Leo and my family were all living by the late 1940s, accents could be pretty fluid either side of the Scottish and English divide. As I grew up I did my own share of accent-switching, or code-switching, to suit my surroundings and I'd become pretty good at it by my early adulthood. I wondered if Francis Leo had practised the same skill before me in his twenties and thirties, adopting a Scottish dialect when he came to live near the border. Maybe, I speculated, I had even inherited my mimicry skills from him. I was yet again getting way ahead of myself, and of the provable facts.

On my laptop I checked in daily to Linda's webpages—and repeatedly had to bear in mind that what I was encountering were examples of hypothesising, as practised by specialists using their insider jargon; I was not seeing reality. It was disconcerting to observe the site's bold and direct graphics begin, purely for the notional, theoretical purposes of making comparisons, to place my mother and her family closely adjacent to Francis Leo's family. I could feel my head beginning to swim.

I am hallucinating, perhaps. But no: right here in front of me on this fifteen-inch screen, some new, diagrammatic graphics have taken shape. It's hard to remind myself that they are only notional, not real: a kind of visual theorising that the experts call a 'floating' family tree. Among the floating elements, I'm jarred to see a straight horizontal line appear between the box marked 'FRANCIS LEO' and the box marked 'HILDA'. Worse by turns now, that line between them sprouts another line drawn vertically downward from them. This new line ends with a box filled with the name 'DAVID'.

It's only a digital drawing, a sketch, I tell myself. Merely imaginary, theoretical. But nevertheless I'm trembling queasily in disbelief and denial. Now I was being confronted with a real-life person, I wanted to reject this man as my father, whatever the evidence so far might say.

Just as troubling, the algorithms of the family tree programme that Linda was using also generated language in obedience to a formula. This resulted in an Artificial Intelligence version of a sparse narrative: what the programme labelled, in its compressed webspeak, a 'LifeStory'. The wording was blunt and seemed disturbingly matter-of-fact, while not of course being wholly factual.

The computer-generated account explained that when Francis Leo was born in 1916, 'his father, Thomas, was thirty-nine and his mother, Catherine, was thirty. He had one son, with Hilda Brown. He died on January 26, 1995 in the county of Lancashire, England.'

'They may look and sound like it, but these are NOT facts,' I almost screamed at the screen, alone in my home-office. It was still a matter of conjecture. This one phrase in particular—'had one son, with Hilda Brown'—felt like salt in a wound and I yelled that this was definitely, utterly NOT a correct description of what had happened.

'Time to just breathe, David,' I told myself.

I was grateful, in those unsteady moments, that I could reach for the professional detachment instilled in me by journalism. I decided to step aside fully and leave the experts, with Linda in her leading role, to get on with their task—including all their plausible but unproven conjectures. It was a task that had to be pursued until all conjectures were proven or discounted.

Chapter 24
Troubles

We should have evacuated. I don't really understand why we didn't. A bomb-threat had been issued, and the bomb had been located. A group of reporters, myself along with older guys from the *Times* of London, the *Daily Mirror*, the *Daily Telegraph* and other papers, eight or ten of us in all, were gathered at a wide, floor-to-ceiling window, to watch the British Army bomb disposal squad go about its exacting work to defuse the device. Directly in our view through the window they started delicately examining some entangled-looking wires that sprouted from a cardboard box. The box sat in a parked car's trunk. Something about the car seemed French, a Citroën or a Renault, but it was hard to tell because its back was to us and its marque was out of sight. The team had lifted up the hatchback and dropped the tailgate. This gave them room to work, and also happened to give us a better view.

We were in the Belfast Europa Hotel's ground-floor pub, the *Whip and Saddle*. It was an undeniably urban bar, looking onto the city centre's Great Victoria Street, but we never questioned its rustic name or the glut of horse-riding and fox-hunting prints that paraded across its walls. As we watched and waited, we ordered glass tankards of Guinness, dark pint after pint.

The disposal team's methodical first task was to check for booby traps. A few of their highly skilled members had been killed by such so-called 'secondary' bombs. The squad all the same retained its collective nickname, 'Felix', taken from the lucky cartoon cat with nine lives or more. Their endeavours this day were a tense process: tense for the bomb-handlers, for sure; much less so for us.

Time was passing slowly with no clear outcome and an urge for mischief rippled in whispers between some of us. Needing a distraction we decided to switch our drinks order. We changed it to an intoxicant that looked deceptively similar. Instead of Guinness we surreptitiously ordered massive black servings of Irish Coffee in the same pint-sized glasses, topped with heavy cream mimicking Guinness's distinctively thick, white foam. The brew was strengthened with many extra shots of Bushmills whiskey (known by some as 'good Protestant spirit') to match— or more than match—the abnormal volume of coffee. Those who weren't in on the swap choked in surprise on their first swallow but were delighted anyway. Others appeared to not even realise they were drinking anything different.

We might have begun to feel some anxiety had it not been for the booze; an estimated twenty pounds of gelignite was being tinkered with, however expertly, mere yards away from us, with only a sheet of plate glass between us and it.

Someone came in with news, unconfirmed but sounding authentic, probably gained by eavesdropping on army- or police-radio traffic. The bomb's timer apparently included one of the many very basic clocks that bomb-makers stole from the automatic switches of neighbourhood streetlights. Such thefts would often send the lighting system askew, rendering a district dark at night and unnecessarily illuminated in daylight. What seemed like merely annoying vandalism in fact had a deadly purpose.

The Felix knew this particular mechanism well. Their challenge now was to isolate it from the bomb's detonator without setting off the whole pack of explosives. We stared intently, those of us with better vision at least, hoping to see how they'd neutralise the circuitry but it was hard to make out any revealing detail as we watched the deft, gloveless hands, some with wire-clippers, reaching into and out of the box, in slow, deliberate motion.

After two hours, maybe a little more, the Army team achieved victory. The impending blast was averted. We greeted this triumph of steely nerves among the soldiery with some slurry cheering among ourselves. But some of us (the most drunken, I'd guess, but obviously I can't be sure) let out disappointed moans of anti-climax. At my own point on the inebriation scale, I think I cheered.

Deep curiosity once overcame me when, aged around eight, I came across a cherished bottle of the Scottish liqueur Drambuie, distilled from a base of Scotch whisky spirit and scoring forty per cent alcohol by volume (or eighty proof). It was kept for tiny tipples by the abstemious adults in my family, and then only on Christmas Day. I found it in a cabinet and not at a childproof level; no climbing was needed. It had an appealing shape, long necked with a bulbously swelling lower part. I wanted to understand why bigger people should make such a special deal about it.

Other drinks, notably milk and orange juice, were virtually forced on me. Both came in one-third-of-a-pint glass bottles that were distributed daily, and free, by Britain's newly established welfare state. The drinks were a measure aimed especially at the poor, part of a national effort to combat juvenile ill-health. What was the difference, I'd quizzically complain to myself, between those liquids and that drink reserved, at Christmas, for grown-ups only?

On that day we all gathered in the front room of my grandmother's home, the so-called 'council house' for which she paid a small, subsidised rent to the local municipality. We had a man-sized fir tree dug up from the back yard. It lived there all year round but we brought it indoors for Christmas week, replanting it into a foot-deep tin box filled with dark soil. After New Year's Day it would go outdoors again, to grow another six or eight inches until next time. In its box it stood like a ceremonial totem over our opening of seasonal presents. String was carefully untied, never cut, and the newspaper pages used as wrapping were removed without tearing and folded for future re-use.

One gift recurred every year: a mandarin orange, one each for both young and old. But my attention was magnetised to the Drambuie and I stared, fixated, as the adults decanted minuscule measures of the strangely thick, slow-to-pour liquid into narrow, short glasses, drank it with solemnity and then reverently put the bottle aside, to stand in splendid isolation on my grandmother's sideboard until it was cleared away at day's end.

I could tell this was nothing like my milk and orange juice. I was being cheated. It wasn't that I disliked the kiddy beverages; they were okay, the milk undoubtedly, though the O.J. tasted a bit gooey on the tongue and was much improved when diluted with water. It was simply the sheer mystery of the exceptional Drambuie that overtook my young mind, a mystery that needed exploring.

The exploration took place out of season; it wasn't Christmas and I have a rough idea it might have been early Spring. After some time spent searching, my discovery was triumphant. I picked up the bottle and downed virtually the entire 24 fluid ounces. Almost instantly I passed out. At some point I came to, everything around me circling, going in and out of focus. My eyes felt like raw eggs slopping in a glass bowl.

I don't remember anything of what may have been said to me. I was aware of an aghast fluttering among the adults—as there should have been, I suppose, over an eight-year-old getting totally trashed. But there was no chastising. I don't recall a doctor being called, either, but I guess there must have been one. I was nursed in bed for two days, with cold compresses and a saline-drip in my arm for hydration, until the massive assault on my diminutive system finally subsided.

Much of my Northern Ireland time now feels unreal and unclear, but some of the scattered pieces that I do recollect can be sharply concrete. My assignments there began in the early 1970s when I was twenty-two and lasted on and off through the whole decade and beyond. Serious, often deadly events were unfolding around me but my sheer youth, with the ebullient company of my fellow-journalists carrying me along, enabled me to take it all in my stride. Or appear to.

It had been entirely novel territory when I arrived in 1971, though in many ways Belfast resembled a familiar British town. I could even feel at home. The city had a Woolworth's store in its main shopping street (ever since 1915) just as Manchester and many other mainland population centres did. It was an airplane ride across the Irish Sea but it was nevertheless, constitutionally as well as in ordinary, everyday ways, wholly part of the United Kingdom.

My initiation began with a jolt. On my first drive to the downtown area from Belfast's Aldegrove airport, I turned into a narrow roadway and realised I was now following a police vehicle. Here was the Royal Ulster Constabulary, travelling in an unmarked, grey Land Rover, armour-plated in military style. Over my steering wheel I was staring into gun-muzzles pointing out the back. I'd later know these weapons to be Sterling Mk 4 sub-machine-guns and the vehicle to be the Land Rover company's so-called Hotspur variant, specially developed for the RUC and built of ballistic steel. I gulped at the fearsome strangeness of it. After all, the mainland British police forces I'd so far known were entirely unarmed. But for all my shock at an unaccustomed kind of menace, by the time I got to the city centre, meeting up with my new crew of elders and betters, or at least more experienced observers, I was already shrugging it off as a commonplace.

Journalists frequently hunt in packs, even more so in crisis zones, so almost all of us were billeted in the Europa. Some called the hotel simply, and a little cutely, 'our rooms over the bar'. We crowded in mainly from London but also from foreign media organisations, especially when big newsbreaks were going on, most often a violent upsurge in the ongoing guerrilla war. The Europa was fairly newly built, influenced by the New Brutalism style of concrete and glass: a 'high-rise', in Belfast terms, in that it initially had all of five floors, later to be increased to a towering twelve. The city's mainly low-slung skyline had traditionally been interrupted only by gigantic cranes at the shipyard that had built and launched the Titanic. We herded together, all in that same hotel, partly because our close proximity was felt to be useful to people who might want to reach us with a story to tell or a tip to give. And anyway, in those days Belfast didn't offer much choice in hotels. I didn't mind. I rather welcomed the company of veteran professionals. They could certainly teach me a thing or two, though rarely if ever by direct instruction. This particular bunch was not the mentoring kind, not any of them. But that was okay; I had come to learn mainly by observation. And something else about our situation, not especially work-related, was reassuring to me. In one of my few and not especially deep moments of self-examination at the time, I realised I was getting to rather enjoy hotel living.

An almost perpetually tuxedo-clad manager named Harper Brown presided over the Europa. I still smoked in those days (part of my chameleon effort to blend in with the older, worldly crowd I now ran with) and I was startled and flattered to have Harper's crisply-trained staff always jump to light my cigarette the moment I put it to my mouth. The manager invented a ritual mark of distinction for his regular customers, more remarkable than any ordinary 'loyalty-points' programme from a hotel chain or airline. He awarded us special Europa neckties; the one I was given went missing in a later house-move and that ugly bit of apparel is still a memento I greatly regret losing. Its synthetic fibre had some coarseness to the touch and it came in what I remember as a dingy yellow-gold colour. Harper awarded you one if you survived a certain number of bombs planted at the hotel. All these years later I can't remember if the qualifying total was ten or twenty or maybe another figure entirely.

It was relatively rare that bombs actually exploded in the hotel. Without exception, I'm pretty sure, they were planted by the Irish Republican Army, and IRA strategy then involved giving telephoned warnings after explosives were placed and primed. They even used agreed codewords recognised by the police to authenticate them as emanating from IRA high command. IRA spokesmen repeatedly briefed us that their primary aim was to inflict economic damage and not to kill. We recognised, though, that any deaths would obviously increase confusion and terror among the population, a familiar and cynical aim for insurgent guerrilla forces the world over; but disarray and turmoil were certainly the result while evacuations and searches were conducted after a warning and the British Army's bomb-squad had moved in. In the earliest part of the Seventies, when my Belfast assignments were at their longest and most frequent, the rate of full-fledged explosions going off at the Europa was kept down to an average of just over six per year.

When security was made extra-tight and bombing attempts became increasingly more difficult inside the building, the IRA naturally took to planting devices outside but nearby. The day of our impromptu Guinness-and-Irish-Coffee party was an example. Another time, I was staying up on the fifth floor and saw from my window flurries of people at street level being herded away from us. No warning had reached us at the hotel's upper levels. The explosion went off with an ear-splitting crash somewhere out of my line of vision, but within perhaps a nanosecond I had my first education in the unpredictable effects of blast. The bomb's wave of compressed air particles travelled faster than the speed of sound, smashing through windows in the building's stairwells. It rushed along the corridors, and the door to my room—maybe left unlatched, I don't know—blew open behind me. The blast pitched me forward onto the carpeted floor. I lay there only a moment, assessing whether or not I'd been hurt. I had not. But my head felt a little, well, not quite my own. To my surprise my window had stayed intact. A neighbour some rooms away on the same floor was less lucky. His window splintered and flew into his face.

I heard his piercing, wordless squeals of pain, and so did a colleague who appeared from another room. Like me he seemed unharmed though he was slapping each of his ears as if to clear his head. Together the two of us carried the injured man downstairs, his blood soaking through the three bath-towels we wrapped around his head. We took him out and across the street to where ambulance crews were already setting up a triage station in the surprisingly undamaged neighbourhood pub, *The Crown*. (Undamaged on this occasion; it was to be more directly bombed, and nearly destroyed, later into 'The Troubles'.)

The *Crown Liquor Saloon*, to use the pub's full name, was a favourite of mine and famous for its Victorian stained-glass windows and exquisite etched-glass dividers between the private booths, known as 'snugs', each with its own small door, where I'd often sit to drink. It had become my solitary retreat, a delicious contrast to the rowdiness of the *Whip and Saddle* back in the hotel. I needed my quiet time among our hectic days and our hyper-vigilance. I took to heart an old adage, occasionally repeating it under my breath while drinking in *The Crown*. It was something I'd first heard when nine years old and sitting at the feet of my great-grandfather and his friends around the fireplace. 'Sometimes Ah just sit an' think; sometimes Ah just sit.' It seemed to help when I was badly jarred by bloody events.

I didn't think the victim we carried to the Crown was one of our journalists' contingent but it was hard to tell: his lacerated face was unrecognisable, and he couldn't voice anything meaningful. He may have been one of the few travelling businesspeople who still visited Belfast even as the violence was mounting. In the chaos of that day I never learned his name or how serious his injuries might have been. We left him on a stretcher under one of the pub's century-old heraldic shields, with a Latin motto carved into the dark oak: *Fortuna audaces juvat*. Fortune, it claimed, rewards the brave.

Bombs and bomb threats affected our everyday life in big and small ways. Along with Belfast's long-suffering native citizens, we visiting reporters would frequently have our cars hijacked for bombing purposes. We may in fact have been more likely than city natives to lose our vehicles, which we rented, since our work took us, perforce, into those parts of the city where paramilitary groups held sway. Once stolen, a car would in the earliest days be loaded with either gelignite or a home-made mixture of nitrobenzene and fertiliser. Later on, the bombers used Semtex plastic explosive manufactured in Communist Czechoslovakia and supplied by Libya's Colonel Muammar Gaddafi. An explosion would inevitably mean a total write-off for the car. If it was successfully defused by the British Army, the vehicle was impounded as evidence for forensic investigation. Every planted bomb was a crime scene, and investigators were always eager to identify the bomb-maker, if they could. Explosion or no explosion, Hertz and Avis had to bear the losses, not we renters, and the companies would simply put them down to the cost of doing business in Belfast.

I developed a stratagem that in effect ensured that none of my cars was ever used to blow things up, although that wasn't my main purpose. At the rental counter I insisted on getting a dark-green vehicle, preferably the biggish Ford model known in the

British Isles as a Granada, though it didn't look the slightest bit Spanish. And I wasn't aiming to avoid a hijack: very much the opposite. I had learned that senior IRA staff officers, as they loftily called themselves, in direct parody of formal military forces, enjoyed being driven around by a Volunteer, the lowest IRA rank, in a roomy vehicle of a hue that evoked the military drab adopted by regular armies everywhere. Oftentimes I would head straight from the airport to an IRA neighbourhood and soon get pulled over by a pair of armed, balaclava-wearing teenagers. They would take my dark-green Granada at gunpoint, commandeering it for their bosses' convenience and comfort. I made a point of keeping a record of the plate-numbers and once, not in Belfast but in Derry, I did see Martin McGuinness, then a local IRA battalion commander (and decades later the Deputy First Minister of a peaceful, self-ruling Northern Ireland) riding in the back seat of unquestionably one of my—that is to say, Hertz's—Ford Granadas. My ploy gained me some notice among the paramilitaries and helped ingratiate me a little with IRA men in both main cities. One of them, reputed to be a Belfast company quartermaster, welcomed me once with 'Well, if it isn't our favourite used car salesman!' When I tried to protest at the label in the bantering way expected of me, he went on, 'Didn't do Tricky Dicky any harm being called that!' Meaning, of course, Richard Nixon. 'Look who won the last election!'

Five, maybe six, of my vehicles went missing but I was never queried by Hertz or Avis about my high recidivist rate as a Granada-loser and I can only presume that this kind of loss, of the non-explosive kind, was ledgered as just another indirect cost in the companies' daily accounts. Once I'd had a Granada taken, I would replace it with an entirely different model and colour, thinking I'd now be in less danger of losing it. And, as I hoped, lightning did not strike twice in the same place and I never had two cars hijacked in quick succession. Once I was driving a new, non-Granada car, my tactic for contacting the IRA would be to drive at dusk to one of the city's 'no-go' areas: no-go, that is, to the army and police. I'd find a quiet spot to park and then take a snooze. It wouldn't be long before a patrolling pair of young men, sometimes masked but often not bothering, would tap on

In Derry with Martin McGuinness, once a local IRA battalion commander.

my window with an Armalite rifle. I might be slow to wake but I don't remember ever being scared. I knew that the 'security check' would happen—and of course it always did.

'What are ye doin' here, Friend?' was the usual challenge, in the Ulster voicing of 'Fri...end', drawn out into almost two syllables, with a distinct upturn at the end. It sounded more threatening than friendly.

'I'm waiting for you,' I'd say, hoping not to sound too cocky. I'd show my press card and say I needed to meet their battalion chief. It usually worked. I would be taken to see 'The Ma...an', another stretched vowel—either promptly or after a wait while messages were carried back and forth, on foot or by car. Only once was I sent packing. That was the one time I let the respect-fulness quota slip a bit and joked: 'Take Me To Your Leader.' The two fifteen year-olds didn't seem to get the standard sci-fi allusion. Or maybe they did and just didn't like it.

Cultivating journalistic relations was harder with Protestant paramilitaries. Many of them regarded us reporters as pliant mouthpieces for the IRA, mainly because we often aired the very genuine grievances of the Catholic population, whom the IRA saw themselves as protecting and serving. (The British Army's regular soldiers, too, often regarded us as pro-IRA but their more professionally minded officers felt it important to maintain at least businesslike and cordial communication with us.) Every side in the conflict could strike me as threatening—they all carried guns, after all—but I found myself more nervous in hardcore Protestant areas than in any other sector of The Troubles' varied landscape.

Even so, I was still at times able to build some rapport. I recall a Protestant heavy (he called himself a Loyalist 'adjutant') who never once removed his ski mask throughout several meetings between us, stretching over two or three months. During one talk, in the anonymous kitchen of a shuttered Loyalist social club, he made and served tea for us both, with his Webley .455 pistol laid aside on the stove. Without asking how I liked it, he poured so much sugar into my tea that a spoon could have stood up in it.

Any such Protestant connections, though, could often get badly frayed or torn. The 'Proddies' never felt the press was on their side. I was present for a street battle between opposing gangs at a contentious point along the inaptly named Peace Line, the walled and fenced division between Catholic and Protestant housing projects. I was weaving about, unsure which way to go and getting more and more scared for my safety as I dodged hails of broken bricks and primitive Molotov cocktails: the Northern Irish variant—milk bottles with their broad mouths stuffed with gasoline-soaked rags. I'd experienced them in previous riots but this confrontation seemed to bring out a more concentrated fusillade. Once set alight, the bottles were tossed so that they exploded in the air or when they landed on the ground or when they hit some unfortunate passer-by. A bulky man in his thirties among the Protestant ranks gestured and beckoned to me—yelled too, but I couldn't hear him over the crashing, the small explosions and the jeers. He signalled that I could take safe refuge behind their makeshift barricade. When I managed to get across to him he used a thickly gloved hand to raise the barricade's barbed wire that was tautly stretched at about four feet high. As I crouched to crawl under and through, he let go and the wire thwacked me down onto the rock-strewn asphalt, the barbs piercing the skin of my right shoulder-blade. The cuts were slight and soon healed, which is more than can be said for the humiliating wound to my gullible pride, and for several days my sore shoulder made me feel a complete fool for being conned. Much worse was the more lasting damage to my precious, though too-bright-for-Belfast lobster-red leather jacket. It was a creation of the then 'swinging London' tailor John Stephen, and its distinctive, somewhat swaggering look had charmed me into wearing it too often. Dull, dun-coloured anoraks were what almost everyone else in the press corps wore, but I had this inexplicable need to wear what I liked, not what was sensible. Inexplicable, I guess, except for my youthful folly—and my obstinate attachment to having come from London's unbearably fashionable Chelsea district and to looking like I did. And maybe, somewhere in my combination of fear and growing familiarity with danger, the jacket was a silent but eloquent expression of my boldness. The goon who ruined it beyond repair would cross my path at several more riots and he always greeted me with a ready smirk. I meanwhile learned to wear less ostentatious clothing for street fighting.

My TV network colleagues and I were grateful to have with us a Protestant cabbie formally named Isaac, but known to us as Ike. 'We like Ike' became our slogan. He was in his mid-forties, lean, tall and quite muscle-bound. He could rev the engine to escape an angry crowd and wrench the wheel into astonishingly tight turns—and this was well before the days of power steering. Ike became our regular driver, albeit only in his own familiar 'Orange' districts. More than once while we filmed, and with remarkable authority, he was able to talk hostile groups out of physically enacting the verbal threats they made against us: threats of roughing us up or even, rather credibly, of shooting us dead.

On one occasion, though, I was doing background interviews on my own with ordinary residents of a Protestant district, people uninvolved in any violent goings-on. I hadn't thought that Ike's protection would be necessary on such a low-profile mission, and I came to regret it. Three masked and armed members of the UDA (the Ulster Defence Association) appeared without warning and ordered me into the back of a van. They blindfolded me and took me to an ill-lighted room which sounded like it was the back room of a pub. They took off my blindfold once indoors and two of them (the third had disappeared) menaced me for an hour or two with very few words ever being spoken. One sat facing me cradling his ancient Martini-Enfield rifle, which was pointed in my direction, and the other much younger one sat to my right fondling an oily Mauser pistol, seemingly more interested in it than in me. In the heavy silence I hoped to suppress signs of my fear. I shifted in my hardback chair now and again, but carefully, making each move very slowly to suggest relaxation rather than anxiety. At one point I crossed my legs at the ankle a little too instinctively. The rifleman jerked his weapon to shoulder height and trained it on me even more determinedly, or at least that's how I felt. I fast separated my feet, planting them firmly at attention and sitting upright. Time dragged. I sensed it would not help to attempt any conversation. And anyway, I blanked entirely on what in hell I could possibly say. I then caught myself imagining the full-metal-jacketed bullet lying in its breech, ready to be expelled in my direction. Inwardly at least, I winced at even the thought of it and tried to dismiss it. I wanted to shake it out of my head but knew I shouldn't do anything so unwise. I made just a gradual, barely discernible sideways turn of my head to the left and back again. Getting desperate now, I wondered if anyone had seen me being taken. But even if they had, I realised, they would surely not report it. The UDA's rule by intimidation always prevailed in that city district. I was trapped; no way out.

Eventually both men stood up. One said, 'We'll be goin', then,' and they delivered me in the van, blindfolded again for the journey, to a point within some walking distance of where I had left my car and they had first accosted me. I gained no notion of what they had wanted with me, except perhaps simply to try out some frightener tactics on someone—maybe on a journalist in particular. If so, they succeeded.

I added this scary afternoon to my growing litany of tense, sometimes life-threatening experiences, which I decided to classify as a succession of term papers. I hoped I might someday graduate with a diploma in crisis-hardened calmness.

Our relations with armed men were sometimes quite open. But even when there was a degree of candour, or even a tone of friendliness in the air, no side in The Troubles was ever free of double-talk, and journalists had to maintain a warily suspicious guard in every direction. For a while the chief PR man for the IRA in Belfast (and he seemed to bask in that job title) was Seamus Loughran, a chummy fellow who traded on a close physical resemblance to one of the UK's most beloved comedians, Eric Morecambe—at the least, he had the same high forehead as Eric, wore the same heavy, black-framed glasses, and ornamented his own wisecracks with the same quick, rising laugh—which in his case, unlike Eric's, was an unwelcome extra garnish.

One warm July day in 1972 Loughran held a press briefing out in one of the city's far western neighbourhoods under IRA control. It was not a very focused briefing; in fact we failed to see any real point to it. Until, that is, we were dismissed and all drove back towards the hotel. We heard on our car radios that a massive barrage of IRA bombs, later turning out to be twenty-two in total, had gone off in and around the city centre. They had all exploded within little more than an hour of each other; nine people had been killed and another 130 seriously injured. The IRA's customary warnings had this time been delivered in a confused or confusing way; in the case of some of the explosions, warnings had evidently not been given at all. We theorised that Loughran's purpose in keeping the media away from the onslaught had been to further crank up the city's shocked confusion. I ended up scribbling notes in a trembling, nauseated state at the Oxford Street Bus Depot while dismembered human remains were being scraped off the pavement with shovels. And whenever I was back in Seamus Loughran's company my skin would crawl and my gorge rise, close to throwing up. It was hard to maintain the requisite civil manner when I had to ask him questions in a press conference.

The day of the bombings, at first headlined as the Bomb-a-Minute Blitz, came to be known as Bloody Friday. And for what it's worth, thirty years later, once peace had finally prevailed, the IRA saw fit to apologise formally for that afternoon's deaths and injuries.

We were obviously wary of the men with guns, whichever side they were on, but we were also wary of each other. We were a mixed bunch. Some were old hands who'd gone into the reporting trade straight from secondary school, a few as early as fifteen. Joe Gorrod, for instance, was a sailor's son from England's Northeast coast, whose voice had been sharply etched by its smoggy, industrial air; he worked for the top-selling tabloid, the *Daily Mirror*, and he believed Biblical language was an essential work-tool, often claiming that 'the Bible is the best bit of tabloid reporting you'll ever see.' Others had undergone a university education, and one or two had advanced graduate degrees. In all our variety we coalesced within the tight community of journalism, from the most sensational to the so-called serious broadsheet newspapers, and we revelled together in a self-awarded title that some of us used with wry irony and others announced plainly and wholeheartedly. We called ourselves the 'ink-stained sons of toil'. The label could loosely include me because although I mainly worked in the electronic medium of television, I could claim a relationship to printers' ink by virtue of my articles for London's political weekly, the *New Statesman*, written while moonlighting from my TV broadcasts.

There were, however, limits to our comradeship. We could be convivial, even friends in some cases, but our work meant that we engaged in intense, sometimes bitter competition—hence the constant wariness. It became ever more clear why it was a good idea to lodge together; that way we could keep an eye on each other. Eavesdropping on our fellows was an essential task for every reporter, and one perfectly legitimate form of spying was to pay close attention to the Europa Hotel's public-address system and its Tannoy loudspeakers. Announcements would emanate from the reception desk or the switchboard and were usually intended for individual guests, and especially the reporters who took calls and received visitors all the time.

My ears pricked up one summer evening in 1972 when, over the Tannoy, the reception clerk informed a BBC reporter that he should come to the desk and meet an outside visitor. The BBC man was a direct rival of mine, and the very nature of who our employers were put us in a state of perpetual competition: his was the publicly owned network; mine the commercial. I needed to know just who my rival would be meeting. I ran and then hovered near the reception desk, hidden from view by a group of new registrants. A lone incomer was not signing the register, merely waiting to connect with his contact. I recognised him as a mid-level British government official and I guessed he was intending to brief the BBC man privately. Something important must be going on, was my inevitable thought—and my professional alarm. What was I missing?

I quickly phoned a couple of my own government contacts. I couldn't get a clear sense of what might be afoot. Our conversations went along well-guarded pathways.

'Anything new happening?'

'There's always something new happening, David, as you know. But nothing earth-shattering, I would say. We continue to monitor the situation carefully.'

'For what, right now? Is there some change in the air, maybe?'

'Well, we're always on the lookout for new developments of significance. Among our daily round of incident reports, meetings, monitoring the level of violence ... all the usual sort of thing.'

'So are there any, at the moment? New developments?'

'Oh, I wouldn't say so.'

'But you'd let me know if anything did come up, huh?'

'Of course I will, David.'

Reading between the lines, and with that word 'meetings' carrying (to my ears at least) an extra-cautious intonation, the possibility began to emerge that some secret talks could be in progress, perhaps even discussions between the government and the IRA. A stunning development, if it was true. I set about trying to confirm it over the next thirty-six hours, learning tantalising snippets along the way, like a rumour from Derry that Daithi O'Conaill, the IRA's Chief of Staff, plus another leader (who later turned out to be Gerry Adams) had made a somewhat cloak-and-dagger trip to a County Derry manor house and there had met British MI6 agents. My informant, a local drinks-and-food supplier, used the quaint Elizabethan term 'hugger-mugger' to describe the gathering he'd heard about. At least one participant, he'd been told, was in disguise. Again, all astonishing if true. I had to check everything out as verifiable fact.

Then suddenly came a newsflash. IRA command in Dublin had issued a formal public statement that they would suspend 'offensive operations' if there was a 'reciprocal response' from the British Army. This duly turned into an actual ceasefire. It even came to involve face-to-face talks between the IRA and the British Secretary of State for Northern Ireland, Viscount William Whitelaw; these talks were held, it so happened, in a London riverside house close to my Chelsea apartment. The negotiations ended in failure after twelve days, as would several more efforts at truces and talks. That on-off process became an established pattern for the war as it continued through three more decades, until the enduring 'Good Friday' Peace Agreement of 1998 was finally achieved.

But back amid the peaking violence of 1972, we reporters were sideswiped by the rapid though out-of-sight manoeuvering that led to the war's first truce, the public announcement of which rendered our competing for leaks and off-the-record tips totally moot. In spite of that, our fierce professional jousting—that competitiveness that had me desperate to scoop the BBC man's possible scoop—remained an unending feature of our presence together. We would fight with each other for the ear of a government minister whenever such an official might fly to Belfast. A very determined correspondent one day locked a rival in a hotel closet to keep him out of an important press conference. Another, in order to maintain the exclusive nature of his interview with the wife of a newly imprisoned IRA commander, spirited her away to a Spanish vacation island. And as the continuing backdrop to our intermittent clashes, there was always the persistent need to keep our ears keenly alert for the sound of the Tannoy.

The hotel public-address system seems, looking back now, a ludicrously open way to have conducted business. In truth, it was tempting to abuse it. At least I thought so. One reporter among those representing the more respected, non-tabloid London newspapers was just two years older than me and an eager newcomer. He would go on to become a widely admired interpreter of international affairs but when he first arrived in Belfast, Bill—let's call him Bill—quickly learned to take special note of the Tannoyed announcements. Sensing an opportunity for some pranking, I decided to bribe the switchboard operators to put out a false message. There was a bench of four such 'lady operators', as we then called them, all aspiring to be Lily Tomlin, it seemed, in her well-loved role as the headset-wearing Ernestine on TV's *Laugh-In*. The four were very happy to share between them my £20.00 (about $300 in today's money), plus a tinge of excitement that might pierce the daily grind. With my fellow-journalists, no financial inducement was needed. I easily persuaded them to pretend for the sake of the ruse not to hear the phony announcement when it came. Bill was meanwhile left in the dark.

The background context was some big news: the city's Crumlin Road Prison, where many IRA captives were held, was experiencing a rash of dramatic breakouts. First came a group of nine rank-and-file IRA volunteers who were instantly nicknamed the 'Crumlin Kangaroos', because their mythologised escape was said to involve some unlikely high-jumping over the prison walls. For the prison authorities insult was added to injury when soon afterwards a trio of leading IRA gunmen also broke out, led by an alleged killer with 'most-wanted' status, called Martin Meehan. Two of the escapees were recaptured but Meehan stayed on the run, fueling a Scarlet Pimpernel image among many in the Catholic population. Only that morning the *Belfast Telegraph* had updated the continuing story with a headline: 'Massive Manhunt for IRA Jail Breaker'.

In the evening we all drank together as usual, Bill included, in the hard-to-avoid *Whip and Saddle*. At my pre-arranged instigation, an operator's voice blandly pronounced: 'Will Mr M (for Martin) Meehan please take a phone call at one of the house phones located in the lobby.' All of us except Bill ignored it: credible enough behaviour amid the bar's raucous hubbub. Bill fought hard not to look startled, quickly checked around to be sure nobody else had registered the announcement and then grabbed his notebook from the drinks table and darted off towards the lobby. We all paused, glasses in hand.

He must have discovered pretty quickly that he'd been duped when no one was in the lobby to take the phone call, least of all a terrorist on the run. And then one of the operators took pity on him, confessing they'd been put up to playing the trick. He returned hangdog to the bar, to our derisive laughter and ironic applause. Then my irresistible, pre-arranged follow-up was broadcast: 'Will Mr M (for Mickey) Mouse please take a phone call at one of the house phones located in the lobby.'

Poor Bill seemed disproportionately distressed, more upset than I had ever seen him, slumped with his drink and close to tears. I could not bring myself to tell him I was the author of the conspiracy against him but let him go on believing it was a spontaneous and entirely communal bit of hazing. Looking back, I feel bad about it: it was humiliating and hurtful. What I'd thought of as a harmless jape was in fact my showing off to an audience of elders I still wanted to impress by my cleverness.

There were some less unkind, friendlier forms of rivalry. We engaged in a continuing contest for which we couldn't all agree on a name, but 'Viable Verbiage' gained favour with some of us. Early on a given morning, but especially when news was slow, we would collectively agree upon a single word—one of special inappropriateness or improbability—and each of us would smuggle it into the reports we sent to our newsrooms that day. We usually arrived at our consensus in jentacular fashion—that is, over breakfast, to employ one of our actual arcane choices. The game's challenge was to get the day's item of outrageous vocabulary past our various organisations' copy editors and out to our general audience. Our choices of verbal contraband became increasingly preposterous during our buoyant, at-times-frantic jockeying for success. But again and again, sober-minded editors would officiously delete our ridiculous offerings, occurring as they did inside weighty reports about IRA attacks, political wranglings, riots, kidnappings and sectarian assassinations. Our overripe vocabulary included lollygagging, kakorrhaphiophobic, oxter, cabotage and many more in similar vein.

The grand award for a clever writer's victory over more sensible editors was never to be won—not for a long time, anyway. And the person who finally did achieve it was none other than Bill. That was gratifying, in view of the drubbing he'd previously suffered at his fellows' hands, or at mine. Bill's victory as a cunning wordsmith was made all the sweeter, for every one of us, by the fact that he bested the stern-eyed censors of one of our nation's staidest, most formal publications.

Our absurd word for the day had been stoat. (That's the small, long-necked mammal, which incidentally doesn't figure much in Irish wildlife observation. For some reason, in Ireland, stoats are commonly and inaccurately called weasels, a little confusingly, since there are no weasels in Ireland.) Bill inserted the little beast not into the day's major news item, which I recall as being purely political, but into a 'colour piece' he had written. He'd had the luck—luck in a reporter's sense and no other—to get caught up in a minor gun-battle in the city's Andersonstown district. His paper had given him a sidebar running down the page for a personal eyewitness account. It gave him the opportunity for some audacious shorthand in describing a British soldier's tactical move: 'The corporal darted stoat-like across the alley and took up a kneeling position to fire.' Maybe his copy editors' attentiveness was somehow a little below par that evening for, overnight, Bill's outlandish turn of phrase came to be dispatched to hundreds of thousands of United Kingdom breakfast tables.

And in the Belfast Europa breakfast room it was cause for jubilation. The prize—a Nebuchadnezzar of Moët et Chandon

Imperial champagne—was ceremonially popped and at least the first pint of its ejaculation went over Bill's joyful, proud head.

Chapter 25
Waiting and Regrouping

Impatient by nature, I generally found any enforced delay insufferable. But the potentially lengthy wait for some definite news about Father Francis Leo turned out to be relatively short: just a little over two months. The news itself, though, landed with a thud.

Linda Lawless was leading the search and co-monitoring the frequent alerts from the DNA genealogy websites we were using, inconclusive though they mostly were. She would log in thirteen time-zones away at her home in Australia; we conferred at hours which were convenient for me but which could hardly have been easy for her, although she always said they were.

One early evening (breakfast time for her) came the blow. Linda was blunt. 'Whoever your dad is,' she said, 'he is not Father Francis Leo. Some DNA for Francis Leo's relatives who I've already identified on his family tree has now become available, and it's completely different from yours.'

I was assailed by a crushing sense of setback. We—that is, me and my investigative teammates Linda and Vincent—had confidently lined up a chief suspect on our notional wallchart, and now forensic science meant we had to eliminate him from our inquiries. Case closed.

My disappointment ran deep. I had nursed high hopes, lulled into believing an end to my paternal mystery was not merely possible but now likely, even imminent, thanks to the modern miracle of DNA analysis. Maybe I'd been naïve; or if not naïve, then possibly too trusting in the science, almost investing it with the power of magic. At the least, I was a sucker for the appeal of an apparently persuasive narrative.

But I turned my disappointment into a newly dogged refusal to be discouraged. I joined Linda on a videocall to review our possible new approaches. As she examined the very few family trees that included people with whom I had some DNA in common, she expressed her usual, cold-eyed genealogist's sort of assessment. 'It's now definitely gonna be a long-haul project,' she said. I allowed myself a short sigh to signal, I hoped, both acceptance and realism.

The research got more detailed. Linda brought on board a virtuoso called Dawn Bennett who was based in Arizona and was even more of an expert in deciphering genetic codes. We also broadened our work, taking in more and more of the fast-growing DNA databases posted online. Linda and Dawn were eager that I submit my own DNA to an especially detailed, specialised database, to obtain analysis centring solely on my paternal line. It would concentrate on the genetic evidence embedded in my Y-chromosome, the one inherited from my father.

Our approach now resembled, to my mind at least, the process of reverse engineering. Previously, when Father Francis Leo was in our sights, we had started with someone who might possibly be my father and then looked for any publicly posted DNA that related to him and also matched mine. Now we switched the order of things. We'd start with all the people out there in the universe of digitally available DNA who might be a match with me. Then we'd drag a net through all of them in search of any trace of a male family member who could have lived in my home area at the time of my conception.

A big surprise came up early on. We kept finding matches for me with people living in Germany, with German names. Several were a near-enough match that they could be my first or second cousins. This opened up a whole new field of inquiry.

Linda set about writing to all the Germans who had posted DNA that matched mine, introduced herself as a researcher tracing my family tree and asked whether they were willing to help us and whether they had a relative, an uncle perhaps, or a great-uncle, who might have been in the England–Scotland borderlands during the late 1940s. We sat back, awaiting replies.

The German connection rattled me. For a start, it cast doubt on my mother's account that my father had been a Scot. But then, perhaps he had been a German who had assimilated really well into the Scottish borderlands, and could successfully appear to be Scottish? Another possibility occurred to us: a Catholic priest in that part of Britain could possibly and theoretically have been German, even though it would have been very unlikely, especially around the time of the Second World War. But a priest who had at least some German heritage could be slightly more feasible. Could we perhaps find such a priest?

We got back in touch with my home area's Catholic diocese, the organisation whose cooperation we now needed again, even though its previous help had been somewhat limited. The always obliging Vincent Doyle, in his role representing Children of Priests, once again posed the inquiry on my behalf. 'Who among your priesthood at the relevant time may have had German family origins?' was the simple question.

The diocese's answer was sufficiently disappointing to anger me all over again, though frankly not a great surprise. 'Unfortunately,' the email said, the diocese was 'unable to retrieve the information you request from Diocesan records.'

Chapter 26
DNA Update

B ackstage in New York's Carnegie Hall, my phone pinged with a message from Australia. It was Linda with news about a fresh batch of DNA matches. I was using Linda as a buffer between me and all the genealogy websites to which I subscribed. I'd got tired and irritated by their alerts. With their algorithms ceaselessly scanning their ever-expanding databases, each platform periodically sent a note exclaiming, 'We have a match for you!'

So often these 'matches' turned out to be of little significance when examined fully, and I ended up turning off the alerts, letting Linda evaluate them and draw to my attention only those she thought worth pursuing.

The growing number of matches with people of German heritage was starting to seem suggestive. One connection in particular, she now wrote, 'might be worth discussing'. Glancing at the screen, I registered only that one tantalising phrase. I

At work in a Public Broadcasting Service video edit room.

would have responded to her immediately but I was in the middle of videotaping for a network TV show. I had to direct the Carnegie Hall crew as they took roaming footage of some young musicians on stage rehearsing intently for their career highlight, a long-awaited recital in this fabled venue. I then took my seat in the audience for the actual performance while the crew covered it from a static camera position, high in the auditorium. Our work continued immediately afterwards, with more candid video coverage of a cocktail reception to fête the youthful performers. The timing of Linda's note about my paternal origins struck me with an odd, maybe even ironic, resonance; my assignment centred on a notable example of family continuity.

The story had long been on my mind—about twenty years, in fact—but it wasn't its family dimension that first drew me to it. Back in the 1990s the internationally renowned pianist and conductor, Daniel Barenboim, an Israeli citizen, formed a rare friendship across his country's bitter divide with the equally renowned Edward Said, the Palestinian cultural critic and historian. Together they ended up creating an extraordinary cross-cultural partnership: an orchestra drawn partly from the country's Jewish population and partly from the Arab community. Against all apparent odds, the orchestra turned out to be a great success, with musical excellence at its core, while at the same time pursuing its social mission to embrace both sides of the Middle East dispute. The musicians, by now known as the Barenboim-Said Divan Orchestra (from the Arabic word for a gathering or an assembly) had performed at some of the world's greatest symphonic venues. And now in early 2020, a chamber-music ensemble chosen from within the orchestra's ranks was to play Midtown Manhattan's historic venue.

The Divan story felt like a complete natural for me. Long stretches of my reporting life were spent overseas covering violent conflicts: those of Northern Ireland, Cyprus, the Arab-Israeli dispute itself, Sri Lanka, South Africa and Zimbabwe, as well as racial killings in the United States. How could I not be excited by this bridge-building exercise employing musicians as peacemakers? I offered the story to public television's *NewsHour* and the show promptly bought it, wanting a fast delivery.

As I got down to the business of assembling all its elements, I now saw the narrative cohering around a newer, generational aspect to the story. The Divan operation was changing over time. Edward Said had died of leukemia at the age of sixty-seven. Maestro Barenboim was ageing; he still conducted the orchestra

Israeli press credentials, 1997.

On location in Jerusalem, 1997.

but much less often than before. Leadership, especially for the smaller chamber-music ensemble, was devolving onto Barenboim's son Michael (or Mischa)—a violinist and professor of violin in the Barenboim-Said Academy in Berlin that trained orchestra members. Now in his early thirties, he bore the title Concert Master for his group of eight travelling string-players.

The whole team's youthful buoyancy couldn't fail to entrance me during their rehearsal, their performance and when we mingled at the reception. Post-performance, Mischa seemed tired but elated. Servers clad in black-and-white circled us with finger-food on trays but the young maestro waved them away. He was eyeing the still off-limits chafing dishes that brimmed with hearty servings of pasta and he caught my eye to beckon me exaggeratedly towards them. In his impatience he seemed positively boyish.

'I suppose we must observe cocktail-party etiquette,' he said, mugging to me, glass in hand with his pinkie in the air.

'Yes—guess we do,' I commiserated. 'We have to wait until after the speeches.' When at last the votes of thanks and appreciation at the microphone were over, he gave me a wink and fast-forked a plate piled high with puttanesca.

While our camera-operator hovered over my shoulder, my phone vibrated again insistently; I'd programmed the device to repeat its alerts for anything from special sources like Linda. But my work demands were pressing; next on our tight schedule was my formal, sit-down interview with Mischa. I put the phone aside and addressed the task at hand; I had to encourage this young man to describe on camera how he was continuing his father's mission.

The shoot had gone well but something seemed amiss. He and I took our seats in facing chairs, silence descended, and from behind the camera came a muttered 'Rolling!'—a procedure as familiar to me as slicing onions to start a casserole. The kitchen analogy comes to me readily. I amassed a repertoire of casserole dishes during my late-teenage years, part of my drive to become a sophisticate (I felt my *coq au vin* was guaranteed to impress people) and the opening rituals at a chopping board have always epitomised relaxation for me. Settling in for a TV interview feels the same; I've even been caught on tape sighing audibly and contentedly at this point in the process. Now, though, facing the young Barenboim, I was the opposite of relaxed. Something wasn't gelling. An awkwardness in me made the interview halting and stilted. Troublesome misgivings, which I wanted to dismiss as banal but couldn't, were taking me over. It was ridiculous but I simply didn't know how to ask this guy about his father.

Here was a man who very evidently did have a father, one inescapably present, and whom he could—what a weird luxury! —choose to emulate or choose not to. It felt like a daunting conundrum, however much I tried to suppress my feeling as irrational and inappropriate to the moment.

I wanted to prise something from him without my really knowing what it was. A distinctly unprofessional track was running in my head, even as I maintained the outward courtesies of a normal interview. As we picked our way through some urbane exchanges, I heard wholly infantile questions surging within:

What was it like having a dad?
And a dad so huge—what was that like?
Did he tell you what to do?
Did he stop you doing what you wanted to do?

Out loud they would have sounded unexpected, to say the least, and maybe even inane and childish. They were also unfair. Mischa could of course have no inkling of my ignorance of what a father–son relationship might be like. I ended up voicing something utterly mundane and a tad unsophisticated, in the hope that it would sound adult enough: 'What made you want to follow your father?'

Mischa looked bemused. He fumbled a bit, saying in an offhand way that 'music is in our blood, of course.' He darted on quickly to a well-practised riff about music's ability to bring harmony between very different peoples, which he added—in a kind of nod to my question—was the core mission, after all, of both his family and his creative community. My grown-up, professional persona started to return to the room. I recognised how much Mischa resembled a lot of people I knew in his age group. He quite naturally took much more interest in cultivating and talking about his horizontal relationships with contemporaries, especially in the case of fellow musicians, than wanting to dwell on vertical links like the connection to his father.

I had to move on rapidly to the interview up next, relieved there was no dynastic inheritance involved. I now sat with a twenty-two-year-old violinist from the octet, the Palestinian, Yamen Saadi. He came from Nazareth, the son of parents with no musical knowledge or interest whatever. When he was ten years old he announced out of the blue that he wanted to play the violin, totally bemusing the family. As he recollected that moment for me, his wispy moustache crinkled into an elfin grin: 'I mean, where I grew up there are not many classical musicians.' On camera he didn't spell it out, but I gained the strong impression (unless I was merely projecting something of my own onto him) that he was in search of a vehicle to take him decisively out and away from his background.

Next morning it was my own background that was again under the microscope. Although in Australia it was already late evening, Linda and I conversed online about her research progress. Among the mounting German connections, the family-name Reidel kept coming up, enough times to sound significant. Everyone's family tree had to be charted. Our shared ancestor had to be found, for they and I must surely have one in common, given that these matches even existed. Identifying that ancestor could lead to my father being spotted somewhere among the branches of those family trees.

As we reviewed all the names, along with whatever additional details were available on the websites, Linda pointed out one name in particular, and my eyes widened: Francis Reidel. I flashed back to my mother's neat, slightly sloped handwriting on the fax she sent me in 2001: I know you just want a name. So here it is. He was called Father Francis. She had underlined the name.

Our newly found Francis, buried deep in a database, was born in 1900 in a location that wasn't yet fully clear but was probably in Lower Saxony, judging by some Saxon relatives who figured on the site. He would have been forty-eight when I was conceived. And though very likely German by birth, his death at seventy-two was recorded in a town within the Catholic diocese in Britain that included my home village.

'This could be our man, couldn't it?' I asked Linda, trying not to sound like a foolish leaper-to-conclusions.

'Really hard to say at this point,' Linda replied, 'but I'm working on it,' and signed off for a while.

Seven hours later, after what I found an agitating expanse of time, Linda came back online. For her it was now deep into the night, getting close to dawn. She wrote: 'Yes, you are definitely jumping to conclusions. I'm almost 100% certain that the name Francis is just a coincidence. There are simply not enough "shared segments" of DNA between the two of you for him to be a closely relation, let alone your father. We need much more directly matching material if we're to come anywhere close to finding your dad.' My heart sank, not to be raised much even as she tapped out a PS: 'Let's say we haven't got the evidence yet, at least.'

Later, Linda went on to promise, she would pore intently over every new possible connection that could pop up, while the various platforms (about a dozen of them now, all in possession of my swabs and spittle) continued their digital trawling through other people's DNA. 'I know this probably won't be much comfort, but I'm used to this,' Linda wrote, voicing a sentiment now familiar to me. 'Just be aware, we'll be in for more of a long slow slog.'

Chapter 27
New Leads

I t was official. There was now, just as I turned seventy-one
years of age, a criminal investigation into my conception.
Children of Priests (Coping) reported my mother's alleged
rape to the UK police. Because child sex-abuse scandals had been
breaking out year after year, severely shaking once-trusted British
institutions including the Catholic Church and even the BBC, a
centralised police clearing house had been created in 2014 to deal
with abuse allegations, however historic they might be. Coping's
Vincent Doyle, as a professional psychotherapist, was duty-
bound to report my case (or, I should say, my mother's case) to
this fast-growing law-enforcement unit.

The unit bore the curious title of 'Operation Hydrant'. No one
gave me a reasoned explanation for the name's origin. I was told
it was a randomly generated title choice, but I was ready to
imagine it represented some determination to firehose Britain's
streets completely clean. By 2020, Operation Hydrant had reported that it had investigated 11,346 allegations, some dating as far
back as the mid-1940s. More than a third of them resulted in
convictions: around 4,000 guilty men from many different walks
of life: priests and teachers, workers at children's homes, sports
coaches and many others who had held positions of trust and
authority. Senior officers labelled the sexual abuse of children as
'widespread', and some sounded buoyant about how many
offenders they were bringing to justice. During the press
conference announcing their report, I heard triumphant sneering
in the voice of a detective superintendent who commented of the
convicted men, many of them now quite elderly: 'They had
thought for years that they'd got away with their crimes.'

Operation Hydrant's national office referred my mother's
alleged rape to the local force in the small city near my home
village: the city from which she told me a priest came to conduct

mass for our village's Catholics, when she was fifteen. The case landed on the desk of a certain Detective Sergeant Richard Massey of the city's force.

Like me, D.S. Massey became seized with the possibility that one priest in particular, Father Francis Leo, was our man. He worked to track him down, following the same trail I had followed, ending with Francis Leo's death in 1995. Examining the man's entire priestly career, the detective learned that Francis Leo had raised 'no recorded concerns' among his successive employers in different parishes. Wider inquiries pursued via neighbourhood police stations and community sources like local newspapers—plus less obvious informants, the occasional local family doctor who might still be alive, or even a known village busybody or gossip—appeared to clear the priest of any wrongdoing. Massey finally reported back to Coping that all his unrewarded digging, along with the unavoidable truth that my mother, both alleged victim and sole witness, was no longer alive, led him and his colleagues to end their investigation: 'The case has now been closed and there are no further lines of inquiry'.

When Vincent Doyle told me of this conclusion, I was far from satisfied. I wanted some discussion of my own with the detective sergeant. But not immediately. I needed to do some prep-work. The prospect of dealing directly with the British police again raised mixed feelings. Much of my reporting life, back in the 1970s and 80s, had involved working with cops, or on stories about them. Early on I was part of the reporting team on a TV programme who produced exposés of corrupt Scotland Yard officers. We also highlighted some wrongful convictions that we established were gained through underhand and illegal police methods.

Understandably, perhaps, my relations with the London force became tense, and once when I had to report a burglary at my house, I encountered downright hostility at the local police station after the duty sergeant recognised me as one of the TV show's reporters. As a member of the public filing a criminal complaint, I was offended by their lack of professionalism. They were all too evidently falling into a stereotype, pursuing the so-called traditional 'Blue Line' of solidarity, which included solidarity even with lawbreakers within their own ranks. For them, contempt was what I deserved. As I walked down a corridor with a uniformed constable and passed the half-open door of an interview room, he made an exaggerated gesture of invitation: 'Take a look inside,' he said. 'You'll see there's no blood on the walls.' As if I'd seriously be looking for evidence of police beatings while in the station.

Naturally enough I had to give the duty-officer my fingerprints so they could be discounted when the forensic team dusted my house for any burglar's prints. The detective in charge made one point so ponderously that it could only have signalled sarcasm—unless it was a threat. 'Of course,' he said, 'we will not retain these prints of yours. We are obliged to destroy them at the end of our investigation. To respect your rights.' Nothing ever came of my reporting the break-in. No one was charged, and none of my stolen property, mainly electronics, was ever recovered. Nor was I ever told that the investigation had been closed; it seemed to just fade away. I didn't think it worthwhile to inquire whether my fingerprints were still on record or not.

This isn't to say my relations with the police were always cagey or hostile. I enjoyed a lot of cooperation with a wide range of local and regional forces, especially while I was charting the IRA's intensive bombing campaign against the British mainland, which prompted a burst of fervent police work up and down the country. And I did build some friendships among individual officers, a few of which were to endure over time.

Forty-five years on from my bombings coverage, Detective Sergeant Massey in the Scottish Borderlands became my new focus. The situation felt a little tricky. I was on a purely personal mission and uncertain about my own status in approaching the officer. I didn't exactly qualify as the victim of the crime; indeed, it might be said that I owed my very existence to it. But I did feel as if I suffered consequentially from it—but suffered quite what I would find hard to itemise, especially to a criminal investigator. It seemed best all round to proceed on the simple basis that I'd be recognised as a party with a stake in the case, even if that stake was one that had little investigatory relevance.

Before talking with D.S. Massey, I wanted as full a picture of him as I could get. I wasn't sure that the now-closed investigation had been conducted by the best of professionals. I also felt a need to check if this officer-in-charge was on my side, wondering if his approach coincided with my best interests. This was difficult, since I wasn't entirely sure what my interests actually were. Bottom line, though: all I really had to know was how good a cop he was.

From the public record he looked effective, with many significant arrests and convictions to his credit. As part of a successful drugs-busting team, he had received an effusive commendation from a senior judge for taking off the streets a dangerous gang of traffickers. He also had a good record for 'putting away' people on illegal weapons charges. Another cop I knew of old, now serving in a nearby force, told me that Massey was something of an athlete, and following that broad lead I discovered he was a dedicated cyclist. Merely clicking through British cycling websites showed me he had clocked up hundreds, maybe thousands, of miles in charity races, raising funds to provide handicapped people with chances to enjoy outdoor activities. My sense of him was piqued by learning that among his fellow cyclists, D.S. Massey was celebrated for his prodigious pedal-power with the nickname 'Massimo'. I got the strong feeling that he could be an energetic, persistent sleuth, even though I was disappointed with the conclusion he had reached.

I emailed him and we traded voicemail messages a couple of times. When we finally got to speak in person, our talk on the phone began with some idle chat, though in my case quite deliberate, about my home village and the picturesque hills around it, just eight miles from the station office where he was sitting. I recalled that those hills had been challenging for a boy-cyclist like me. He didn't rise to the bicycling reference.

I tried something that might stir his experienced investigator's pride. 'I know you concluded there are no further lines of inquiry,' I began, 'but can I suggest that this may turn out to be a mistake? In the light of new information, I mean.'

'Oh really? What new information would that be?' he asked.

'Well, although you've said there are no further lines,' I said, air-quoting again his own report's language, 'there could indeed be one. The new information that's emerging comes from my DNA searches online. Genealogy websites.'

In the slight pause that followed, I sensed a professional's eye-roll at a civilian amateur in the throes of their enthusiasm for, even obsession with, a case. But his voice stayed steadily in neutral when he asked: 'so what exactly is new?'

I told him that, quite separate from Father Francis Leo (now discounted as a suspect), growing DNA evidence was connecting me to families in Germany. I suggested—more emphatically now but still maintaining proper respect, I hoped, for his expertise— that there was reason enough to investigate further—to inquire especially, I insisted, into whether any of the priests in his city at the relevant time, early 1948, might have had German origins.

I explained that Coping and I had asked the Catholic diocese whether there might have been any such priest, but they told us they were 'unable to retrieve the information from Diocesan Records'. I pressed the notion that if he, as a law-enforcement officer pursuing a criminal investigation, were to ask for the same details, the diocese's answer might be different, and quite possibly more accommodating.

'They did after all promise something,' I said, reaching for my diocesean letter. 'They said they would, and I quote, fully cooperate with the police or any statutory agency if they approach us for assistance in the course of enquiries.'

D.S. Massey thought for a moment or two, and then was persuaded. He said he would indeed pursue this new line of questioning with the Church bureaucracy.

From here on, more informality settled on our quite frequent phone exchanges. He was happy for me to call him Richard. He discussed his modus operandi a bit, as well as the constraints on him. 'You realise, don't you, David, that even if we discover a name that might be relevant in the course of our investigation, I couldn't reveal that name to you? I could only do that if someone was actually charged with an offence, in which case it could be made public. And you'll know of course that that's very unlikely to happen.' He meant, I took it, that arresting the alleged perpetrator was unlikely.

I should say on this point that British police procedure differs a lot from America's. City and state cops I've worked with in the US have been astonished to learn of the typical formula—anonymous, stiff and euphemistic—that the British press has to maintain while reporting on a crime, often using a phrase which is designed to prevent prejudice to any future court proceedings. 'A man is helping police with their enquiries,' journalists will announce vaguely, and little, sometimes nothing, more. In America, police officers have invariably given me, for public use, an extraordinary amount of detailed information about possible suspects and 'persons of interest', not merely individuals who've been charged.

I told the detective I understood the British rules completely and we came to a friendly, informal agreement. 'My job is to conduct a criminal inquiry,' he pointed out, just a little officiously, only to ease off again into some kindly-sounding warmth: 'But I certainly appreciate your wish to identify your father. And I'll definitely do what I can to help you in that.' We agreed that if there turned out to be no diocesan priest at the time who had any German background, he would, just between us two, let me know. I could then drop my search for him.

If, on the other hand, he discovered that such a priest did exist, then his own investigation might, just might, proceed further and track the man down, even interviewing him if he was alive. Given that faint possibility, I found myself asking, now a little imploringly: 'In such a circumstance as that, could we then perhaps talk afresh about my being informed of that new name?'

'Well ... we'll see how it all goes, shall we?' said D.S. Massey.

Meanwhile, 'in another part of the forest', other developments were emerging. (I'm not sure why this much-quoted stage direction from Shakespeare should come to mind as I switch scenes. Maybe it's because the playwright's Forest of Arden is often said to carry a promise of truth and honest dealings, as opposed to the artifice that prevails in the aristocrats' court. That said, the forest can also be seen to represent a place of disturbance and confusion.)

On the DNA front, in what I felt was a somewhat drama-filled battle for the truth, my trusty genealogist, Linda Lawless, was finding more people with whom I shared some genetic markers. Her research now centred on a man in Germany with the closest matches; his name was Christoph Seidel. The degree of overlap in our genes meant he could be a cousin on my father's side. So far, though, he hadn't answered messages sent to him through the genealogy website where we'd found him. Nor was he replying to emails sent to the business in Osnabrück, Lower Saxony, where Linda had resourcefully discovered he worked. He appeared to be an IT specialist and had become a junior executive in a marketing company. The common ancestor we almost certainly shared could have been a great-grandparent.

Given how comparatively close to me he was in a familial sense, it was disappointing he didn't respond to any of our repeated efforts to reach him online. I found it odd, I complained to Linda, for him to take the trouble of enrolling in the genealogy network in the first place, and to give his DNA sample to do so, but then not bother with any follow-through.

'It's not so much of "a thing" in Germany, this find-your-ancestors-online business,' reasoned the experienced Linda. 'And everywhere, even in countries like America where it's getting really popular, people's engagement can flag. A lot of people sign up, swab their cheeks and then lose interest.'

We decided on some more direct nudging of the man we were now calling 'young Christoph'. We were getting to know him a bit. Still in his twenties, he had an active social-media presence from which we could derive intel. 'Sometimes I feel like a stalker,' Linda joked. We learned, for instance, that he had recently married, was building a new house, apparently visited the US periodically, and claimed among his resumé details to speak English well. In his posted selfies he had an earnest, fresh look, with neat dark hair.

I discovered a number for his cellphone, surprised and momentarily amused to learn that Germans call the device *ein Handy*. With sweatier palms than I expected for someone who spent his whole working life cold-calling complete strangers, I dialled the number.

After just four European ringtones a recorded Teutonic female voice invited me to leave a message. I gave my name, spelling it out as always, and said I was phoning from New York about my sharing DNA with Christoph. 'I'm very interested in researching my German genetic background,' I said, 'and I hope you can tell me something about your family.' I just had time to dictate my number, though his phone would presumably register it anyway, before a piercing peep cut me off.

I put my phone down, and leaned back in my chair to begin again that part of the research process that I always hated the most: the waiting.

Chapter 28
Ellies

In Africa I always headed towards elephants. Whatever professional task brought me back to the continent, I always made every effort to ensure that I had some downtime to pursue this compelling private enthusiasm. If elephants could be seen, I would go watch them.

It had started in 1972 when I'd just escaped the violent wrath of Idi Amin and ended up in his neighbouring country of Kenya. My London TV bosses gave me a bonus as reward for my part in making the film that our team brought out of Amin's blood-spattered Uganda. It wasn't money. It was a far better prize: a whole six weeks to myself on the equator, with no deadlines and no stories to cover.

I rented a battered Volkswagen Bug in a faded approximation of white. All vehicles in Kenya seemed to be white, except perhaps the safari-going mini-buses, all unconvincingly 'camouflaged' in zebra-inspired wavy black stripes on white. The buses were ubiquitous while the country was fast developing its wildlife tourism industry. I was bent on avoiding such ungainly and unwelcome people-carriers, and plotted my own route across the unmetalled, red murram roads[1] of the country's two biggest nature reserves, Amboseli and Tsavo.

I packed the Bug with supplies. Foremost among these was booze. By the time I was twenty-three I had already developed what I then nonchalantly called a healthy dependence on liquor. Several crates of beer were piled up on the back seat, plus a few strategically chosen spirits of high alcohol percentage by volume,

---

[1] Murram roads have a covering of any combination of compacted gravel, crushed rock, silt, earth and sand, all being derivatives of a laterite or lateritic rock, which is rich in iron (and aluminium) and consequently red. Editor's note.

clear liquids for the daytime, brown tinctures for the night. The car sank heavily on its back axle and, when the motor was running, it sounded uncannily like my grandmother's old treadmill Singer sewing machine—and sometimes every bit as halting and stuttering when the going got tough. It had an air-cooled engine (a water-filled radiator would have fast evaporated) and its filter periodically got clogged with the red dust kicked up from those murram roads. This called for periodic manual declogging by using a foot-long, narrow stick which came with the rental, to clear out the air-hose, and which was made from mahogany, of all things. The frequent stops were also a welcome opportunity for my own rehydration from the reserves on the back seat.

My lone trek, after the tension of dealing with a mad dictator's flailings, felt both calming and invigorating. I had planned to meet a London girlfriend who would fly to the old trading port of Mombasa on the Indian Ocean, and the idea was that we'd take a beach vacation together—but for now it was just me and the bush.

Advisedly, I drove only by day, stopping before nightfall at the scattered and in those days decidedly informal campsites: some tented, some with wooden huts provided by the government wildlife agency. I greatly preferred the latter. They could be basic to the point of bivouacking but were comfortable enough. Comfort, in any case, was ultimately unimportant; my nights were deeply sunk in sleep; in the daytime this boy from the pleasing but unspectacular Scottish Borderlands was entranced by the vastness of the savannah, by the alternation of dense vegetation with open dry prairie, by the searing but wholly welcome temperatures in the upper 90s Fahrenheit, and most of all by the compelling, endless variety of animal life.

I largely avoided the huge game lodges, ugly transplants into pristine, wild terrain built by the international hotel chains that were all too familiar from my work-life. There were occasional exceptions when I got bush-weary and took a meal at one of their restaurants, but at one particular, still new, Hilton-operated lodge, my distaste overcame me afresh. The company had drilled its own waterhole to attract animals, as a feature to add spice to the lodge's open-air cocktail-bar. Totally thwarting the hoteliers' hopes, examples of the Big Five (the loudly publicised tourists' must-see list of elephant, rhino, lion, leopard and buffalo) made only paltry appearances.

Whenever any sizable wild beasts did show themselves, they provoked ridiculously enthusiastic human excitement at the bar and a desperate mass snapping of long-lensed Pentaxes.

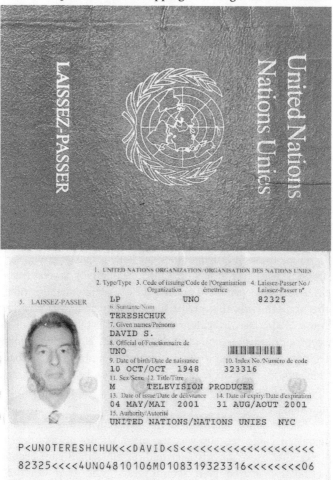

My United Nations 'Laissez-Passer' travel document, valid for 193 countries.

Unsurprisingly the animals would then take off—in disgust, I fancied.

A mere fifteen miles away I found an ancient waterhole that, by contrast, continued to draw every kind of animal—not least the elephants, to whom all other creatures deferred when they arrived, regular as clockwork, in the early mornings and evenings. So began my lifelong fascination with the massive pachyderms. Starting in simple wonderment at their majesty, I soon became engrossed in the subtleties and complexity of their social organisation. The cohesion of the group includes much special care being taken with the young offspring. Most of the animal kingdom expects newborns to become independent quickly; the amount of time they spend being especially vulnerable to predators or to accidents has to be reduced to a minimum. Elephants follow a different course, more in common with humankind's approach to children, and take their considered time over rearing their young. There is a lot of elephantine education to be imparted, and elephant mothers generally share their infant-raising with other females, usually younger adults, whom naturalists label with an odd piece of jargon: allomothers, with the prefix taken from the Greek αλλος (allos) meaning 'other'.

I took irresistible delight in seeing such a female group, each around eleven feet in height, gently encouraging several frisky, three-foot-tall juveniles to practise the use of the unique attribute they're born with, that prehensile and ultimately very powerful trunk. I later learned with astonishment that the trunk is made up of more than 40,000 individual muscles. Not unlike human children taking about a year to first crawl and then walk, baby elephants can take six to eight fumbling months of flipping and flopping before they gain full mastery of their complicated appendage.

The presiding authority over every activity was the oldest female; I could see she was the most senior, in every sense. Experts on Tsavo's herds later told me she would have been in her sixties, maybe even seventy years old. At a waterhole especially, there's no doubting that elephants are a matriarchal society. On reaching maturity, bull elephants leave the family group to live a solitary life or in small gangs—and I saw several singletons come to the water on their own, and then respectfully allow the women and children to go first (if I may briefly use anthropomorphic terms). As I watched each twice-daily visit by the females and their young, the elderly leader would, after about an hour or so, simply raise and stiffen her shoulders but make no other overt sign nor any sound—none audible to my ears, at least. Almost instantly, everyone else would stop in mid-action. After an apparently empty pause that, in those first days at least, I found eerie in its quietness, they would all troop off back into the bush, with the matriarch herself moving forward to lead the column.

My intentness on their behaviour surprised me. The attention I'd previously paid to any of my non-human fellow creatures on earth had amounted to little more than acknowledging the undoubted smarts of Border Collies, along with what I unthinkingly judged the dumbness of sheep, herding up on the low hillsides of my childhood surroundings. These African creatures were something else altogether—wildly exotic of course, and on a stunningly enormous scale. But they presented me, for all their hugeness, with an intricate, endless range of small details to watch for in their interactions with each other.

The waterhole had a clutch of government-provided huts above it for human visitors. While spare and utilitarian, they did offer the precious amenities of a solar-heated shower and a small propane-powered fridge. Basking in this new-found luxury, I stayed on longer than planned and continued keeping my appointments with the elephants. Part-way down the slope to the water, just about fifty feet away from them, I would sit unmoving on my haunches throughout their entire stay, keenly observing the splashing, playing and drinking. Sometime into my residence —four or five days out of the full two weeks I spent there—I noticed that I hadn't opened a single bottle of booze. It felt a weird thing to realise; a day without alcohol had not happened since my earliest college days. I didn't dwell on the oddity, brushing it aside in my overall state of delight in finding each day some fresh discovery about my gigantic visitors' behaviour.

On the road once more, I miscalculated the driving time to

my planned overnight stop. I was still driving by the time the ultra-brief twilight descended—and then pitch blackness. I crested a hill, only to have my headlights suddenly illuminate a single great mass blocking my path. It was one of those lone bull elephants, exiled from the group; fourteen feet high, standing rock-solid and monumental in his isolation. I was driving slowly enough that I could brake sharply to a stop just twenty feet in front of him. He turned towards me unhurriedly and gave me a widened, forward fanning of his vast ears. This was what I'd later learn to be just a warning signal, some gradations below an actual threat—but I didn't understand that then. I backed out fast, downward. I waited another forty minutes at least, and then crept up to the hilltop again to find him mercifully gone—and raced ahead to my intended campsite.

Rattling once again along the rutted murram surface, my hand automatically reached in the dark to the back seat and took a bottle—a tall one, not a stumpy beer. Strong, distilled spirits. And opaque or clear, it didn't matter.

Some years later, in Tanzania, I took time off from reporting a human story I can now barely recollect, except it had to do with economic development of some kind. I made for Tarangire National Reserve, not as famous a safari destination as the Ngorongoro Crater or the Serengeti Plains but pretty rich in elephants all the same, and especially attractive to me because their herds would be easy to find. They'd be concentrated near the sole source of water, the region's River Tarangire.

I've often wished that my education had been different, that it had given me the scientific grounding to become a professional pachyderm-observer. I dreamily imagined myself setting up camouflaged hides, sometimes entire biological stations, working for years in devoted attention to a single community of animals. As it was, I can't claim my relations with elephants ever became exactly close; they never really extended beyond those of a visiting dilettante. But in Tarangire I did have the benefit of a well-connected go-between, a ranger called Joseph Ndagala. He was lean and wiry, in his thirties, probably (I guessed) a member of the Datooga tribal grouping, but he wasn't disposed to talk much about himself. He was far more eager to dispense his understanding of the elephants, as social beings and as individuals. He knew intimately every member of every group of ellies that came to the stretch of river that my rented thatched cabin conveniently overlooked. ('Ellies': not a word Joseph would ever use; it's the product of my own and other visitors' over-familiar presumption.)

Joseph wasn't a formally educated scientist, but at several points in his ranger training he had adopted a practice that was widespread among the animal behaviour specialists he encountered. He was impressed by the rigour with which they labelled and classified the objects of their study. Out of the scores of bush guides who helped me across sub-Saharan Africa, Joseph was the only one I ever heard using the word taxonomy, for naming and classifying creatures. The scientific approach he most happily copied was allotting to each elephant group a letter of the alphabet, and to each single group-member a name beginning with that letter. 'Our' group, the one he and I saw most often, was the B-Team, comprising a leader, Bushra, and then less senior females including Bertha, Bupa, Boba and other B-names my memory can't retrieve.

Among the infants, the youngest was the ever-present Big Ears, a four-month-old male. He did seem somewhat overwhelmed by his own ears. Joseph said that his actual mother was Bertha, but Bupa, Boba and a couple of others all played their part in mothering, or at least nannying, him. One morning I saw Big Ears slip on a crumbling part of the riverbank and tumble sideways into the water, which submerged him so completely that he disappeared—for a whole minute or more. There was a sudden rush of adult females in his direction. His head came into view again, thrashing from side to side and upwards, his trunk flailing about uncontrollably. Maybe his lower body, or just his feet, were stuck in mud or among roots and rocks—we couldn't tell.

'Should we help?' I asked in a panic. 'Can we?'

Joseph frowned briefly and then grinned, very slowly shaking his head, and gestured me back towards the action. One female

(I think Boba) put her huge and of course perfectly controlled trunk to Big Ears' forehead, barely touching but lightly stroking him with its tender, lip-like protrusions. This didn't seem to soothe him much and he kept on thrashing. We saw mother Bertha, who'd been browsing among trees a short distance away, come pounding along to join the rescue party, but before she could get there, Bupa and another female both waded into the river and took up positions facing each other on either side of the youngster. They probed a bit below the surface with their tusks, and then together lifted him up, cradled by their interlocking ivories—his stubby legs paddling madly in the air—and onto dry, safe land again.

Bertha enveloped his neck with her trunk and pushed him under the great overhang of her belly. Joseph told me that as soon as his skin dried, within minutes, it would burn in the sun without his mother's shelter. I was blinking in that fierce sun— blinking back tears of relief.

I made a friend of one of those elephant scientists I found so enviable. He was an animal ecologist in South Africa called Gus Van Dyk. A sturdy Afrikaaner, he displayed that single-minded concentration so common to experts in their various disciplines, but he was also widely read, intellectually versatile, naturally convivial and a caring family man. He always had his wife and two daughters living with him in whichever reserve he happened to be posted.

A good many years into my friendship with him, in 2013, my wife and I visited his then-new and somewhat forbidding work-place, an isolated reserve deep in the Kalahari Desert. Melissa and I played with the girls in a boma, an enclosure where they got us acquainted with some juvenile animals being reintroduced to the territory as part of a biodiversity programme: mostly baby brown hyenas and two-month-old wild dogs. After the human juveniles left for an early supper and bed, we remarked to Gus that his children seemed very happy. He nodded but grimaced a little.

He told us about a recent trip he'd taken with the kids to the city of Kimberly, more than two hundred miles away. Their rare weekend treat had been to see *Frozen* in an actual movie theatre, not a home video setting. He overheard the younger girl react to one disturbing plot point by asking her big sister, 'What kind of parent keeps their kids shut up in a castle?' Gus said he was mortified to hear the older one snap back: 'Well, Dad does, doesn't he?' He resolved then to make sure his children saw more of the outside world beyond their desert reserve.

The reserve where Gus and I originally met in 1997 was the fairly lush Pilanesberg, not very far from Johannesburg. I'd heard from contacts in the elephant studies field that his wildlife management team was experiencing a baffling problem with their animals. I got in touch with him, became fascinated by his approach to the problem, and made him a central character in a documentary about it all. It eventually aired as a co-production between the Science section of *The New York Times* and the National Geographic Society's TV channel. It was the one and only occasion when I had the chance to bring together my work-life with a favourite leisure occupation: elephant-watching.

There had been a spate of mysterious rhinoceros deaths in Pilanesberg. Mysterious, since human poachers could not have been responsible; the rhinos' horns had been left intact and their fatal injuries were not from gunshots. Instead, they'd suffered slash-like lesions and severe cuts right through their thick, leathery skin. Suspicion fell on young male elephants, with their sharp tusks. Some males who had come to Pilanesberg as orphans, Gus worked out, had developed into troubled teenagers, adolescents with surging levels of testosterone. It was an unusually severe and premature form of musth, the condition in which developing young males experience a frenzy of sexual arousal and aggressiveness.

In normal elephant society, this frenzy would be held in check by mock battles played out with older males throughout the younger ones' period of puberty. But this society was not normal. The youngsters' lives had begun in the distant, very large reserve of Kruger Park and had been severely disrupted when their mothers were shot dead. This was a crude park policy in the 1980s, formulated, ironically enough, in reaction to the park's own wildlife conservation success. Happy elephants were breeding happily and this had led to overpopulation, with bigger herds than the park's land could support. Herd-dispersal to other reserves would have been a more humane response but it wasn't possible with the older, bigger individuals. Sedatives were not strong enough at that time to knock them out completely and their sheer bulk was too big for the animal-transporter trucks that existed then. So they were killed—'culled' in the park management's vernacular. The young, smaller survivors were transported to Gus's Pilanesberg Reserve.

But as they grew into their teens these young males had no older bulls as companions or rivals to engage with, and they ended up attacking rhinos instead. (I was tempted to say in my TV script that these 'criminal', indeed 'murderous', delinquents did not have the benefit of 'big brothers', still less fathers, to teach them how to conduct themselves until I decided to avoid such simplistic humanising language. It was the bane of far too much wildlife coverage on TV, I believed, and still do. Let the audience decide for itself about any animal–human parallels.)

In searching for a solution, Gus alighted upon a theory, which became an experiment. He decided to anaesthetise some bigger bulls in Kruger and bring them to join the troubled youngsters. By now veterinarian medicine had developed potent enough drugs for these massive animals—and very much bigger transporter trucks were also being manufactured. These were all brought into play, together with enormous, powerful cranes, which hoisted the unconscious monsters onto huge eighteen-wheelers. The Kruger park ranger, Johnson Nyoka, described the whole venture to me as 'a mammoth project'.

And the project seemed to go well. After getting used to their new surroundings in Pilanesberg, the big bulls were soon being accosted by the younger existing residents. They reacted to the youngsters' provocations by sparring with them tolerantly but decisively, and a new calm began to prevail.

Meanwhile, in a smallish game reserve far to the north, a field ecologist called Jock Macmillan was suffering from similar problems, but the acreage he had available wasn't enough to provide habitat for any imported bigger bulls. Gus's experiment couldn't be attempted in this cramped territory so Jock opted—remarkably, and maybe foolhardily—to act as a human stand-in, believing he could mimic the older male pachyderms in staring down and subduing the truculent teenagers.

During our filming at his reserve, Jock's authoritative shoulder-squaring, expansive arm-waving and loud yelling appeared, amazingly, to have their desired effect. Most of the aggressive teens seemed to be cowed. Except, that is, at one alarming moment when a disgruntled, five-ton seventeen-year-old called N'gama reacted with freshly aroused anger at Jock's shouted orders to 'Stop that now!', 'Cut it out!' and (a little weirdly) 'You're still not bigger than me!'

At the time I was standing with Jock, conducting a taped interview. Our recording had so far been interspersed with his emphatic but now decidedly ineffective commands. N'gama suddenly came lumbering towards us, surprisingly fast and with determined menace.

In retrospect, the footage looks hilarious to me now, though it retains some of our terror in the moment. 'Get in the truck; this interview is over,' Jock shouts to me and to Russell, my cameraman. We all scramble and flee, our driver revving the Land Rover, as out the back Russell's wide-angle lens captures N'gama steadily pursuing us until we can eventually, with our engine roaring, put on enough speed to outdistance him. We soon made it, shaken but safe, to Jock's stockaded camp headquarters.

Back in Gus's larger reserve, with its ample territory for bigger bulls, the elephant-to-elephant stand-offs continued to a point where the youngsters' musth subsided and facing down by the older pachyderms was no longer needed. Violence against other species—'rhino mortalities' in Gus's wording—quickly declined all the way to zero. And the clincher for me came when I accompanied Gus on one of his trips to examine the young elephants' massive dumps of excrement. Analysis of their cannonball-sized droppings showed that their hormonal levels had stabilised. No longer were there any raging spikes of testosterone.

QED, Gus and I both agreed. *Quod Erat Demonstrandum*, the

Latin tag for 'what had to be shown'. It was one of those deeply satisfying stories from science where a problem is in need of a solution, a theory is proposed, tested and proved.

And for me, in my deeper heart, it's now poignant to think that the one time I ever got to meld my professional skillset with my most fervent personal fascination should end up as a reflection on family, community and the troubled young male.

Chapter 29
Mozambique

I had been finagling to get to see it for over three years, and now here it was—towering above my dwarfed figure, 1,000-feet wide and 600-feet high. To be strictly accurate, it was still under construction and so it hadn't yet reached that precise height but it was already by far the biggest newly built structure I'd ever seen and was destined to be even bigger. I was awed and appalled.

I glared up at what I saw as a moral monstrosity: what was then called Cabora Bassa hydroelectric dam (now named the Cahora Bassa). It was rising steadily in the Northwest of Mozambique, a country that in 1973 was still one of Portugal's so-called 'possessions' in Africa. By then I'd gained some reporting experience around the continent, and felt a gut-wrenching sense of outrage at Europe's historic and continuing rape of Africa. There were many occasions when I'd wanted to vent out loud how I felt but instead projected an image of professional, even lofty, objectivity, sometimes to the point of chilly remoteness, I now fear.

Researching the dam's significance much earlier on and from afar, in London, I was struck by its economic and geopolitical importance. Once built, it would generate electricity for all of what remained of white-ruled Southern Africa, reinforcing colonial power while upsetting the lives of tens of thousands of black residents whom the project would displace, and probably killing many. South Africa had advanced northward from its natural geographic border to take a lead in building the dam. It was also paying the lion's share of the project's costs and would in return take the largest cut in the electricity it would produce. Meanwhile the white-run economies of Portuguese Mozambique and Rhodesia next door would also share great benefits in this capital exploitation of Africa's natural resources. These benefits would come from the gigantic development programme in which the dam served as an essential centrepiece.

But I had to be tactical. I was writing story pitches for editorial bosses down the corridor who ran a global news show that I didn't yet work on but dearly wanted to. I needed to keep my vocabulary cool. I could have framed the Cabora Bassa story as an insidious white partnership between the forces of apartheid and international finance. But that would have been way too dialectical and unduly emotional. As a young researcher only recently emerged from academia, I was nervous about being dismissed as either hysterical or doctrinaire by the world-weary, determinedly fact-centred editors in charge. I wanted to build a career, not wreck it.

At the same time, I was a sucker for puns and couldn't resist describing the dam as a concrete symbol, literally and figuratively. Looking back, I am embarrassed by how much my draft memos exuded smart-aleck cleverness but maybe this was how I kept my passion tempered. Had I given it free rein, I'd have been painting my proposed documentary as an unmissable chance to highlight and condemn a nefarious plot by white racists to entrench their control over a corner of the world where they had no right to be, and which they had already brutalised far too long.

With cooler phrasing my pitching turned out to be relatively effective; I was at least told to work further on the story. It took a long time before I was officially hired by the international show and sent to Mozambique but when I eventually arrived, the site's massive reality persuaded me that I had been right about the dam as a monumental embodiment of evil.

My destination was a spot on Mozambique's map called Songo, a town established at the eastern end of the dam in 1969 to house its construction workers and made up of a series of loosely connected barrios. From here I was determined to portray even the unbuilt aspects of the project visually, on screen: what was yet to come and what I took to be the hateful significance of the venture. The problem was, how? It hadn't taken me long to learn that, in TV, there will often be elements in a story that are well-nigh impossible to capture with pictures alone: the broader social or political implications, for example. You can't film

British and South African newspaper articles about and by me in the 1980s.

abstractions. What you can do is build up a mosaic of all available images, to add to the verbal testimony of people with direct experience or well-informed knowledge. Beyond that you can add written narration of your own—with animated graphics, sometimes, if they'll help—and maybe music, too, if it's available on site or you can dub it in, subtly and without overdoing it, where it seems appropriate. With Cabora Bassa I was dead-set on employing all those devices and more: all the arrows in my expanding televisual quiver. But at the heart of it I was convinced that the most powerful element in my film would be that one dominant and, to me, highly sinister visual: the massive dam itself.

My journey had originally begun 12,500 miles away, and in temperatures seventy degrees Fahrenheit cooler than the torrid conditions of the River Zambesi in its deep ravine. It was winter in London, and I was still that brand-new, purely metropolitan journalist, eager to burst through the confines of local reporting. Previously, at college and aged eighteen, I had joined Britain's nascent Anti-Apartheid Movement and donated a little cash: quite literally the minimum single penny requested by the Movement's so-called Penny Pledge. I possessed only limited resources to draw on: a state student grant plus an academic scholarship from my college and some patchy earnings I amassed as a housebuilding labourer during my college vacations. But I was convinced that whatever little I could afford must surely go to fighting the scourge of white supremacy.

The Movement's fundraising was in support of a letter-writing campaign; it collected letters of protest written by individual members like me and forwarded them *en masse* to South Africa's apartheid leaders. The letters demanded the release from prison of Nelson Mandela and other liberation struggle leaders. By 1969 the Anti-Apartheid Movement had mushroomed sizably as a lobbying organisation and I was still volunteering to write letters; I was now also able to contribute a bit more financially, since I'd suddenly become a well-paid young professional. At a central London meeting to rally the letter-writers, I met a Mozambican, Fernando Honwana. He was a strikingly eloquent figure in a natty jacket and tie. He'd come to persuade us to write also to Portuguese colonial authorities, demanding the release of his country's freedom fighters, the liberation movement called FRELIMO, the Front for the Liberation of Mozambique. At that point they had been fighting their war of independence for six years; they were mainly a black African movement, also including sympathetic whites plus members drawn from the country's small biracial population known as *mestiços*.

Honwana's grandfather and great-grandfather had fought against the colonists and his father and elder brother were recently imprisoned by Portugal's hated secret police, the PIDE. If there was anything we could do to help reunite his family, he told the meeting, he would personally be deeply grateful, as would his fellow cadres. Moreover, he insisted, it would help the overall cause of freedom all across Southern Africa.

I joined a group of supporters who took him to a neighbourhood pub that I was familiar with, and which I greatly enjoyed using because of its singular (and not easily explained) name: The Queen's Head and Artichoke. I was surprised to find that Honwana was younger than I was; he seemed so much older. He was an undergraduate studying at York University, 200 miles to the north. As the other sympathisers drifted off home in ones and twos, he and I both lingered, drinking. Blessed with the miraculous novelty of an expense account, I asked if he was hungry. He nodded assent: 'I've learned that shepherd's pie goes well with your English beer.'

I wanted to correct him—'I'm Scottish,' I would have said—but I let it pass. He didn't need to know about British identity politics; and I certainly couldn't disagree about the shepherd's pie. As we each tackled our hefty portions, he broached a new topic. 'I didn't want to talk about this earlier,' he said. 'I had to concentrate on our Release-the-Prisoners issue. But I learned yesterday that some of my family were probably killed last week. Cousins, and an aunt on my mother's side.'

I couldn't answer, couldn't even form a real question. I picked on a single word. 'Probably?' I asked.

'Reliable news is hard to get out of our country, especially from the northern region. We're from Moamba in the south, but my aunt married a man from the north, in Tete Province, and they moved up there.' His English was slow and careful, almost stilted. 'We simply heard that the PAF [the Portuguese Armed Forces] killed all the people in their village—part of the "pacific-ation" of Tete.' He spat out the army's term, assuredly aware that I'd recognise it as a mendacious euphemism for slaughter. 'The village held a protest meeting against being curfewed, and soldiers simply shot into the crowd. Two hundred people killed. All the houses burned.'

He allowed himself a pause, staring emptily towards the pub's pebbled-glass windows. I felt wholly inadequate to the moment. The evening was getting late and drinkers around us were downing their pints with a near-closing-time urgency.

Thinking that I could at least be practical with my sympathy, I offered him an overnight stay on my sofa. 'My flat's just a taxi-ride away,' I said, 'in Chelsea.'

'Thank you but no, my friend. I must take a night train from King's Cross Station. I have class tomorrow morning.'

I gave him my business card and bade him 'Goodnight, Senhor Honwana.' He genially chided me: 'Fernando, please—or Comrade if you like. Goodbye, Comrade David.'

Fernando and I were not to meet again. Shaken by his story, I put myself on alert for news of Mozambique's liberation conflict, as well as the globally better-known South African struggle. Fernando graduated from York the following year and returned to his homeland to fulfil a role in the freedom-fighting. He went on to serve as presidential aide to Mozambique's first president, the Marxist-Leninist Samora Machel, and died in the same plane crash that took Machel's life in 1986.

Mozambique's war against its Portugese rulers was not widely or deeply reported at the time. Newspaper accounts were thin, though they appeared a little more often in continental Europe than in the UK; I came to rely more on international wire-service dispatches for occasional news of battles. Through the early 1970s, I read increasingly of wartime atrocities. A French North African order of Catholic missionaries, the White Fathers, was forced to leave Mozambique and carried disturbing stories. The fathers detailed exactly how the conflict was being increasingly waged against civilians. Their English spokesman described it as 'a series of massacres, for ghastliness each rivaling that of My Lai'. These had taken place in the area of Mukumbura, in Tete Province, between May and November of 1971. Cross-checking the dates, I realised this was probably how the members of Fernando's family met their end.

The issues at stake broadly echoed those in South Africa's anti-racist struggle but there was also a more dramatic dimension: the Mozambique conflict had become a full-fledged war and the horrible truth is that, however awful it was for those caught up in it, I was hungry to observe it, as were all those reporters who volunteered to cover it. The haphazard backstreet gun battles of Northern Ireland had counted as useful experience but career ambition urged me to get into the thick of complete battlefield conditions overseas: I was hungry for large-scale military action.

Actually, what I really wanted was to be assigned to Vietnam, the world's most prominent war in those years and the war in which the most prominent foreign correspondents made their names. It may be revealing of the callousness of the news trade but if you could get to cover Vietnam, you had made it in journalism. In my case, in spite of my desperation, I was repeatedly denied the chance to go; my network sent its more experienced staffers, not me. But I thought my bosses might take a risk on me in some less well-known region of combat.

Covering a war seemed to me an essential rite of passage. I think now that this feeling was not only driven by careerism; in the years before my prefrontal cortex had fully developed its risk-assessment role, I hankered after dangerous excitement and cared little for my personal safety (though fear did inevitably grab me in the most extreme situations: a handgun held directly to my head; rifle-shots flying around me during Derry's infamous bloodbath). On a daily basis I drove cars at breakneck speed and pooh-poohed any possibility that it was risky. I performed ridiculous tightrope-style walks along the stone parapets of tall buildings to horrify and impress others. Put simply, I loved to feel my pulse race and I loved getting accolades.

I also felt I had a compelling personal link to this African war since I had known, if only briefly, a man of my age whose family had been butchered in it, so I sought out all the arcane pieces of background material I could find. From these more analytical studies the colonists' broad strategy for the native population emerged clearly: a forcible herding of rural inhabitants into tightly controlled centres. The Portuguese playbook was borrowed from British colonial troops during Malaya's insurgency of the 1950s, creating what they called 'New Villages', and from the US in Vietnam with its Strategic Hamlet Program. American reports I saw about Mozambique, though even less frequent than European accounts, were especially sharp and down-to-earth. They made very direct comparisons with Vietnam; the My Lai massacre was again frequently invoked.

The Portuguese version of controlled communities had the name *Aldeamentos* ('Established Villages'). They enabled the military to maintain tight surveillance over residents, and to deny them the chance, or so officers thought, to provide support—especially food, concealment and useful intelligence—to FRELIMO's guerillas. I pursued this education in Mozambican matters on top of my day-job of reporting London's rolling news. But in the newsroom one day I had to drop all my immediate municipal work; I received a call, made locally, from a Mozambican who'd just arrived in the UK, someone I did not previously know. I rushed out to meet him.

His given name was Afonso; he didn't tell me his African family name. From his pocket he drew my business card, crumpled and stained now but the same one I had given to Fernando many months earlier, even though Afonso said he had never met him. How many hands had that card passed through, I wondered, and in what remote, arduous, maybe war-torn conditions?

We met, I felt appropriately, back in the smoke-clouded *Queen's Head and Artichoke*. He looked a year or two older than I was and he brought more specifics from the war. He described, albeit at second hand from a frontline comrade, killings by the PAF's Sixth Commando in a village near the Rhodesian border. It was, we both understood, a relatively minor atrocity by the baleful calculus of this conflict: just seventeen deaths. Evidently the villagers' lives were destroyed, viciously and indiscriminately, in reprisal for a FRELIMO attack that had killed some Portuguese commandos. On a handwritten list Afonso had names for each one of the corpses left in the village's main meeting-place. Two were men, seven women, eight children or babies.

Afonso also told me about one aspect of the *Aldeamentos* programme that I hadn't fully appreciated. Well to the north of the Mukumbura area, where the murders of Fernando's relatives had probably taken place, even more aggressive and much wider population clearances were being enforced. In that part of Tete Province, violent removals were more than a military strategy: they had the broader purpose of clearing territory for the building of Cabora Bassa, the colonists' new pride and joy that

274

promised a vast economic powerhouse to serve all of white-ruled Southern Africa. As with earlier massive constructions across the continent, notably the Aswan Dam in Egypt and Kariba Dam in Rhodesia, the plan would involve massive flooding. In Cabora Bassa's case a 1,000-square-mile valley would be submerged to form a huge artificial lake; it would displace incalculable numbers of local people (some estimates were predicting hundreds of thousands), plus of course the area's wildlife.

Afonso's report deepened my disgust at the colonists' tyrannical practices and their determination to entrench white supremacy. A few white colleagues of mine, even some who sympathised with the freedom movement, had suggested the dam at least represented some progress—electricity for a poverty-stricken region, for a start—and so maybe had some positive value, objectively speaking. But such objectivity was lost on me. A vicious, oppressive war was being prosecuted around the dam and I simply had to make my way there to expose this outrage; I had to enlighten those in our Western world who were still unaware of Southern Africa's brutal realities.

FROM LONDON TO TETE PROVINCE

I was still obliged to mount my Get-to-the-Dam campaign on the sidelines of my regular local duties: London's homelessness crisis; periodic scandals in the Mayor's office; the latest daring heist in the Hatton Garden diamond district. For my more distant goal I employed the professional tool I probably appreciated most, my seemingly limitless expense account; it still felt new to me but I quickly learned to bask in it. I began by wooing António Rato Potier, inviting him to luxurious lunches in a sumptuous old-world eatery: Rules in Covent Garden. Rato Potier was the Portuguese Embassy's veteran press counsellor, though 'veteran' barely begins to match his status; his London posting went back to the 1940s. According to my work-calendar of the time, we took eighteen lunches together in total, as attested by my expense claims, which I entered pretty much bi-monthly.

Counsellor Potier was an incurable Anglophile, who constantly extolled the Treaty of Windsor, between his country and England, as the world's oldest alliance: a pact of mutual support between the two nations. It dated back to 1386 and he spoke of it as 'the medieval flowering of a friendship bound to last between two peoples sharing the same values and ideals'. I saw it differently, as merely a tactical *entente* between two monarchies that felt threatened by the cooperation of two other rising powers at the time, France and Spain. Of course, I didn't say so out loud. For reasons of expediency, the Anglo-Portuguese treaty had survived into the twentieth century despite Portugal's government being, by the 1970s, widely condemned as Europe's last fascist regime. Its dictator, Marcelo Caetano, fully deserved his placement alongside Italy's Mussolini and Spain's Franco.

I always invited the counsellor to Rules because I knew it to be (for he had told me) his favourite restaurant on the planet. Rules hadn't existed quite as long as our two countries' diplomatic partnership, but it was venerable enough (founded in 1798) that it suited my purpose ideally. We must have presented a comic pairing to the crisply waistcoated waiters. An eager young man pressing his case urgently to a silver-haired Iberian of aristocratic bearing in his exquisite Savile Row three-piece suit and florid silk tie, or an aquamarine ascot if it was a rare day when he chose to dress less formally. I always sported a smart but deliberately conventional suit and tie, and would defer to him with studied politeness whenever he said anything—which wasn't often. He mostly listened in a non-committal fashion as he knife-and-forked his food delicately. When I gushed admiringly about the 'world-class engineering' of the Cabora Bassa project, he merely nodded sagely and concurred in a light murmur, as he stretched out the whole process over many rounds of the game. 'We will consider what you say, David,' he often reassured me. 'And I will convey to you our thinking when you and I next meet.'

I suppressed my youthful (and I'd still say well-justified) righteousness about the dam's iniquity. I fawned unconscionably on Counsellor Potier. I stressed the value of getting his country's grand plans more widely known—indeed greatly celebrated internationally, I weaseled. I now grimace to remember myself saying, 'Let us show everyone in the world how it's even bigger than Aswan on the Nile!' But eventually I succeeded, and we clinched the deal over our last Dover Sole Meunière. More than two years after launching into my campaigning, I finally gained official government permission to travel to Portugal's southern-most African colony and film its notorious dam.

International argument about Cabora Bassa was getting louder. It became a touchstone for indicating on which side of Africa's racial divide the global business community saw its interests lying. In neighbouring Zambia, free from white colonial rule at that point for nearly a decade, President Kenneth Kaunda denounced Cabora Bassa as a 'crime against humanity'. Many other countries' leaders in the developing world agreed with him, citing the ruthlessly violent population-clearances the Portuguese were conducting, and the broader effect they feared: that the dam programme would strengthen white supremacist rule in the region. In spite of that, a cabal of German, French and Italian companies (plus some subsidiaries of British ones) came together to play a major part in the construction programme being led by the South Africans. In contrast, a Swedish electrical manufacturer, ASEA, was forced by public opinion to withdraw from its early entry into the venture. Scandinavia's populations always seemed to me better informed about Africa than other Western countries; as small nations, perhaps, they cultivated a wariness, even cynicism, about bigger rich countries.

Getting myself to Cabora Bassa's location wasn't easy. I made my way with little difficulty to the regional capital of Tete, a sizable Portuguese garrison town, but then my effort to accomplish the last, short hop to the dam, aboard a flea-like Piper Aztec, ran afoul of the most dramatic tropical thunder-storm I have ever experienced, before or since. The winds blew up from the east wholly unexpectedly. I was the sole passenger, sitting alongside the pilot, a non-English-speaking Portuguese, and I watched in mounting panic as he rode his bucking, shuddering machine through and over thick, dark clouds with rain lashing and lightning striking on all sides. The fuel gauge dropped steadily and alarmingly towards the 'E' mark, convincing me that he'd lost any way of navigating in the storm, and was ploughing on blindly.

Our flight time was meant to be just twenty minutes but by my watch we were now enduring an hour, an hour-fifteen, and then an hour-forty-five of this terror. With whitening knuckles I clutched my seat-arms but I was tongue-tied. I did not want to break in on the pilot's intense concentration. His sallow face was grim, tightly set, also saying nothing. We were doomed, I was sure. I threw up twice—mainly bile, few solids—aiming unreliably into my narrow-necked puke bag while we repeatedly jolted and rolled.

Suddenly an opening of a kind appeared in the clouds— enough, mercifully, for the pilot to make out below us a thin landing-strip, of all things. He brought the plane down in a fast, bumpy return to *terra firma*, both of us shrieking with laughter and slapping each other's shoulders.

But we were not at Cabora Bassa. Somehow or other, my new-found hero of all pilots had taken us the entire way back to Tete, where we'd started. I spluttered a made-up piece of Portuguese, *Sensacionale!* and mimed to him not just my gratitude, but astonishment at just how he had pulled off his incredible achievement. His few words left me none the wiser. But his emphatic shrug, with raised and upturned palms, could have meant his success was really down to sheer dumb luck.

I waited a few more days for the storm system to clear and eventually arranged to travel not by air but with one of the military-led, overland convoys that transported supplies to the dam. (It would take me several years before I could willingly endure a light-aircraft trip anywhere.) To reach agreement on the detailed terms for my passage by road, I ended up drinking in the dusty garrison town's sole and shabby nightclub—inevitably named Copacabana—with the Portuguese Army captain in charge of transportation. Since neither of us spoke the other's language, we made faltering efforts in our haphazardly shared French.

It proved to be one of the few times when I could be grateful for having spent my teens, however reluctantly, in Manchester, England. We were trying to swap basic biographical details and when the captain tapped his chest and said 'Oporto!' I answered simply, and with much less civic pride, 'Manchester'. He promptly let out a delighted, extended and raucous near-yodel of 'MANCHESTERRR UNIIIIITED,' to acclaim the legendary football team. We local schoolkids knew it simply as 'United' but its name was celebrated in full the whole world over. In Africa's southern tropics, our adult man-to-man bonding was assured.

Next day in his role commanding the convoy's security detail, the captain had me sit precariously alongside him atop an open munitions truck. He insisted that I wore an absurdly ill-fitting steel helmet as we drove the tense seven-hour journey. We were running the gauntlet of guerrilla attacks by FRELIMO, who repeatedly carried out landmine or machine-gun ambushes, or both. As I squinted into the dense bush on either side of the badly cratered road, I reflected ruefully on how much I'd cultivated good relations with representatives of that guerrilla force throughout the years I was working my way towards this assignment. I even had the anguished but fantastical thought that somewhere between the trees, dressed in camouflage fatigues and aiming an AK47 at us, might be Fernando or Afonso, or someone else who had handled my business card. Those good relations wouldn't be any help to me now, of course. I was beginning to learn some of the discomforting ironies involved in reporting both sides of a conflict and getting to know people who were each other's sworn enemies. With the help of rudimentary sign language, I asked the captain if the helmet would really protect me from high-velocity gunfire. His face twisted into a non-committal wince and he gestured that it might at least save my skull if (or when?) I was thrown from the bouncing truck onto the rocky road-edges. This was evidently an occupational hazard for the escorting squaddies, quite apart from injury and death in combat.

I kept anticipating what I might find to film when I finally reached my destination. I was still set upon exploiting to the fullest the dam's emblematic value. That phrase 'concrete symbol' would not leave me. I also expected to see an equally solid (and heinous) unity prevailing among the white people engaged in its construction. My mental tableau of international capitalism clasped in an embrace with white racism would, I thought, become animated in reality before my eyes. It would take filmable form, offering scenes of diabolic collusion acted out among real human figures bent upon evil deeds. I wasn't naïve enough to think that groups of multinational experts would willingly acknowledge, while on camera, that their work was intended to shore up white supremacy, but I still imagined I might entrap them with some skilful prodding.

But in any case white unity turned out to be in short supply. During my forthcoming stay in the dam's artificially created township of many nationalities, I was to inhabit a seething cauldron of conflict and division.

DEEPEST MOZAMBIQUE, ON MY OWN

Songo was the township, a newly minted company town built to house all the white workers imported for the dam-building. Its creation had involved forcible removal by the Portuguese Army of the area's entire indigenous population, all of them relocated to arid and stony territory well beyond the project's perimeter and rife with malaria. All of them, that is, who survived the machine-gunning and hut-burnings that drove them out.

Songo's residential areas had a range of different housing styles graded from communal dormitories for the lowest-ranking journeymen and mechanics to comfortable three- and four-bed-room, suburban-style bungalows for white-collar staff. There were also administrative offices to service the construction site, plus ancillary facilities of all kinds from auto-shops to dry-cleaners. And inevitably the entire settlement was wholly white-run.

It sat many hundreds of feet up the ravine above the African labourers' compound, which I was barred from visiting by a rider to my official permission for being onsite, requiring that I never seek access to the compound. The agreement I signed gave no reason for the restriction; it's a fair assumption that the Portu-guese simply didn't want me to see, still less film, the black living conditions. I voiced no objection before signing the document. After the time it had taken negotiating to get to Songo in the first place, I knew that any insistence on penetrating the *Composto de Trabalhadores Negros* would result in my whole endeavour being cancelled. Once there, I saw company security guards and Portuguese soldiers making very sure of the compound's separateness and segregation by colour. All the same, though, I felt I should get into it. I needed as full an understanding of the whole place's functioning as I could get. And of course, it's never OK for a journalist to be told that there's somewhere they cannot go.

Atop the ravine also sat the headquarters of the South African-led consortium, ZAMCO, and those of the Portuguese authorities who oversaw its operation, the two opposing (as it turned out) poles of the entire venture. It was here that I first appreciated the stresses and strains gnawing at the white unity I'd naïvely expected to see. An entire two miles separated client from contractor. 'Who else but the fucking Portuguese would make themselves so inaccessible?' an exasperated South African engineer complained to me.

Afrikaaner professionals like him, who often proudly proclaimed their Dutch ancestry, saw themselves as rough-and-ready, get-it-done types and viewed the Southern Europeans—'dagos', as they referred to them in private—as an infuriating mix of both haughty attitudes and inefficiency at work. They repeatedly applied the phrase 'lazy and feckless' and blamed 'the Portos' (a locally invented shorthand) for interfering needlessly in matters that should be conducted straightforwardly in their own brisk, Hollander fashion. ZAMCO men spent much of their time fuming about the Portuguese, who for their part appeared quite blithe to the annoyance they caused. I never heard any Portuguese officials say anything critical about another nationality.

They did insist, though, that all official communication should be in the Portuguese language; in their minds, after all, it was their country and their dam. A ZAMCO administrative assistant from Johannesburg showed me his desk; it was covered with memos that he'd translated between the different languages of consortium members. He moaned, 'These are quite enough work in themselves, and this is without the Portuguese.' He had the misfortune to be the only multilingual translator in the Babel-like throng and had laboriously turned all the documents into German, Italian and French as well as English. The clerk became more plaintive: 'Some detail might have to be referred to the Portuguese,' he whined, 'or the Portuguese might suddenly take an interest in something specific, without any warning. And then I've got to work through every one of these memos all over again, just to get everything into their goddamn language.' The most obvious option—to South Africans like him, at least—of employing English as a common language was imperiously prohibited by the Portuguese authorities.

I observed the South Africans' contempt for all things Portuguese getting incorporated into their broad-based, everyday racist outlook. The township manager, a stout Afrikaaner with few graces, called Clem Gething, showed me around Songo with a proprietary flourish and freely expressed his judgement that the Portuguese were 'worse than kaffirs', the general Afrikaans term of abuse for black Africans. One major complaint for these apartheidists was that while the Portuguese may have been colonists by policy, their personal attitudes and behaviour towards native Africans lacked the codified viciousness that white South Africa displayed as its culture's signature behaviour.

There was little to do in the Songo evenings but there was the so-called Songo Social Club. In actuality just a glorified bar, it aspired to being family-friendly by serving food, and it placed flowers, plastic ones, on the tables. Since I had to probe all aspects of the enclave's insular existence, the Club became a frequent location for my research. I would go in mid-evening and chat with individuals and groups in the hope of gaining their confidence. I might even, I hoped, score an agreement to profile on film a 'typical' white worker and his life there. Such hopes became increasingly forlorn: one blunt refusal to be filmed was followed by many more.

South African-style attitudes were becoming dominant. One night a white Portuguese surveyor entered with his black wife; they were only very recently married, I learned later. The couple's arrival provoked a swift muting of bar noise, then a wave of dismayed but unspoken outrage along previously rowdy tables of Afrikaaners. Forks were dropped, fingers were pointed and broad muscular backs were turned away. The newlyweds sat in silence, speaking not a word to anyone, or to each other.

The Whites' employment contracts were often lengthy, some up to three years long, and the township engendered its own form of claustrophobia. In the main, residents could travel out of Songo only by the twice-weekly military convoy, and needed special permits, not easily granted. The six-seater airplane service, the one I'd initially tried for reaching Songo, was expensive even for the higher-paid Europeans. Portuguese military officers had spoken to me proudly of concentric 'triple steel rings' of defence that their army had established around Cabora Bassa, providing impenetrably secure protection for the dam-building work. FRELIMO had sworn equally confidently that its guerrillas would destroy their oppressors' dam. And day by day those guerrillas succeeded in capturing more villages, and sometimes substantial towns, thereby driving out Portuguese troops and freeing whole communities from colonial control. Not for nothing were they called a liberation army—and now that army was getting closer and closer to the dam.

Like all the regular residents of Songo, I lost contact with outside news sources but everything I had previously learned *en route* there, unofficially from informants in the capital city of Lourenço Marques (now Maputo) and in more detail at Tete's regional garrison, confirmed for me the seriousness of FRELIMO's continuing advance. Here, though, at the very centre of the circles of defence, the Portuguese kept insisting that everyone in Songo was completely safe from 'the terrorists'. But this safety came with constraints, and these were greatly resented. I heard the bitterest complaints from the dedicated big-game hunters among the South African contingent; they weren't allowed to venture out into the bush and indulge in their lethal hobby during their downtime. Clem Gething got himself into trouble with the Portuguese for his openly expressed sarcasm. He was called in to the Portuguese commander's office for a telling-off after he was heard saying that maybe he should apply to FRELIMO for a hunting licence.

None of the fighting was ever close enough for us to witness it directly, so it was easy for Songo's Whites to be blasé, or affect to be. In my Club conversations and in the other bars where I talked with every rank of white worker, from architect to engineer to electrician and plumber, it became clear they had no conception of either FRELIMO's advances or of what the Portuguese military was doing 'out there' to counter FRELIMO. They knew nothing about the destruction of villagers' homes or the forcing of families into *aldeamentos*, while men of working age were rounded up to come and labour on the dam in slave-like conditions, housed in the dismal compound deep in the ravine below us.

Dismal was certainly how it looked from the outside, with its forbidding defences, but I still hadn't seen inside. I heard that the accommodations resembled the barracks that generally prevailed in South African coal and gold mines, long rated by human-rights observers as among the worst workers' housing in the world. The men billeted here weren't technically enslaved, I suppose; they received wages. I never learned exactly what the wages amounted to but no white man in charge ever claimed that they were any more than rock-bottom rates. And every labour gang I saw was supervised by a gang boss with a shotgun slung over his shoulders. 'For safety's sake,' one of the bosses, a Rhodesian, told me. He didn't elaborate any further when I asked, 'Safety from what?'

Breaking, or least gingerly testing out, my prior agreement with the Portuguese authorities, I made one effort to enter the black compound. I was waved away decisively by a troop of suddenly agitated infantrymen. They were manning, and then swiveled menacingly in my direction, two American-made, NATO-issue M60 machine-gun emplacements. My still-limited experience of covering wars had given me enough tradecraft to identify the weapons, but I'd half-forgotten that Portugal was a NATO member and had access to the alliance's multinational range of munitions. For all I knew, its troops might even be using British arms made in my own home-country to conduct their war of oppression. In the face of this high-grade weaponry, I made a tactical withdrawal from my incursion attempt.

Songo's bars—very functional (much cheaper than the Club) but somewhat dreary—were never less than fully packed, and I often saw the Whites' fenced-in frustrations spill into alcohol-fuelled violence. I once had to escape in a hurry when a fist-fight between a German and an Italian (possibly over a football issue—or maybe something less vital) multiplied quickly into a wild donnybrook of at least thirty men with flying punches, broken bottles and one whopping 40-ounce beer can, opened but still full, that crashed at head-level into the doorframe just as I ran out through it. It exploded and soaked the back of my shirt. I gave that particular drinking-spot a wide berth thereafter. I later re-encountered one of its regulars, a South African pipefitter, when he made a rare visit to the Club, still sporting a livid black eye from somebody's uppercut on fight night. He told me that the super-sized container which narrowly missed me—a frequent missile of choice, he said—was known familiarly in that bar as a Man Can.

The Yukon goldrush atmosphere might have been moderated by the fact that many of the workers were settled onsite with their wives and children. But as a potentially steadying feature of Songo life this actually brought a different set of problems. Single men had their separate quarters: long, low-slung huts subdivided into cubicle-sized units usually shared between two men. The contrast between these and the much more comfort-able family houses provoked strong resentment.

Social facilities were also separate, and much of the security-guards' energy was taken up with ensuring that the bachelors, who frequently worked nightshifts and spent aimless days in the sun, would keep to their own swimming pool and did not 'fraternise' with their colleagues' wives. That seemed to me an odd official euphemism, since there was nothing remotely brotherly about their overtures to the women. I stayed at a discreet distance from the female swimmers and sunbathers, and not just out of respect or propriety; I didn't want to risk com-promising my precarious presence in the enclave. But I watched, inwardly squirming, embarrassed by my own gender, whenever a solitary male, often an Italian or Portuguese but just as easily a German or South African, moved in all-too-leeringly on a group of women and offered to buy drinks all round. I saw only groups; women never seemed to come to the pool alone—an understandable precaution, I supposed. Usually the women said a firm 'No thanks,' or just sometimes a guardedly encouraging 'Yes, please' might be voiced. But always—without fail, during my scrutiny at least—a guard then appeared in almost no time, demanding to see the man's area-coded ID card and expelling him back to his own sector.

An earnest, almost combative South African Calvinism characterised the township's administration, despite its cosmopolitan citizenry. Whenever a prostitute was found to have slipped in, usually by favouring a pilot or convoy-driver, she was promptly shipped out. I never saw this happen but I heard about it often enough. Some Italian men, who were especially cohesive as a group, collared me one afternoon and berated me insistently (as some sort of external resort of appeal, maybe?) about this infringement on their personal rights.

I found it bizarre how the Afrikaaners tried to police this multinational community as if it were a Boer *veldt* town, like the farming communities on South Africa's treeless plains with names like Jagersfontein, Ficksburg or Kroonstad, whose social values were summed up in the word *ordentlik*, a precept that combined notions of being well-ordered, respectable, modestly clothed and pure. To even begin to qualify for such decency you did have to be white, of course. I shouldn't have been surprised by Songo's efforts at moral strictness, I suppose. I often sensed that under apartheid there lay a creepy sanctimony, along with its innate defensiveness and deep existential fear.

I had to absorb a good deal of personal hostility: deliberate snubbing; refusals to engage in any discussion at all, even unofficial, casual chat; walking away when I arrived on a scene— all that kind of micro-aggression. The animus was greater than I've encountered on any filming assignment, unless it was among the die-hard Protestants of Northern Ireland (Calvinists there too, I can't help recalling). Many Songo residents could not believe that the Portuguese had allowed me in; they saw no sense, unlike Portugal's globally ambitious senior diplomats, in publicising their massive enterprise to the wider world. So when it came to negotiating for on-the-record, filmed interviews onsite, I was totally blocked by their wall of refusal and resistance. Clem Gething shared the common angry incredulity that I was there at all but he was under orders to cooperate, and he did so, although minimally and sullenly. He gave me a clipped, barely articulate interview that laid out basic facts and figures about the operation, and very little more. 'There are 510 million cubic metres of concrete and metal,' he summarised at one point, as if to put an end to our talk, 'We'll create over 2,000 megawatts of electricity via five generators.'

As for logistical cooperation, he at least let me have my own form of transportation to get around the widely sprawling site: a relic of a Chevy pick-up truck, for which he charged me a gouging rental rate in US dollars. This went into his own pocket as cash, not into the company ledger.

I was housed, too, but in a dilapidated and infernally sweltering example of the smallest company-issue, tin-roofed hut that was available. It wasn't long before I fell ill with a slight-to-medium case of malaria, and was unable to leave my billet. The hut's Styrofoam ceiling tiles served as flimsy separation between me and whatever animals had the run of the space between ceiling and roof. There was constant scratching and some disturbingly sudden and frighteningly heavy thuds. Lizards and gigantic insects were everywhere, of course—on floors, walls and ceilings: mostly harmless and unthreatening. But the unseen and heftier-sounding wildlife above the tiles really troubled me. I could have sworn that a tile was at times being lifted at the corner and that a pair of reddish eyes was staring down at me. I fully expected whatever creature or creatures were up there to drop on my head at any moment. I cannot rigorously vouch for any of this, of course; delirium may be a better explanation.

I was still on my own at that point; my film crew hadn't yet arrived and in my lone and feverish state I couldn't move or seek medical aid, let alone work. I sweated it out, copiously, writhing on my two-foot wide cot and vomiting into a tin bowl. A few days later the crew turned up and our film director, a burly and amusingly officious man whom I liked a lot and who was blessed with a British Raj-sounding name, Peter Tiffin, was appalled at my conditions. Peter's outrage ('Not even a fan? For a sick man in 100-degree heat!') more than equaled Clem Gething's obstructive surliness and it won me a transfer to more comfortable accommodation, plus some welcome medical attention. I was up—up and at 'em in my mind!—within a couple of days, a quickly recovering, healthy youngster bursting to get our film shoot finished, whatever level of cooperation, or its opposite, might face us.

DEEPEST MOZAMBIQUE, NO LONGER ALONE

The dam-builders' animosity was immovable, but I now had the relative comfort of sharing it with colleagues. All of us knew each other from previous shoots mainly in Britain or Europe, but our current unity was different, thrown together 2,000 miles south of the equator in a decidedly hostile environment. The others, as usual in any team I then belonged to, were all older. Our leader, the stocky Peter, had fifteen years on me. Ray, the cameraman, tall and spindly and always wearing a neat, if rather out-of-place neckerchief secured with a gold ring, was just about a decade older; as was Reg, the compact, sometimes unkempt sound-recordist. It quickly became less tiresome, even irrelevant, that our 'hosts' were so against us; we ourselves got along together just fine.

As often on location, it was a delight to be alongside professionals each endowed with their own special skills, and to see them combine in their interdependent ways, creating as a result something collaborative and unique. My longtime friend in print, the foreign correspondent Bob Chesshyre of London's The Observer, once reinforced in me my gratitude that TV journalism is, of necessity, a team effort. I had met Bob on various stories in different parts of the world, and when off-duty at home, too. Some months before the Mozambique trip, we were both sent— without realising the other had also been assigned—to report on conditions in a grim refugee camp near Vienna. Bob was standing alone with his reporter's notepad by the camp gates when he spotted me with my crew and gave a broad, sweeping wave, happy to recognise me. When our team finished our interviewing and picture-taking in the front courtyard, I peeled off and accompanied him to a nearby bar. I hadn't previously appreciated how uncomfortable he must have been with being alone. Toying with his drink, he said wistfully, 'It must be nice to be always with a band of other guys.' I had to think a moment, and replied: 'Well, I'm not always with the others. I do a lot of solitary research and note-taking just like you. But yes, when the others do join me, it certainly can be nice.' Not an exact term for it, nice; but it sufficed.

At Cabora Bassa's highest point, Peter, Ray, Reg and I conferred over one shot we felt we simply had to get. Conveying the sheer scale of the dam for our viewers required something special. The solution, when it came, was Peter's brainchild. He voiced what was already becoming a defining catchphrase for him: 'I know just how to show this.'

As usual, he was right. The imagery we captured from our elevated standpoint—or that Ray captured—was to become the dramatic opening sequence for our finished broadcast. The audience first saw a tight close-up. Filling the frame was what appeared to be nothing more than a domestic-sized bucket containing bits of crumbled cement and debris. The bucket was then lifted up by a hook and cable. Ray widened his zoom lens outward and slowly tilted his classic 16mm Arriflex camera upward, all in exact time with the bucket's journey; only then would the viewer see that the bucket was an object travelling from the bottom to the top of a thousand-foot-deep ravine, with ant-sized human workers now appearing around it to provide a new sense of scale. Only then were the scene's true dimensions fully revealed, in a form of cinematic gigantism. The 'bucket' was in fact a tapering cylindrical dumpster, thirty-five feet tall and almost twenty feet across the top. In our planned final cut of the film, we would insert a brief pause here to allow the utter hugeness of everything to register as the background setting for our report. After this attention-grabbing ploy, our full, rather involved story could then begin to unfold.

We needed multiple takes to get this opening shot right. Thankfully, the dumpster was brought up full, then up-ended, emptied, and sent back down again a dozen times through that sultry morning. We had started just as dawn broke, hoping we'd only be exposed to the day's least searing heat. Each time the emptied dumpster went back down to the ravine bottom, more broken concrete was again dumped into it by a pair of Caterpillar backhoes and the lifting would begin again, enabling us to record another version of the same movement.

Anyone else might have thought that Ray had already fully caught all the elements of the scene but, ever the perfectionist, he kept saying: 'Let's cover one more, just for good luck.' I think it was Take Seven that we ended up using in the final broadcast. We filmed until almost noon, when the temperature hovered around 112 Fahrenheit. The scene, we all agreed, was well captured.

Another day it was Reg whose skill came to the fore. We had given up on ever accomplishing a regular-Joe kind of interview with any white workers and their families. Talking with African workers remained off-limits, of course, and they were seen by our camera only as silent and probably unwilling contributors of their labour to the racists' grandiose venture. Only later, and elsewhere, would we hear from black Mozambicans—the leading members of FRELIMO pledged to destroying the dam.

We wanted some ordinary white workers' voices and so we tried a subterfuge, a last-ditch effort in the face of all the non-cooperation that had blocked us. In the Songo Social Club, Ray set up his tripod and camera behind a gap in a curtain—or maybe he cut a secret slice out of it. The curtain fronted the Club's small entertainment stage, which to my knowledge never showcased any actual performances. We had bribed the Club staff to gain this access in this clandestine way. They were scared to cooperate and would do so only once and for just one hour flat; US dollars in sufficient quantity were what made them agree: a hundred for each of the three janitors, I recall—a hefty sum for us, and a total outlay of roughly $1,500 in today's money. We also promised that, if discovered, we would claim to have rigged up our position during the staff's off-duty hours and without their knowledge.

From his hidden position Ray could film mainly wide shots, but could also zoom in close on groups of clubgoers when required. Reg and I meanwhile roamed the room, with me engaging small drinking-schools in conversation. Playing the role, glass in hand, of an over-talkative semi-drunk felt a lot harder than doing proper interviews with a notepad or microphone. My repertoire of openers was undoubtedly clumsy: 'How are you doing?' or 'How'd your day go?' or even on occasion 'That glass looks low—can I buy you another?' Responses ranged from 'S'okay. Same as ever' to 'Fuck off, ya skelm' or sometimes just a sullen grunt or blunt silence. But if given even the slightest of encouragements, I would then try to manoeuvre towards the nub of my matter: 'Do you ever worry about your safety, with the war going on out there?'

Reg was carrying a Uher mini-recorder in the deep inside pocket of his safari jacket; a cord ran from it, down his shirtsleeve to a tiny directional microphone taped to his watchstrap. We thought we'd look suspicious if we moved around the Club as a couple joined at the hip, so he was sometimes close to me, but more often kept his distance, relying on the powerful capabilities of his Unitra mic, a legendary instrument sold by its German manufacturer with the slogan Making Things Work.

To the unwary it might appear as if a mime-act was in play; at unexpected moments Reg would sharply readjust his elbow's angle whenever a different person spoke up in response to my questioning. He had the unrelenting need for audio-capture of the highest clarity, whichever direction a new voice might suddenly come from. He tried to make his odd gesticulations look casual, as if merely checking the time on his watch. But I felt it happened a little too often to be entirely believable; I worried he might overdo it and start to look like a semaphore messenger.

I had my own problems too. In my interviewer's task I elicited very few meaningful answers. On the personal danger question, their assessments went only as far as 'Never think about it'—plus perhaps 'That's the Portos' job, not ours. We're not soldiers.' These were far from substantive contributions to our coverage, but their tone did sum up the temperament of this insulated community.

After a total of more than three weeks for me, and one intense week of work for the crew, we had gathered as much material as realistically possible. We said a relieved goodbye to the truculent white population of Songo and left the country, hopping (myself very leerily) onto a succession of small planes, first back to Tete, then via two hops to the bigger airport of Beira on Mozambique's coast. There we caught, a little more reassuringly, a DETA plane, one of the colonial airline's few Boeing 737s, big enough for 120 passengers. This took us to Blantyre, the commercial capital of

Malawi. From there we chartered a sizable but rickety plane I couldn't identify—it might have been a re-configured 1950s Viscount, built in England—to get us finally to Tanzania.

We landed in the capital, Dar-es-Salaam, which translates as Place of Peace. The change in climate we sensed was as much mental and subjective as meteorological. After Cabora Bassa it seemed we were now breathing free, fresh air. We relaxed into the spirit of a country that had thrown off the shackles of white colonial domination a full twelve years before our little party arrived.

DAR-ES-SALAAM: FIRST IMPRESSIONS

Here was FRELIMO's heavily armed headquarters-in-exile, a part of the self-proclaimed city of peace devoted entirely to waging war. I was staggered by its expanse and its assertively maintained separateness. It seemed like a militarily ruled state-within-a-state, with everyone speaking Portuguese and indigenous Mozambican languages, a big contrast with the spoken English that prevailed throughout Tanzania. The camp was our primary target once we arrived. We needed to hear directly what the Cabora Bassa dam meant to the forces arrayed against it.

I had been warned long before our arrival that Dar would buzz incessantly with rumours; the first I heard was a new theory being promoted from abroad by South African commentators. The claim was that FRELIMO troops were now finding it difficult to reach the dam and had in fact decided to abandon their attempt to destroy it, in recognition of what the commentators called 'the new realities of war'. It sounded doubtful to me, totally out of key with what we'd learned inside Mozambique, but I needed to check it out. The answer came hard and fast.

We rolled up to FRELIMO HQ in a rented van with all our equipment, and Peter was the most amazed. 'It's a hell of a lot bigger,' he said, 'than any Portuguese emplacement we've seen,' meaning both the colonial garrison for Tete province and the various command posts we'd observed up close to the dam. We were told that FRELIMO in Tanzania amounted to a boots-on-the-ground presence of 10,000 troops or more. The camp we were entering did not house their full complement; far from it: many more battalions were dispersed in camps spread across their host-country, some very close to the border with their homeland. Barracks security in Dar was tight, with high perimeter walls well-patrolled, and with doubled (almost airlocked) doors at the main entrance. All new arrivals, whether persons or deliveries, were subjected to rigorous searches. It was three years after FRELIMO's first president had been assassinated. Having led the movement from his founding of it in 1962, Eduardo Mondlane suddenly met his death by mailbomb—most likely dispatched by Portugal's PIDE agents. As we unloaded our gear, each item underwent a more diligent piece-by-piece examination than anything we had encountered at any of our many checkpoints since leaving London. Such careful precautions might have reassured us about our own safety going into this citadel but I still harboured some misgivings. Since white supremacists had used mailbombing to terrible effect, might they not now try some other deadly avenue of attack, maybe from the air? Not while we were inside, I hoped.

The minute we had rigged up our camera and interview mics, the top commander launched straight into addressing the dambusting issue. This was Major-General Joaquim Chissano, a FRELIMO founder-member and currently number two in the movement as a whole, charged with running the army and conducting the war. A trim, wiry man, thirteen years older than me, he looked tidy, even fastidious in his dress, even though it was simply military fatigues. He reminded me of the equally neat Fernando Honwana, the first Mozambican I'd met in London, the serious twenty-something who campaigned for his nation's freedom during breaks in his college studies. Like that young volunteer, the General's manner when at rest seemed quiet but was utterly different when barking orders at his men. He was brisk in refuting the rumours I wanted to check.

'Cabora Bassa unquestionably remains a major target for our guerrilla forces,' Chissano said. I didn't need to quote the new South African line to him; he was well up on it. But I did tell him what some European dam workers—in particular a group of engineers from the German Siemens company—had told me on site. 'They say they feel they're safe,' I said, 'because they reckon the dam itself is neutral. They see it as a project to enrich whoever runs the country in the end, Portuguese or Africans.' Chissano shook his head, I couldn't tell whether in sadness or anger. Then almost tonelessly he said: 'To leave the dam alone during our war would be like ignoring our enemy's military headquarters simply because one day, after independence, we might like to use the building.' It was chilling to hear, but it made a flat, inescapable kind of sense. These were the 'realities of war' as FRELIMO saw them. I would learn more about those realities later.

I may have given the impression that our Chissano interview was the first thing we filmed in Dar. That doesn't take account of some other realities, political ones. To begin with, there was a good deal of etiquette to observe, not least an appropriate recognition of just whose country we were now working in. Before we could spend much time with FRELIMO we were directed by Tanzanian officials towards filming a government ceremony. It was to be a formal celebration of pan-African unity, to showcase Tanzania's active support of other countries' liberation movements like FRELIMO. The event was to be hosted at the highest level; by the President himself, in fact.

I had come to regard President Julius Nyerere as an archetypal hero-figure. This dated from my time hanging out at London's rendezvous for the continent's many exiles, the Africa Centre. Almost every African I met there referred to Nyerere with the affectionate nickname or honorific, Mwalimu, meaning 'teacher' in Swahili. The white supremacist leader in Rhodesia, Ian Smith, inevitably regarded this honoured teacher in very different terms. 'Africa's evil genius', Smith called him. My African friends wanted me to understand Nyerere's towering example in achieving liberation for his country after a century of colonial dominance, first by Germany and then by Britain. And more, I should appreciate the distinctive quality of his victory: he had won that freedom through peaceful political means, not by revolution or war. His peaceable approach made it all the more remarkable to me that, as soon as he was in power, he invited into his country fighters from other countries who were conducting armed struggles against their colonial oppressors. As well as FRELIMO, Mwalimu Nyerere was also lending great stretches of territory to liberation armies from South Africa, from South West Africa (which would eventually become Namibia), and from Rhodesia (Zimbabwe).

My aim was to get him talking on camera about the hospitality he gave to FRELIMO, so I lodged an interview request with his office and looked forward to our meeting. It didn't happen. Helping black-nationalist freedom fighters was a major priority but it was not his absolute top priority. That of course was governing his own sometimes-factional population, and his appointment diary was filled with domestic concerns. Who knew —I certainly didn't at the time—what internal problems and pressures might be awaiting him?

His staff told me I had to be content with filming Mwalimu as he made his already scheduled speech at the upcoming solidarity celebration. I could see that the event might offer us a chance to gauge, if only impressionistically, how important FRELIMO's fight was to black Africa beyond Mozambique. At the ceremony, FRELIMO was represented by its current leader, President Samora Machel, successor to its assassinated founder-president. Other liberationist organisations from abroad sent lower-ranking officials to the event as ambassadors-in-waiting, so to speak. Machel, on the other hand, was treated as a soon-to-be head of state.

So there came to be two Caesars in the room. I sized up both Nyerere and Machel with the inescapably intertwined sensations —awe plus curiosity—of a young man coming up close to older men of great authority. I looked on intently while Ray and Reg filmed Nyerere mounting his steep podium with care, and looking out at the audience. We were in a crowded stateroom in his official residence, the Ikulu or State House, a grand, white-turreted building previously occupied by British governors. The high-ceilinged chamber was aswirl with a kaleidoscopic mix of dazzling kitenge robes and elaborate, bemedalled military uniforms, plus a solid leavening of plain soldierly camouflage. Television journalism inevitably involves a considerable amount of pomp and circumstance; I had done my share of covering official pageants such as, for instance, the state opening of parliament in London. But this Tanzanian gathering was very different from that stiff array of MPs alongside elderly members of the House of Lords in their white miniver and ermine furs. Here in the Ikulu there prevailed a comfortable looseness, an unforced joyousness even, which cheered and thrilled me alongside the unquestioned gravity of the gathering's formal purpose.

And there was no pomp about the man in charge, only straightforwardness. A local journalist whispered to me just as the presidential speech was beginning that Mwalimu had recently moved his personal living quarters away from our current surroundings, not caring for their imperial resonance. He opted instead for a humbler private home in a coastal suburb that was still in essence a Swahili fisherfolk's village.

Nyerere's exact age was unknown because his parents, who'd been leaders among the Zanaki people of Tanzania's northern lakeside region, neither read nor wrote and so did not register his birth with colonial officialdom. I guessed him to be in his mid-fifties. He was slightly built and seemed at first diffident, standing only five feet, six inches tall. He had a narrow, Chaplinesque moustache that might have been comical had it not been for his compelling speaking voice and authoritative bearing. His words emerged in a clipped, precise manner, with an element of emotion occasionally tingeing the rising timbre of his voice as he made vehement pledges of unending support for the continent's liberation fighters. I thought I recognised the clear-cut tones of a graduate from Edinburgh University, which is where he'd studied.

By contrast, FRELIMO's much taller Machel, at least a decade younger, delivered his formal vote of thanks to Nyerere in tones that sounded a little rougher at the edges, albeit duly respectful. Like Nyerere, he was drawn from that broad class of the continent's black nationalists whose upward mobility in their colonised societies propelled many of them to the Western world's colleges.

Their generation of liberation fighters—and I was to meet

many of them in those final decades of last-gasp colonialism—came to have a special fascination for me in whichever country they originated. I found it inspiring how many of them scaled the structures of their oppressed societies and grasped the tools of resistance from the oppressors themselves, attending their universities, mastering their language and customs, learning their political ways and turning them into levers against the powerful. My own mobility, from rural disadvantage in the Scottish Borderland to Oxford's gilded academia and then into a position of some influence via the world of media, carried only the faintest echo of theirs, but I couldn't help sensing a small degree of identification with them. One enormous difference, though, was obvious. Their life trajectories had entailed, when necessary, taking up arms against the power structures that had held them back. I could never see myself as that kind of rebel, if indeed I was any kind of a rebel at all. I was a persuader, not a fighter, I reflected, as resounding words of war from the Mozambican leader were reaching their crescendo.

Machel gained rousing applause from the crowd—though for not quite as long (because orchestrated, I wondered) as that which greeted Nyerere when he magisterially closed the whole event—but I was well satisfied that we had captured, along with the occasion's rhetoric, a palpable measure of FRELIMO's favoured standing among other Africans.

DAR-ES-SALAAM: EXILES

The solidarity ceremony was a one-day event woven into the liberationist warp and weft of Dar-es-Salaam life. Dar reveled in its identity as a black city leading a free black nation. As four visiting Britons, we each enjoyed it in our own fashion, going our separate ways to carry out our different tasks.

I had to get to know the city politically and place FRELIMO in its wider African context. I also had to carry out my customary chores: some journalistic, some logistic. This mostly meant finding and pre-interviewing potentially useful people before pinning them down for filmed interviews. It also meant setting up ritual drinks meetings with the usual round of staff members from foreign embassies. Who they all were has long disappeared into the deepest thickets of my memory, along with the legions of diplomats in almost every capital I ever worked. Their job was to keep an alert but discreet ear to the ground in their host country and they'd invariably insist on anonymity when we talked. Such a round of meetings was a social requirement for any international newcomer, and the background knowledge they yielded sometimes turned out to be of real use, especially when I was still an inexperienced reporter.

On the logistics side, I had to survey all our possible shooting locations in the city and make practical arrangements for access to places and events we needed to cover. It could sometimes feel humdrum but I enjoyed the effort to secure apt visual scenes to illustrate our editorial ideas. As I paced the streets, slowly and carefully to limit my sweating, I couldn't stop my pulse from thrumming—as it always has in African cities—with the heat, light and blazing colours, so excitingly different from the damp, cold grey of my Borderlands upbringing, best described in our dialect as *dreich*.

Separate from me, Peter, Ray and Reg could feast on capturing the 'atmos'. They wandered the old port city's streets, a riot of scarlet flame-trees at that time of year and garlanded with purple blossoms of jacarandas, collecting material that carried our trade's abbreviated label of GVs (general views). Reg sometimes split off and walked around alone with his Uher to tape the city's soundscape: traditional East African *taarab* music, Muslim calls to prayer, street vendors spieling their wares, drum-driven *mchiriku* tavern-songs—all the city's noises that caught his ear. I don't think I ever saw Reg so happy in his work, through nearly six years of repeated assignments with him.

In Ray's painstaking hands and eye, Dar's GVs combined to convey a bustling city of growth. Early twentieth-century art-deco buildings in pale shades of tropical yellow and cream were now overshadowed by the inevitable glass-and-concrete high-rises of the 1970s. And all the while the redolent flavour of an Arab and Indian trading post, which Dar had historically been, remained irradicable. All of us wished, often repeating it to each other, for the impossible: that the mingling smells of sharply differing spices in the open-air market could be captured on TV, along with the hurly-burly of our images and sounds.

Since Tanzania's independence in 1961, Dar had attracted a constant flow of visiting leaders from throughout the continent, giving the city its reputation as a seething epicentre of sub-Saharan politics, a real-life version of the Bogart movie, *Casablanca*, with all its spies and skullduggery. And the epicentre of this epicentre was the bar-restaurant of the New Africa hotel, where leaders could often be seen conferring in twos and threes or sometimes larger groups. I was thoroughly taken with the New Africa's palm-fronded décor and its slinky, crisply-uniformed wait-staff; after all I'd just spent nearly a month in Songo Township's very much rougher-and-readier conditions. And there was to me a thrilling purposefulness in the air as well as a sophisticated look to the clientele. The waiters moved about soft-spokenly to serve the eminent figures who exchanged confidences at table or bar. Then and since I have read many a visiting reporter, seduced like me by Dar's conspiratorial atmosphere, struggling to convey the spirit of international intrigue. They'd often quote verbatim the veteran Polish foreign correspondent, Ryszard Kapuściński, from one of his books:

> One can spot sitting at one table Mondlane from Mozambique, Kaunda from Zambia, Mugabe from Rhodesia. At another, Karume from Zanzibar, Chisiza from Malawi, Nujoma from Namibia, etc. ... all planning courses of action, calculating their strengths and assessing their chances. We, the correspondents, come by here frequently to pick up something. We already know all the leaders, we know who is worth sidling up to.

I really doubt that those leaders would ever have been all so conveniently positioned in the same space (on the hotel's broad terrace) at the same time. In my own case, the only top-line visitor I ever recognised at the New Africa was President Kenneth Kaunda—'KK' to his supporters—and only from a distance. Like Nyerere, he'd been a great luminary for London's Africa Centre habitués, including me. In fact he was the main speaker at the Centre's inauguration. In Dar I would dearly have loved, in

Kapuściński's words, to 'sidle up' to him but I didn't have the nerve. The crowd of courtiers was too dense and intimidating.

In later years, when I entered my thirties and came to be on first-name terms with him, I could look back with a smile on my youthful timidity in Dar. When KK and I were meeting in his State House (architecturally quite unlike Tanzania's; more akin to America's White House), he developed the habit of calling me David and unexpectedly asked me to please call him Kenneth. I couldn't quite do that, sticking instead at the 'Mr President' level. His own middle name, between the Ks, was David. His father had also been a David, an ordained minister in the Church of Scotland. He told me he liked bearing the name as much as his African birthname, Buchizya, meaning 'the unexpected'. He saw our shared name as a link to Scotland, recalling the explorer David Livingstone—the Scot who supposedly 'discovered' Zambia in 1855 and who still has a town named after him in the country's South. 'These David names of ours—yours, mine, my father's—mean in Hebrew that we are beloved of God,' he said. 'Never forget that.' I couldn't fail to be touched by his fond familiarity with me. At the time, he was broken-hearted and would long remain so, following the death from Aids of his thirty-year-old son, Masuzgo. HIV/Aids was then just beginning its death

Meeting President Kenneth Kaunda of Zambia, with presidential aide and trademark presidential white handkerchief.

march through Africa. It had already stolen a thousand lives per year in Zambia alone, and would eventually claim millions.

In saying I was touched, I'm being literal. KK repeatedly patted my forearm and emphasised special points by gripping me tight on one bicep or the other. I puzzled over such personal attentions and wondered if he was equally demonstrative with other journalists, but it would have felt awkward for me to ask them. One afternoon, though, after a State House press conference, the veteran *Financial Times* Africa columnist, Dick Hall, brought up unprompted the president's well-known emotional temperament; we laughed together at his familiar habit of carrying a huge, floppy white handkerchief and dabbing his eyes whenever the stories people brought him had sad endings. I took the opportunity to ask Dick if the president ever got touchy-feely with him. He winced slightly and spluttered, 'Good God, no!'

I remained mystified by KK's singling me out, if that's what he did, but perhaps I represented some kind of filial presence for him; maybe I even stirred up echoes of his lost son—but why me, compared with some other young man? Our shared Christian name perhaps made the difference but it seemed a tiny, incidental tag among the crowds of admirers who surrounded him. He was evidently greatly loved; his Father-of-the-Nation image was more than mere political mythmaking.

When visiting Dar back in the 1970s, KK and his entourage stuck close to the New Africa hotel, like most other delegations, but I discovered that the Mozambicans of FRELIMO forged their own separate path. They favoured The Canton. This was a Chinese restaurant just a stone's throw from their base. One of my embassy sources had passed on a bit of hearsay that it was a front for Chinese espionage. I wasn't sure what that meant in practical terms. Were the waiters all spies, eavesdropping on their customers at dinner in hope of gleaning strategic data and conveying it all to Beijing? It was a far-from-hidden military fact (possibly related to the spy-rumour, possibly not) that much of FRELIMO's weaponry, notably shoulder-fired anti-aircraft missiles, came from China, supplied at prices well below the global market rate. It seemed a stretch, however, that The Canton ran a covert quartermastering operation. In any case, the waiters I tried communicating with appeared singularly unskilled in English. Ordering a dish was best done by pointing at the menu's helpful pictures, all printed in unappetisingly saturated colours.

The cuisine available from the illustrated menu was standard international Chinese; think the chop suey and spring-rolls of your local Golden Dragon or Peking Palace. The mid-ranking Mozambican officers I ate with there were usually more fluent in English than any of their Portuguese enemies I'd recently met in the theatre of war. They were also more genial companions. Our conversation was light-hearted though now impossible to recall, given the hefty doses of alcohol consumed. I have a vague sense that international sports events figured in it—plus freewheeling stereotypes and jokes about different people's national character. Some of these provoked a lot more laughter than they deserved, and some I didn't totally get but grinned at all the same.

Undying British–Mozambican friendship was frequently toasted, most often in *mofru*, a somewhat fortified local pineapple wine, which these exiles had adopted enthusiastically and which I kept trying to get a taste for. What became very obvious were the limits set on our conversation. The others all grew deadly serious, and quiet, whenever I broached anything concerning their mission in war. 'We fight to free our country, that is all,' was the sum total of their comment. For any more detail, they made clear—in strict observance of the chain of command—that I had to speak with their chief officer.

THE COMMANDER

I got to spend quite some time with Major-General Chissano. Aside from our filming, he briefed me off-camera with historic and current background detail and we found ourselves chatting in general, almost amiably, for hours at a time, spread over several days. This led me to hope I'd also get to meet, and ideally interview on film, the supreme leader of the movement, President Machel. But it wasn't to be.

The PR team members were canny operators. At first I had assumed that they'd nominated the less senior Chissano to be our main interviewee because our topic of Cabora Bassa was a tactical, military matter rather than a question of wider policy, like achieving political control of their entire country. But their reasoning proved to be more circumstantial than that, more a matter of presentation. These media experts had judged that for us British broadcasters, President Machel's English would sound 'too African', according to one of their team. For both men, English was their third language but Chissano's English had an easier, more colloquial lilt. Such attention to detail was noteworthy; the leadership's advisers had given much more thought to their spokesman's impact on a British audience than I had.

A trusting if purely business-like relationship was being built between us. It felt very different, and of course a great deal more enjoyable, than the outright hostility we encountered at Cabora Bassa. There are times when professional detachment and objectivity can slip a notch in the scales of importance. I wouldn't say we were wholeheartedly taking FRELIMO's side in their struggle but we did sense that we were in each other's good graces and that there was a shared cordiality and respect.

During our one-on-one conversations I warmed to Chissano. He told me how he'd learned his English when studying in Europe, before becoming a FRELIMO member. His offices were spartan; evidently no special comforts came with a position of command, and there was an atmosphere of quiet efficiency in the corridors. He and I talked on his veranda over a snack he offered of badjia (fritters made of black-eyed peas), lubricated with some greatly watered-down tipo tinto, the Mozambican answer to rum. He broke off once or twice to yell a sharp corrective to an alfares (the loose equivalent of an NCO in regular armies I knew) who was drilling troops some 200 feet from us.

My previous work had conditioned me to think of an army as a highly formal entity—official and national. I had of course also known the less regular Irish Republican Army in Ulster but even the IRA's leaders insisted, to me and every other reporter, on formal-sounding and rather old-fashioned ranks such as Chief of Staff, Divisional Commander, or Brigade Commandant. They also adhered to a patriotic sense of national unity as a mission. But their clandestine soldiers on the ground had remained, to my eyes, a loose, back-streets organism more than an organisation. FRELIMO's well-regulated force of guerrilla fighters was a complete contrast. I don't know exactly what else I might have expected but I was surprised by the depth of its discipline. The men trained and drilled all hours of the day in 90-degree-plus temperatures, fast-running their obstacle courses with multiple sets of vaulting-bars and rollover logs. They undertook rope-climbing and daunting watercourses, too, sometimes wearing heavy backpacks, sometimes carrying only rifles. The firing-range emitted stiffly regimented commands and bursts of both small-arms fire and occasional heavy artillery. As befitted a force dedicated to asymmetric warfare often conducted covertly, the training continued through many night-time hours, too, when the temperature cooled only a little to 80 degrees. I watched both daylight and nightly training sessions but we were not allowed to film at night. Our use of lights would alter the training environment for the fighters. There may have been other concerns, too, of course—security came first to my mind—though I doubted that anything we filmed would have helped an enemy. But who knows? Military intelligence is often a matter of small, overlooked details.

The rank-and-filers were young, all looking to be in their late teens, and they seemed unnaturally intense to me, with fixed stares that they held so much of the time. Evidently none spoke English and once again I was told I could talk only with senior command. I decided to take full advantage of my verbal access to Chissano. I asked him personal questions about his background, and he pointed out that when he formally committed to FRELIMO he was just about the same age as me. Before that, his studies had him headed towards a life in medicine. My simple-minded reaction to this, which I cautiously left unspoken, was that it seemed odd for someone set upon a career of saving lives to switch to the business of ending them. I framed my question a tad more delicately. I said, 'Medicine and the military—aren't they very different callings?' Even as I uttered it I wondered whether he'd be familiar with the idiom. I needn't have worried. His English was well up to it; he indulged in a little wordplay on my use of 'calling'.

'I had no choice,' he said. 'I responded to a greater call, the call from my people.' For the first time in our talk his face lightened a little into a half-grin. 'And there is not so much difference as you think. As a doctor I cared for my people. As the military commander, I am still caring for my people.'

His demeanour just once shifted into some brusqueness with me. I naïvely (and unprofessionally) asked a question that I thought might ingratiate myself with him. I wondered out loud —helpfully, I thought—if I could offer him some of my freshly gained knowledge about Cabora Bassa and Songo from the inside. I clearly wanted to step outside my professed impartiality, to volunteer myself as an intelligence source. My willingness was pointless. His terse response: 'You cannot tell us anything we don't already know.'

The judicious way Chissano talked when we ranged over policy and his vision of a future egalitarian society prevented me, several years later, from being at all surprised when he did something that startled many other observers, and many followers, too. After FRELIMO's eventual victory, he served two terms as president of the young, independent Mozambique. But he declined a third term, which the constitution would have allowed him. In this he was prefiguring by some years his much older South African friend, Nelson Mandela, who could easily have enjoyed two presidential terms but served only one, willingly giving up power. Chissano also initiated his country's first multi-party elections; black-ruled Mozambique had initially been set up as a one-party state—with FRELIMO of course as that one party.

In our filmed interview, after he'd flatly reaffirmed his army's determination to destroy Cabora Bassa, I broadened the issues under discussion. I raised a question journalists often ask during wars of guerrilla insurgency. It was, for instance, a commonplace in our interviews with the IRA. We needed to confront 'the terrorists', as the UK government always labelled them, with the fact that Irish Republican 'freedom fighters', as they saw themselves, too often ended up killing innocent civilians with their bombs, not just British soldiers.

'Does FRELIMO include civilian workers at the dam as legitimate targets of war?' I asked him. Under internationally accepted rules of war, I was suggesting, the engineers and surveyors imported from, say, Italy or Germany simply for their professional, non-military expertise could be said to have no role whatever in the conflict. If killed by FRELIMO soldiers, they would be (in the language of military handbooks) 'collateral damage', and how justifiable could that possibly be? He paused a little wearily and then spelled out his answer with care: 'We cannot give instructions to our bullets saying this is so-and-so, don't kill him. The people who are involved in building Cabora Bassa are the same as the soldier who is conducting the war against us.' Another chilling but clear statement of purpose from the chief man-of-war. Another reality of war, in a conflict that we knew to be merciless on both sides.

My colleagues and I concluded that the white dam-builders, a community already far from at ease, would surely be getting their nerves frayed much further. I couldn't know how realistic or otherwise this might be, but I did find myself envisaging a FRELIMO advance through the bush getting close enough for their guerrillas to start shelling the dam itself, maybe even getting a rocket-propelled grenade through the roof of the Songo Social Club. I didn't want to consider the real-life consequences of that. My memories of burned and bloodied body-parts strewn across Belfast's pavements were still raw.

RETURN TO BASE

Finally back home in London, we edited and broadcast our film—opening as planned with Ray's extraordinarily long, unforgettable single shot to demonstrate Cabora Bassa's vastness. Our team sat together with our inevitable champagne bottles watching the programme spool out its story. I have rarely found so rewarding any broadcast's interweaving of filmic imagery with strong verbal testimony. We conveyed persuasively how the region's racist regimes hoped the dam would help them hold on to power, and showed clearly just how determined FRELIMO's guerrillas were to prevent that from happening.

Britain's major political weekly, the *New Statesman*, asked me to write a personal eye-witness account of my time inside the dam's embattled white community. The magazine put on it a straightforward and apt headline: 'The Cabora Bassa Stockade'. Although both these TV and print versions of the story had, in all, taken me more than forty months to collect and deliver, I believed it was all worthwhile, however difficult the effort at times became. Through some robust journalism we had successfully brought the Mozambique struggle to the attention of a wider world.

Barely two months later, coverage of Mozambique exploded further. I picked up my morning copy of the London *Times* and saw a heart-clutching story. A priest I was familiar with had compiled a detailed exposé of a monstrous Portuguese army massacre of civilians, committed in a village named Wiriyamu.

Father Adrian Hastings was that rare creature, an independent-minded English priest who had joined a predominantly French missionary society, *Les Pères Blancs*. These White Fathers were already well-known for infuriating Portuguese colonists with their condemnations of military brutality, and inevitably they were forced to leave Mozambique. Hastings settled back in a British home-base but still diligently worked all his deep Mozambican connections. He was in his early forties, slim and tall, wearing half-rimmed spectacles halfway down his nose and a white 'dog-collar' that looked at least one size too big. But despite his innocuous appearance he had an incisive manner. I had gotten to know him in 1970 when I was first learning about Cabora Bassa; he handed over a lot of background research. He may have been pious in his beliefs but in our every exchange he seemed to me worldly and hard-headed.

Now in 1973, months of communicating with his on-the-ground informants had built up a mass of compelling evidence about Wiriyamu. It was just about as bad as or worse than any atrocity previously reported; but the big difference this time was that, thanks to his and his fellow priests' hard work, the documentation was unprecedentedly complete. The dead numbered 380 named and verified individuals. And the killings were revealed as no loose-cannon aberration by hot-headed soldiers but part of a deliberately planned army operation. It bore the official military label: *Operação Marosca*, or Operation Hustle. On cross-checking the dates cited for the killings, I realised with a shudder they had taken place just when we were filming, at a mere 110 miles from us across dense jungle.

At first, the Portuguese authorities denied it all, even claiming there was no such place as Wiriyamu. There was angry debate about the killings, not least in the UK: the Portuguese had their supporters among prominent conservative-minded Britons, devotees of that ancient England-Portugal alliance. They made it their business to cast as much doubt as they could on the report. My own contribution was to jump into print again. I wrote in the columns of the *Times* that while I hadn't personally witnessed this particular outrage, the priest's account of it comported fully with my own reporting work on the Mozambican war. The uproar continued, from heated sessions in the British House of Commons to special hearings in the US House of Representatives and Senate and urgent resolutions in the United Nations. Portugal was roundly condemned in all quarters.

Things happened fast from that point onward. Less than a year later, in April, 1974, Portugal's own army rebelled and brought down the right-wing government in Lisbon with a remarkable, totally bloodless coup. It was called 'The Carnation Revolution', memorable still for its repeated imagery of joyful citizens placing red carnations by their stems into the barrels of their soldier's rifles. Within a year, Portugal had withdrawn from its colonies. Mozambique was handed over to FRELIMO. The Cabora Bassa Dam and the electricity it would produce was now to work for a new nation. The freedom fighters I had interviewed had been completely earnest in their determination to destroy the dam but in the end they hadn't needed to. To me this seemed at the least a neat irony; perhaps more than that, maybe even poetic justice being delivered upon the white racists. The Portuguese after all—succumbing to mounting international pressures along with continued attrition by the guerrillas' jungle attacks— had simply surrendered, giving up to FRELIMO both the dam and the country.

Unsurprisingly, at Portugal's London embassy, there was a lot of hurried change. Senior diplomats of the former regime had to leave and go home. These included my main contact there, the

In CNN's New York studios.

press counsellor, António Rato Potier. He and other top staff were being replaced by new officials—no longer white-supremacists. I walked by their elegant, late-Georgian building in Eaton Square to see two big removal trucks being loaded up. My mind inevitably strayed back to the seemingly endless series of lunchtime meetings I had sat through with Potier, over always elaborate dishes, before he finally granted me my passage to Cabora Bassa. However grateful I felt to him for having made that journey possible, I did not step inside to offer the counsellor any parting good wishes.

Chapter 30
Plodding Onward

I was enjoying my life. Another year had passed, another birthday had arrived and I was once again among good friends in the Colorado Rockies to celebrate. I relaxed, put all journalism work aside, even went horse riding.

Less happily, though, there had been no real progress in nailing down my father's identity. Even in the easeful pause I was enjoying out West, I felt moved to take stock of my ongoing search. The mystery over my origins had not been top-of-mind while pursuing my work-packed everyday life for the past year, but I had nonetheless devoted about three or four hours in any given week to researching into the topic. And the truth was, I had not gotten very far at all.

The UK police force may have been investigating the rape my mother had alleged, even though it dated from seventy-two years previously, but there was no news emerging from its probe. And no news, either, had come out of the genealogical research which Linda Lawless was patiently conducting into the family trees of people in Germany who we were discovering shared DNA with me. No new clues had emerged about just how I might be related to them. I was feeling a lot less patient than the steadily persistent Linda.

With the UK police, I was annoyed at the lack of results from Detective Sergeant Richard Massey as he made inquiries into the Catholic diocese that might have employed the priest who possibly (and violently) fathered me. Detective Massey had begun well enough; he had asked the diocese the critical question I wanted posed: 'Did any of your priests in the city at the relevant time—early 1948—have German nationality or German heritage?' But he had not gotten anything like a satisfactory answer. To my mind, Massey's investigation should have been proceeding expeditiously, in person of course, and preferably with a hefty rapping of constabulary knuckles on diocesan doors. All too predictably that wasn't the way it was happening.

The questioning was in reality somewhat unhurried, conducted by email rather than in a dawn raid. And more distressingly, external events and conditions—in my view, sheer excuses—also conspired against us.

'After my email it took a month for them to get back to me,' the detective reported. 'And they stated that they would check their records when they went back to work in the office, as they were working remotely due to Covid-19.' Massey said we should wait another two months before pressing the Church authorities further. I thought this was a little over-indulgent of the diocese's administrative difficulties; this investigator, whose incisiveness had at first so impressed me, now disappointed me. Though he didnt know it, I was suddenly pinning on him a name from a series of famous English children's stories, a fumbling police constable called P.C. Plod, who patrolled the fictional world of Toyland, and whose name in British popular culture has become a mocking trope for cops of, let's say, a somewhat slow outlook.

Massey-Plod didn't agree with me about his patience with the Church. 'Everyone is under pressure in this pandemic,' he pointed out to me rather too obviously, and too sympathetically towards the diocese for my liking. But rather than antagonise him over a case which was so clearly not a high police priority (and which he'd earlier made very clear to me was very unlikely ever to result in criminal charges), I agreed to the wait.

At least, I had to admit, the diocese's response to this officer-of-the-law was already proving to be quite different from the wholly unhelpful way they had answered us civilians, myself and the Children of Priests group, when we had asked the same question. It was understandable, I reluctantly acknowledged, for the Church office to cite Britain's national shut-down and stay-at-home as reasons for now kicking the can down the road. It did, though, leave open at least the chance of some progress at some time—whenever the world was finally virus-free, I inwardly harrumphed.

As for the German genealogy angle, there was a turn for the better. I had a German contact: Thomas—someone I had known for twenty years or more. We once lived near each other in Manhattan, friendly if not especially close; certainly good neighbours at the least. He kept a set of my keys and would often check on my place for mail and suchlike when I was away working. More recently he'd moved back to Berlin and now crossed the Atlantic only rarely. We had hardly spoken in years but he was happy to hear from me again and quickly became eager to help. Our research in Germany badly needed a German-speaker, and Thomas—a publisher by trade—was well-suited to the pursuit of information; he even harboured a previously unexpressed hankering for the role of private investigator. He was a gently tolerant soul with humour of a wry and detached kind—not least about his country of origin, and especially after taking up residence there again full-time. He scoffed at Teutonic attitudes of strict formality and exercised an idiosyncratic trait, claiming the right to call his fellow citizens 'Krauts', an epithet that I and almost all my British and American friends would have been leery about applying.

Thomas assiduously chased all the thin leads Linda found as she plumbed the depths of online DNA databases. In one particular case the young digital-marketing man, Christoph Seidel, who shared enough genetic material with me to suggest we had ancestors in common, was proving hard to communicate with. He seemed to be ignoring our efforts to contact him. We tried many ways: messages posted at the DNA website where we'd first found him, inquiries via an email address that was to be found among his social-media accounts, and voicemails left at a phone number we had located for him. I phoned him myself and left a message, since his professional résumé online suggested he was a fluent English-speaker. But this and every other form of outreach to him produced only silence.

Thomas's entry into our small team transformed the search dynamics. Unlike Linda and me, he was of course well-accustomed to German officialdom and familiar with the district residence records that are held in every town hall and the country's comprehensive phone directories that are updated annually. He found new avenues for approaching 'C. Seidel' (our new abbreviated, less chummy tag for him) and he eventually struck a kind of gold when the silent target suddenly fired back from an email address we hadn't previously known. But the information he sent was sparse and limited. In response to Thomas's explanation that it was a British man lacking knowledge about his family background (i.e. me) on whose behalf he was inquiring, C. Seidel wrote back: 'Unfortunately much is unknown about my family, too.' That tolled a rather plaintive bell for me.

Christoph was able, after a couple more promptings from Thomas, to say that his mother and the few other members he knew about on her side of his family all came from the Saxony region. He knew less about his father, saying merely that the older Seidel had been born in 1945 and that he'd 'been told' that his father's family also came from Saxony. Then came a juddering halt. When Thomas asked about any further parental details, Christoph answered: 'Unfortunately I have not had any contact with my parents for several years, so I cannot ask them anything.' I wondered what family tension or bust-up or unexplained mystery (like mine, I wondered?) could lie behind his flat and empty summation.

We all wanted more. I wanted a story; Linda wanted details: the full names of Christoph's relatives, maiden names in the case of females, plus dates and places of birth for everyone. These could all help her to plot a comprehensive family-tree and discover if any of its branches in the generations before Christoph led to someone who could have been in Britain in 1948. Thomas passed on to him these detailed requests for information. We went through a process described in Linda's sharp South Australian tones as 'jest pooling taith' (just pulling teeth) and over several weeks we learned, in fits and starts, just a little more from Christoph. This amounted essentially to his mother's family name being Reidel (confusingly similar to Seidel for me) and that his mother was much younger than his father, born (he now 'thought') in 1969, and that he knew the forenames of only a handful of Reidel family members.

And then after six weeks or so of this, when Thomas was on the point of sending another and, we hoped, much easier, set of questions (now to establish merely some rough windows of time, not exact dates any more) Christoph's email address went dead. A 'Mailer Daemon: Unable to Deliver' message was all we got. He appeared to have deleted his email account with .de, the national internet domain for Deutschland. Diabolical news from the daemon, I thought at first.

I mulled further on Christoph, though. Here was a young man with tenuous links to his family—not unlike me in my twenties and thirties, but with more interest in his family background than I had ever demonstrated in those more youthful days. He was certainly interested enough to enroll in an online DNA database. He must have wanted something. What he was now getting was a barrage of questions that he couldn't answer. I theorised, without having any way to know if this was true, that we were perhaps only making him more frustrated and even annoyed about possessing so little in the way of family awareness.

Elsewhere in the DNA constellation of cyberspace, Linda discovered another young German man with a genetic connection to me (a third or fourth cousin, perhaps) and matters here took a similar course to those with Christoph, only quicker.

His name was Otto Kausche and he lived in Hamburg. Curiously enough, or just coincidentally, he happened to work in marketing, as Christoph did. I wrote him a message via the website where our respective DNA samples had been matched up. He was prompt in replying, saying in adept English that he was on a business trip but would contact me when he got home and would provide all the information he had that I might want. He had obviously taken time to look me up online, since in his parting words he delivered a professional compliment about my journalism: 'It's very valuable to see work like yours in these troubled international times.'

A week passed and I heard nothing so I wrote again, only to find that Otto's account had been closed. Thomas tried hard but couldn't locate him by any other means. There was no phone listing. All we had was an extant Instagram account in his name which stopped having pictures posted to it.

I had to wonder what it was about my (albeit distant) German family connections that made them seem to hide once I contacted them? It was baffling, frustrating and piquantly intriguing.

Chapter 31
South Africa, 1994

Nelson Mandela's exhaustive press conference, a cannonade of questions from international journalists, was being brought to a determined end. I knew what was to happen next. Mandela would be hustled away from the press at large and beyond our reach—an infuriating manoeuvre for most of us gathered there to chronicle a world-changing chapter of history. South Africa was about to plunge into a whole new era, in which its 300 years of racist, white-minority rule would be replaced by a future of democracy and majority rule.

Somewhere else, secluded in a part of Johannesburg's Carlton Hotel quite separate from its large ballroom where the general 'presser' was concluding, Mandela would sit for three successive, one-on-one interviews with—who else?—the major US network news anchors, in those days comprising the triumvirate of ABC's Peter Jennings, NBC's Tom Brokaw and CBS's Dan Rather. Along with hordes of other hopeful reporters I had naturally enough requested my own interview. But Mandela's savvy media representatives, all party stalwarts of the African National Congress that he led, knew what mattered most. Their target audience was Wall Street; their immediate task at this vital, sensitive moment in South Africa's existence was to keep the country's position steady in the world's financial markets, as it went through its unprecedented political upheaval. For the ANC's news managers, the American networks had to take precedence. The reassuring voice of Mandela, the carefully spoken sage, was to be channeled through New York's broadcasters. All other reporters including me were boxed out.

To my mind, it was some kind of miracle that I was there at all. Mandela had been released from prison in 1990 after serving twenty-seven years of a life-sentence for sabotage; and after three years of testy negotiations between the ANC and the white supremacist government, agreement now seemed close on the extraordinary prospect of national elections that would include more than the existing whites-only electorate. Eventually a date, 27 April 1994, was announced as voting day. For the first time since Europeans began colonising the country in the seventeenth century, Black South Africans who made up four-fifths of the nation would have a democratic say in choosing their own government.

I was in a turbulence of excitement about the country's utter turnabout. I was obsessively convinced that I was owed (by whom?—the universe, I guess) the right to witness this pivotal moment and report on it. I had covered the liberation struggle ever since 1969 and gained entrée to many of the principals involved across the entire spectrum of South African politics. These ranged from white supremacist leaders in their deep intransigence and denial, to white liberals who wanted some limited reforms, to the ANC members who fought for a complete overthrow of the status quo. In my own assessment, I embodied the ideal individual to be charting and analysing the dramatic climax that was now imminent.

However, I was at that time a freelance Manhattan-based journalist with a UK career behind him, badly damaged by his alcoholism. No longer accredited to any journalistic organisation, I was reduced to grabbing whatever meagre assignments I could find. They ranged from writing dry dissections of the Clinton administration's Africa policies for a business newsletter's private subscribers to throwing together 'documentaries', barely worth their name, about American serial killers for a tabloid-tending cable TV channel. Since the cable service was owned by CBS, I could raid the network's ample news archive for infamous murder cases, creating out of them some gruesome historical narratives. They began with Ted Bundy in the 1970s, who cunningly seduced or simply abducted scores of young women (exact number unknown, though he confessed to thirty-six) and then killed them, keeping their heads as trophies, sometimes to practise necrophilia on them. With my fellow professionals I affected nonchalance at the horrors we were cataloguing. We left a three-minute space for some on-air commercials and then moved on to Jeffrey Dahmer. In his case, during the 80s, the victims were young men, and as well as dismemberment there was now cannibalism, over which I had to stifle my revulsion. Then we ended with Aileen Wuornos in the early 90s, a very rare female variant of the serial killer species. As well as her gender, her modus operandi marked her out: she hitchhiked along Florida's highways and shot dead male drivers who picked her up —seven of them in total.

But God, how I struggled to get myself back to work that better suited me. I tried relentlessly. I knocked on the door of every news organisation I could get to, in print, radio or television (journalism hadn't yet moved fully into the World Wide Web) and laid out all my impeccable credentials for the South African assignment. To no avail. Every news editor already knew exactly who they wanted to send: usually someone already on their staff; certainly not me.

All the same, I strove doggedly to win the impossible gig. At one point I tried building on my thin connection with *Details*, the mainly men's magazine in New York, where I counted as a contributor low on its totem pole. The glossy monthly carried some serious, even hefty material, but it was much better known for its emphasis on lifestyle and fashion. I pitched to its editors a feature story about South Africa's political parties as seen through their visual electioneering styles. I even offered the gimmicky idea that I could make an informed, headline-ready prediction for just who would be South Africa's 'best-dressed campaigner'. I didn't know who that might turn out to be, but I was sure I could make some calculated, well-informed guesses.

There was some basis for my adopting a style-based approach. Vast crowds were already expressing party affiliation by wearing vibrant party colours, something never seen before in South Africa. An ANC slogan conceived in visual terms gained wide currency after it was first used for summoning supporters to a massive rally. It urged attendees to 'Paint the Stadium Yellow!', meaning that everyone in the 30,000-capacity crowd should wear the predominantly yellow ANC tee-shirt. Bandanas, elaborate hats and neckerchiefs, too, all mushroomed in yellow, combined with the black-and-green stripes that in full made up the official ANC logo. A friend in Johannesburg had sent me an arresting photograph of four male Congress rally-goers all wearing exactly matching, formal three-piece suits, but with a twist. The outfits were a witty take on staid European styling, tailored in a geometrically printed fabric that repeated the colourful logo all over the jacket, pants and waistcoat. Female supporters far outdid the men's finery with their own voluminous and dazzling *imibhaco* gowns of brilliant yellow and green. But my bold pitching of this original journalistic angle didn't bring me anywhere close to getting what I wanted, and neither did any of my other clever ideas.

My frustration led in time to a sense-talking session over breakfast with a musician friend, an orchestral and Broadway bass-player well used to gigs failing to land in his lap. 'It's time to recognise reality,' he said. Along Columbus Avenue I trudged the eight blocks from our favourite diner back to my apartment, saying to myself through gritted teeth that, while I wasn't one jot or tittle happy about it, I may as well resign myself to not going to South Africa and witnessing freedom's momentous triumph in person. A wretched, miserable fact of life. But that's what it was: a fact. It had to be accepted.

When I opened my door, the fax machine on my desk was sounding its distinctive whirr, just completing a message from the United Nations, where I had done some occasional reporting over the previous two years. It was wholly unexpected, coming from a source I'd regarded as unpromising among other more obvious news-gathering organisations, but there in black and white was a job offer. I was to cover South Africa's earthshaking transition in a UN documentary to be made and distributed globally by the world body.

So I was back in the Carlton once more, something of a home from home. It was the sole Johannesburg hotel I ever stayed in for the many trips I made to the city, trips that began back in 1971 when Mandela was 'only' seven years into his prison sentence for life.

On one early trip I arrived without a reservation, after I was summarily expelled from the neighbouring white-ruled country, Rhodesia (now Zimbabwe). I'd been trying to report on efforts at military and economic coordination between the remaining white regimes in the region but, for my pains, Rhodesian police took me to the airport and dumped me on the first flight out, which happened to be headed to Jo'burg.

Never demurring for a moment, the Carlton's staff quickly found me a room, even though the place was fully booked at the time. It helped that they knew me well from previous visits. After I settled in my room they surprised me with a generous package of toiletries including the all-important toothbrush, and even a change of clothing, its sizes all well-guessed. It was welcome beyond words in my dishevelled state and was delivered with a smile by a bellhop named Andrew Makwetu; he and the desk clerk had noticed—couldn't fail to—that I was luggage-less. Somehow during my forced expulsion, my bags had been wrongly routed to another country entirely: Malawi. It was probably just an extra little gratuitous punishment by white officialdom. A local journalist I knew imagined for me some dialogue the *pote* (cops) could likely have voiced: *Stuur sy kak an ander kakgat.* (Let's send his shit to some shithole.)

A few days later the same beaming Andrew, in his forties and of Xhosa heritage, shared in my pleasure and amusement when my suitcases finally showed up. He brought them to my door, saying he had to explain some damage to their locks. He pointed out it was not his doing or anyone else's at the hotel. I guessed that anyway from the messy duct-tape that now held the cases together. Andrew helped me rip off the tape and on top of my rifled belongings inside one case was an official receipt for some missing items—a typed and officially stamped document from the wonderfully apt acronym, BOSS, the South Africans' BUREAU OF STATE SECURITY.

Andrew translated the bureaucratic Afrikaans text for me. My luggage had previously contained two suspicious books, now confiscated as illegal contraband. One was a predictable seizure: Alan Paton's great anti-apartheid novel *Cry, the Beloved Country*. The other was initially puzzling but only until we gave it a little thought. The mere two-word title of this second book must have activated the Afrikaaners' puritanism. It was Kate Millett's *Sexual Politics*. Each word on its own would have been a red flag. Andrew laughed even louder than I did. He knew the Paton book well (through underground connections, no doubt) and when I asked him if he knew the Millet work he said he had certainly heard of it. This came as no surprise. Andrew was a solid ANC supporter, though he hid it from his white employers, and the party had long embraced women's advancement along with its anti-racist campaigning. I would have ditched both *Sexual Politics* and *Cry* if I'd known I'd end up in South Africa. But I was part-way through reading them both when I had to leave London, so they came with me on the Rhodesian assignment. Kate Millett was at the time essential reading for feminist women in the UK, and for men with any sense. I expected to finish it undisturbed in Rhodesia, where the security police were oppressive but isolated and backward-looking; they probably wouldn't have even recognised it as an example of progressive international publishing. They lacked the cosmopolitan awareness of a Johannesburg hotel worker.

The Carlton became election publicity headquarters for the ANC, now that it enjoyed the freedom to campaign openly after three decades of being a banned organisation. I hoped to enjoy some special 'in' with the party. I had, after all, cultivated its senior leadership since the late 1960s, the start of my engaging with South African issues. I had enjoyed the hospitality of Oliver Tambo, who during Mandela's imprisonment had become the movement's overall leader at liberty, though forced to live in exile. I often sat listening to detailed if idealised visions for a free South Africa's future delivered from the kitchen table of his Edwardian house in the unassuming London suburb of Muswell Hill.

The Tambos were a welcoming family though, in truth, Oliver himself was rarely there, travelling the globe most of the time. He was generally studious in manner, smiling only when giving a warm greeting and rarely expressing mere light-heartedness. He had trouble relaxing, I felt. He once spoke to me in a tone more compellingly serious than I had ever heard at first hand from any politician—not threatening, just sounding like a statement of

Arriving on assignment at Hosea Kutako Airport, Namibia, 2008.

plain, unavoidable reality. He explained in slow, emphatic beats that if the white regime did not lift its suppression of the ANC and its supporters, 'we expect rivers, rivers of blood will flow.'

By contrast his stately, well-proportioned wife, Adelaide, was a decade or so younger than him and often belted out hearty, pealing laughter. She would sail among us in her ample, diagonally patterned *shweshwe* outfit, often topped—even indoors at home—with elaborate *isicholo* headgear. When Oliver was around she often took pains to remind him about taking his hypertension pills. Originally trained back home as a nurse, she worked long hospital shifts during their London years, looking after mainly geriatric patients. Their sociable son, Dali, nine years younger than me, was the one who most often invited me to the house. He was a wry jokester. At a central London party I took him to, he drew breath for a moment when an Englishman asked him if his name had any 'special meaning' in his 'native language'. 'No,' Dali said impishly. 'My parents named me after the Spanish artist, Salvador.' I didn't think that was true. In the Xhosa language there's a cluster of similar-sounding names, like Dalindela (He who paves the way), Dalivuyo (He who brings happiness) and the Dali part alone can mean 'maker', but when I pressed him about it, he kept insisting on his painterly namesake.

During travels through the countries surrounding South Africa, the connections I made with exiled ANC people there were more purely business-like than those I maintained with the Tambos. Brisk arrangements were also made for me to have, inside South Africa, surreptitious meetings with the movement's covert agents, some of whose identities are still kept secret all these years later. Through their help and that of more overt ANC operatives in Zambia, Mozambique and Tanzania, I was able—in addition to filing periodic short reports on news developments—to make plans, little by little, for a broad-ranging film documentary. From original idea to final completion and international broadcast, it took me fourteen years and it amounted to a detailed television history of the Congress, traced from its origins back in 1912.

One reason it took so long was that I could not persuade any British broadcast organisation to back the project. I needed such institutional support, and most of all finance; it was an expensive venture. But the UK's prevailing political atmosphere was discouraging for such an enterprise. Every broadcast organisation knew that Prime Minister Margaret Thatcher was deeply opposed to the ANC; at an international conference she dismissed the Congress as 'a typical terrorist organisation' and constantly insisted that the media should deny such terrorists what she called 'the oxygen of publicity'.

I was finally able to bring the documentary to fruition, under the title 'Spear of the Nation', by forging an alliance between the International Broadcasting Trust, the non-profit production house I had come to lead by then, and the television company where I started my London career, Thames TV. I felt sure that that particular company would be courageous, whatever the political climate. I wasn't wrong; we were eventually able to broadcast a probing and illuminating study of the movement.

A national magazine devoted to television matters highlighted the surreptitious nature of our documentary-making, noting that I had 'made much of the film inside South Africa, despite the emergency regulations'. I had barely noticed those new regulations, because the regime already ruled, in so-called normal times, with a such heavy hand. It was true, though, that during the year I was filming, the white president did declare a nationwide state of emergency. The club-wielding and gun-toting *pote* were put on even higher alert than usual. We, for our part, were already determined to be ultra-cautious; we could hardly have been more anxious to keep our filming secret.

For the only time in my career I assumed another identity to enter the country. The name I was given was a common-or-garden English name. (I couldn't possibly pass as Akrikaans.) Because the need for secrecy was paramount, I in effect placed myself entirely in the hands, for a while, of my subjects. I did so with some reluctance, fearing it would tarnish my professional nonpartisanship, but it was necessary. Undercover ANC workers provided me with my false papers and my film crew was made up

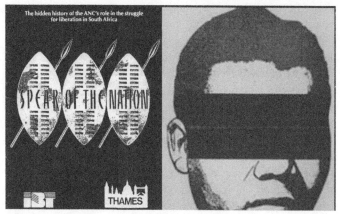

Educational booklet accompanying my African National Congress documentary, 'Spear of the Nation', broadcast by Thames TV in 1986. The cover shows the face of ANC leader Nelson Mandela obscured under a South Africa 'banning' order. (Published by International Broadcasting Trust.)

of party sympathisers—different ones in different towns. It didn't seem wise to travel in company with cadres, as they called themselves, no matter how deep their cover may have been. Simply being a white man on close terms with two men of colour could attract unwanted attention, my sources and handlers warned me. Trying a little brashly to have some influence on their cloak-and-dagger logistics, I reminded them (as if they didn't know) that Mandela himself, while he was operating undercover and needed to travel with white comrades, sometimes posed as their chauffeur with papers in the name of 'David Motsamayi'— so couldn't we maybe do something similar? They pointed out the awkward fact that when Mandela was arrested in 1962 he was wearing his driver's uniform and cap. The surveillance state was not easy to beat.

By the time I was on my covert mission, the apartheid regime had placed Mandela's wife, Winnie, under a so-called banning order which prevented her from meeting more than one other person. Somehow or other—I wasn't told how—she was spirited from her home to a friend-of-a-friend's house. I met an intermediary several blocks away and was led, through a series of backyards with helpful gaps in their fencing, to the house's rear door. Inside, Winnie was waiting for me, with a crew of two young men on camera and sound, plus three other supporters.

She spoke about her rarely allowed visits to her husband in Robben Island Prison, South Africa's Alcatraz. While I'd hoped for some individual emotion I instead heard deep ANC loyalty, expressed in a controlled but still moving generalisation about the fellow-wives of the movement's imprisoned leadership. In precisely-voiced phrasing she told me, 'There are times when one has felt ashamed of having dampened spirits when we visited them—because instead of us going to inspire them in prison, it's the other way round.' More fully, she explained, 'We go there for the inspiration our leadership gives us from behind bars. They exude that, just as they did those many years ago.' By 'those many', she meant the full twenty-two years that had elapsed since political and guerrilla activity led to their menfolk's arrests.

The wariness that my contacts and I maintained during our filmmaking paid off; neither this conversation with Winnie nor any of our other stealthy interview sessions ever ran afoul of BOSS's heightened intelligence gathering.

Five years after Thames aired the documentary in the UK and sold it overseas, there came a telling footnote. The company had its government-controlled licence to broadcast taken away. This was widely interpreted as an act of retribution by Mrs Thatcher. It wasn't provoked by our ANC material, at least not directly or primarily. She was known to be already infuriated by Thames journalists and their habit of exposing secrets her government didn't want revealed. The exposures came most powerfully in Thames's determined coverage of Northern Ireland, reporting in which I was proud to have once, earlier on, played my part.

The notion of making 'Spear of the Nation' was born out of my desire to explore a troubling incongruity, something of a paradox. The ANC may have been the oldest liberation movement in the entire continent of Africa, dating back as it did to before the First World War, but by the 1980s it looked as if it would be the very last to achieve its aim, if it ever did. This was a powerful demonstration of just how fully dug-in, institutionalised and militarised the white regime's suppression of dissent had become. And there was more, beyond that unavoidable domestic truth. Internationally, too, South Africa received support in its intransigence, especially from the Reagan Administration in the US and the Thatcher government in the UK, both of which needed to be subjected to public scrutiny, to my mind. The governments of those two so-called 'advanced economies' employed the same overarching excuse: however odious the racist white regime of South Africa might be, it still formed a desirable 'bulwark against Communism' in the continent at large—and I found that insupportable.

I hit on 'Spear of the Nation' as our title because it was a direct translation of the name, in both the Xhosa and Zulu languages, of the ANC's military wing: uMkhonto we Sizwe, or MK for short. Researching and shooting the film brought me close to the movement's army personnel for the first time. To meet them I journeyed around several of what were called the Frontline States, the already Black-ruled countries surrounding South Africa, where MK always had a presence. For a while I accompanied an MK detachment whose members had undergone basic training in Russia, East Germany or Algeria, and were then moulded into cohesive units in camps spread across those frontline nations. Observing a strict agreement with ANC leaders never to reveal exactly where I'd been, I embedded with one unit as it made a cross-border sortie into South Africa-controlled territory. The reconnaissance team scoured a dirt roadway running about thirty miles across scrubby savannah where, they told me, SADF (South African Defence Force) convoys would frequently transport munition supplies. I have never walked so far in any African setting, nor sweated so copiously. I was glad to be carrying only a notebook and water-bottle—in contrast with the scouts' full kit, a weighty rucksack and either an antiquated SKS rifle with bayonet or a more modern AK-47, plus cumbersome bandoliers and magazine pouches for their 7.62 mm ammo.

We were on a wary lookout, wanting to dodge any SADF patrols (I was inwardly, foolhardily disappointed that we didn't actually encounter any) and I watched, fascinated but edgy, when an attack location was decided upon and we stopped. The team used machetes and an oddly narrow spade to dig several holes, into which they laid some alarmingly battered-looking, Soviet-made TM46 landmines. Each time a mine's arming pin was pulled, I tried to disguise my involuntary winces of fear that it might prematurely explode. As evening fell, a couple of old, mud-caked Land Rovers and a nondescript grey van brought us twelve more guerrillas as reinforcement and I was bundled away in the van in company with four scouts, back to presumed safety. After a mere ten miles we crossed a national border—an unmarked bush crossing, but legally speaking beyond the SADF's reach. I was told that the next morning our minetrap became a full-on ambush, and a firefight that resulted in five South African personnel being killed, plus a haul of enemy armaments acquired for future MK use. They said, though of course I could not verify this, that there were no MK losses.

My most senior ANC contact was in Lusaka, Zambia's capital: the enigmatic Thabo Mbeki, who was in essence the chief propagandist in exile. He was a Mandela protégé, the son of an ANC veteran, Govan Mbeki, who spent years as a fellow inmate with Mandela on Robben Island. Looking into the future, the younger Mbeki would eventually become Mandela's immediate successor, as the second president of a free South Africa. During his Zambian exile I found him a curious individual, capable of being simultaneously aloof and companionable. He had a fondness for tweed sports-jackets with leather elbow-patches, and he smoked a pipe—an unusual habit among his guerrilla peers and certainly puzzling to me. Tweed was decidedly out of place in Lusaka's temperatures of 90-plus degrees Fahrenheit. And with his varied range of meerschaum pipes, most notably an elaborate 'Bent Applewood' model by Dunhill of London, he could have been auditioning as Sherlock Holmes.

Mbeki had a master's degree in economics from Sussex University on England's South Coast and I ascribed his affectations to the time he spent there. He expressed an odd pride about the picturesque English site where he had married his South African wife, Zanele, who was a psychiatric social worker based in London. It was a grand palisaded castle in the countryside, built in the twelfth century and home in the fifteenth to the English judge who—Mbeki told me with incomprehensible glee—condemned Joan of Arc to death by fire. This same man was a revolutionary who enjoyed being addressed as 'Comrade' and had a reputation as a kind of Pimpernel desperately sought by BOSS but so far never captured or assassinated by its undercover agents. Such a fate was happening all too frequently to other ANC exiles. Ruth First, an ANC political organiser and writer (and the wife of Joe Slovo, Chief of Staff in the MK military wing) was killed by a package bomb in Mozambique; Albie Sachs, an ANC legal expert and activist, also based in Mozambique, had his car booby-trapped. The explosion tore off one arm and blinded one eye, but Sachs lived on to continue the struggle.

Mbeki and I established a professional relationship, but with some personal touches, you could say. Essentially it was transactional; I needed information, both current and historical, plus interview access to people under his authority, and he dispensed such information and access, sometimes openhandedly, sometimes sparingly. Eloquent and precise, Mbeki was without doubt an important interviewee in his own right but he made me wait several long months before agreeing to sit for some filming with me and then would do it only in London and not in Lusaka. He cited unexplained 'security concerns' as his reason.

On the personal side he expressed interest in my Eastern European surname. He had attended the Soviet Union's guerrilla training-camp in Skhodnya, near Moscow, and said he had known people with variants of my name. He seemed disappointed when I told him it came from my Ukrainian stepfather but then he got interested afresh to learn I had Scottish origins. 'Zambia is full of Scots,' he said. 'I know many. Scots invented the best drink in the world.' But he professed consternation that he heard no trace in me of a Scottish accent. I vaguely blamed Britain's educational system for ironing out regional differences. 'Ah ... Oxford,' he murmured knowingly. I hadn't told him where I'd attended college but he could easily have learned my background from the ANC's intelligence division, iMbokodo, meaning 'the rock' or 'the grindstone'.

Our exchanges sometimes had an unexpected spontaneity. I didn't ever count myself as exactly a recluse during my stays in African capitals, but at Lusaka's Pamodzi Hotel he once unnerved me by showing up a little after 4 am, chiding me by phone from the lobby for having already gone to bed.

'Come down. Come out,' he almost yelled, 'I have something to show you.'

I staggered downstairs. 'Where are we going?'

'On the town. You might be familiar with that phrase.'

I didn't want to go out. I was dog-tired. But this was Thabo Mbeki, head of the ANC's Department of Information and Propaganda—already Mandela's right-hand man in exile, according to many, and someone in whose good books I needed to remain. So we embarked together on the first of several drinking-tours of the city's nightspots. Every time we went out he drank nothing but Scotch—single-malt if the bar carried it. To begin with, I thought he and I paced each other pretty evenly in quantities consumed, but there were nights when I was startled at how much his intake could exceed mine. Maybe Thabo has a problem, I thought at the time, with a lack of self-awareness that carries some irony for me now.

At one of our rest-stops he introduced me to two alleged sisters who worked as hostesses. With some exaggerated formality, he said, 'David, may I present to you Faith. And this, this is her sister, Hope.' He then looked around in a display of disappointment and burst out with what I thought might be mock anger but couldn't be totally sure. He complained to the girls that, 'on a special night when I bring my friend', their third sister appeared not to be working. There evidently was a third— and neatly enough she was said to bear the name Charity. Faith and Hope apologised insistently for her absence. On another, somewhat later visit I finally got to meet Charity in person.

A decade later, on the very eve of the Free South Africa which my time with Mbeki was spent earnestly anticipating (when we were not carousing), I dared to hope that our familiarity back then would now pay off for me professionally. Of course it didn't. The demands of 1994 were different—especially the massive influx of international journalists who swooped in for the elections. They all wanted special access to the ANC. My drunken bonding of earlier years, even with the highly influential Thabo Mbeki, would not really count for much now.

My United Nations assignment was to cover the entire transition process. The UN had a two-fold mission in South Africa. It first had to supervise the ceasefire between the previously warring sides. It then deployed its globally experienced Elections Unit. The Unit coordinated the many contingents of specialist poll-observers sent by democratic organisations everywhere: the European Union, the Organisation of American States, the Organisation of African Unity (later to become the African Union), the British Commonwealth and several other international and regional groupings. The United States sent its own observer delegation headed by Bill Clinton's choice of Reverend Jesse Jackson, who dutifully presented his credentials to my UN colleague, the electoral unit's chief, Reggie

Austin, a goatee-bearded Australian civil servant. My report was to take its place alongside others in a long-standing UN tradition, observed since the organisation was formed in 1945, of documenting on film (and later on video) history-making events where the UN itself was involved or exerted responsibility. While I was shooting I occasionally gained some usefully close access to ANC workers on the ground, thanks to my well-established connections. Mostly, however, my work consisted of criss-crossing the country laboriously, like every other journalist, capturing whatever my crew might come across as the raucous, many-sided juggernaut of campaigning rolled towards Election Day.

Conventional history now emphasises the impressively peaceful transformation which this election represented, from cruel oppression to successful democracy. But the peacefulness was hard-won. It was in fact a disturbingly tense time. Right up until almost the last moment, when Mandela himself came to project onto the entire country an extraordinary, personal calm-ing effect, long-bubbling grievances and paranoia, heightened by the hectic electioneering atmosphere, produced some shocking violence. Chris Hani, a senior strategist in MK and one of the steadiest and most far-sighted people I knew in the movement, was assassinated in the street by white extremists. My document-ary reported the calculation, confirmed through independent sources across the whole nation, that politically motivated murders were taking place at a rate of ten per day.

In the very centre of Johannesburg, in Bree Street, white men planted explosives in a car that killed nine people and injured a hundred, a bigger bomb than any that the ANC had used in its guerilla warfare. In the east of the country, where the popular mood was souring dangerously and some intended polling-places were burned down, I was for the first time in my reporting anywhere forced to put on a bulletproof vest. It was more serious than the strong advice often meted out to me in active war zones; here I was compelled to vest up by police and army officers in charge of the electoral district's security. If my crew and I didn't obey the order, we couldn't even enter the district. Then, as often, I gained little reassurance from wearing Kevlar: it was bulky and restrictive and served mainly to reinforce the notion that I was a potential target, which I found deeply unnerving. This was an election, that very essence of democratic normality. I'd be walking with my crew alongside a banner-waving street march—normally the most humdrum kind of TV news work—with the security men's orders fresh in our minds that we must watch out for snipers on the high vantage points around us.

It was just 24 hours before voting stations were due to open when Mandela gave the final ANC press conference at the Carlton. He told us again, as he often did, that 'Years of imprisonment could not stamp out our determination to be free.' He was asked about the risk that violence might prevent the vote from taking place in some areas and he answered firmly: 'Years of intimidation—and violence—could not stop us. And we will not be stopped now.'

Madiba, his clan-name as used familiarly by his supporters, was then huddled out of a door to the side and, as he moved towards that door, the world's cameramen swarmed around him in hope of a last word uttered in their direction. But I left with my crew through a door on the opposite side. My long acquaintance with the hotel and its staff—in this case the especially helpful kitchen team—came to my aid. I had paced the back corridors the previous day and, directed by a guileful commis-chef, learned that to get privately to the US networks' assigned interview-room, Mandela's security men would have to take him through the kitchen's storage area. So among towering shelves of industrial-sized tomato-cans and flour-sacks we now waited to accost or, in our newshounds' term of art, doorstep the man destined very soon to be president.

'For the United Nations, Sir, can I ask: how big a turn-out do you expect in tomorrow's election?' was my first, not especially probing, thrust.

'Ah, yes, the United Nations,' Madiba said, as his left-side guard glared in my direction and started to angle a shoulder between me and his boss, only to be motioned aside by an almost imperceptible, patrician hand gesture. 'The United Nations deserves our great gratitude for the extraordinary assistance they have given our country during the preparations for this important day.' The deliberation in his delivery was insistent; I thought that that was maybe his normal way of talking, rather than one he adopted when having to perform. I found myself absurdly flummoxed, to an extent that I've never experienced in the company of any other public figure, and I lost my train of thought. My mind offered only, 'I'm here with Mandela, in the kitchen!' In the half-light of the shelving, his features took on a sculpted quality and though his guards were all big men, and at seventy-five he himself was developing a stoop, I still felt him somehow to be towering above us.

My questions now spilled out as if on autopilot, raising details like possible regional variations in the turn-out percentage, the awkwardly late addition of new candidates onto the ballot, the obvious security and safety concerns, and more. I probably ended up taking six minutes of his time. His answers didn't quite address any question straight-on (he was already an expert at that) and it was he who brought the exchange to a polite close. As we shook hands I uttered possibly the most anodyne and, if I'd thought about it, wholly superfluous phrase I could possibly have expressed.

'Good luck for tomorrow, Sir.'

He won, of course, by a massive landslide.

Chapter 32
Remembrance — 'Arch'

South Africa's Archbishop Desmond Tutu was dead. It was December, 2021 and the world seemed to be falling over itself to pay tribute. The Reuters global news agency described him as a 'moral giant', the United Nations Secretary-General said he had been 'an unwavering voice for the voiceless' and his own country's president hailed him as 'the spiritual father of our new nation'.

My own memories of Tutu flooded back in bits and pieces. We originally met in the usual way for a prominent figure and a reporter. He was in the vanguard of campaigners determined to defeat white supremacy; I was covering that movement and naturally interviewed him about it. Undeniably I was a sympathiser but, aside from that central issue, he and I were on very different wavelengths: he so decidedly and obviously spiritual, at times even mystical; I with my fixed roots in a materialist world. He had many acolytes or disciples, formal and informal, but I certainly wasn't among their ranks. I would not bow down and sit at his feet to catch the pearls of wisdom he might drop, as others did, but as I look back I can see that he did educate me to some degree.

Above all, perhaps, he taught me about the sheer, unstoppable power of a good idea. He would talk in terms of faith and prayer, while I more prosaically would have labeled it simply conviction and determination. But whatever tag it should carry, he firmly implanted in me the message that a deeply held belief in justice and the equal value of all human life can ultimately win the day, even when apparently overwhelming odds are stacked against that belief.

He died at ninety, when I was seventy-three. Quite a few celebrated people I had known were then ageing and bound to die around this time, if they hadn't already. But Tutu's death saddened me more acutely than others, as one small recollection or another kept coming to mind. I couldn't ever describe us as close friends. He was a largely open book to just about everyone. He seemed to like people in his circle using a nickname for him, 'Arch', but I didn't feel comfortable with it; it carried the whiff of a manufactured familiarity. As for him, he knew next to nothing about me. But for all my clinging to formal convention, the very real warmth in his greeting whenever we hadn't seen each other for a while has stayed with me indelibly. His broad beam of a smile shone out wholly unforced; his handshake fluidly morphed into a stretch up towards my shoulders and a squeeze with both arms: very nearly a hug. Sometimes a complete hug—tight, too, and lasting palpably longer than I could comfortably take. Especially early on in my adult life, I was generally on guard against anyone trying to win me over, as I suspected he was, and was deeply suspicious of anyone who was effusive. I was either stiffly protecting my professional objectivity as a reporter or just a cautious young male uneasy with emotional displays. Whichever sort of guardedness it was, the fact remains that in the end I relaxed inescapably in Tutu's likable company.

Undeniably, then, he was a warm man, but that didn't stop our encounters from being prickly at times. The very first memory that rushed back as soon as I heard his death announced was, fairly or unfairly, one of our prickliest moments. It occurred when I raised with him the subject of Robert Mugabe. I had got to know Mugabe in Zimbabwe much earlier on, at first respecting him, growing later to despise him. With Tutu, I had come to enjoy some openness of connection. That emboldened me to try and explore the relationship between Tutu and Mugabe—what attitudes the two leaders harboured towards each other.

'President Mugabe has called you an embittered, evil little bishop,' I said, knowing full well I was being provocative, as a journalist must often be and which I unabashedly enjoyed being. 'What's your reaction, Archbishop?' He blinked hard. It looked like his answer might go any one of several ways. After an intake of breath he chose to laugh the insult off.

'Oh,' he said, 'I learned in the apartheid days to develop the skin of a rhinoceros.'

A good line. That capacity for quick, neat turns of phrase was one of his most appealing qualities.

Our meetings recurred periodically through the forty-plus years I reported on South Africa and the broader Southern African region. We called them our 'catch-up interviews'. The rhino-hide quip came during a 2008 taping and, once he'd made his joke, we moved on to review the whole region's disturbingly mixed fortunes at the time. Worst of them all was the economic and political disaster that Mugabe presided over in Zimbabwe. The South African sighed, more in sadness than anger, about the calamitous condition in the neighbouring country. Time was, he recalled, that their two peoples had been unified in similar, ultimately successful struggles against white rule. Now, nearly thirty years after the Zimbabwean had won power, Tutu felt personally betrayed by the ugly change he'd seen overtake his former comrade—Mugabe's mutation into a cruel autocrat.

'He is someone I used to have a very high regard for,' Tutu said quietly, 'and he must be given credit for what he did. But it's an inexplicable aberration that has taken place.' His voice rose and turned into a near-splutter: 'This, this almost, you'd say, perverse determination to destroy his own country and bring about huge suffering.'

I reflected that the Nobel Peace Prize laureate was no stranger to human aberration. After his long career of protesting against the atrocities of apartheid, he was asked by Nelson Mandela, as first president of the now free South Africa, to chair the nation's Truth and Reconciliation Commission, the TRC. It began work in 1995, a brand-new country's bold and innovative attempt to move on from the violence of its previous history by facing it squarely—and, wherever possible, healing some of its worst effects.

Spread over three years, the TRC's often harrowing sessions were broadcast live on coast-to-coast television. Viewers saw Tutu break down in tears as he heard testimony from victims and bereaved families about barbarous cases of torture, disappearances and killings.

The hearings had various purposes. First, the atrocious human-rights violations were to be investigated thoroughly, after which the commission would issue recommendations for making restitution to victims and their families. Then, remarkably and controversially, the TRC was also tasked with assessing whether the agents of apartheid should be criminally prosecuted for what they had done—or (astonishingly to many observers) be given amnesty. The ANC was always nervous throughout its campaign, and even during its all-out war, that revenge-seeking might break out into mass-action rampages of murderous vigilantism; the new government therefore wanted to forestall any appearance of seeking vengeful retribution against the former regime. Its leaders wanted to be exemplary, showing that the new order would dispense justice fairly and evenhandedly. But freedom from prosecution was not meant to be granted on a broad, blanket scale. Tutu wielded authority to grant amnesty only to individual agents, not to whole classes of people such as the police or army commanders as a category, or to BOSS itself, and there were supposed to be strict conditions. These conditions were hard to formulate but, in essence, amnesty could be considered if a person's actions, even their killings, beatings or kidnappings, could be classed as 'politically motivated'.

To cite the TRC's commissioning mandate, the definition of what was political included actions committed by any employee of the state (or any former state) in the course of his or her duties. But this notion that state agents carrying out a brutal attack on a liberation supporter could possibly be excused because of their official position came perilously close (certainly to my mind and in the minds of many others) to accepting the weasel-like defence used by Nazi torturers and executioners that they had only been obeying orders.

Overarchingly, amnesty was meant to be allowed only if the perpetrators disclosed exactly what they had done in full. And here perhaps lay the toughest truth in the 'Truth and Reconciliation' formula. The commission presented to us a succession of perpetrators giving more and more evidence of the heinous crimes they had committed, and the closer they came to winning amnesty by doing so, the more outrageous it became that they should receive it.

My most vivid memory of the process was a paunchy,

nondescript police officer, Captain Jeffrey Benzien, who was later amnestied. He described his interrogation techniques while one of his many victims, a veteran ANC member named Peter Jacobs, was sitting in the same hearing room.

'If I say to Mr. Jacobs I put the electrodes on his nose, I may be wrong,' Benzien testified. 'If I say I attached them to his genitals, I may be wrong. If I say I put a probe in his rectum, I may be wrong. I could have used any one of those methods.' To everyone's horror, Benzien was suggesting that since all of those repulsive forms of assault were just a workaday part of his job, he simply couldn't remember which one, or more than one, he might have carried out against any particular prisoner. Besides electrical torture, he also graphically demonstrated on a mannequin on the hearing room's floor his 'wet bag' technique for suffocating detainees almost to the point of death. He offered his apologies to Jacobs and other victims, however stiff and legalistic it might have sounded:

> I apologise to the people whom I assaulted during interrogation, namely Peter Jacobs, Ashley Forbes, Anwar Dramat, Tony Yengeni, Gary Kruse, Niclo Pedro and Allan Mamba.

A few of the victims, I didn't learn exactly how many, said then or afterwards that they accepted the apology. Jacobs himself even shook Benzien's hand, for reasons I couldn't fathom, and I never got the chance to ask him. But Jacobs also told the commission that he believed the torturer had not been telling the whole truth. I felt we could reasonably infer that the policeman had committed other acts of depravity to which he was not willing to confess. There was a twenty-year-old student activist, Ashley Kriel, who was shot dead while in Benzien's custody. The officer apologised to his family for the death happening but denied playing any personal role in it. No one was ever charged with the crime.

Few people would claim that the TRC finally brought a perfect solution to South Africa's violent legacy but it did impress many across the world with the way it helped to keep South Africa's momentous transition calm and relatively non-violent. Tutu told me he was quite naturally pleased by the number of visitors from the world's many divided and troubled societies who came to consult him on lessons to be drawn from the TRC. But at this point I also received a dose of his publicly well-hidden bad temper. He emphatically contradicted me when I quoted to him press reports that he viewed the commission as 'a paradigm' for other nations. Indeed, his response came close to fury.

'No, no, no, no, no,' he said, thumping the table vigorously. 'No one should ever make out that we have provided the world with a universal paradigm—that we are saying this is one size that fits all. That would be arrogant in the extreme. In very real measure, it is something that is ad hoc. It must be specially designed for each country.'

He sat back in his chair, subduing his own outburst. 'But,' he added slowly, 'there are certain principles that you could say might be of universal application.'

And as we then discussed what those universal principles might be, they inevitably chimed with what I saw so clearly in the commission's hearings and, I could recall, in my own interviews with survivors of the apartheid regime's cruelty. 'There is an incredible generosity and magnanimity on many people's part,'

With sister Julie Tereshchuk.

he said. 'Almost everyone who has suffered is not so much desperate for revenge. More important, they want to hear the truth. And most want to be able to tell their story. And when perpetrators admit their guilt, it's far more healing.'

I would hardly disagree with Tutu about any of that. Indeed, considering him altogether I could find little fault with him at all, even as I maintained my reporter's sceptical probing and held at bay any hero-worship. I couldn't fail to be impressed that, way ahead of many other churchmen in Africa, he voiced vigorous support for LGBQT rights. There was a personal dimension to his public stance. The youngest of his four children was a daughter, Mpho, who made a mid-life career change after first trying electrical engineering; she suddenly become the second pastor in the Tutu family. She and her father went on to collaborate in authoring a couple of religious books, *Made for Goodness* and *The Book of Forgiving*. I found it heartening to see them work together, demonstratively affectionate and lovingly respectful of each other. Mpho then also made another change; now divorced from a man she met at college and with whom she had had two children, she came out as gay and married a Dutch woman. Tutu gave his father's blessing to the marriage and he rounded rapier-like on the homophobia that was endemic in the Church. He announced that if, by any chance, he got to Heaven's pearly gates and discovered LGBQT rights were not respected there (as many conservatives in his flock evidently believed), 'I would refuse to go to a homophobic heaven.' He paused, and with typical timing added, 'I would say "Sorry, I would much rather go to the other place."' Another of his neat jibes, still zestily spilling forth in his eighties. I could well imagine Tutu making a querulous nuisance of himself in Hell.

It was when he grew older that I noticed more cantanker-ousness, but there were times, right from the beginning when he was still relatively young, that he would sometimes sharply correct me when he thought it necessary. In hindsight I can admit contributing some tetchiness of my own whenever our conversations turned adversarial. As the completely assured non-believer I considered myself to be, I could get irritated simply by his deep piousness. Or was it that I found his combining of piousness with such expressive amiability just a little too much of a challenge for me?

He had to put me straight (in his terms) once in the 1990s, during the uneasy period between Mandela's release from prison and the eventual elections that sealed the country's complete transformation. As soon as Mandela was freed he went to stay at the Archbishop's Residence in Cape Town, even though the men had never met before. How could they have done? Mandela had been behind bars for twenty-seven years, much of the time in solitary confinement. The two of them, by then aged seventy-six and sixty-three, seemed to form a bond very quickly. How personal, as opposed to how political a bond, I couldn't be sure.

During the uncertainties of that post-release, pre-election period, I expressed my amazement that Mandela not only seemed capable of putting behind him the brutalisation he had often suffered from his jailers but also of showing strong signs of guiding his entire country's citizenry on a journey to democracy without widespread recrimination or violent revenge.

Tutu said I should not be surprised at the promising way events now seemed to be heading—and, indeed, as they later turned out, when South Africa's reconciliation process did impress much of the world. There were nonetheless dark times when political murders were taking place and that outcome was far from certain. I pushed Tutu on why, even with blood being spilled at a disturbing rate, he maintained the complete confidence he was now professing in Mandela's stewardship. 'David,' the Archbishop said, 'you must never underestimate the power of prayer.'

I felt stung into correcting the cleric. I imagined him thinking that Mandela, like himself perhaps, believed God would bring about peace across the land. It seemed preposterous to me. I had spent much of the previous decade interviewing many of Mandela's friends and one-time fellow prisoners, plus Winnie and his personal physician, Nthato Motlana. I had inquired quite searchingly into his overall philosophy of life. 'I know for a fact, Archbishop,' I said confidently, 'that Mandela is not a praying man. I don't believe he's even a Christian.'

Tutu was now shaking his head and smiling. 'I was not

talking about Nelson,' he chided me. 'There have been millions of people around the world praying for him, and for a peaceful outcome to the struggle.'

Chapter 33
Oral History

The UK police inquiry suddenly jerked with alacrity. Or at least faster than I'd resigned myself to expect. Perhaps Detective Massey had been spurred by my impatience during our last exchange. He had clearly pushed harder and quicker than he said he would for the answer we needed from the Church diocese; and an answer came quite promptly. I received an unexpected email from the detective announcing there was news and when we later talked on the phone he filled me in, speaking in abbreviated, conclusive-sounding tones.

Church records, he explained, had finally been unearthed relating to the year I was conceived and born; and in those records there were definitely no priests employed by the diocese who had German nationality or heritage.

Unaccustomedly, the diocese had now gone some extra distance to help. It hadn't merely opened up lists of its own clergy to a careful examination; it also facilitated a search through all churchmen belonging to autonomous Catholic orders who might have worked in the diocese's area at the relevant time. All in all, and in short, there was simply no Catholic cleric who fitted the bill.

I was deflated, even while grateful for eventually getting an answer—any answer. I recognised my disappointment as being much like the common reaction of a reporter when a promising theory gets contradicted by evidence. More, though, an air of finality hung over our talk. 'I will update the crime report regarding this case,' the detective said, 'and the case will be closed, again.' That again was a reminder of the delicate pressure (or maybe less than delicate) that I had exerted to have the case reopened.

So this is how the story ends, I said to myself. 'I hope,' said the detective, 'you eventually obtain the information you desire.'

That certainly sounded like the end of a road. A sinking feeling of defeat began to steal over me.

But it didn't have time to consume me completely. Within days I was embarked on a whole new line of inquiry.

A h canna jes remember, pet.' Warm nostalgia washed through me at the phrasing and intonation, so characteristic of the Scottish Borders. The familiar dialect delighted me, even while the words' meaning might seem discouraging. In more mainstream English it would be: I cannot quite remember, my dear.

I was on the phone with Ruth, ninety years old and one of the eldest living residents of my one-time home village. And this conversation marked a very different, unforeseen turn in my long hunt.

My sister had told me about her. Though Julie may have technically been my half-sister, with a different father, she had become nothing less to me than a wholly full sister. One of my life's delights was that we had such a close friendship as adults, despite the eight years' age gap that once separated us somewhat as kids. We used to connect on pretty much a weekly basis, she at home in Texas and I in New York, and on this occasion we were

With sister Julie, left, and mother Hilda, right, late 1990s.

343

speaking just after the police investigation into the diocese was shut down. Together we ruminated over whether any other leads could possibly exist. We agreed there were none, certainly not among members of our immediate family; everybody was dead. Sometime before our youngest uncle, Norrie, had died I questioned him closely but he had no notion at all of who my father might have been. He deeply regretted not knowing, he said; he really wanted to help me. Then after him, our mother died, finally wiping out that entire generation.

'But maybe,' said Julie, 'Auntie Ruth knows something. She goes back a long way!' It's a measure of the distance that I'd allowed to grow between me and my family and community of origin that I was taken aback to even hear of this elderly person's existence. I might have wished that Julie, always one to maintain family connections, could have told me sooner about this possible lead. But she hadn't, until now—and it certainly seemed worthwhile to try talking with Ruth.

Just how we were related was a little abstruse. She wasn't my aunt or Julie's but she had always been 'Auntie' to a clutch of our cousins, technically their great-aunt. I almost certainly met her when I was twelve and she was thirty, though I had no recollection of her. Our meeting would have been at the wedding of my Uncle Hector, who along with Norrie had seemed like my older brother when I was a child, as I recalled earlier. Hector was marrying a local young woman, daughter to the nearby country estate's chief gamekeeper. It was this young woman's uncle who had married Ruth. Like I said, an abstruse connection.

In her young days, Ruth had lived a mile or two out of the village. Her father had been a farm labourer whose compensation included a tied cottage on a corner of the farmland. While not fully in the middle of it, Ruth was a part of our village community and would have been just two years older than my mother.

My intermediary to reach Ruth was our cousin Janet, Ruth's grand-niece and the first child of that uncle's marriage that I had attended six decades earlier. Janet regularly checked on the old lady at her bungalow in our home village where she still lived independently; at my request she now asked Ruth if she'd take a call from me. 'I told her David's hoping to find who his dad is,' Janet reported to me. That sounded jarring. It would have come perfectly normally to Janet's lips but it was the first time in our family that I'd ever heard the word Dad being used for my possible father. Janet said Ruth was enthusiastic in her reply: 'I'd be more than willing to help.' Even at second hand, that rang to my ears with a hint that Ruth might know something, something significant.

She had said, 'Tell him he can phone me anytime,' but she voiced one small caveat for Janet to pass on: 'Ah'm a wee bit deaf, mind.' The two of us ended up having a series of lengthy phone conversations. And however hard of hearing Ruth may have felt herself to be, there was no great difficulty. I can get quite loud; I was certainly slow and deliberate, pointedly repetitive in my questions. In return her answers came full of verve, her voice cogent and sharp. She warned me that as well as her hearing, her memory was also failing; in spite of that, she turned out to have some crystal-clear recollections.

She remembered one early evening in particular, when she was seventeen, walking to her home from the village bus stop after arriving from a day's work in the city. She told me she noticed my mother strolling near the village church, which lay along her route, not far off the road.

'I didn't exactly know her, ye ken, but I knew who she was. I knew her by sight. She was Hilda.' She pointed out that while they both had attended the same village elementary school, their paths had since diverged, she finishing her schooldays at fourteen, my mother going off to high school. I asked what she remembered of Hilda in general. Was she reserved or outgoing? Good-tempered? Lively? Ruth was imprecise: 'She was an ordinary girl, like any of us. A good lass.'

On the evening in question, Ruth told me, she saw that my fifteen-year-old mother was walking with a much taller, older man. Trying to picture the scene, I asked how far away she was from the two of them but she couldn't exactly gauge the distance. It was close enough, though, for her to say in an oddly emphatic manner: 'He was very tall. Very dark. And handsome. A good-looking fella.'

She also knew that he was Hilda's 'young man'—that they were, in the country idiom of the time, 'walking out together'.

'How did you know that?' I queried, maybe in too quick and pointed a tone. She said, 'Ah just knew. Ah knew.' When pressed she reasoned: 'Ah must have been told afterwards that they were walking out. Ah'm not sure now who would have told me, but Ah knew.'

This was stunning new information. But my perceptible reaction was little more than a quiet intake of breath—and I turned in my studied, ingrained fashion to some meticulous question-framing and careful notetaking.

Delving for particulars to fill out this sparse picture wasn't easy. Ruth couldn't specifically recall any elements of the couple's appearance, any more than she could substantiate her idea they were girlfriend and boyfriend. I asked what they had been wearing (I had a memory from childhood that couples 'walking out' tended to dress in their best when together) and how they related to each other and what kind of mood they seemed to be sharing. Were they holding hands or not? But such useful detail hadn't been recorded in her mind's eye.

When I pursued whether she had seen the couple actually meet each other, we established that she did not witness an actual greeting, but she figured that Hilda had been coming from the village, while the man had come in from further out, and they must have met midway. She was certain about this because she recognised the man and where he came from.

'Ah knew him from the farm,' she said. 'He was one of the prisoners in the Nissen huts between our farm and the river.' She meant the rows of humpbacked steel shelters (Americans call them Quonset huts) that were originally erected to billet Royal Air Force trainee pilots early in World War II. The structures were afterwards used to house prisoners of war, pending their repatriation.

'He did work on the farm for my dad, and Ah think on ither farms as well.' She described seeing him as he went between the Nissens and she also had a sense—not any detailed recall—of him 'carrying stuff about' for her father on the farm. She'd also seen him walking in company with his fellow POWs. 'They were allowed to take walks, sometimes in groups, but they weren't permitted to go into the village, Ah dinna think.'

I remembered talk of German prisoners who proved valuable to local farmers, initially under guard by British soldiers; Ruth's quaint euphemism was that the squaddies were 'lookin' after' the Germans. Many lasting friendships had evidently been formed. Across Britain as a whole more than a quarter-million such prisoners were retained until a full three years after the war had ended, indeed until the year of my birth. One contemporary estimate said a fifth of all British farm work was being carried out by POWs, paid at an average rate of a shilling per hour (in today's US money perhaps a quarter per hour). From the 1950s onwards local newspapers often carried articles about repatriated Germans coming back to the area to renew their friendships and to express gratitude for the hospitality of Border people.

And some did not go home; they made new homes instead. One notable transplant featured in local papers was Fred Sichert, a German paratrooper who'd been captured in the battle for Normandy and ended up as one of our village's POWs. While delivering milk from a Border farm to local customers Fred met and fell in love with a girl and—after overcoming bureaucratic hurdles to get a special licence—he was able to marry her, stay in the area and raise a family of several children. That was quite obviously not the course my father followed, if indeed he was a POW like Fred.

For her part Auntie Ruth was convinced that this 'good-looking fella' was indeed the person who fathered me. But proof? Of course she had none. I pressed her again on how she could be sure—and still she couldn't provide any supporting basis for her belief. And she didn't have any actual memory of Hilda becoming pregnant. 'As Ah say, Ah didn't really know her. Ah jes heard sometime afterwards that she'd had a baby boy.'

At the time when Hilda was pregnant with me, Ruth had started working in the city branch of Woolworths while still living where she called 'out of town', meaning at her family home on the farm. 'Ah wasn't in the same village crowd as Hilda,' she said, 'Ah didn't know about any scandal, never heard gossip about her. Ah didn't go to the same dances, or the same films as that crowd.' The village had its own little movie theatre, functioning as quite the busy social centre, even though its screenings were scratched copies of Hollywood releases that arrived long delayed—sometimes by months, sometimes by years. The cinema was named The Lochinvar, after Sir Walter Scott's bold Borderland hero. In childhood I'd often chanted along with other kids a couplet from Scott:

> O, young Lochinvar is come out of the west,
> Through all the wide Border his steed was the best!

It felt poignant to be talking with someone about our old picture house and recalling the historic local verse, but that seemed as far as we could go with Ruth's recollections, for the moment at least. Hoping for more, I asked her as we were hanging up to keep a notepad handy for any newly remembered thoughts that might come up.

In my next call several days later there were new memories for us to discuss, memories that she was 'not a hundred-per-cent sure of but Ah'm fairly certain.' We spent some time on incidental matters like who had owned which village stores at the time, good for context but not satisfying my thirst for detail about the prisoner.

Eventually, of her own accord, she mentioned that she had an idea, while not able to give a source for it, that the German she'd seen with my mother had been an officer, and in the Luftwaffe at that. I felt we could be on shaky ground here but she ploughed on even while she was clearly tiring a bit; it was evening for her, afternoon for me. She suddenly said she even had a name for the man, long buried in her mind but now surfacing. 'Only a Christian name, mind ye. He was Rudi.'

She had become thoroughly wearied by this stage. For myself I had no more well-focused questions left in me beyond the odd 'Are you totally certain?' or 'How do you know that?' We said goodbye and I put the phone down, drained and perplexed, even exasperated. Rudi, indeed. I'm not exactly sure why but the name itself struck me as comical, ludicrous.

When we spoke again after some more days I changed gear a

little. I'd previously been wary about putting thoughts into Ruth's mind or words into her mouth. I wanted to avoid any chance of triggering whatever suggestibility she might be prone to. I'd been well trained in this by strict academic advisors when I first started making historical documentaries. We adhered to the cardinal rules of oral history and strove to keep the witnesses' own memories pristine. What trial lawyers would perhaps call 'leading' questions were absolutely banned. But I needn't have worried because Ruth knew her own mind very clearly. And so, for this latest conversation, I softened my policy a little and tried spreading before her (as at some point I would have to, I felt) the alternative story that I'd been given twenty years earlier. 'My mother told me,' I said, 'that she was raped by a Catholic priest.'

'Och, no—Ah never heard anything like that,' Ruth replied, quite sharply. 'Never heard that mentioned at all.' She pointed out there was no Catholic church in our village at the time, as I knew, and that 'We didn't have any priests.' And then she recalled, without my bringing it up, that small Catholic masses were celebrated informally at the village doctor's office. Here at least she was matching my mother's account. But rape? By a visiting priest? She was mystified. No, more than that; she was downright sceptical. 'How could they have been together for him to do such a thing?' she asked.

There seemed little point in telling her Hilda's details about the priest offering to walk her home and attacking her on the way, after enticing her into a neighbour's garden. Ruth clearly had no knowledge of this story and exploring its specifics with her would serve no purpose. She had only her own experience to go by, experience that in essence centred on one indicative but inconclusive observation on a winter's day long ago. Once more we hung up, letting the matter rest awhile, promising that we'd report to each other anything new that might arise: new memories in her case, fresh research discoveries in mine.

Ruth's memories so far had left me with some wholly new, stomach-turning disquiet. I'd been kept in the dark for half a century about how I was conceived. Was what my mother finally told me after that long wait—her account of being raped by a priest—now turning out to be, another two decades later, simply more mystification? Worse than that, was it an outright, elaborately detailed lie?

Chapter 34
Mother of Lies?

I'm snatching at ways to steady my swirling thoughts in the wake of Aunt Ruth's startling revelations. I need to stay calm and retrace my progress with some collected, rational thinking, if progress is the right term for the zigzag that has now come to light. I have a short series of possible fathers. In consecutive order they are:

> Initially—Unknown male, for fifty-two years.
> Then—A rapist priest called Father Francis, for nineteen years.
> Now—A German POW called Rudi, for a handful of days.

Was my mother simply lying to me with her priest story of 2001? It's a hard notion to take in, my mother as a liar. If I scan back over our life together, do I see her ever lying to me? I really don't think so.

Hell, though, she could without doubt be evasive. After all, once I started the effort to ask her about my origins, she managed to avoid answering for several more years before telling me the priest story. Along with that evasiveness about the specifics I was interested in, she tended to keep all our talks firmly contained within the realm of little or no substance. Few of our transatlantic phone calls, and none of our short emails after life turned digital, would ever extend very far beyond the subject of the weather in our respective localities. Such avoidance of anything meaningful is a long way from lying, of course.

And to be truthful myself, I aided and abetted what I'm now calling her evasiveness with my own form of co-conspiracy with her. I waited an unconscionably long time, after all, before I actually raised the question of my paternity, telling myself all the while that I wasn't that interested, that it didn't matter that much.

I'm reluctant to accept that when she finally agreed to tell me something, it was to simply invent the entire 'Father Francis' account. But I cannot see any way to reconcile her report of a priest raping her with Ruth's account of a German boyfriend. Hold on, though. Maybe she could still have been telling the truth, at least about a rape.

Perhaps, I conjecture, it was Rudi the German who raped her. But against that conjecture, Ruth had provided a plainspoken message that the German was Hilda's 'young man'—not that this would totally preclude rape, of course. Ruth's conviction that they were in a relationship had been firm and clear enough to sway me towards believing that Hilda was indeed, in a fully consensual way, 'walking out' with a man, but that he was a lover whose identity she couldn't admit to. In other words, I feel Ruth must be right. She certainly sounds convincing every time I talk with her.

On the other hand (there is constantly another hand), I remember how utterly persuaded I was by Hilda back when she told me those few but, to me at the time, persuasive details about the predatory Scottish clergyman. The man's name itself, a first name only because he was a priest; his being young, 'not an old priest'; the attention-catching oddity of a Catholic mass held at a doctor's premises; 'Moor Road' as the location, well-known to me, of the garden where she said it happened—these all stick out like handholds on the narrative, offering a grip of credibility.

But if it was not true ... just why would she make it up? Let me take this piece by piece. One piece is pretty clear. I can understand that back when she was a teenager, she'd have good reason for not admitting to a relationship with a POW. Captured enemy soldiers were not necessarily welcomed by every local family, even though they provided help on the farms. After all, we had lost a young soldier in the war—my uncle Tom of the Border Regiment, killed in Norway—and several more family members served on other fronts in that same war. Other families all around us also had young men killed by the Nazis. Village children in my day still played battle games in the street, with Germans as the brutal foe to be vilified and destroyed. Ruth herself had had something to say about this. She briefly stepped out of her unadorned recollections and allowed herself one short piece of speculation, about Hilda's possible motive for lying: 'Maybe she jes' didn't want people to know she'd been wi' a German,' was her simple assessment.

I recognise that in my self-consumed bafflement I had scarcely spared a thought for Hilda's shame. But if I replay our pivotal, long phone call in my mind, her sad but rather generalised reflection, 'In those days, everybody looked down on you having a child out of wedlock,' can barely hint at the full weight of visceral guilt and disgrace she had to carry as a teenage girl. My grandmother's injunction that Hilda must pretend to be my older sister would, I recognise, have been an additionally exacting burden. I have no recollection of just when it might have been that I learned she was indeed my mother; was it at five years old? Seven? No way of knowing. All I know was that I felt deeply unsure about things, about the people around me, about how I fitted in. But for her, how could it have been anything but utterly intolerable. Her saying on the phone 'I found I wanted people to know you were mine; I couldn't keep up the pretence' now poignantly suggests to me just how painful the subterfuge must have been.

Perhaps, as her life went on, after marrying and leaving the village, Hilda thought fate was granting her a respite from questions and judgements, especially since her son seemed wholly uninterested in knowing his father's identity. Until he reached his forties, that is. When I did bring up the question, was all her shame then horribly resurrected, along with a panicky need for yet more secrecy, that all came out with the concoction of another deception? I really should acknowledge the power that shame would have exerted over her. After all, my own brand of shame—whether self-generated or inherited, whether cringeing at any inquiry that might bring up my fatherlessness or concealing evidence of our family's poverty—was undeniably hard to shake; it held me in its silent grip for all of those forty-plus years. But to recognise her shame, along with my own, doesn't take me to a full understanding of it.

Why couldn't Hilda, all those years later, finally reveal to just me (no prying villagers or others to 'look down' on her) that my father was a German prisoner instead of deepening my distance from the truth with a lie about a priest? If indeed it was a lie. If … if.

Godammit, I need to talk this through with my sister. I phone and reach her voicemail. She calls me straight back and in her typically crisp but gentle way, says she can readily see Hilda's need to hide a liaison with an enemy German and even her clinging to the concealment for decades. Julie goes further and presents some supportive reasoning, if it can be labelled such, for why Hilda might pick on a clergyman as a decoy to draw me away from the truth. 'I wonder if it was related,' says Julie, 'to all that news about Catholic priests' sex-abuse? It was very much in the headlines at the time.'

I'm confounded and embarrassed at not understanding my own mother. I cannot feel that I know her now; perhaps I never did. Julie's pointing to the Church's sex-abuse scandals could well be valid. At the time Hilda told me her story, horror over children being sexually assaulted by priests was indeed running high, sensationally so, in both the British Isles and the US. She always followed my career, so she knew that my journalism often covered abuses of Church power. I don't, though, remember her commenting much on such work, apart from her once appearing impressed to have seen me sitting down for an hour-long TV interview with England's foremost churchman, the Archbishop of Canterbury. I never myself reported in detail on any individual sex scandal but I frequently covered the powerful institutional impact of those repeating exposés of abuse, not least the massive financial hit the Catholic Church was taking in costly lawsuits filed by victims. Was Hilda's sketch of a clerical attacker meant to carry some added, special force for me? Maybe she hoped for greater credibility by appealing to my ingrained journalistic stance—always prone to be suspicious of authority and perhaps especially Church authority. I recall again how her terse fax contrasted her own vulnerable girlhood with her alleged attacker's adult and elevated status: 'He was a Roman Catholic priest and he raped me when I was an innocent schoolgirl.'

My pressure on her for a decade or more may have built up within her. She was being dogged by her own son, now an adult, familiar with the world's wicked ways, perhaps even intimidating, forcibly pursuing and interrogating her, however subtle he tried to be about it. Perhaps she was driven to desperate measures in her frantic effort to avoid the truth or get me off her back. I can imagine her grabbing at a fresh stratagem: she wouldn't have used my words but her thinking might have been something like, 'Let's throw him off the scent with something he can't resist running after'.

We siblings cannot hope to know the unknowable. Our mother's thought-processes have long been a mystery to both Julie and me. But I recollect an earlier remark of Julie's, not during this immediate discussion but at an earlier time soon after Hilda's death, a moment when we were puzzling over a shared uncertainty about her, exactly what I can't remember. Julie had said, 'Hilda could seem a very quiet person but she did like to have her dramas.'

It was a little cryptic but I take it now as a reflection on Hilda as someone choosing to live in her own world, perhaps designed to resist being punctured by other people's reality. She and her second husband certainly led an isolated life, appearing to have few friends; and whenever she or he made new ones, they rarely lasted long. Several times she told me about meeting someone who seemed to have gotten close to them, only to tell me a few months later when I asked about them: 'Oh, we're not friends anymore.'

But on the current question—was Hilda's priest story just fiction?—Julie of course could not be definite. Instead she voiced a conspicuously open-ended assessment. 'I wouldn't put it past her,' she says. I feel the same misgivings—as well as my anchorless state of utter not-knowing. I simply have no way of judging if my mother could be a skilful liar; whether she constructed a lurid fantasy of self-dramatisation or whether something else entirely was going on. I am hurled back into my childhood memories of obscure helplessness: staring up covertly at Hilda through half-closed eyelashes, trying to figure out the inscrutable expression on her face as she looks down at me.

I end up furious with the witches' brew of inconsistency that swirls around in my head but I can't aim my anger directly at my mother. Even if I could be sure she lied, without knowing her motive there is no fair way to pronounce judgement on her. Late on in her life I recognised (and Julie apparently appreciated this much earlier) that she was increasingly inclined to believe that others were lined up against her and her husband, a shared conviction that they were constantly being let down or mistreated. Is it an overreach for me to see again the power of shame at work? Did our family's perpetual anxiety about what others, like our neighbours, might think of us morph for Hilda into some form of a persecution complex?

I once experienced her in such a disordered state when Julie and I were both back in our old homeland for Uncle Norrie's funeral. I phoned Hilda to discuss our timetable for the forthcoming days (the burial and what we would all do afterwards) and at one point she suddenly yelled at me: 'Is that Julie listening in on the line? Are you two cooking up something together?' I had to assure her that Julie was somewhere else entirely—asleep in her hotel, in fact.

When I described this episode to Julie next day she took it as the behaviour of a woman in or very close to clinical paranoia. To me Hilda did sound like she was in some kind of untethered space, maybe buffeted by grief at her youngest brother's death. Reflecting now, I can certainly see there's evidence here of delusional thinking; but this doesn't mean, does it, that she could have been an out-and-out fabulist? Did she tell the priest story to others, at any time, early or late? I have no evidence that she did. Perhaps it was for me only. Oh God, who can tell?

My thinking now swerves into the downright wayward. It occurs to me, given my track-record of investigative leads getting crushed, that the still-fresh explanation (my-father-as-POW) could also turn out to be just another red herring. It's entirely possible, isn't it, that some further, completely different account can be waiting for me in some other, still-to-be-revealed direction?

And then suddenly this thought: what if both stories are true? They could be, couldn't they? They don't have to be exclusive of each other. The scenario: Hilda was in a relationship with the prisoner (getting pregnant with him, as my German DNA

356

matches indicate) but she was also raped by the priest. Maybe she didn't know which of them was my father. Oh, my.

I have never been exactly happy with the hypothetical or the suppositional but now I'm fiercely appalled at the way my own mind is running wild with speculation. It's time to halt the spinning brain, breathe carefully, admit and accept that I am—yet one more time, it seems—thoroughly, totally baffled.

I'd better turn to a preferred approach, since I know it always works. I should simply settle myself back within my familiar, comfortable territory: that of attainable facts. Then I'll at least be able to get a grip and focus calmly. I'll get to work, checking out records of German prisoners of war.

Chapter 35
Prisoner Hunt

Finding POW records was harder than I'd imagined. The UK's National Archives occupy a squat concrete pile of a building in Kew, a suburb to the southwest of London which is also home to the most beautiful botanical gardens in the world. The archives, uninviting enough as architecture, seemed to me even more off-putting when I read their blunt online notice intended for researchers in my new area of investigation:

> Very few lists of prisoners of war in British hands have survived and documentation providing biographical information is equally scarce.

After a short menu of the POW-related documents that they did offer—mainly historic administrative papers like the detailing of Britain's duties under international law—the guidance went on to stipulate in specific terms what could not be searched for. Prominent among the restrictions: 'It is not possible to find records using a person's name.'

Ah, well. But then I only had a half-name anyway: the almost tauntingly commonplace forename, Rudi. Even if it had been a searchable term, there might well have been thousands of Rudis in British captivity. What other sparse information I had also turned out to be of little practical use. I knew that close to 1,100 camps were spread across Britain, all identified by a number, and that my village's POW Camp had been No. 692. But scrolling through the catalogue of official documents revealed that not a single record existed from that particular camp.

The Archives had a final message for me, which I couldn't help but interpret as a kiss-off: 'It may be best to contact another organisation—particularly if you are interested in records from the Second World War.'

I was broadly aware that the Geneva Conventions obliged warring countries to swap their prisoner lists at the end of hostilities. I hadn't realised this meant the capturing nation would then destroy its own copies of the lists after its captives had been released and returned to their home country. In Britain's case the practice was supported by the Labour Party, which was resoundingly elected in 1945 as a radically reforming postwar government. I was told by party historians that expunging individual Germans' prison records helped to buttress Labour's reputation internationally as defenders of human rights. Seeing myself as also a supporter of individuals' civil rights, I guess I approved of the policy in theory but I was annoyed with how it frustrated my personal search.

Occasionally narrow slices of prisoner records did survive, perhaps through some civil servant's oversight or mistake, and I was momentarily excited to see them. But when I checked into them more thoroughly, they amounted to little more than a few highly specialised listings of prisoners who had, for example, worked as camp teachers or been taken to hospital at a certain point. I scrolled through them all anyway; none of them included a prisoner who might correspond in any way to 'my' man, nor did they even refer to any camp in my part of the country. It took only a few days of online work to be persuaded that the British repository was completely barren ground for my purposes.

So I switched the locus of the hunt to Germany. Thomas, my determined Teutonic truth-seeker, got to work again. But the Bundesarchiv (federal archives) turned out to offer as slim a set of pickings as my own birth-country's records. All Thomas could find initially was a list of Germans who had died in British camps, a list held at a branch of the Archiv in an outer Berlin district. In keeping with the handing over of documentation to the opposing side, the list of deaths (dating from 1945 or 1946) had been catalogued as an *Englische Liste*. And of course, as Thomas expressed it in his familiar dry manner, the list was 'not very helpful to us, since clearly your father was not dead in England when he met your mother.'

Thomas made more useful progress in identifying what appeared to be a comprehensive list of all repatriated prisoners.

To be precise, though, what he discovered was simply that the list existed; it totalled, remarkably, a quarter-of-a-million men, and Thomas could not consult it personally. Any search had to be conducted by the archivists in charge and, to do so, they needed specific details from us. For instance, both last and first names of the person being sought were essential; and another absolute requirement: the person's exact date of birth.

The reason for applying such strict search filters was that even eighty years after Europe's desperate population upheavals of the Second World War, the archive keepers were still receiving over a thousand individual inquiries per month from people hoping to locate ex-prisoners. My puny offerings of detail like 'Rudi', along with the vague suggestion that he might have been a pilot in the *Luftwaffe*, cut no ice whatever. Thomas said, with an emphatic grimace of sympathy that was somehow enlarged by the screen during our FaceTime call, 'I'm afraid this is another stop to your quest.'

This whole area of research recalled my frequent encounters with the International Red Cross during warzone reporting in the 1970s through the 80s and 90s. I'd been moved to see its teams working persistently—in the Balkans, the Indian subcontinent, the Middle East and various parts of Africa—to gain access to prisoners of war and to set up lines of communication to them for their relatives. Their work inevitably continued into the aftermath of wars, too, helping to reunite families that had been separated and scattered by conflict. So I turned to them now in my search for a one-time German POW who had found himself in Britain's Borderlands several wars ago. The organisation was still in the 2020s working on cases of family disintegration from that war. It was a humbling reminder that my hunt for my father was merely one of hundreds of thousands, quite possibly millions, of ongoing family searches.

Staff at the International Committee of the Red Cross HQ in Switzerland were also finding themselves overwhelmed by research requests, many of them going back to the 1940s and beyond. The sheer volume of work had recently reached the point, they told me, that they had had to call a halt to new inquiries. The delay would last for an undisclosed length of time, though informally they said they hoped to reopen for searches within, say, a couple of years.

But one goodhearted ICRC official pointed out that I could plead for my search to be taken up and pursued even in spite of the new shutdown, on the grounds that I fell into a category of special cases they classed as 'humanitarian'. (I had assumed, in my underinformed way, that all their work was humanitarian but for the experts, it seems, there are degrees of humanitarianism.) A humanitarian exception to the freeze on new searches could be granted for an applicant, like me, seeking what the ICRC called a 'natural parent'. However—and there's always a however with bureaucracies—even in the most deserving cases, making a decision on whether I would be awarded expedited action could inevitably take some time. No surprise there; I was again in a waiting pattern.

But I felt less irritated than usual by this latest hold-up. Language lay at the heart of it. Through much of my life I had built a carapace of mental defences in response to labels like bastard, illegitimate, whoreson, base-born, misbegotten and son-of-a-bitch. That last epithet has in America weakened over time to become a generalised insult or an untargeted expletive or even a term of approval, peeling off from the literalism of its use in English literature of the past, when 'son-of-a-bitch' still retained its original connotation of bastardy. In its earliest recorded uses it meant quite literally the offspring of an unwed or loose woman (to quote one dictionary definition). It occurs in this same sense throughout the works of Shakespeare, deterring me slightly from a more total reverence for the Bard. In King Lear, most notably, the Earl of Kent spells it out, yelling 'son and heir of a mongrel bitch!' at the hapless Oswald, before starting to beat him, while the villainy of Edmund in the same play appears to flow from his bastard status. I can't help resonating to Edmund's complaint on behalf of all our kind: 'Why brand they us with base? With baseness, bastardy?' Such is the curse of having studied English at university.

So it was soothing—strangely comforting even—to linger over the less loaded, even kindly, terminology of the Red Cross. I signed my application form for exceptional humanitarian status, making sure to check one box in particular, the one identifying me as simply the 'Natural Son' of a man from 1940s Europe. I liked the label.

Chapter 36
Local Knowledge

Through all the sixty-plus years since I left the place, my original home village has rarely hit the headlines. It has broadly retained the anonymity its residents seemed to like when I was a boy

Despite our generally low profile, however, we did produce a crop of local historians, few in number but zealously dedicated to researching the events and people of the area. It was to them that I turned after I was completely upended in my paternity search by Aunt Ruth's story, pointing my search in a wholly new direction.

Scottish Border historians turned out to be both helpful in supplying detailed information and engaging in their enthusiasm. First came Gordon Routledge, who had published a profusely illustrated, large-format, 150-page first volume of a historical work titled *The Olde Border Town*. It took the reader from the Ice Age that formed a glacial ridge where our elevated parish church has sat (since 1601) to the Roman occupation and an outpost camp established while Emperor Hadrian's wall was being constructed to keep out the scary Scottish tribes, arriving eventually at the 1939–1945 war, when our local armaments factory fulfilled a patriotic role by supplying weaponry to beat the Nazis. It also included the setting up of our local prisoner-of-war camp, and the arrival of the BBC to make a radio broadcast that celebrated our community for having 'a personality all its own, belonging to no particular country, its people a strange, tough, Border breed'.

Within a week of Aunt Ruth telling me my father had been a POW, I had read Gordon's first volume and located him through his publisher. He was busy, already deep into researching Volume Two, but was ready to help me with anything I needed. I had only to tell him that he and I were from the same village, that I had been born in 1948, that I had never known till late in life who my father might have been, and that I was now struggling with two remarkably different versions of my identity. Could he help to clarify my story? 'Oh certainly!' he said, and I heard the eagerness in his voice. 'I'm up for the hunt.'

I was as surprised as he—and delighted—to find we had been born within three months of each other (I'm the younger) and had lived, amazingly, only 1,500 feet apart as children. His first home had been on the main east-heading road, just around the corner from mine in the sidewards-curving Crescent. Unlike me, he had stayed in the village all his life, ending up in a house right at the very centre and serving as a member of the local council. Oddly, or perhaps not, neither of us had any recollection of each other as children, even though we both attended the same small elementary school. His last name of Routledge was very typical for the area; it certainly rang familiar and I felt, as I enjoyed hearing his Border burr on the phone, that I'd grown up surrounded by the sound of Routledges.

From Gordon, fascinating details tumbled out that predated anything that I could remember. A few days after our first talk, he sent me a photograph—evidently the only picture in existence—of the POW camp where my alleged father would have spent his captivity. It appeared to have a brick-built or concrete watchtower and yet oddly, to me, there were also thick rows of trees at its edge. I would have expected levelled, open space as a necessary security measure but perhaps security was less a priority as the years unspooled after the war's end.

Gordon knew of several local families where POWs had become part of the household as they worked on the family farm or in a local business or store, often connected with farming. He started digging into whether any of these families—survivors from the 1940s or their children or grandchildren—had any information about a Rudi among the Germans they'd once hosted. That individual character did not immediately leap out of anybody's reminiscences but Gordon was building up for me a vivid overall scene of POWs interacting with villagers.

This new flow of information, coming from such a close contemporary, brought me mixed feelings. It was encouraging, even exciting, and I had a warm sense that my hunt might be quickening its pace, but at the same time a disappointed, self-reproachful annoyance grew in me. I had journeyed through a life that took me away, eventually settling in a home thousands of miles across an ocean, and only now was I learning things that had all the time been sitting, unknown to me, within a two-mile radius of where I was brought up. How ridiculous it seemed in retrospect. Of course I still couldn't be sure that what I was learning so regrettably late in the process was the truth, instead of what I had been told nearly twenty years earlier. But all the evidence now surfacing locally was tilting me towards belief in the POW story.

And then came Dr James Bell, another very common Border-Country name. He took me a little longer to find, having retired and moved to another part of our 'Debatable Land'. Gordon had recommended him but the two had lost touch.

I located him by searching through the UK's registry of companies, in case he'd ever been involved in a business. He had. Just one and it had recently folded. I took an educated guess that the officially registered address given for his company—somewhere much further south in England—was the address of his accountants, as often is the case in financial records. I found that an accountancy firm did indeed exist at that address; I wrote to them asking whether Dr Bell had been their client and, if so, whether they would put me in touch with him. They did. 'Sounds like Investigative Journalism 101,' my lawyer friend Walter said, when I told him about my progress.

Dr Bell wasn't strictly speaking a published historian but over the years he had compiled a rigorously thorough lecture that he had delivered in many public forums. Not unlike Gordon's book, it was a lavishly illustrated presentation, with close to a hundred slides. I read it with fascination, a lengthy PDF laying out the story of the Border Reivers, men who from the thirteenth to the seventeenth centuries gained notoriety for both rapacious cattle-rustling and forming themselves into bands of ruthless mercenaries to be hired by both the Scottish and the English armies.

James Bell was a multidisciplinary wonder to me. He must be the only man I'd ever known to hold doctorates in both biochemistry and medieval history. His biological science background led him to a career in the development of clean-energy resources. In retirement, he had become dedicated to historical work and, like Gordon, he warmed to my family mystery as a goad to ever more intense digging. 'You've really got me going,' he said.

He told me that being dedicated to research was a hereditary trait. His father had been our area's veterinarian; his research in the 1970s into the transplanting of bovine foetuses, widely hailed at the time, had helped to further experimental work into *in-vitro* fertilisation in humans. On top of his enthusiasm for the distant past, Dr Bell eagerly confessed to me that he pursued another time-consuming hobby, and one that I found endearing: the upkeep of a thirty-two-year-old Jaguar XJS Convertible with a V12 engine. Not exactly antique but certainly vintage.

Dr Bell offered some powerful input into my search—and he did not have to look far for the material. His own father-in-law, one Mark Richardson, was still living at the age of ninety-five. Mark turned out to have grown up in the Crescent, just eight doors away from my grandmother's house. I remembered the Richardsons but only as a name and a general sense of their presence, without recalling any specific exchanges between them and my family.

By contrast, Mark retained very clear memories, according to his son-in-law. I didn't speak to him myself; but Dr Bell's report on his questioning of the older man was succinct and to the point. Mark apparently remembered my mother well; 'a smart, good-looking girl,' he had said. And he delivered some more information which had resounding impact, though no real surprise—not in light of how my search had recently been going.

Mark recalled that Hilda had a boyfriend who was German. 'He was called Rudi.' And my ageing, one-time near neighbour gave an unprompted description of the boyfriend. Rudi was, he recalled, a 'tall, good-looking man'. The sketchy portrait, if a little vague, was getting repetitive and thereby the more credible.

Chapter 37
Return to the Scene

In February, 2021 I drove a late model Opel sedan—the rental company listed it among its 'executive saloons'—along a little-used Scottish lane. When I ran along that same lane back in the 1950s, tiny-footed and trying to match my fast-walking grandmother, it had been a stony track. Now it was smoothly asphalted. It had also been widened to accommodate cars. But the lane's edges still squeezed tightly inward where it crossed the narrow humpback bridge, unchanged with its low sidewalls of stone. Cars could go over it only in single file. Patiently, one car at a time, sometimes having to let a driver coming the other way take precedence.

The tide was far out and the coast of England was just about visible across the sandy firth. In the distance I could see an extraordinary addition to the landscape, unimaginable in my young days: a small wind farm of half-a-dozen turbines standing tall, too far to tell whether their blades were turning to generate clean energy, though they must have been doing so, and very fast at that. Gusts of thirty-miles-an-hour buffeted me as I stared out from what I still inwardly named our clifftop, though in reality it was just shy of thirty-feet high.

The ten houses of White Row were still there, unaltered and still mostly white, though now with a soft cream or yellowish tint on a few of them. I carried absolutely no memory of how big my great-grandfather's cottage might have been but I could recall its layout. What was once configured as a couple of pinched bed-rooms with a living room and a scullery-kitchen would all have been contained within no more than 800 square feet; that's not to count the old dry privy outside at back, probably now a storage area or a utility room. I felt no wish to look inside the cottage; never even gave it a thought. I suspect I wanted my ancient memories of the warm, tranquil home simply left pristine.

I registered the seafront sights without emotion: they were neither cheering nor saddening. Location in itself didn't seem that important in the journey I was on—not as important as the people of the area I was headed to and their recollections of the years immediately after World War Two.

My great-grandfather's village, by the sea, was only seventeen miles away from where I had grown up with my grandmother and where a few residents still had memories of my family. The two villages stood, however, on opposite sides of the English-Scottish border but the border was porous and the surroundings, the lie of the land between them and the look of the area's vernacular buildings were all very similar.

A forgotten feature of the territory on each side of the border came back to me as I drove the country roads: the military atmosphere that existed in my young days. Back then, the whole area had been dotted with an array of war-related installations, including a large munitions depot, various army camps and barracks, a displaced persons' camp with British soldiers helping to run it, and of course (newly significant to me now) a still operational prisoner-of-war facility for Germans, Prison Camp Number 692.

There were very few private cars in those days. Most vehicles were those of service personnel. I recalled khaki-coloured, troop-filled trucks growling along our winding roadways. Sturdy British soldiers, standing unsteadily, gripping onto each other under tall, hooped-canvas covers, would often wave to my stubby figure as they lumbered past, tailpipes belching black oily smoke at about my chin-height. Here and now in twenty-first-century Border country, my aim was to learn more about that military force's enemy prisoners who were still being held captive in the late 1940s. One of their number, after all, might have been my father.

My hopes had been raised, not entirely rationally, by some of my more historical research. I had come across heartening instances of the Red Cross helping to locate lost members of families who had been divided by war, indeed by a number of wars. A case in point was a search by a certain Chris Weekes, who lived in the English county of Essex and had sought information about his great-uncle, Wilfred Livermore. His family knew that way back in 1914 seventeen-year-old Wilfred had enlisted in the army, becoming a member of the Machine Gun Corps (the MGC, known to its veterans as 'Emma Gee'). Wilfred served with distinction and was awarded a medal for bravery in carrying messages under fire; it was a job with a high casualty rate, hence its other moniker in some war narratives: 'The Suicide Club'.

Wilfred progressed to the rank of sergeant during the four years he was in action. But he went missing in March, 1918 in a battle around Ervillers, a Northern French village that was completely destroyed in the fighting. Thanks largely to Red Cross records, Weekes learned that his great-uncle had become a prisoner of war, albeit briefly. Two months after being captured in March, Sergeant Wilfred Livermore had died, evidently in a German field hospital, from injuries inflicted during the battle. He was only twenty. Weekes wrote in the online regimental record I consulted: 'I am grateful for the help I received in bringing to light the bravery of my great-uncle, who with thousands like him joined up in the patriotic fervor of 1914, only to die a few months before the end of the war.' His words of appreciation inevitably reminded me of my Uncle Tom, killed in the last days of our war on Hitler.

The Red Cross was in recent years able to help with this kind of tracing because of an intensive project mounted in 2010 to collate its astonishing total of over five million individual POW records from the First World War, with the aim of making them all fully searchable. Such a mammoth effort at indexing had not yet been attempted for POWs from the Second World War. All the same, the fact that the search for Sergeant Livermore had been resolved satisfyingly encouraged me to believe that a revealing result might also be possible in my case, even though it dated from soon after a different, more recent war.

It was several months since I had submitted my own request to the International Committee of the Red Cross. The restrictive public-health measures introduced to combat the covid-19 pandemic were inevitably making all kinds of research efforts more difficult. I felt fortunate, though, that my inquiry was being fast-tracked because my hunt was for 'a natural parent'. Being classified this way by the ICRC as a humanitarian priority also enabled me to claim exceptional status as I travelled, if and when I was ever stopped and questioned at checkpoints; this was during an especially tight period of the UK's covid lockdown.

When news eventually arrived, just I was setting off for my on-the-ground investigations, the answer to my Red Cross inquiry was a distinct let-down. The archivists' message said simply:

> We have searched our archives of individual prisoners of war.
> However, we could not find any information about your father.

The Red Cross team restated one obviously appreciable point, that their task was made especially hard because, when it came to names, we had only a first name to go on—that now distinctly baleful-sounding, single word: Rudi. They had naturally wanted to narrow the field and had therefore tried to find records based specifically on my locality, the particular prison camp in Britain that would have held the man I was looking for. But here again they came up empty-handed:

> Unfortunately we were not able to locate any lists of prisoners of war in British Camp Number 692.

No explanation was given for why no prisoner list could be found; there was only the stark fact that no such list had survived for 'our' camp. There must have been one once, complied by the British military, but it had disappeared.

All of this was deflating, of course. But there were other developments to be followed up. Dr James Bell had told me before I left New York about what seemed like a wild coincidence. While travelling in Europe for his energy business years earlier, he had met an engineer from Essen, in Germany's industrial Ruhr region, who turned out to have been a POW in our village until he was repatriated home in 1948. The engineer was called Harry Werner; we speculated that he had adopted and then kept an English variant of his German name, Heinrich, during the five or six years he had spent in Britain. He must have been a prison camp contemporary of Rudi, we realised; maybe he actually knew him.

More than sixty years later, in 2014, when Harry was aged eighty-four, Dr Bell had even helped him make a sentimental return trip to the UK. At my urging Dr Bell was now busily trying to re-establish contact to see if he remembered a Rudi in the camp. Harry would now be aged ninety-one and, we soon learned, was seriously ill in hospital. Then, on my way to Kennedy airport for my transatlantic flight, I heard from Dr Bell that Harry Werner had died.

The disappointments mounted. As I arrived in the old village Dr Bell sent an email in which he stepped back from extending any further help. I had asked him—carefully and considerately, I hoped—if I could have a conversation of my own with his father-in-law, Mark Richardson. I wanted to pursue Mark's memories of my mother around the time she gave birth to me, and see just what else he could recall of Rudi, whom he had so clearly labelled as her German boyfriend. I'd suggested doing this by phone, or preferably—but only if this might be feasible under the covid-19 restrictions—in person. We would observe all necessary health precautions, with face-masks and 'social distancing' correctly maintained. I told Dr Bell I had just tested for covid and was found negative for the virus.

I wish now that we had used phone calls to conduct this exchange more informally, but we didn't. In an uncharacteristically brief note, Dr Bell now simply emailed: 'We are presently in lockdown and also shielding ourselves from any contacts outside our households.' He made no mention of his father-in-law, and then broadened his message to cover my mission overall. He cited again the saddening death of the ex-POW he had got to know: 'We're not able to help you any further with your search now that Harry has passed.'

I felt crushed. The whole world over, covid and the clamp-down measures necessary for its defeat had made conditions burdensome for everyone. And by that stage, it was hard to ignore that covid had caused the death of more than two million people; I was ashamed about feeling so stymied in my one individual, personal quest.

Dr Bell's shift from his previous enthusiastic helpfulness was unexpected but emphatic. I questioned my methods. I had— hadn't I?—just shown up in our once-shared home territory, not exactly without warning but somewhat precipitately, at a time when most other people couldn't travel at all. And I carried hopes of even entering his household. As my mind tried to read his mind, phrases came up in echoes of what I often heard in the UK after I based myself in the US and returned to Britain only occasionally, usually in professional pursuit of stories. Pushy American ... Pushy journalist ... Ease off, can't you?

In something near panic, I nearly called him to backtrack and suggest afresh the halfway measure of my having only a phone conversation with Mark, rather than our meeting in person. Then I abandoned the notion, thinking it most likely that he would recognise my number and choose not to answer. His email had the inescapable expression of finality about it.

I read the email again carefully in the small woodman's cottage I'd rented as an isolated base for my local explorations. I tried composing a reply asking Dr Bell if he would kindly quiz his father-in-law on my behalf, posing a range of telling questions carefully designed to gain as full an account as possible of my mother—and of my conception and birth, if Mark recalled those events.

Pre-scripting an interview for someone else to carry out is rarely either satisfying or effective, as I ruefully knew from my years of television work. I obviously did not stress in my request something I was painfully aware of: that Mark was already ninety-five years old, that another of my possible father's nonagenarian contemporaries had just died and that I needed answers quickly. Yes, I was being pushy, I could see that. I recognised that my journalistic juices were racing. More than that, I'd say they were the juices of someone who'd been long denied the truth and was now feeling tantalisingly close to it.

In the end all I wrote was that I understood Dr Bell's caution, and that his exemplary observance of anti-covid measures was fully justified. I said I would repurpose my visit and use it merely to re-familiarise myself with the geography of my childhood. 'My on-site interviews will have to wait until our public-health crisis is over,' I wrote. 'May that be soon, for all our sakes.' In fact, though, no interview ever materialised; Mark Richardson died the following year.

My relations with Dr Bell had undergone a complete (and for me puzzling) turnaround from when the versatile scientist-historian had cheerfully kept up my spirits with encouraging messages like 'We are on track to find your father' and 'I have a lot of contacts here who may have relevant information.' His most immediate past email had said, 'We are well along the trail now!'

I resignedly put the good doctor's troubling change of mind to one side and turned to different elements of my quest. They were not a lot easier. Great-Aunt Ruth also declined to see me because of covid, no matter how eagerly she had wanted to. The pandemic had hung in the air while we had previously been making our tentative plans to meet. 'We'll certainly get together in person,' Ruth had said, 'if it's at all possible.' But by the time I arrived in the area, the authorities' lockdown suddenly tightened, because of a new surge in covid cases and deaths. Ruth's wish for complete isolation was entirely understandable. She was another village resident in the most vulnerable age-cohort, due to celebrate her ninety-first birthday in just a couple of weeks.

But she and I did at least get to talk further—fully and enjoyably. We were now on a local phoneline and we chuckled about the crackling audio quality compared with our crystal-clear international conversations from earlier. Ruth voiced the local self-deprecation that I remembered so well among our villagers. 'Typical o' this place,' she said. 'It's harder to hear ye now, jest one end o' town to th' ither end, than when ye were on th' ither side o' the world.'

We chatted but no new memories surfaced—not about my father's identity, anyway. She did tell me how, among her several brothers-in-law, two of them had been gamekeepers. And I was able to tell her that I remembered one of them very well. A large-fisted man called Dud, he had taught me how to catch salmon and trout with my young bare hands, crouching shoeless in the flowing river, a skill that was called 'guddling' in our local dialect. Further south, the English, less catchily to my mind, call it simply 'tickling'.

Since I wasn't allowed to be with people, I switched back to places. Thankfully the lockdown rules didn't stop me from visiting buildings. I went first to the parish church. It had no special importance to me, I didn't think, but it was always the village's most prominent landmark, half a mile due south of the centre and the only local feature ever singled out in regional guidebooks. It claimed some misty connection with King Arthur and his Knights of the Round Table, an unlikely fantasy, since most experts agree that the real-life model for Arthur would have reigned at least 400 miles away, much further south and west.

The church was still beautiful to my eyes in its sturdy rectangular way, its stonework even more ingrained with lichen than I remembered. Its rather squat tower didn't exactly strive towards heaven, standing just three storeys high, and its battlemented parapets were like a set of squared-off teeth with regular gaps between them; they suggested defensiveness more than any aspiration for holiness. A tall spire would have better achieved the upward aim of piety, I now thought.

The crowded graveyard's headstones proclaimed the slim range of names native to the area, repeating and intermingling the English with the Scottish: Armstrong, Baxter, Bell, Brown, Carruthers, Graham, Kirkpatrick, MacCready, Murray, Routledge, Roy. That was about the sum total.

The church door was locked. Framed as I was by the doorway's Gothic arch, an unexpectedly sharp memory rushed back of being photographed there at the age of eight for my mother's wedding to my stepfather. My *boutonnière* came into focus: lily-of-the-valley, repeating the predominant flower from Hilda's bridal bouquet, her favourite flower all her life. On my lapel the miniature, bell-shaped white florets were set against the green backing of a leatherleaf fern.

I drove back into the village itself and turned into the

Crescent, where my grandmother's house, Number Six, looked strikingly different from when I had lived there. No longer publicly owned, an owner-occupier had painted it pastel blue, with a sharp line dividing it from its 'other half', the attached Number 5 that boasted a different pastel shade: pale yellow. For most of their lives, all thirty-four homes were uniformly coated with an institutional grey pebbledash. In front of her house Mam had devotedly clipped a privet hedge with her wooden hand-shears, keeping it to a tidy height of five feet. I provided my own proud bit of assistance, ensuring the front-facing side of the hedge was always clipped straight and flat, to whatever height I could reach. In place of the hedge there was now a low beige-coloured stretch of a product that, in my teenage, construction-site days, I knew as 'reconstituted' stone walling, or just plain factory-made. Interspersed every couple of feet along it were small openings lined with cement tiles, and its entire length was topped with some pressed-steel replication of wrought-iron filigree. Gratifyingly, one element of the small garden enclosed by the low wall still looked familiar. A well-rounded white-flowering rosebush stood near the gate. I blinked in surprise, but it could not have been our original bush, whatever I may have thought for a fraction of a second. Such roses, I was aware, would rarely last more than thirty years in the Border Country climate.

I had slowed the car down to take in all these details, and a bald man in a fluorescent yellow road-safety vest stared out at me from just inside my grandmother's front window. I drove halfway round the oval tract of housing and stopped diametrically opposite Number Six, now with the central Green between us. The bald man was still staring. I drove out and away from the Crescent. On a previous visit (for either our uncle's or our mother's funeral, I now can't be sure) my sister and I had knocked at the house's front door but no one opened it, even though we'd been sure somebody was inside. I didn't feel disposed to make the attempt again.

I drove on further, as far as the farms on the village's outskirts. There were two in particular where many of the prisoners of war had been put to work. According to Great Aunt

Ruth, the POW named Rudi had helped out at the one called Hill Farm. (The other was named Burn Farm, for the burn, the Scots word for a small stream that ran though the farmland.) Working from Ruth's description of the scene as it had been seventy-plus years earlier, I gained a rough sense of where the prison camp must have been: it was most likely sited between the two farms and our village's main river. Cartographic evidence, I knew, was sparse and vague. English Heritage, the national organisation dedicated to recording and preserving buildings and monuments of interest, had tried in 2003 to chart all the country's one-thousand-or-more wartime prison camps. It was part of an ambitious survey published under the workmanlike title, 'Twentieth-Century Military Recording Project'. But regarding the exact placement of 'our' camp, all that English Heritage (now renamed Historic England) could offer was: 'Precise location not identified'. There was certainly no footprint left visible these many years after the camp was demolished. A multi-digit mapping reference that EH had assigned to the camp was far from exact. It covered nearly a square mile, could take in both sides of our river and included stretches of land that belonged to each of the farms.

Both Hill Farm and Burn Farm were now merged under the ownership of one family, a family whose help I'd been trying to obtain. Some time before arriving in the village I had talked by phone to the registered owner, a woman called Julia. In the post-war period her father, now long dead, both owned and ran Hill Farm; on site he would have been the POWs' boss.

My first approach to Julia was a cold call, with no inter-mediary to prepare the way for me. Whenever beginning with someone new, my describing the nature of my inquiry would take on a different tone for different people; that much was a given in my professional practice. For this current, very personal, perhaps sensitive kind of interviewing, probing into family background, I sometimes spoke in rather broad and general terms, saying I was trying merely to find extra historical detail to fill in some unclear elements of my ancestry. At other times I'd be upfront and specific, as I was with Julia. I said to her: 'I was brought up in the village but I left when I was eight years old and I've never known who my father was. I think your family might be able to help me discover something about him.'

During that first phone call, Julia listened politely while I laid out more specifically what I was searching for: any information concerning the Germans who had worked on her family's land. I told her I'd heard my father may have been among those POWs. She was quick to say that she was way too young to have any memories herself. I said I didn't expect her to but that there might be bits of family lore that harked back to those earlier times—anecdotes or people's names that might have been repeated down the years.

After I had aired my hopes for a minute or two, she acknowledged that she had an elderly aunt who might remember the POWs and came around to saying that she would talk to her. She disclosed, hesitantly, that her aunt's name was Margaret but seemed reluctant to take a note of my phone number. I dictated it carefully all the same, emphasising that I'd be very happy to hear from her whenever she and her aunt had spoken.

I left the matter for five days, during which no call came. Then I phoned her again, after which began an episode of non-communication that was familiar from my reporter's work—not an overly common experience but frequent enough for me to recognise a pattern. It was that of a reluctant source who was avoiding me.

My follow-up call rang out four times at the farm before going to voicemail. Naturally I left a message. I called again an hour or so later. This time the call was answered, but in silence, before whoever took it hung up. I made a couple more tries, leaving voicemail messages again. I let another day pass, then rang again, but got no response at all, neither machine nor human.

I'll admit, and it's a clenched understatement, I was frustrated. I was now about halfway into the two weeks I was to stay in the area.

I penned a handwritten letter in which I outright begged, while hoping to sound restrained and polite, and took it into the village to post in the familiar red pillar-box, the slot of which I remembered being too short to reach when gripping a handful of my grandmother's letters that I insisted I could mail for her.

I had written:

Dear Julia—I'm so sorry that we didn't get to connect again by phone. But let me please repeat how much I would appreciate your telling me anything your family might recall about the POWs who worked on the farm. Anything at all, even just a small, apparently insignificant detail, might help me as I try to build a picture of who my father could have been. Please phone or text, or email, or send me postal mail, if there's anything you might feel able to say.
—Yours sincerely, David Tereshchuk

Sitting in my rental car a few days later, in clear view of Hill Farm down its muddy driveway, I was wrestling with my feelings. There had been no answer to my letter. My instinct was to play the unstoppable journalist, stride down the driveway and hammer on the farmhouse's front door. What stopped me was the force of the covid lockdown, with its rule barring visits to other households, and the wholly unambiguous evidence that this farming family felt they had no information to give me and didn't believe they needed to tell me so.

An utterly different exchange was to prevail between me and the local historian Gordon Routledge. He and I did get to meet in person, while observing the public-health strictures; we kept our regulation distance of two metres apart, and wore masks the whole time we were together.

Rarely have I seen more clearly demonstrated the truth of an axiom all journalists and researchers know: that nothing beats a live, one-to-one conversation. You can bat questions, answers, old knowledge, new thoughts, puzzlements, possible solutions and fresh angles back and forth—and sometimes wholly extraneous matter will fly in from left field. It's infinitely better than any amount of phoning, emailing or exchanges of documentary evidence.

I'd also say that the extra alchemy of walking as well as talking can somehow add value. Gordon and I walked and talked our way along wooded pathways, sometimes crossing deep ditches by stepping—very carefully—onto the heavy timbers of railway cross-ties that foresters had laid down to create makeshift, ten-inch-wide bridges.

Having already told me about Harry Werner, whom we had lost, Gordon had more to say about German prisoners. From his notes he had dug up details of a prisoner called Georg Ziegler who was befriended by a local woman called Eva and her husband. Georg only lived for twenty years after being repatriated, dying at the age of forty-five, but some twenty years after his death, his son Gerhard journeyed to the village to retrace his father's steps. By now it was the early 1990s and Gordon interviewed both him and the now-widowed Eva, as she welcomed the son of her dead German friend. This seemed to me a rather hopeful lead but it turned out that no one, not even the careful Gordon himself, he sadly confessed, had kept any contacts for the younger Ziegler. And Eva herself was now long dead, passing away at ninety-four, just as the twenty-first century dawned.

While Gordon and I walked, through what he called 'Good Border winter weather'—dustings of light snow and bursts of heavier sleet—one detailed memory led to another, including a recollection of a POW called Clem. He was another detainee who had had fond feelings for the village and had made a trip back there in later life. But like the younger Ziegler, he too had left no traces that we could follow up and his last name was unknown.

Gordon was peering down a length of pathway that ended at a gate onto the edge of a metaled public road. 'There's a name I can't remember just now,' he said, 'but I'll have remembered it by the time we get to that five-barred gate.' And sure enough, when we were about thirty feet from the gate, he let out a triumphant roar: 'Polczynski!' It was the name of a Pole, not a prisoner of war but one of the many displaced persons billeted to our area. Gordon said he'd been an entrepreneurial fellow, setting up a specialist food-store in the village. It catered to Central and Eastern European tastes (specialising in sausages, to no surprise) and consequently he got to know many of the POWs, many of whom he befriended. We conjectured that it must have been a very informal kind of store, maybe just a temporary stand, because when Gordon went later to look it up in the municipal records, there was no sign of it.

There was also no traceable record of any kind for Mr Polczynski's whereabouts, or those of the local woman he had evidently settled down with. But together they raised a son called Stephen who, Gordon believed, became a physician. I resolved to look up every Stephen Polczynski I could find listed among medical professionals across the world. I was eventually to email or direct-message a total of forty-three. Unsurprisingly, I wasn't deluged with replies. In fact I received just one response: from a medical technician in Minnesota, regretfully saying he was no relation to Stephen. His father, named Piotr Polczynski, had emigrated from Poland to the Twin Cities before the war and had no connection to the UK whatsoever.

During our lengthy and productive walk, Gordon drew one more slender arrow from his quiver of ideas: a Dutchman this time, by the name of Lucas Van Nuil. According to Gordon he had settled in our region because he possessed skills honed in his native land that were especially useful in our Borderlands.

Northwest of the village lay an ancient peat bog, the Solway Moss. In history it was notorious for two things. One, a bloody cross-border battle (what else?) in 1542; the English happened to win that particular encounter. And the second, a horrific disaster in 1771 when freakish torrential rainfall led to massive floods, and a catastrophic earth movement described at the time as a 'bursting' or eruption of the bog. Countless humans and animals were said to have died in the surging black ooze. By the twentieth century, wholesale draining of the Moss was deemed essential, and Lucas Van Nuil, from low-lying, flood-prone Holland, had just the right experience in directing such work, recruiting German prisoners, most likely to keep labour costs low.

Here again was someone who had to be found; if Lucas was still alive he might have memories that included my supposed father, and Gordon had an idea that he was indeed alive, though he was likely to be frail. So it was decided that Gordon would put out the word that we needed to speak to Lucas. In another impressive feat of walk'n'talk memory-delving, Gordon recalled that there was a daughter and that her name was Tracy and that she worked in the field of optometry somewhere in the wider Border area. Our quest would go on—and it did for several more weeks, continuing in Gordon's hands after I finally departed back to New York.

What Gordon already knew about Lucas's operation suggested the Dutchman could be a very informative source, once he was found. He had supervised a system arranged with the British Army for a daily delivery of POWs to his various worksites on the Moss. The men became part of a human payload being trucked around on military vehicles under the watch of British soldiers in what was called 'the farm run'. It was an apt enough name since, besides draining the Moss and some casual labour at the local sawmill, farm work was what POWs mainly did outside their camp. The same army trucks that had deposited them would pick up the men when their day in the fields ended—which in the long summer evenings could be close to the camp curfew of 10 pm. Amid all this daily coming and going, Gordon felt sure that Lucas would have had plenty of opportunity to get to know the Germans—perhaps a great many of them, and not just those who worked directly for him.

The picture Gordon painted stirred memories of my own 'farm run'. Between the ages of six and eight I remember being a well-tolerated helpmate to George Bell, the village grocer. He let me drive around with him as a favour to my grandmother, I believe, taking me off her hands for a few hours. We travelled in his dull brown van, rigged in the back with pale wooden shelving to hold sliding trays of sweet-smelling, freshly baked bread. For each sizable grocery delivery that we left at farmhouse after farmhouse, the centrepiece was a loaf. I would often get a tip from the farmers' wives, maybe even as much as a tuppence. It was, I feel sure, my first experience of a bigger world and its riches beyond our village.

Chapter 38
And so ...

I was once again in a state of waiting, the kind of limbo I used to find so hard to endure, waiting to learn if any new evidence would emerge in my old Borderland village about my father. Would the local historian Gordon Routledge locate the transplanted Dutchman, Lucas Van Nuil, who had known those German prisoners who continued to be kept in our area after World War Two ended? I needed to know if he had known my father.

In fact it wasn't unbearably long before Gordon established that Lucas, now well into his nineties, was living in a nursing home. That was the good news. The bad news, his daughter told Gordon, was that he had lost not only most of his memory but also the capacity to talk coherently about anything at all.

I felt devastated. After a trip to the Borderlands in which every promising lead had come to nothing, I had allowed myself to believe that Lucas, who was clearly my last remaining line of inquiry locally, might prove to be the key that unlocked my lifelong mystery. The prospect of meeting him and listening to him reveal the truth had become a tantalising reverie. And now, the edifice of hope that I built up was crushed.

Under other circumstances, I might have found this latest in a relentless succession of dashed hopes almost comic: worth a bitter laugh, anyway, at the irony of it. So much had been promised by each of the prospects that had been dangled in front of me and, one by one, each of them had failed: they might have known something but couldn't be found, they might have known something but wouldn't reply, they might have known something but wouldn't talk, they might have known something but couldn't talk, they might have known something but had died. If I were a superstitious man, I might have felt tempted to believe that I was being tortured or tested by a malevolent spirit.

That is the reality that I have had to accommodate myself to since then, and I have done so by reverting to a perpetual holding pattern in which, instead of ever touching down on the runway of revelation, I am left to circle round and round, with no obvious prospect of ever reaching my destination. It is a condition that has often characterised much of my life, and one which I now seem to be stuck with indefinitely. Here I am, thwarted again—perhaps permanently. There's no way down.

For sizable periods I can shrug off my frustration and concentrate on going about my day-to-day work as if there is nothing in the background to plague me. But beneath all my mundane preoccupations, I still quietly harbour the hope that one fine day, somebody's DNA will pop up on a genealogy website, probably from Germany, and yield some connection to a man who could have engendered me. The fact that no one's has, however, is an irritant that makes me feel cheated, in the way that an expectant beneficiary might feel on discovering that they have been written out of a will.

To some extent, I've gotten used to my predicament, to the extent that my not-knowing now feels normal. Ever since my doughty genealogist, Linda Lawless, first started checking on all my emerging matches and counseling me that it would likely be 'a long haul', I've become accustomed to living in this familial no man's land. I still routinely check in with Linda, devoting a couple of hours a week to reviewing whatever new matches might have appeared. We carefully trace lines from each new individual along the branches of their family tree, in the belief that we might find an adult male who could have been in the UK at the relevant time. But undeniably now, my hunt is no longer an active one, as it once was. In essence I now wait passively for my genetic prey to come to me, rather than going out to find it.

Discouraging thoughts assail me all the time. The most obvious is that the man I seek is now dead. This does not prevent me from finding things out about him but as so many people involved in this story have been ageing, and some dying, I recognise that there might never be a full resolution to my search, in the sense of having a definite fix on the man—an identity and, more important than that, some well-founded sense of what he might have been like. I recognise that I am probably going to have to resign myself to never fully shedding the weight of this seemingly endless secret. Some cautionary words resonate for me, voiced first by Thomas in Berlin at a time when we still hoped we'd quickly home in on my mother's alleged POW boyfriend. 'Let's face it,' he said, 'whatever you do find, it won't be as much as you would want or as much as you have every right to know.' I have a profound recognition of just how true that prediction is turning out to be.

It's well-nigh certain that even if my father were eventually to be identified, I wouldn't be able to question him or in other ways gather a meaningful life-story from him. While I have undoubtedly gained odd bits and pieces of information—some later discoveries contradicting earlier ones—there are still times when I see myself as merely a much older version of the young boy I once was, silently perplexed about there being no man in our house. Put very simply, perhaps even childishly, I know I'll never know him. In the face of this realisation, I need to call on whatever adult self-awareness I possess to put aside the disappointment that dogs me.

There is also of course the intractable puzzle. Why—after my fifty-plus years of complete ignorance—would my mother have thrown me what now looks like a gigantic red herring, as if she were some clumsy, devious mystery novelist? Or maybe not so clumsy. It does look like she diverted me very effectively for twenty years. Perhaps, though—again just a perhaps—she didn't mislead me at all, since it is still just about feasible that a priest called Francis did rape her, despite my finding no evidence to support her story and much more evidence to suggest its falsity. And let's not forget that the other account of her evidently 'walking out' and getting pregnant with a prisoner-of-war boyfriend has not been proved either.

But if my mother did spin me a false tale, maybe I failed to give full weight to her possible motives. I have to remind myself how very different the moral atmosphere was, not just *when* she was young but *where* she was young. In the same era into which I was born, so great was the shame of bastardy that in countries that considered themselves the most advanced in the world, people working in such institutions as the church and, in Britain, the National Health Service, sometimes forcibly removed the children of single mothers and sent them away for adoption or to orphanages, where abuse was common, known about and accepted. The unhappiness caused to a mother and a child by their separation was thought preferable to the unseemliness of an unmarried woman being known to have become pregnant and then raising the child that she had conceived.

On top of that came the shame of there being no known father, or a father who couldn't or wouldn't be identified, and the uncomfortable suspicion that Hilda may have been made pregnant not just by one of Hitler's soldiers but by a soldier from the same hated army that had killed her older brother—and even that she hadn't minded. If such suspicions were true—and gossip always thinks the worst of people—the neighbours would doubtless have had much to condemn her for in all that.

I can appreciate, too, that in my mother's young day society's mores were patrolled by authority figures who could barely utter the word 'sex', so painfully embarrassing was the thought of it. It should be no surprise to me that my grandmother would be horrified simply by her teenage daughter having lost her 'innocence'. A girl's virginity, including her supposed unaware-ness about sex, was a precious social commodity without which she'd be reduced to a non-person, a young woman with a soiled reputation in the community.

But I don't have to go all the way back to a time before the vaunted sexual liberation of the 1960s, to understand such a social affront. Marriage rates are collapsing and more babies are now born to cohabiting couples in the UK than to married couples. Teenagers also seem to be more sexualised or more exposed to sexual material, and yet sexual activity between an adult and a teenager is defined as statutory rape and is perhaps more widely condemned than ever. By any modern definition, whether in the 1940s or today, Hilda was raped.

The truth of what exactly happened is hidden among several overlapping pairs of possibilities. I still do not know whether her assailant was a priest or a civilian, a prisoner of war or a displaced person, a friend or someone unknown, and whether what happened between them was forced or consensual. Perhaps she loved a man who was taboo. Perhaps she was naive and believed entreaties that were made to her. Perhaps she even encouraged the assault upon her; for children do not suddenly become sexually curious only when such curiosity is legally permissible. Perhaps it was her own willing participation that Hilda could not confess to me. Whatever the truth, she was evidently ashamed of what she had done, or what someone had done to her, and she perhaps in some way never stopped blaming herself for me, the living proof of a moment in time that she could never put right. And this could be true even though she insisted to me how determined she was to both give birth to me and raise me, and that she never regretted for a moment refusing to give me up.

My logical mind is tempted to label her later behaviour as irrational but I can nonetheless understand how her pain contin- ued to control her through the decades, even half a century later, when she talked one-on-one with her son, someone who had come of age in an apparently less moralistic, less judgmental time and who had no World War Two memories or anti-German bias.

What I feel overall about my mother is dismayingly hard to pin down. My emotions ebb and flow when I look back on her secrets, evasions and lies. How much easier it would have been, surely, for her to have told me, simply, what really happened.

But maybe it was my fault. I am beset by a recurring recrimination. I should have probed more fully into her rapist priest story when I first heard it from her. I could have probed it more fully. But I didn't. I'm a journalist. I have all the apparatus needed to elicit information, even from the most unwilling sources, and then to test what I'm told. Why, in Hilda's case, did I fail to check her account much earlier on? In a distressing exception to my habitual way of working, I took my mother's word for everything she said. In hindsight, considering what I have discovered since then, that omission looms heavily over me as the mistake of a lifetime.

Maybe, also, there's a lesson in this. While the detached professional in me is reluctant to accept that I let myself down, I have to accept that there are limits to how we engage with those we are close to—that in every relationship there are appropriate and inappropriate behaviours and that these are tightly defined. To anyone else, Hilda would have been just another a source, someone to be quizzed and pushed and then appraised as either reliable or unreliable. A mother—one's own mother, that is—is something else; even I (with my mixed feelings about my mother) see full well that there are greater sensitivities. In both cases there are proprieties but the proprieties are different. In my case, I was a son in search of an answer, and my mental and emotional system was utterly roiled by my mother's priest-rape story. I don't believe, though, that I stifled my critical faculties simply because I was shocked and upset; rather, I sensed limits to what can be talked about between a parent and a child. At a certain level, I feel sure, we recoil at the total exposure of a parent, just as many of us would turn away from their bodily exposure.

And then there was the nature of our relationship. I had won an Oxford scholarship, become a highly paid television performer and ended up living in Manhattan with a second home by the sea. Hilda represented not just what I had left behind but what I had rejected. Maybe she resented me for it. I do remember an unexpected remark of hers, voiced soon after I'd moved to the US and in a surprisingly critical tone, that we each lived 'very different lifestyles'. It's possible too that she felt intimidated by me—and her evasions were a form of self-protection. Maybe the truth was the one thing she could hold onto and not let me take from her, however well-regarded I might be in my public arena for asking questions and getting answers.

Or maybe, again, behind my failure or reluctance to probe deeply enough, there was something much simpler, even matter of fact: that I had other things on my mind, that I was building a new life for myself, that I was focused on being sober, on living in a new country, on being married and on caring for my wife through an illness that eventually killed her after seven years. I can now fully delve into the mystery of Hilda because so many inescapable, everyday things that preoccupied me then no longer do so. It is telling, I believe, that only after Melissa died did my most earnest and dedicated phase of searching for a true father begin. Perhaps I have been trying to cope with a devastating, irreversible loss by throwing myself at another lack in my life that could just possibly, if I was really lucky in my efforts, somehow be reversed.

Chapter 39
To my Mother

I was about to turn forty-nine. You were sixty-five. In New York I asked you—straight out loud for the first time ever, to my conscious knowledge—who my father was.

You said then that you would tell me. Not immediately, but sometime soon, when you were more comfortably back home in the UK. I know it took some time, almost another five years, but I was thoroughly relieved when you finally did tell me something. First in your fax and then in our long talk on the phone, you told me the terrible story of how you were raped by a visiting Catholic priest.

And you described how the cover-story got invented in our family, presenting me to the world as your little brother.

I believed you. I remember, though, the slight tingle of incredulity that pricked me. A priest? A rape? Against a fifteen-year-old girl? The sheer outrage and horror of the crime you described was enough to trigger doubts. None of us wants deep down to believe such terrible violations can happen. As you knew about me at the time, I had been well trained in exercising a reporter's scepticism; but all the same, I didn't press you for anything to support your story, even supposing there could be any such thing. And I didn't then look for any other kind of proof, from any other source.

Not until more recently. And now, years of work have unearthed nothing to confirm your account, although my searching has been diligent, as I feel sure you'd known it would be. And I have discovered a different story (one which can't be proved, either) that you had a boyfriend who was a prisoner of war.

Although our family subterfuge, making you pose as my big sister, may have fooled a few villagers, I've heard that at least a few local folk knew about your being pregnant with me and that the father was that prisoner-boyfriend. A name, too, has been mentioned for him more than once: Rudi. What am I supposed to do with this information?

Yours was a life of hiding the truth from me. But as you know, much of mine was spent conducting interviews with people who made a practice of hiding things—and with no need between us for me to be modest, I'll say I steered them skilfully and incisively. I steadily got the truth out of a head of state who tried to deny he'd ordered mass killings of his countrymen. I confronted the abusive father of two small children with the evidence that he burned them with a firebrand. Similarly—in pursuing a story that's twistingly repellent to recall in our present context—I exposed the self-justifications of the populist community leader who claimed that his rapes of women were a political act. But all my experience and probing skills seem no use at all as I attempt to frame questions for you, questions that obviously cannot be answered. I see you start to tighten and jut your jaw. Please don't jerk your head upward and turn away, as you seem about to. In my mind's eye, at least, let our gaze be held steady between us. For my part, my inevitable anger won't stop me from trying to be fair.

Let me pose what I consider the simple, basic query: is it true that my father was a prisoner of war? And if he was, why did you tell me, half a century after the fact, that it was someone else entirely? Why cite a priest, of all possible identities?

And for that matter, to borrow some blunt phrasing once voiced by our cousin's wife: 'Just why the big damn secret in the first place?' Oh, I know times were different then, especially concerning illegitimacy. That I understand. But why continue with the secret, and for so long? I have to acknowledge my own part in that ongoing secrecy. I never went near the topic even after I'd reached an age when I was mature and independent-minded-enough to do so. I was ashamed, I think, of your shame. Ashamed of a lot about my family, in truth: our poverty as well as the unspoken mystery of my origins. That was unnecessary and unfair of me, I'll admit. I feel acutely sorry for it.

Maybe I don't really deserve an answer from you, since I didn't work very hard for one when I might have had the chance —and instead I was all the time consigning you and my whole family background into what I silently labelled as an unimportant and irrelevant past. That, too, I am sorry for.

I want to ask you more about the POW. And with a different kind of question. Let's assume for the moment that this is the true story. Were you happy with Rudi? I'd like to think you might have been. I feel sure that your guilt and terror about being pregnant at all at fifteen—and about your mother's fury, which you so compellingly described to me while telling your priest story—were all very real and deep. But even with the horror and upheaval you went through, was there any delight in your relationship? While I know that, because of your young age, my conception was from a legal view a statutory rape whatever the man's identity, I hope that it might have in your view been consensual. Can you say it was? For a fifteen-year-old, we might both now be careful with the word I will use, but all the same: were you in love with him? You learned, when I too became a fifteen-year-old, that I could be stubbornly confident about what was good for me in relationships, however right or wrong I might have been at that age. Is it fair to think that might have been true of you, as well? You felt you knew what you were doing, and that it was right?

Can you tell me anything about that relationship of yours— anything at all about him? Was he kind? Was he overbearing? Was he creatively minded or a workaday soldier? A man of flair or a grunt?

I'm dismayed by the absurdity of my questions, getting more ridiculous as I press onward. On the page, though, I can attempt even the preposterous. Can I somehow entice you into admitting from beyond the grave that you lied to me in my fifties, as well as keeping me in the dark as a youngster?

It's just as preposterous to consider another fanciful scenario. In it you are continuing—wherever you might be—to maintain that my father was a priest. Does respect for your memory mean I should keep that possibility open? Scrupulous logic, too, might remind me that while a priestly paternity for me cannot be proven, it cannot be decisively disproven either. It seems neatly apt that our unique legal verdict in Scotland, the one saying 'not proven', applies here.

It remains an open possibility. But in the realm of possibilities it surely belongs in the highly unlikely subdivision. And situated immediately opposite is another, contradictory possibility: the maybe stronger Rudi story.

Do you remember reading to me when I was, oh, around seven? I would often refuse to accept a story's ending that I found puzzling or in some other way not to my taste. There was the Aesop's fable in which the hard-working ant so resoundingly wins out against the leisure-loving grasshopper. But why could not both be right, at least part of the time? For many of my story-book disappointments, some perhaps sharper than that one, you had a general, rather pat response: 'Sometimes there is no easy answer.' It gave me no comfort at all. Unwelcome though it may have been then, however, it now stays inescapably true. It even brings, in the present day, some soothing calm.

Perhaps more tellingly than anything I have to ask or let you know, there is this. Despite all my fury at the iniquity of your concealments and evasions, and despite my gut-twisting frustration at not finding a way past the obstacles that keep me from achieving what I want, I quite simply cannot blame you. Mind you, I'm in no position to absolve you either; I'm not sure who would be. Sadly, I see you as always alone—no confidante, no guide in life—to share your agonies with about conceiving me and in your different ways denying me: initially forced to deny I was yours, later deciding to deny me knowledge of what happened.

Between my unanswered lines of inquiry, darting in and out, there flows a current of greater warmth than I once could ever imagine in myself. Not of understanding, exactly (that still seems beyond me) but certainly a way of reimagining my unfulfilled quest as simply a matter of indifferent fate and not anything of your making. Rape or no rape, priest or no priest, maybe in fact an enemy prisoner. All the uncertainty calls for compassion towards you far more than any frustration or anger. You have it in full.

Chapter 40
To my Father

Framing questions for a mother now dead may be difficult but questioning a never-identified father is way harder. I'll try all the same. I do have a deep attachment to questions. They've been an essential tool of my work for just about forever. I know as well as anyone observing me at work that questions will often divulge truths about the asker, not just the askee.

How to start? Well, fairly obviously: Who are you?

You might be a priest, as my mother told me. But if you are, I've come to believe you're probably not called Francis. And it's almost a hundred-per-cent sure that you're not the Father Francis who, according to the Church's answer to police inquiries, was in our area at the relevant time. My DNA doesn't match up with any of that Francis's family members. I'll acknowledge, if I'm to be persnickety, that there's a tiny margin for error here, but it's so minuscule that I'm going to take as definite my total lack of genetic connection to this Father Francis. Maybe, then, you're a different priest? Did Hilda get the name wrong? Did you give her a false name?

Whoever you are, did you rape my mother?

Do I expect an honest answer from this possibly illusory criminal? Obviously no—but this is the sharpest, most urgent of the many remaining questions darting about in my brain.

And since repeat offences are all too common with sexually abusive priests (and abusive men in general), I have to ask if you committed this crime against other young women? Did you perhaps create half-siblings for me, scattered across other parishes? When, or if, your attack on my mother became known, did you make a run for it? Did your fathers superior dictate that you go? Were you punished in any way?

I'm guessing at things here, and maybe I'm wrong, but did you even know about me, as I suspect you didn't?

These are agonisingly pointless questions. The whole thing is a pointless exercise. Except that it might help me refine the riddles that confound me most. And there is definitely some refining going on. I am steadily coming closer to the belief that you were definitely not a priest.

Maybe you'll agree and say that you never were a priest, that your name was Rudi and that you were a prisoner of war. In the movie running in my mind, you'll give me your full name, number and rank, I suppose.

In which case I need to ask exactly how you came to meet my mother and just what attracted you to her at the age of fifteen. Whether her appeal lay in her youth and innocence—whether this inspired a transgressive excitement in you. Actually, this is what I least want to hear about the event that created me: whether you were the predator I fear you might have been.

Or were you caring and attentive? Loving and affectionate? Perhaps not much older than her, but with a very different life-experience already behind you: military service in a bloody war.

Some of my notional questions can of course be addressed to the supposed priest as well as the possible prisoner. Did either of you (I'm fancifully detaining both suspects in adjoining interrogation rooms now)—did either of you learn anything from Hilda about her recent history? That for five of the seven years before you met her, she had lived separately from her family— that is, removed from her mother and without a father, who had died? Did you find her deprived of affection and therefore vulnerable? Did that make her easier to prey on? More appealing in her vulnerabilty? My disgust at the thought is hard to contain but I'm giving you the opportunity to fess up. You've probably never done so before. You'll feel better if you do.

Or do you feel the need to defend yourself? From your side of the interview table, perhaps you want me to understand your own separation from your family, possibly since your mid-teens when you entered the Reichswehr, and then of course the time you spent being held in military captivity. Did you feel as estranged as Hilda felt? And was it that which brought the two of you together? Not love, necessarily, but the need for love?

Afterwards—if you were the prisoner of war—were you not

prepared to step up and be a father? Were you relieved to be repatriated to Germany and escape responsibility, never to return? If, however, you were the priest, then I suppose that embracing parenthood wasn't an option anyway, but were you relieved or regretful? I feel I should tell you, by the way, that today, in the twenty-first century, under Pope Francis, priests who produce offspring are supposed to provide for their welfare. Do you feel you had a lucky escape?

If you were the prisoner, some less antagonistic, even lenient questions come to mind. Did you actually know how young Hilda was? Did she say—as I recall girls saying when I was going through my teen years—that she was older than her real age? Did you perhaps want to take responsibility but couldn't? Did you offer? Or did the crime, once discovered, make that impossible? Did Hilda's family, in the single fierce personage of my grandmother, whose son was killed in the war against your countrymen, simply not allow it?

Were you perhaps not even told Hilda was pregnant? Did you ever know that I was on the way?

We're veering into fantastically impossible territory now. But I also have to ask ... just what, in me, comes from you? Quite obviously I won't get an answer from you on this; only my own imagination can provide one, through the prism of my own speculation. I know, or think I know, one thing: I used to be, until I lost the skill in later life, a fairly adept verbal mimic, especially of accents. Were you a mimic? As either a priest or as a prisoner in a foreign land, such an ability would have been useful to you: a help in blending in better with your surroundings.

About my physical characteristics. Everything I see in the mirror I recognise from my mother's side: my mother's nose, my maternal uncles' hair and eye-colour, my height and the set of my shoulders. I cannot assign anything to you, which is strange and disappointing. If there was something distinctly different in my appearance, I might feel it was a clue. Does this mean (and I find this a bit odd, even creepy) that I want to be like you?

There's one intangible attribute that I feel inevitably, almost unquestionably, must have come from you. It certainly did not come from my mother. It may not, though, have been genetic at all, and instead developed in me simply because you are so much an unknown quantity, one that I have wondered about, on and off, all my life. Were you by any chance an avidly curious person? Were you possessed, as I am, with an insatiable thirst for explanations? Is that your legacy to me? If so, the least you can do is to tell me. I need answers.

Chapter 41
To Myself

All the uncertainties that I have been trying to probe have made my brain feel like someone else's. I am reminded of a brain belonging to a much-scorned politician, a brain that a team of magazine writers once sarcastically suggested should be mounted in a museum. Stashed in my journalist's memory lies that politician's best known remark, voiced in a familiar venue for me—a press conference—when he was doing his own wrestling with imponderables:

> There are known knowns. There are things we know we know.
> We also know there are known unknowns. That is to say, we
> know there are some things we do not know. But there are also
> unknown unknowns, the ones we don't know we don't know.

That mental minefield may have been all about the limitations of intelligence reports in 2002, but Donald Rumsfeld's effort at epistemology rings a pounding bell for me now, in my purely private, individual bewilderment.

The known knowns that I've gathered about the man in my life who was never in my life are few and far between. The known unknowns are more various and more daunting. But how can I ever, with any clarity, pick a pathway through the unanswered and unanswerable mysteries that constitute the things I do not know I do not know? I am tormented by I know not what.

Given the continuing absence of answers, I guess I can wave goodbye to establishing any truth beyond a reasonable doubt. That's distressing since, along with many of us living and working under Anglo-American common law, I'm enduringly influenced by the 'reasonable doubt' maxim. I am not conducting criminal proceedings here; but if I were, any case I might present against either one of my potential 'culprits'—the rapist priest or

397

the prisoner boyfriend—would surely get tossed out of court by the jury on the grounds of reasonable doubt.

There is of course an alternative route. I could draw my analogies from civil law. There, my guiding precept would have to be 'the preponderance of evidence'. Legal experts have explained this to me, most pointedly when I was once being sued in the civil court for defamation—unsuccessfully as it turned out. The lawyers defined the preponderance notion this way:

> To base a judgement on what is the more convincing evidence and its probable truth or accuracy—in contrast to the more severe test of beyond reasonable doubt which prevails in criminal cases.

That does seem applicable here and so I feel bound to conclude, on the basis of a preponderance of evidence, that the man responsible was our German prisoner of war.

But hey—let's stop this legal flimflam. I am definitely not putting anyone on trial here. Not the first suspect nor the second, nor my mother, though at times I have been tempted to invoke charges of a cover-up or obstruction of justice. And for that matter, although this idea has been lurking here all along, I too am not on trial—except perhaps for the regrettable but mercifully not punishable offence of not living up to my normal reportorial standards.

Trial or no trial, I believe I have been released on my own recognisance. The conditions of my freedom amount to my being under an obligation to learn something from all of this. The learning might be that I have ended up on better terms with what I do not know than I ever was at the start of my search. I was convinced earlier on that I must achieve a state of perfect certainty, a notion from which I am now content to retreat. Instead, I am settling into a frame of mind that I heard first mooted long ago by a family friend. She exhorted us to practise an oxymoron: 'Flounder comfortably in a sea of uncertainty' was her suggestion. It went deeply against my inclinations.

But here I am, subsumed in uncertainty. I may be floundering in it but at least I'm not drowning.

Am I totally comfortable with my lack of certainty? Of course not. But the aching intensity, that fierce need-to-know which once wrapped its coils around me and threatened to strangle me, has been substantially loosened. I am immeasurably more comfortable now than ever in my seven decades of life. Not free but freer. I'll take that.

END

Acknowledgements
To All

There is much, close on everything, for which I have to thank other writers. Notably: Orlagh Cassidy, Chris Howard, Josh Lehrer, Kathleen Sullivan, and most of all our fearless group leader, Kate Lardner. This book couldn't have happened without them. And the contribution made by Envelope-Books, especially the indefatigable Stephen Games, has been unparalleled. Thank you, all.

Figures are indicated by the letter 'f' following the page number.
The relationships mentioned within parentheses are with reference to
Tereshchuk, David (born Brown, David).

superheroes 64
TV shows 32
Amin, Idi (Ugandan President)
108–9, 115–20, 255
attack of foreign reporters/
'Amin's Dungeon' 118–19
expulsion of Asians 112–14,
115
the tyrant 109, 115, 116, 118–19
ANC (African National Congress)
315–18, 320–31, 336
election publicity at Carlton
Hotel 315, 320, 331
electioneering style 317–18
First, Ruth (political
organiser/writer) 327
intelligence division
(iMbokodo) 328
Mandela's press conference
315, 331
members 316, 326–7, 337
military wing (uMkhonto we
Sizwe/MK) 325–6, 327, 330
news managers 315
Sachs, Albie (legal expert/
activist) 327
'Spear of the Nation'
(documentary) 322–5, 323f
Tambo, Oliver (leader/
politician) 320–2
workers 323, 330
see also Mandela, Nelson
(South African President);
Mbeki, Thabo (South
African President)
Anglicans/Anglicanism 2, 150,
154
apartheid 106, 268, 282, 286, 319,
324, 334–6, 338
see also Mandela, Nelson
(South African President)
Arab(s) 240, 298
-Israeli conflict 76, 240
army/Army
British 21, 23, 59, 78, 95–6,
100, 215, 216, 220, 222, 231,
352, 381

Irish (see IRA (Irish
Republican Army))
liberation 193, 283, 295 (see
also FRELIMO (Front for the
Liberation of Mozambique))
Pakistani 74, 75, 78, 79, 82
Portuguese 271, 274, 278–9,
307
Zimbabwean 202
see also soldiers
arrest(s) 176, 250, 324
of reporters 70–2, 104, 118–19,
175–6, 194–5
of women 174–5 (see also
Burton, Susan (law-reform
campaigner))
Asia/Asian(s) 79, 110, 112–13, 115,
116, 159, 200
assassinations 150, 234, 293, 295,
330
Australia/Australians 77, 192, 211,
236, 239, 245, 313, 330
Sydney 79, 192
Austria 21, 113
autocracy 116, 203, 335

Bangladesh 47, 73–84, 90, 104
Bengalis 73, 75, 77, 80–1
Choudhury, Ajit
(secessionist) 75
Dhaka 73, 75, 77, 78, 82, 83
floods and cholera 76, 77, 80
massacre by Pakistani
military 75, 77–8, 80–2
Operation Searchlight 73–5
separatism from Pakistan
73, 75, 83
Sheikh, Mujibur Rahman
(Bengalis' leader) 73
Barenboim, Daniel (Israeli
pianist/conductor) 240–3
Barenboim, Michael/Barenboim,
Mischa (s/o Barenboim,
Daniel) 242–4
Barrymore, John 50, 52–3
BBC (British Broadcasting Corp-
oration) 45, 134, 192, 247

Liberation of Mozambique
libraries 32, 42, 79, 133, 195
Loftus, Elizabeth (Professor in
the US) 99–100
London 43, 51, 52, 270
Africa Centre in 195, 294, 299
homelessness in 66, 275
Londoners 66, 200
news 45–6, 192
Regent's Park Mosque 158f
Speakers' Corner, Hyde Park
58

Machel, Samora (Mozambican
President) 272, 295, 296, 297,
302, 303
Macmillan, Jock (ecologist in
Africa) 264–5
magazines 68, 90, 104, 157, 192,
197, 306, 317, 323, 397
Malawi 291, 299, 319
Manchester 30–9, 64, 218
Boggart Hole Clough (park)
31
curry-houses/Indian
restaurants 110
football 278–9
musicians/band 33, 34
neo-Nazis' march 67
schools 26–7, 30
slum housing 24–5
Mandela, Nelson (South African
President) 323f, 328, 330
imprisonment 270, 318, 320,
324, 326–7
interview of 315, 331–2
letter for release of 270
President of South Africa
305, 335
press conference 315, 331
release from prison 315, 340
and Tutu, Desmond 340–1
Winnie (wife) 324, 340
massacre(s)
Bangladesh 75, 77–8, 80–2
Derry 87–8, 92–4, 93f, 96–9,
101–4, 168

Mozambican 105, 271, 272,
274, 280
My Lai 105, 272, 273
Poland 69, 70
Rosewood 105, 133–4
Sharpeville 105
Wiriyamu 307–8
Zimbabwean 202
Massey, Richard (Detective
Sergeant) 248–52, 310–11,
342
Mazrui, Ali (Professor in Africa)
115–16
Mbeki, Thabo (South African
President) 326–9
Middle East, the 120, 240, 360
military
British 13, 59, 87, 88, 97, 100,
102, 103, 370
coup 109, 308
munitions depot 22–3, 368
North Korean 202
Pakistani 73–4, 75, 77–8, 80
para- 87, 222, 223, 225
paratroopers 87, 88, 97, 100,
102–3, 347
Portuguese 192, 274, 283–4,
307
rape by 78, 81
Rhodesian 191, 194
see also army/Army; soldiers
Millett, Kate 320
monarchies 154, 276
Mormons, the 155–6
Mozambican(s) 105, 290, 297,
301, 302
Afonso 274–5
Honwana, Fernando 270–2,
274, 293
massacre of 105, 271, 272,
274, 280, 307–8
Mozambique 267–309
Aldeamentos ('Established
Villages') 273–4, 284
ANC operatives in 322
black-ruled 305
dam 267–8 (see also Cabora

Non-fiction from EnvelopeBooks

www.envelopebooks.co.uk

A Road to Extinction

JONATHAN LAWLEY

When Britain colonised the Andamans in 1857, the welfare of its African pygmy inhabitants was of no concern. Nine tribes died out. Dr Lawley now assesses survival prospects for the three remaining tribes and weighs up the legacy of his grandfather, who ran the colony in the early 1900s. EB2

Spy Artist Prisoner

GEORGE TOMAZIU

Artist George Tomaziu half-expected to be imprisoned and tortured for monitoring Nazi troop movements through Bucharest during the Second World War but thought that his heroism would be recognised when Socialism came to Romania in 1950. He was terribly mistaken. EB10

Postmark Africa

MICHAEL HOLMAN

Made an Amnesty Prisoner of Conscience while he was under house arrest as a student in Southern Rhodesia, the author went on to document Africa's emergence from colonialism as Africa Editor of the *Financial Times*. EB1

Why My Wife Had To Die

BRIAN VERITY

There is no known cure for Huntington's disease, a wasting condition that sufferers acquire from a parent. In this painful account, the author vents his rage at society, lawmakers, health services and the church for not grasping the need, as he sees it, to legalise compulsory sterilisation and assisted dying. EB9

Other titles from EnvelopeBooks

www.envelopebooks.co.uk

Princess Brr-rainy

STEPHEN GAMES

She couldn't help being clever and couldn't help being hated for it but it didn't help that her mother was modern and that her father had banned the fairies. But what was she meant to do when disaster came to Rainland and the rivers dried up? Accept her deadly fate or get sacrificed to the revolution? EB16

From Bedales to the Boche

ROBERT BEST

Bedales, the progressive boarding school founded by J.H. Badley in 1893, instilled values that sustained many of its pupils through the rest of their lives. Robert Best recalls its influence on him as an enthusiastic army recruit in 1914 and, from 1916, in the Royal Flying Corps. EB3

My Modern Movement

ROBERT BEST

London's Festival of Britain in 1951 marked the belief that Modern design was visually, morally and commercially superior. Robert Best, the UK's leading lighting manufacturer, thinks the dice were loaded. This is his memoir. EB8

The Hopeful Traveller

JANINA DAVID

A collection of short stories about—and told by—single women who have put the past behind them but are still looking for their anchor in the present. It includes bitter-sweet accounts of the freedoms of postwar life, of foreign travel, of the rekindling of old friendships and of the search for new ones. EB4

Fiction from EnvelopeBooks

www.envelopebooks.co.uk

Frances Creighton: Found and Lost

KIRBY PORTER

Love demands trust but trust is a lot to ask for victims of abuse. Having been bullied by two teachers in Belfast as a boy, Michael Roberts suppresses his childhood pains until the death of a girlfriend years later forces him to revisit lost memories. EB7

Belle Nash and the Bath Soufflé

WILLIAM KEELING ESQ.

In the first volume of *The Gay Street Chronicles*, bachelor Belle Nash attempts to navigate bigotry and corruption in Regency Bath without compromising his boyfriend, the nephew of Immanual Kant, or the legal talents of Gaia Champion. BB1

Lagos, Life and Sexual Distraction

TUNDE OSOSANYA

Twelve short stories, mostly focused on the struggle to survive in Lagos, Nigeria's commercial capital, illustrating the tensions that exist between the generations, between the sexes and between the country's different social classes and ethnicities. EB13

The Attraction of Cuba

CHRIS HILTON

Chris Hilton went to Cuba to escape the boredom of everyday life and to make money, only to be entranced by the beauty of the country and of Yamilia, a street girl who brought meaning to his life but who could not help him from falling into an inevitable downward spiral. EB14

More fiction from EnvelopeBooks

www.envelopebooks.co.uk

Belle Nash and the Bath Circus

WILLIAM KEELING ESQ.

In Volume Two of *The Gay Street Chronicles*, bachelor Belle Nash returns to Regency Bath from Grenada, inspired by a new love that leads him into various pretences that may compromise the ambitions of black circus impresario Pablo Fanque. BB2

The Train House on Lobengula Street

FATIMA KARA

An anguished but life-affirming novel, set within the Indian community in Bulawayo in Rhodesia of the 1950s and 1960s, about the capacity of women to gain the same advantages as men in the modern world while remaining faithful to traditional Muslim values. Affectionate and passionate. EB12

A Sin of Omission

MARGUERITE POLAND

An emotionally intense novel, set in 1870s South Africa at a time of rising anti-colonial resistance. The book examines the tragedy of a promising black preacher, hand-picked for training in England as a missionary, only to be neglected by the Church he loves. Winner of the 2021 *Sunday Times* CNA 'Book of the Year' Award in South Africa. EB6

Mustard Seed Itinerary

ROBERT MULLEN

When Po Cheng falls into a dream, he finds himself on the road to the imperial Chinese capital. Once there he rises to the heights of the civil service before discovering that there are snakes as well as ladders. Carrollian satire at its best. EB5

Made in United States
North Haven, CT
24 September 2024

57886298R00264